LEWIS CARROLL

LEWIS CARROLL

A Portrait with Background

DONALD THOMAS

John Murray
Albemarle Street, London

A catalogue record for this book
is available from the British Library

ISBN 0-7195-5323-7

Typeset in 11/13pt Monotype Garamond by
Rowland Phototypesetting Ltd,
Bury St Edmunds, Suffolk

Printed and bound in Great Britain by
The University Press, Cambridge

For Laurence and Menna Davies

Waiting among the flowers and tremuloes,
It scarcely seems the place to pray,
Knowing you thought it all untrue.
A sense of etiquette dissolves
The chattered codes of requiem.

Yet loss abhors a vacuum more than nature.
Beside the living in the pale oak pews,
Your subjects rise to tenant empty thoughts.
Debussy, Franck, and Henry James,
And Vincent d'Indy, minted new by Proust.
La Belle Otero, Cléo de Mérode,
Stand tactfully apart from Alice James.

In them the duty of occasion fails,
So may you hear the music of the spheres,
Debussy's *House of Usher*,
Verdi's new *King Lear*,
Read Scott Fitzgerald's latest,
And H. L. Mencken's opposition press.

The bets are down, as Pascal would have thought,
The wheel spins till we learn.
Whether the mushroom puff of flame
Burns for the dawn.

Contents

Illustrations

Preface

THE ASSUMPTION OF this book is that a man who bequeathed to the world three such treasures as *Alice's Adventures in Wonderland*, *Through the Looking-Glass*, and *The Hunting of the Snark* may be forgiven anything. But what is forgiven ought not necessarily to be forgotten or overlooked. There is, as it happens, little chance of that. Charles Lutwidge Dodgson is one of those figures, like Sade, who tempts every age to revalue him. The works of the Reverend Dodgson seem particularly hazardous to critics, whether the psychoanalytical school, so piteously hoaxed in the 1930s, or the later schools of sterner critical theory and practice. Such diligent hunters of the seminar room, waddling along with nets and traps in the wake of the Cheshire Cat and its companions, are apt to take a prisoner which uncannily deconstructs itself, leaving only a grin for their contemplation.

There is more to Dodgson than the figure of the man alone, not least in the background of such family and individual interests as law, psychiatry or the 'great social evil' of prostitution, all of which concerned him as surely as mathematics and photography. He was one colleague removed from Krafft-Ebing in the small realm of nineteenth-century scholarship. Despite the supposedly cloistered world of an Oxford college in which he lived, both life and literature were his stimulus. The courtroom scenes of his greatest work were a tribute to family interests, eminent friends and major changes in the legal system, yet the justice of the Queen of Hearts is recognizably that of the Roman underworld in the sixth book of Virgil's *Aeneid*, as seen from Oxford in the 1860s.

There are, of course, two personalities in one mind, the Dodgsonian and the Carrolingian. If the Reverend Dodgson had on occasion looked more carefully at what Mr Carroll was doing or writing, he could scarcely have concealed a shudder, as in some of Southey's original verses famously parodied in 'Father William'. Most of the time, however, he was self-consciously Dodgson and so he appears in these pages.

Among debts of gratitude incurred in writing this biography, my first is to the University of Wales, which provided me with the opportunity to complete it.

As a novelist, my initial encounter with Dodgson was fostered by the enthusiasm of Lord Hardinge of Penshurst, as Macmillan's Crime Editor, for an idea which became a novel in 1983 as *Belladonna: A Lewis Carroll Nightmare*. At the time I thought that Dodgson and the blackmailer Charles Augustus Howell were, in truth, complete strangers. I now find that hard to believe.

I have also been assisted by individuals and institutions in finding and gathering the material for this book and by others in its progress to publication: Mr Ben Bass of Greyne House Books; the British Library; the Bodleian Library, Oxford; Darlington Local Studies Library; Eastbourne Reference Library; Guildford Muniment Room; the London Library; Mrs Caroline Knox and Miss Kate Chenevix Trench of John Murray; Mrs Janet McMullin of Christ Church Library, Oxford; Father Kenneth Macnab, Archivist of Pusey House; Mr Clive Ogden of Meads Books; Mr Alan Tadiello of Balliol College Library, Oxford; and Mr Michael Thomas of A. M. Heath. I am indebted to the Principal and Chapter of Pusey House for allowing me to quote from the manuscript diaries of Henry Parry Liddon.

I was privileged to know, as a fellow member of the Bibliographical Society, the late Graham Pollard, whose mother, as Catherine 'Katie' Lucy, was among Dodgson's last child-friends, albeit in her teens, and his companion at Eastbourne.

Without the encouragement and forbearance of family and friends, this book would still remain a good intention. It is a great pleasure to commemorate in the dedication a long friendship with the late Menna and Laurence Davies. As a pianist, Laurence Davies was one of the last pupils of the late-romantic Mark Hamburg. By profession he was a psychologist, in his writing a musicologist and biographer. In his conversation he was a kindly and genial authority on French and American culture, one of the most distinguished scholars of his generation, in Wales and beyond, whose knowledge recognized no frontiers. My lines in the dedication are reprinted by arrangement with H.G. Publications.

I

The Prisoner of Conscience

The little girl was walking along with her two sisters, when the clergyman, who was passing in a car, stopped beside her and invited her to get in. A few kilometers further on, he dragged her into a field, undressed her, and then photographed her. The kidnapper admitted having behaved with children in the neighbourhood in a similar way twice before.

'I wonder how many people who knew something about Lewis Carroll thought of him when they read that,' wrote Jean Gattégno four years after the report of the incident, one of three in Sarthe and Mayenne, appeared in *Le Monde* in July 1972. 'Carroll's relationships with little girls undoubtedly represent the most sensitive problem his biographers have to tackle.'[1]

The greater sensitivity belonged to the Reverend Charles Lutwidge Dodgson, whose reputation on the evidence of such comments now lies somewhere between that of the public creator of Alice and the private admirer of Lolita. Even in photography, he was neither seducer nor intriguer, refusing to act against the wishes of parents or their daughters. Perhaps in a labyrinth of emotional compulsions there lay desires not essentially different to those of 'the clergyman, who was passing in a car'. If so, they were drilled into submission by conscience, conviction and intellect.

His true failings showed him to be as much a subject of his time as any man or woman a century later. He was, for example, a snob who described as 'roughs in the gallery' those unable to afford a seat in the theatre stalls where he sat. He was in public a political reactionary, who was awkwardly kind and humane in private. Those unenfranchised classes who demanded the vote in 1868 were 'roughs', like the gallery audience, as were the marchers of the Salvation Army. He himself had two votes in parliamentary elections, one at Guildford and another at Oxford as a member of the University. From time to time the press heard of the loutish behaviour of Christ Church undergraduates, the deliberate destruction in 1870 of statuary stolen from the college library, including a fourth-century BC Aphrodite and Eros. Their wealth and ancestry, however, exempted them from being 'roughs' in Dodgson's view. In their defence, he published a letter in the *Observer* on 5 June 1881 insisting that no young men were 'more gentlemanly, more orderly, and more pleasant in every way to deal with' than his undergraduates.[2]

He was also a prude and, as he wrote in the *St James Gazette* on 22 July 1885, glad to be one. He was not guilty of what his contemporary, the Baron von Krafft-Ebing, first described in 1886 as 'paedophilia erotica'. There is no evidence that Dodgson ever knew of that terminology though, curiously, one of his colleagues in the little world of Christ Church High Table and Common Room, Max Müller, received an honourable mention in Krafft-Ebing's *Psychopathia Sexualis*.

Dodgson's neurosis was more akin to 'onomatomania', as Krafft-Ebing called it. This compulsion to fill the mind with endless problems, puzzles and calculations, in order to crowd out unwholesome bedtime thoughts is, as Dodgson makes plain in *Pillow Problems*, his antidote to erotic images and impulses. Two of Krafft-Ebing's early patients in the 1880s tried precisely that means to quell sexual desire. Their failure led them to the great psychiatrist's consulting room. Dodgson, the insomniac, triumphed over lustful thoughts where those men failed. Yet he described himself laconically to Edith Rix in 1885, the year when Krafft-Ebing's most famous work was in the press, as 'a severe sufferer from *Logical* puzzles of late'.

At the end of his life he still lay awake devising in his head such tricks as the rapid division of 8678159224857031527640092 by 9993. Others might protest that 'the former number would never exist in a real world and would never require division by so strange a divisor as 9993.' They missed the point of his puzzles, which Dodgson described as intended to protect 'the fancy that would fain be pure'. While libido withered, the uneasy sleeper in his college bed performed self-imposed feats of mental arithmetic, honing the keen edge of his mind to a precision that might have graced an electronic calculator.[3]

Dodgson was born into a world that was not so much pre-Freudian as post-romantic. Within a few years of one another, Robert Browning in *The Ring and the Book* (1868–9), F. Winslow in *Obscure Diseases of the Brain and Mind* (1863), and the German philosopher Karl Robert Eduard von Hartmann analysed morbid sexuality in terms far removed from the romanticism of Wordsworth or Keats. Despite St Paul's suggestion that marrying or burning might be the human alternatives, asexuality was not anomalous. Sexual desire might appear, not to puritans alone, as a distraction from the important matters of life. Even sexual love was not a self-evident good to the post-romantic pessimists. 'Love causes more pain than pleasure,' wrote Hartmann in *Philosophie des Unbewussten* in 1869, 'Pleasure is only an illusion. Reason would demand the avoidance of love were it not for that fatal sexual instinct. Hence it would be better to be castrated.' Setting piety aside, Dodgson was not quite the oddity he was to seem to a Freudian creed of innate and universal sexual ambition. Castration was not the sole remedy, however. Mathematical calculations protected the fancy in the sleepless hours of night. Even love was possible, without sexual desire, when provided by 'child-friends' in its least demanding and most easily controlled form.[4]

Many children loved him their entire lives; a few, like Edward Gordon Craig, thought him a bore. Among adults, he had numerous friends in the world of art and the theatre, as well as those at Christ Church who found him an amusing companion at High Table or in Common Room. In his lifetime he was already an Oxford legend, slim and upright in his clerical black, with a white cravat and a top hat worn rather on the back of his head in the manner of the Mad Hatter. Even at the seaside he dressed in black. On the river, however, he appeared in white flannels, jacket and a straw boater. Despite the formal clerical dress there was something about him that seemed not far removed from the look of a dandy of the 1860s. A. S. Russell remembered him always looking as spruce and neat 'as if he had just emerged from a hot bath and a band-box'.

The famous stammer, open-mouthed and with his tongue 'wagging in vain,' as Margaret Mayhew recalled, mellowed into the hesitation of the raconteur. Though he outlived Browning and Tennyson, whose voices were recorded for posterity, nothing is certain but that his tone of voice was precise and pedantic. His more serious poetry suggests the inflexions of a north-country childhood, which pronounced 'trance' with a short 'a', tempering the Oxford voice that pronounced 'were' as 'wear'.[5]

Despite his suspicion of a 'levelling tendency' as the nineteenth century drew towards its end, there was much about him that might commend him to a later age. He was ahead of his time in opposing vivisection and most forms of hunting, and as a clergyman of the Church of England denounced the doctrine of eternal punishment both as a contradiction of the love of God and as a mistranslation of New Testament Greek. He was personally kind and generous. Most important of all, his genius bequeathed to the world a treasure beyond all computation.

Because time so often makes fools of social orthodoxies, the late twentieth century was not to find him a comfortable companion. Those passages in his writing which might cause the politically sensitive to squirm with greater agility than even the rumours of paedophilia, when written, represented inoffensive and good-natured banter. 'You would think from that that my servant is a nigger,' he wrote to young Mary MacDonald in 1864, 'but he isn't – only I admire the niggers so much that I've taught him to speak broken English, and I call him Sambo ... and every morning I do his face with the blacking-brush.'[6] He was no more a racialist in dealing kindly and helpfully with a Christ Church undergraduate from Sierra Leone than he was a sinister collector of child-friends. His jokes on race or class or the flogging of ill-behaved children in the nineteenth century embarrass the twentieth as the chatter of the twentieth will make its own successor wince.

Dodgson remains one of the few historical figures, like Sade, or Marx, or Freud, who suffer the popular fantasies of succeeding ages, sometimes benign if fatuous, sometimes malevolent. In 1993, Gordon Thomas described the use of children in pornography as a 'growth industry of our age.' The market for child pornography is, on the evidence, small however repellent. Yet there is no doubt of the name at the centre of the cult, giving a sardonic pseudo-respectability to the aberration. US Customs Agent John O'Malley details the activities of his target, a man known as 'Tetcher', in Gordon Thomas's account.

> He publishes *Wonderland*, the quarterly publication of the Lewis Carroll Collector's Guild. In *Wonderland* the 'delights' of 'transgenerational sex' pepper the pages. Operating out of Chicago, the Guild describes itself as a 'voluntary association of persons who believe nudist materials are a constitutionally protected expression and whose collecting interests include pre-teen nudes.'[7]

4

The enforcement of the present law, as surely as the crimes against children, is apt to recall Dodgson and his world. At dawn on 28 January 1993, for example, Ron Oliver's home in west London was raided by a squad from Scotland Yard with military planning that might have been reserved for an international drugs baron. The Obscene Publications Squad of the Metropolitan Police were armed with search warrants under the Protection of Children Act 1978. Mr Oliver was a professional portrait photographer, who also worked for such magazines as *Vogue* and *Harpers & Queen*. From his premises the police now took 20,000 negatives, transparencies and prints, his work for the past sixteen years.

Like the Reverend C. L. Dodgson, Mr Oliver was sure that he had never taken an indecent picture. His work was praised at the Victoria and Albert Museum in London and for its 'freshness and purity' by the Bibliothèque Nationale in Paris, where it is in the Department of Prints and Photography. He had never taken a picture of a child without being asked to do so by its parents, indeed being commissioned. The great majority of his subjects were clothed and posed in family groups. Like his famous predecessor, he had never taken a photograph where he sensed the child might be reluctant, since the result was likely to be unsatisfactory. His words echo Dodgson's. He took photographs only on commission, each one costing some £4,000. Not surprisingly, his clients were among the titled and the wealthy. They, not least the children themselves, were pleased and proud at the results. Many of the photographs were displayed in the homes of their owners.

Mr Oliver differed from the Reverend Dodgson neither in his attitude to his subjects nor in his artistic aspirations but only to the extent that he made his living as a photographer. The author of *Alice in Wonderland* could afford not to.

After interrogation, Mr Oliver was released to await a decision as to whether criminal charges would be brought. In the view of the police, any posed photograph of a naked person under sixteen was criminal. That would certainly have applied to such photographs of Dodgson's as that of seven-year-old Beatrice Hatch in 1873. If upheld, it would logically apply to the two-volume Oxford University Press edition of *The Letters of Lewis Carroll* which includes the photograph. No questions of artistic merit are permitted under the Protection of Children Act and even private possession of such material is a criminal offence. The good opinion of the Victoria and Albert Museum or the imprimatur of a university press is no defence. An absurdity of this, of course, is that the photograph of Beatrice Hatch would not be out of place in a collection unkindly entitled 'kitsch'.

Mr Oliver could not recover his negatives and was unable to continue working in England, despite a mass of letters in his support from his clients and their children. Indeed, the letters merely prompted the police to demand a list of his clients' names and addresses. He withdrew to work abroad, still not knowing whether there was to be a prosecution.[8]

When the provisions against pornography were debated, as the Protection of Children Bill passed through the House of Lords, Lord Houghton of Sowerby voiced doubts which are closest in spirit to comments in Dodgson's diaries and letters. 'Some people's minds are like cesspools and they cannot see anything beautiful about some aspects of behaviour and human form.'[9]

Yet despite such misgivings over the new *fin-de-siècle* alliance of prurience and prudery, laws exist to be enforced. If Charles Lutwidge Dodgson had behaved in the second half of the twentieth century as he behaved in the second half of the nineteenth, his rooms at Christ Church would surely have been turned over by the Obscene Publications Squad, and his thoughts by the Equal Opportunities Commission. He himself might have been free only on police bail. Christ Church might have kept him but he would more probably have shared the ordeal of a highly regarded head teacher who faced dismissal in March 1994 for such crimes as allowing a small child to sit on his knee during the morning assembly.

The degree of suspicion with which Dodgson's life is now viewed seems characteristically Anglo-American, the glum censoriousness of a society ill at ease with its own children. The suspicion, or the degree of it, is not universal. On 29 January 1993, *The Times* reported a complaint by the Advertising Standards Authority in London over an advertisement for the 56th Mode Enfantine international trade show of children's clothes in Paris. The poster showed a girl in a bathing costume, looking over her shoulder with – as the keen eyes of the standards officers thought – 'her bottom stuck out.' Mode Enfantine were puzzled. In sixty-eight of the seventy countries attending the show, no one had noticed this or could see anything wrong with the picture. From London there rose a chorus of 'Offensive', 'Irresponsible', and the newly-minted moral code-word 'Inappropriate'. Under the insistence of the Authority and the belatedly awakened British clothing industry, the puzzled French cropped the picture to head and shoulders only. Ironically, the objection was almost the same as Dodgson himself had made to the illustrator of *Sylvie and Bruno Concluded* in October 1893, when he demanded that a rear view of the children must be more amply clad and, in the same month, made an identical criticism of a drawing that Gertrude Thomson had done for him.[10]

Not even his most famous creation herself is free from stigma. On 3 March 1994 the *Daily Mail* apologized for feeling that it must publish three pages of pictures showing adult fashion models in Milan wearing clothes that resembled those once worn by schoolgirls in England: 'High Fashion or Low Decadence?' The decisive evidence was presented by a young woman in her twenties wearing an 'Alice band' to keep her hair in place. 'A look that amounts to little more than paedophilia.'

Alice as a fictional creation is also made to take her retrospective share of blame for child prostitution in Victoria's England. A coffee-table version of *Oscar Wilde's London* summons her to hear the indictment: 'Child prostitution, furthermore, may have been justified by the Victorian cult of the little girl of which Lewis Carroll's *Alice's Adventures in Wonderland* (1865) and its sequel *Through the Looking-Glass* (1871) are the best known expression.'[11]

Child prostitution in the late nineteenth century was not on the scale suggested by the legend that no girl-child was safe from the predatory male. It received what justification it needed not from Dodgson or Alice but an age of consent which was twelve until 1875, thirteen until 1885, after which it was raised to sixteen by the Criminal Law Amendment Act. W. T. Stead, whose zeal for the suppression of such prostitution resulted in his own imprisonment, remarked that even before the raising of the age of consent there were very few children indeed under that age on the streets. His commission of inquiry made him an undoubted judge of the truth of this. 'There are children, many children, who are ruined before they are thirteen; but the crime is one phase of the incest which, as the Report of the Dwellings Commission shows, is inseparable from overcrowding. But the number on the streets is very small.' Ruin took place in rooms often shared by more than one family in the 1880s, where *Alice in Wonderland* or little-girl cults seemed as remote as the customs of the furthest continent. Under-age prostitution existed in the late nineteenth century, as indeed in the late twentieth. And, as in any age, the authorities found it cheaper and more convenient to rouse

7

indignation or alarm over the scale of sexual aberration than to improve the living conditions of the poorest members of the population.[12]

A century after her story was told, Alice was for a while noisily elbowed aside by what Dodgson might have thought of as a guttersnipe *alter ego*, in the form of Dolores Haze, better known as Lolita. Each seemed an icon of her age. Vladimir Nabokov admired Lewis Carroll more than he liked the Reverend C. L. Dodgson. Nabokov had, of course, translated *Alice in Wonderland* into Russian in 1923. Yet even his admiration would have been ill-received. 'I always call him Lewis Carroll Carroll because he was the first Humbert Humbert,' Nabokov told *Vogue* in a 1966 interview. 'Have you seen those photographs of him with little girls? He would make arrangements with aunts and mothers to take the children out. He was never caught, except by one girl who wrote about him when she was much older.' For good measure, there is a reference to Dodgson's 'wretched perversion and to those ambiguous photographs he took in dim rooms.'[13]

This was self-evident rubbish. A man who tried taking a wet collodion image in a dim room would get nothing but a blank plate. Dodgson never used any other process. Even in good summer light, an exposure might require a full minute. As for the ambiguous subjects, it might have disappointed the readers of the *Vogue* interview to learn that Dodgson consistently refused to take a photograph without the permission of the child's mother and without the mother or a chaperone being present.

As a photographer, it was not his deeds but his words which made him a questionable oddity. Dodgson was innocent, while also his own worst enemy. He was among a handful of great Victorian photographers, his subjects including Tennyson, Ruskin, Millais, the Rossettis, Ellen Terry, bishops and princes, as well as children. Had he said plainly that he wished to photograph the daughter of a friend naked or in the nude, he would have sounded more honest. Yet prudishness required him to use such phrases as 'in her favourite dress of nothing to wear', or the discreet French of '*sans habilement*'. By this evasion of plain speech, he at once made the proposal sound more furtive or shifty than it was. He who would never have harmed a child for the world, anticipated in his prudishness something of the prose style of Humbert Humbert.

On his reputation as a photographer, one voice is seldom heard, that of the child model. Most of those who recalled being photographed naked by him voiced no opinions as distinct from what they felt about the other photographs. One who made her feelings known was Ella Bickersteth, daughter-in-law of the Bishop of Ripon. As Ella Monier-Williams she had posed nude for him in childhood. She did not much like being posed naked. Not that she felt exploited, or manipulated, or belittled. It was the 'boredom of being posed in the nude' that she disliked. While she stood, or sat, before his camera, her mind was occupied by thoughts of a cupboard in his room which contained a collection of exotic costumes, many of them acquired from the wardrobes of theatres where they were no longer wanted. Every minute spent posing in the nude was a minute lost from 'the delight of being dressed up' in one of these treasures. Nudity was tedious whereas dressing up was something children loved to do. It seemed the worst that any of his photographic 'victims', as he laconically called them, could say of him.[14]

Elsewhere, the judgement of his genius for friendship with young girls was described by Ethel Rowell, who was an undergraduate by the time Dodgson died. 'He gave me a sense of my own personal dignity. He was so punctilious, so courteous, so considerate, so scrupulous not to embarrass or offend, that he made me feel that I counted . . . he was never for a moment patronizing to women or to children.'[15]

*

The author of *Alice in Wonderland* bears the unsought reputation of being a 'Great Victorian'. Yet 'Victorian' is in many respects a simple-minded summary to apply to Charles Lutwidge Dodgson, concealing more than it reveals of him. Victoria's reign covered a period approximately equivalent to that from Roosevelt's New Deal, or Hitler's first seizure of territory in Europe, or the abdication of Edward VIII, to the beginning of the twenty-first century. The majority of those who were alive when the young Queen came to the throne in 1837 would not live to see the mid-point of her reign, let alone its conclusion. Most of those alive in 1901 would have known nothing of its earlier decades.

Dodgson, who was five when Victoria succeeded William IV and who died three years before her, lived through a succession of 'Victorian Englands'. The 1840s were the decade of a starved and diseased urban proletariat, a ruling class which contained a good many self-confident Regency survivals. During the 1850s, chastened by reverses in the Crimean War and Indian Mutiny, for which 'days of humiliation' were ordered, there was a new seriousness. Indeed, in 1865 Victoria offered the Secretary of State for India a plan for getting rid of the empire: 'India really must not be the grave of all our best men.' The tide of Evangelicalism and Sabbatarianism ran strongly in Parliament and outside. 'At this moment cant and puritanism are in the ascendant,' wrote Charles Greville, Clerk to the Privy Council, in February 1856.[16]

By the mid-1860s, Prince Albert was dead, Victoria had withdrawn behind the veils of widowhood and the young Prince of Wales was to be the focus of fashionable society. There was a new bohemianism in the arts and a succession of new young writers. The 1870s and 1880s saw more leisure and greater affluence, though not evenly spread. Aestheticism and Art for Art's sake, which would have seemed intolerably self-indulgent in the 1840s, now formed an avant-garde. Other movements in society would have fitted into the earnestness of earlier decades. The rights of women were advocated by Mrs Fawcett and her supporters in town hall lecture-rooms and monthly magazines. Sydney Smith had once asked whether any woman would desert an infant for a quadratic equation. It seemed after all that she might. University extension lectures brought learning to the slums. Child abuse, as it was later to be termed, gave cause for concern. The more lurid manifestation was in tales of white slavery and Stead's *Maiden Tribute of Modern Babylon* in 1885. More important was that general movement which, for example, led to the evolution of the National Society for the Prevention of Cruelty to Children in the 1880s.

Dodgson's 'merry noontide', as he called it in the dedicatory verses to *Sylvie and Bruno*, was a period between the publication of *Alice in Wonderland* in 1865 and the end of his photography in 1880, when gossip and a threat of scandal led him to resign a certain freedom as well as his camera. There was, indeed, at least one unappealing aspect to the final years of the century, perhaps the obverse of the concern for women and children. A new prudery was abroad. Whatever might offend women – Dodgson's own criterion for theatrical propriety – whatever might be unsuitable for children, was suspect. This was in part a matter of time passing. As J. W. Mackail noted, looking back from 1925, 'the reformers of the 'sixties were insensibly becoming the Conservatives of the 'eighties.' So the National Vigilance Association kept a watch on the welfare of young women arriving in London but also prosecuted Henry Vizetelly, and had him sent to prison, for daring to publish Maupassant and Zola in England. Where censorship was not exercised through the courts, it was increasingly imposed on literature in private and arbitrarily by the bookseller and librarian.[17]

The nineteenth century was rich in resolve, denunciation and harangue during its last fifteen years. The *Pall Mall Gazette* in 1885 advocated a new respect for female sexuality, urging young men to form 'vigilance associations' to horsewhip any scoundrel they saw offering unwelcome invitations to a woman. It was unlikely, in this view, that a court would convict them of any offence in respect of their public-spirited conduct.[18]

What is often called Victorian is in truth characteristic of this later period, an age which might seem as strange to some who were young in the 1860s as to the 1960s. It was policed by a coalition of evangelicals and progressives, and some who were both. Those at Oxford or Eastbourne who had regarded Dodgson's interest in children and his photographic enthusiasms as innocent, or at worst eccentric, twenty years before would have done so no longer. As surely as the alleged freedoms of the 1960s were followed by the recriminations and resentments of the 1980s and 1990s, so the youthful mid-Victorian bohemia steadied into sobriety.

Curiously, for so prudish a man, Dodgson now described himself as the victim of prudery in his frequent references to the frowning figure of 'Mrs Grundy.' This totem of moral disapproval had first appeared in Thomas Morton's play *Speed the Plough* in 1798 with its constant admonition of 'What will Mrs Grundy say?' Dodgson seemed to sense her everywhere in his dealings with his child-friends in the 1880s and 1890s. Indeed, he first mentioned her when arguing with Mrs Mayhew that it would be more becoming for him to photograph her daughters in the nude than in bathing drawers. Worse was to follow. Within a few years, Mrs Grundy was reinforced by the *Psychopathia Sexualis.* Forms of behaviour that had seemed harmless, even if they were odd, acquired newly descriptive titles from Professor Krafft-Ebing. Paedophilia, which if it meant anything at all to England before psychopathology simply indicated a love of children, soon denoted a deformity of character at which decent people shuddered and pulled their offspring protectively closer.[19]

As a century draws to its end, there is a natural tendency to put away childish things in the contemplation of mortality. Despite the encouragement to celebrate its successor, most of the revellers know the only certainty is that they will be dead long before the next century is over. The nineteenth century was not unique in such manifestations as Mrs Grundy and the National Vigilance Association. The ending of the seventeenth century heard a stern call to moral renewal from the Society for the Reformation of Manners, founded in 1692. The last decade of the eighteenth century saw the routine hunting of indecency and blasphemy through the courts by the Proclamation Society, overtaken in the last year of the century by sponsors of the Society for the Suppression of Vice.

Faced by Mrs Grundy in his own later years, Dodgson might rebel or withdraw. He was no rebel and he withdrew. Others fought. The young novelist George Moore was outraged by the news that his book *A Modern Lover* had been withdrawn from library shelves merely because 'two ladies from the country' had objected to one of its passages. In *Circulating Morals: or, Literature at Nurse* in 1885 he denounced the hidden censors of the book trade as the nannies of public taste who allowed into circulation only those novels written to a pattern of what was to be known a hundred years later as political correctness, 'a callow, a whining, a puking brood of bastard bantlings, a race of Aztecs that disgrace the intelligence of the English nation.'[20]

The ultimate revolt against the current philistinism of prudery was the advent of Art for Art's sake. Dodgson, by then in his sixties, kept his distance from it. Indeed, in 1888 he managed to couple such 'gaudy and ostentatious vulgarity' with 'unmanly men and unwomanly women.' Rebellion was not entirely silenced by the tragedy of Oscar Wilde but its teeth were drawn. At the least, it went underground. The jubilation of newspapers like the *Daily Telegraph* and the *Evening News* on Wilde's conviction was cultural as well as personal. The latter, on 25 May 1895, denounced those writers who despised 'the emotions of healthy humanity and the achievements of wholesome talent.' Next morning, commenting on Wilde's imprisonment, the *Daily Telegraph* warned the dissidents that 'No sterner rebuke could well have been inflicted on some of the artistic tendencies of the time.' The paper cited the style of 'paradox and unreality' as having received its just deserts.[21]

*

In his character, Dodgson is one of those figures who appear most clearly when seen against a background of the years through which they lived. He was a man of rectitude and moral authority who seemed to walk a tightrope of respectability with heaven above and hell beneath. He lived, as Browning's Bishop Blougram describes it, 'on the dangerous edge of things.' Despite the wish of his successors to unearth some hidden vice, the evidence is not that he was a lonely prig tormented by secret sensualism nor a soul enthralled and horrified by images of children as sexually desirable. Had he been, he would be much less interesting.

Dodgson, however innocent, was certainly not ignorant of the shabby world that surrounded him. Despite the image of the neatly turned out prig who chose to live in the solitude of his rooms within the isolation of an Oxford college, the contents of those rooms were instructive. His bookshelves contained such volumes as *The Physical Life of Women*; William Acton, *On Prostitution*; James Greenwood's *Seven Curses of London*; the fourth volume of Henry Mayhew's *London Labour and the London Poor*, in which a criminal class of prostitutes, thieves, beggars and their kind reveal their lives in their own words; the sexual freak-show of Nathaniel Wanley's *Wonders of the Little World*. Ironically, this man who died a virgin knew more about the sexual physiology of women than the great majority of husbands – or wives – of his day. To that extent, his public prudence was a poor indication of his private curiosity.[22]

No greater mistake could have been made than to regard him as the pampered and unworldly don whose eccentric ways protected him from the social realities of his time. At regular intervals he left Christ Church for the theatrical and social pleasures of London, in neighbourhoods offering a parade of sexual vice that was a by-word throughout Europe. The curiosity inspired by reading was to be satisfied by observation. 'There was,' wrote Jean-Jacques Mayoux in 1977, 'something of Leopold Bloom in the imagination of Lewis Carroll.'[23]

The evidence is that he was unusually well acquainted with many things which he might instinctively have found the most repellent. The motive was not dissimilar to his determination in 1857 to witness the amputation of a man's leg at St Bartholomew's Hospital in order to test his nerve in the face of such sights. Pain, madness, crime, punishment and the law were the stuff of fact and fiction to him.

The world, quite rightly, forgave everything to a man whose genius bequeathed it *Alice in Wonderland*, *Through the Looking-Glass*, and *The*

Hunting of the Snark. Yet despite the almost universally saccharine descriptions of him at his death as 'The Patron Saint of Children' and the like, he was by no means always amiable. A good many adults found him pedantic and querulous, 'the most prolific malcontent' among his colleagues at Christ Church. His child friendships seemed to his critics egotistically absurd, at the best suggestive of sadness in a man who could find no more durable relationship with adults. A few parents thought his suggestions or invitations to their daughters would be disapproved of by bourgeois society. Yet neither parents nor their daughters ever found his conduct sinister and almost all remembered him with gratitude and affection.

What of Dodgson and the clergyman in the car who enticed little girls away to photograph them – or Nabokov's figure taking ambiguous photographs in dimly-lit rooms?

As in the case of his afternoons of photography at Christ Church, the best evidence is not conjecture but the memories of women who had been his child-friends and who, if they had reservations about him, need only have remained silent. Edith Maitland, daughter of the Reverend E. A. Litton, Vice-Principal of St Edmund Hall, was one of many who recorded memories of him after his death. She, who had once been a photographic subject as well as a child-friend, was by this time a married woman. Her recollection embodies an affection common to almost every girl whose reminiscences were to be published in adult life. 'My father died on August 27, 1897, and Mr Dodgson on January 14, 1898. And we, who are left behind in this cold, weary world can only hope we may some day meet them again. Till then, oh! Father, and my dear old childhood's friend, *requiescatis in pace!*'[24]

2

Ancient and Modern

WHEN THE REVEREND Charles Dodgson, father of the author of *Alice in Wonderland*, became perpetual curate of Daresbury in 1827, it seemed almost like a step back into the eighteenth century and a step down in his career. Twenty-seven years old, he was a 'Double First-Class Man', what was later called a 'Double First' at Oxford, in Classics and Mathematics. Until that spring he had been a Student of Christ Church – the equivalent of a 'fellow' in other Oxford colleges – and a Lecturer in Mathematics. His later writings dealt with theology rather than mathematics but they showed him to have a solid, methodical intelligence, tenacious in argument and quick to see the fallacies and possibilities of paradox.

His appointment at Oxford was one in which he might have passed the rest of his life. However, on 5 April 1827, at Hull, he had married his cousin, Frances Jane Lutwidge, whose father, Major Charles Lutwidge, was Collector of Customs for the port. The Dean and Chapter of Christ Church, as clergy of the cathedral, were free to marry. The Students, like the fellows of other colleges, were bound to celibacy. The elder Charles Dodgson put love and family duty before ambition and so lost his post. It was a common enough occurrence in Oxford life and, as usual, Christ Church looked after its own. The College had some ninety livings in its gift, including the perpetual curacy of Daresbury in Cheshire, which it bestowed on Mr Dodgson.

The new curate was later described by his son as a High Churchman of the traditional kind. He was a conservative rather than one who sympathized with the Oxford Movement's catholicizing of the Church of England in the 1830s. The ritualism that was to develop from this movement in the more aesthetically conscious decades of late century

15

was unappealing to father and son alike. Even if he lacked the plain taste of the evangelicals, the new curate's strictness of moral belief and observance was beyond question.

He represented a new earnestness of the Established Church in an age of political and social instability. He believed in charity as a practical duty. The observance of the Sabbath and the avoidance of any but the most devout reference to the Bible were central to his own conduct and that of his children. Such attitudes testified to a revolution in the half century or so since Parson Woodforde had bet a fellow student of divinity at New College, Oxford, that the latter could not drink down three bottles of wine at once and then write correctly three biblical texts in the next three hours. In the riotous aftermath Woodforde won his bet, his opponent being incapably drunk within five minutes.

To Charles Dodgson, as later to his son, such impious use of Holy Writ lay somewhere between profanity and blasphemy. Moreover, the Church now took knowledge of divinity as a serious matter. Woodforde, examined viva voce at Christ Church for his degree, was disconcerted that the examiner asked him questions to which he could not reply simply 'Yes' or 'No'. And while Parson Woodforde might have seen nothing amiss in the game of trying to get the garters off the legs of two young ladies, it seems safe to assume that the new curate of Daresbury had never so much as seen a young lady's leg. His grandfather, Christopher Dodgson, while a Northumberland vicar, was more familiar with such limbs, writing to his patron about the impressive size of his maidservant's legs and their unsuitability for wearing stockings. A century later, when the creator of *Alice in Wonderland* came to a stile with a female companion, he would extend a helping arm but kept his back turned during the inevitable display of ankles.[1]

The moral tone of the clergy, as the Reverend Charles Dodgson represented it in 1827, had certainly improved. Yet a brief survey of Daresbury would have suggested that his perpetual curacy was far from handsomely endowed. The scattered village lay on the borders of Cheshire and Lancashire, some seven miles south of Warrington, and almost within sight of the Mersey. Liverpool and Manchester were fifteen and twenty miles off respectively. By 1827, the first railway of the new industrial age had reached Warrington, within sight of the hill above the parsonage, but Daresbury might have been waiting for its first stage-coach. On its horizon, beyond the fields and occasional farmhouses, the Bridgewater Canal and the Trunk Canal now linked Liverpool and Manchester with London. Daresbury in its remoteness and isolation seemed linked to nowhere. The dwellings themselves were for the most part well separated. There was such stillness over the fields and hedgerows that even the occasional passing of a farm cart on its way to market brought excited children to their doors.

The contrast between the rural solitude of Georgian England and the life of Christ Church seemed complete. During the 1830s, Daresbury still reflected a landscape from the fiction of Goldsmith or Fielding, while modern readers were immersed in the London of *Oliver Twist* or *Sketches by Boz*. As for Mr Dodgson's cure, the medieval village church of All Saints with its later additions was one of two in the area to which Domesday Book appeared to refer. The church building was, as Thomas Hughes had called it, 'A pretty Parish Church', with the remains of a medieval rood screen and a fine Jacobean pulpit. Almost the whole of the structure was to be destroyed when the building was 'improved' in 1870. It was not a parish church in its own right but a 'chapel of ease' belonging to the mother church of Runcorn a few miles away. In the eighteenth century it was still known as 'Daresbury Chapelry' rather than by its grander title of 'All Saints'. Two centuries before Charles Dodgson's arrival, there had been great difficulty getting either a preacher or a teacher under any circumstances, according to the wills of those who left money for such purposes.[2]

All Saints served the two hundred inhabitants who were scattered over this area of farmland. The parsonage itself was almost two miles from the church, at Newton-by-Daresbury, standing among the fields of its 'glebe farm', as the church land was called. Its isolation was of the kind commemorated by William Morris's 'lone house in the midst of the corn' in 'Summer Dawn'.

To this parsonage Charles Dodgson and his bride came by the ancient toll road, which was Daresbury's sole connection with the world of the industrial revolution. It was a plain late-Georgian house, built in 1819, with a schoolroom where the new incumbent was expected to play his part in the education of the local children. The Double First and Mathematical Lecturer became the village teacher of reading and writing. There were seven bedrooms, which the pro-creative energy of the Dodgsons soon filled. Adjoining the house were outbuildings for cattle and poultry, stables, a gig-house and a laundry. Water was drawn from a well in the forecourt. The fields immediately surrounding the house grew the crops intended to make the family self-sufficient.

The most important landowner in the area, Lord Francis Egerton, was to be a good friend to the Dodgsons while their immediate neighbours were minor gentry. On higher ground nearby stood Daresbury Hall, a redbrick manor house with stone quoins built in 1756, the property of the Reverend George Heron, Canon of Chester Cathedral. Above the tall trees with their clustering rookeries, it looked north-east over the flat farmland of the Vale of the Mersey to Halton Castle and the Lancashire hills. The moated grange of Morphany Hall stood closer still to the Dodgsons and gave its name to the muddy track of Morphany Lane, the nearest byway to the parsonage. In such surroundings, Charles Dodgson was to combine the tasks of his curacy with those of schoolmaster, smallholder and patriarch.

In 1827 many of Daresbury's village customs had scarcely changed since the middle ages. The 'bawming' or miraculous flowering of the thorn, which had long been famous at Glastonbury, was reported locally as late as 1844 in a case at Daresbury Sessions. May Day was still celebrated by the young men with 'Birchen Boughing'. Foliage placed over the doorways of the houses was meant to relate to the character of the inmates. Some were complimentary, others not. The foliage was taken from a tree which rhymed with the character symbolized: an owler branch meant a scowler, a nut branch indicated a slut.

The curiosity of these survivals was that they should still have preoccupied Daresbury at a time when, twenty miles away, ocean liners were steaming out into the Irish Sea on their way to New York, leaving behind the squalor of dockland prostitution – much of it juvenile – which Edwin Chadwick and his investigators were conscientiously documenting. For the next ten years, Daresbury turned out to watch a farm cart, while travellers elsewhere ate breakfast in London, lunch in Boulogne, and dinner in Paris. The life of the age was changing with a speed that would soon overwhelm such village communities. Country life of this kind was regarded by Victorian pessimists as having been destroyed long before the nineteenth century was over. Leslie Stephen, looking back in 1893 on its description in the novels of George Eliot, remarked, 'Its last traces are vanishing so rapidly amidst the changes of modern revolution that its picture could hardly be drawn again.'[3]

With the publication of *Alice in Wonderland*, it seemed that the grin of the Cheshire Cat was one survival from the antiquities of Daresbury, nurtured in the mind of the county's most famous author. The sources of inspiration for this, if they were needed, proved numerous enough. The sign of the roadside inn at nearby Stretton was the 'Cat and Lion'. A ferocious cat was shown spitting at a mild-looking lion. Round this design was an inscription of the sort that might well lodge itself in a child's mind. 'The lion is strong, the cat is vicious, my ales are good and so are my liquors.'

Perhaps the Cheshire Cat was a tribute to the medieval carving of the grinning cat at Brimstage or the tradition of the cat on the coat of arms of John Catheral of Chester in the fourteenth century. Cheshire cheeses were made in the shape of a cat to commemorate this, grinning in the manner of Catheral's rictus smile. The image, however, may not have been seen by the Dodgsons in Cheshire but in the church of St Peter's at Croft, where Charles Dodgson senior became incumbent when his son was eleven. On 7 July 1992, *The Times* reported the discovery of 'a rough-hewn carving of a cat's head' close to the altar of the church. 'From the front, it looks like a cat, but if you go down on your knees and look up, you can see only the grin and not the cat.'

The creature of Alice's dream may simply reflect the reputation of the local Daresbury girls among their neighbours for grinning 'like Cheshire Cats', or discussions of the phenomenon which were to appear in *Notes and Queries* not long before *Alice in Wonderland* was composed. Dodgson was a regular reader of the journal and had a bound set on his bookshelves.

*

Even before their most famous member was born, the combined families of the Dodgsons and the Lutwidges had long enjoyed substantial prestige in the North of England. They represented that professional class, in Church and State, which is apt to be much respected but little rewarded.

Christopher Dodgson, the new curate's grandfather, had risen to become Bishop of Ossory and Ferns, then Bishop of Elphin, dioceses of which most people had scarcely heard. As a young man, he had been tutor to the son of the Duke of Northumberland, who rewarded him with the Northumberland living of Elsdon.

There was no parsonage house for Christopher Dodgson. He and his household lived in the vestibule of the castle, above the stable, as his letters to his patrons in the Percy family described it. Bedrooms were an unnecessary luxury. In an arrangement which might have shocked later generations, the curate, the curate's wife and the maid slept on 'two little beds joining to each other.' Christopher Dodgson occupied the parlour, lying between two more beds 'to keep me from being frozen to death' by the winds that swept into the stable block. 'I have lost the use of everything but my reasoning, though my head is entrenched in three night-caps, and my throat, which is very bad, is fortified by a pair of stockings twisted in the form of a cravat.' In such circumstances, the vicar and his wife produced four children. When Christopher Dodgson became Bishop of Elphin, he received a letter from George III, congratulating him on having found better stabling.[4]

Remarkably, under such circumstances, the Bishop lived into his seventies and two of the four children survived. Elizabeth Anne married Charles Lutwidge of Holmrook in Cumberland and became the mother of Frances Jane Lutwidge. Charles Dodgson, the Bishop's son and father of Charles Dodgson of Daresbury, married Lucy Hume and rose to the rank of captain in the 4th Royal Irish Dragoon Guards. As if to complete a marital minuet, his two sons each married a cousin. Charles Dodgson of Daresbury married Frances Jane Lutwidge in 1827. His brother Hassard Dodgson married Caroline Hume. By the middle of the nineteenth century, the Dodgsons had become a complex and numerous family.

Charles Dodgson of the 4th Dragoon Guards never rose from the rank of captain. In December 1803 his regiment was in Ireland. Its immediate duty was to track down the suspects in the murder of Viscount Kilwarden, Lord Chief Justice of Ireland, during the uprising by Robert Emmet and the United Irishmen, in the summer of that year. A message was received that one of the suspected assassins was prepared to surrender personally to Captain Dodgson. The rendez-vous was to take place during the night at a derelict hut near Phillips-town in King's County, some forty miles west of Dublin.

Captain Dodgson wrote a letter to his wife and set out with his party to keep the rendezvous on the night of 16 December 1803. The arrangement was that his men were to remain at a distance of a few hundred yards and that he was to go forward to the hut alone. As he approached, there were two shots from the darkness and he fell dead. Whether deceit, panic or misunderstanding caused the firing of these shots was never established. A curiosity of the incident was that his wife, in England, was said to have heard two shots fired during that same night and to have been sufficiently disturbed to make inquiries. No one else heard them. Shortly afterwards, she received her husband's last letter.

Captain Dodgson left one son at his death, the future curate of Daresbury then three years old. But Caroline Hume was pregnant with a second child, born two weeks after his father's murder. Hassard Dodgson was to make his mark on the Oxford Union Society and, after a successful career as a barrister, to become a Master of the Common Pleas.

On the Lutwidge side, the ancestry was more picturesque and more reminiscent of the royalty of Alice's Wonderland. Mary Skeffington, great grandmother of the couple at Daresbury parsonage, married Sir Charles Hoghton who was descended from Matilda, the natural daughter of William the Conqueror. Among his ancestors had been Richard Hoghton, at whose table James I was reputed to have knighted a sirloin of beef. Three and a half centuries later Alice was to be introduced to an even more famous joint of meat, the leg of mutton in chapter nine of *Through the Looking-Glass*, with a subsequent reprimand by the Red Queen that 'It isn't etiquette to cut anyone you've been introduced to.'

The Curate of Daresbury and his wife were well liked. The gentle virtue of Frances Dodgson was reflected in her private correspondence and in her love for her children. Her great-nephew, Stuart Dodgson Collingwood, cites a description of her by a family friend at the time of her death.

> One of the sweetest and gentlest women that ever lived, whom to know was to love. The earnestness of her simple faith and love shone forth in all she did and said; she seemed to live always in the conscious presence of God. It has been said by her children that they never in all their lives remember to have heard an impatient or harsh word from her lips.[5]

Frances Dodgson loved others easily because she had found contentment. She confided to her aunt by marriage, Mary Smedley, that her life was the perfection of earthly happiness. It was almost alarming to her to realize that she had not an unfulfilled wish. Such serenity prompted her impulse of duty towards others. In the early years of marriage, her husband's inadequate stipend might have seemed a drawback, but even that was to pass.

The cousin she had married was less at ease in his curacy after the sophistication of Christ Church. He shared with her the grace of piety and charity but seemed 'of a somewhat reserved and grave disposition.' As time went by, he also grew concerned at the circumstances of his growing family. He was not a man to complain constantly of his situation but in 1832 he presented it bluntly to his patrons and former colleagues at Christ Church. His income was £191, from which he had to pay for the upkeep of the glebe farm. On 23 January, he informed Dr Bull, Canon and Treasurer at Christ Church, that his position was 'precarious' and that he was obliged to forgo 'domestic comforts.' This frankness was aided by the knowledge that his wife was within a few days of giving birth to a third child at a time when he had lost two paying pupils. Like many incumbents, he took pupils in classics or mathematics to supplement his stipend. He asked the College to secure the payment to him of a potato tithe, worth almost £200 a year. At present he fell far short of the average annual stipend of incumbents, which he calculated at about £300. 'The Revenues of the Perpetual Curacy of Daresbury certainly *admit* of improvement,' he added laconically. Worse still, he had spent £30 of his own money to have the fields of the glebe farm manured. In the long term, the manuring was more likely to benefit his successor than himself. Perhaps Christ Church would also like to give that matter some 'consideration.'[6]

He described himself to Dr Bull in 1832 as having no prospects. Preaching at Manchester seven years later, he pointed out that even wealth and poverty are relative. At the time, working men and their families in London were living on £25 to £30 a year and the weavers of Spitalfields were soon reduced to half that amount. The city in which he was preaching was within a few years to be the subject of Engels' *Condition of the Working Class in England*, replete with descriptions of mortal disease and starvation.

Charles Dodgson thought it hard for a clergyman to be impoverished, given 'the great expenditure attending the peculiar Education required.' With a certain edge of self-pity, he reflected that 'the mental refinement, the habits and connexions necessarily formed, all bringing him into immediate contact with the higher walk of life, tend only to enhance the privations of narrow worldly means, and to unfit him for the rough encounter of those coarser hardships of Poverty.' Mortality might touch him too. He was now within a year of forty, the average age of death in the Victorian period, with a wife and eight children dependent on him. In his youth, he had been shown the good things of life until, at twenty-seven, they had been taken from him. Given his birth and background, perhaps he could not believe he was destined to lose them forever.

Yet he thought of others more frequently than he asked favours for himself. His predecessor had done little for his flock. As the churchwarden noted, by the time Charles Dodgson left the parish he had revived the Sunday School, there were addresses to the parish on three days during the week, the poor and the sick were ministered to once more. The congregations at All Saints had grown. Most of all, his attention to the poor and the afflicted, even to the extent of donations from his own ill-lined pocket, had impressed the people of Daresbury. Years later, elderly parishioners remembered him as one 'whose lips, now long silenced, used to speak so kindly to them; whose hands, long folded in sleep, were once so ready to alleviate their wants and sorrows.'[7]

Yet, despite his generosity of spirit, Dodgson was a somewhat intimidating figure, a man of undeviating virtue. In private, he had a natural geniality. 'In moments of relaxation his wit and humour were the delight of clerical friends. He had a rare power of telling anecdotes effectively.' Of course, there were limits to his humour. 'His reverence for sacred things was so great that he was never known to relate a story which included a jest upon words from the Bible.'[8]

In personal and domestic life, a later or an earlier age might think his rules of religious observance oppressive. But as he and his children followed them, they were rational and enlightened. To make biblical texts or sacred subjects the butt of casual jokes was foolish as well as irreverent. In the great crises of life, those texts brought comfort and strength to men and women, often in circumstances where no other comfort was to be found. The loss would be incalculable if the bereaved or the suffering turned to the great words and found their moral resonance distorted by the associations of a shallow joke.

Sabbath observance was a touchstone of moral renewal prompted by George III's Proclamation 'For the Encouragement of Piety and Virtue' in 1787. Most of the document dealt with His Majesty's command to judges and magistrates to enforce the Sunday Observance

Acts. A Proclamation Society was formed to act on this. Among its eminent founding members were seventeen peers, two archbishops, seventeen bishops, the philanthropist William Wilberforce, Christopher Dodgson's patron the Duke of Northumberland, and the Dodgsons' kinsman Henry Hoghton. They urged the nation 'to check the rapid progress of impiety and licentiousness, to promote a spirit of decency and good order, and enforce a stricter execution of the laws against vice and immorality.' They sought not to oppress but to protect the 'happiness' of the people. The new mood touched even the easy-going Parson Woodforde. On Sunday morning, as he was stropping his razor, it broke in his hand. This was plainly a divine rebuke. 'May it be always a warning to me not to shave on the Lord's Day,' he noted self-consciously in his diary.[9]

To Charles Dodgson, Sabbath observance was also a political and humanitarian issue. With his friend Wilson Patten, a Lancashire MP, he sought improvement in the conditions of working men and women. Sunday was the one day on which servants, still the largest employed class, might be free of household duties. The struggle to improve their lives would be undermined if employers insisted upon their own Sunday pleasures and indulgences. Their selfishness affected livery stables, railway companies and public facilities of all kinds. Forty years later, holidaymakers were still being urged not to walk on the pier on Sundays, since this would force men to work seven days of the week. If so many others lost this day in the industrial culture of the 1830s, might not manufacturing labourers lose it also? The curate of Daresbury and his wife would have been surprised to find themselves regarded as anything but a progressively minded couple whose practice was civilizing as well as devout. Their son, in chapter twenty-five of his novel *Sylvie and Bruno*, paid tribute to their enlightened Sabbatarianism, arguing that 'whatever is innocent on a weekday, is innocent on a Sunday, provided it does not interfere with the duties of the day.'[10]

Against this social and genealogical tapestry, in which the Dodgson ancestors appear like faded figures in the background of a novel by Fanny Burney or Maria Edgeworth, Charles and Frances produced their children in steady succession. There were to be seven girls and four boys in the next nineteen years. Parents and children alike must have thought themselves blessed in the lottery of survival. Secluded in the open farmland of Daresbury and later in the Teeside village of Croft, the entire brood grew up to become healthy adults. In

Manchester, twenty-five miles across the fields from Daresbury, infant mortality by 1840 was 57 per cent. Of those who survived infancy, many more would not outlive their teens, the average age of death being seventeen.

All the children except the Dodgsons' eldest son were to survive into the next century, even he failing to do so by only two years. The first child was Frances Jane, born in 1828. Her sister, Elizabeth Lucy, followed in 1830. On 27 January 1832, four days after his father had written to Christ Church about the need for a potato tithe and the cost of manure, the first son was born. In order that he should perpetuate the two family names and the most common of their Christian names, he was to be called Charles Lutwidge Dodgson. Thirty years later, linguistic sleight of hand would change the first two names to 'Lewis Carroll'.

Despite his future reputation as the creator of a distinctively Victorian world of fantasy, the younger Charles Dodgson was born among late-Georgian crises. The nationwide phobias of those early months of 1832 were revolution and disease. He was two weeks old when the cholera, which the government had mapped in its progress across northern Europe, reached London. Two weeks more and the Reform Bill was passed. William IV was hissed by the crowds as he left the capital. Charles Greville thought gloomily that the old King was evidently going mad and that the 'revolutionary spirit' was gaining ground in the north. Richard Carlile had been convicted and William Cobbett acquitted after siding with the insurgent labourers who were setting fire to the crops. Yet Daresbury saw nothing of cholera or revolution, nor for that matter very much reform. As for the new baby at the parsonage, he was so robust an infant that the formalities of his reception into the Church seemed hardly urgent. Six months passed before the Reverend George Heron of Daresbury Hall baptised him at All Saints on 11 July.[11]

*

Charles Lutwidge Dodgson, known to the family as 'Little Charlie' in his early years, seems to have shared the contentment of his parents in the remote and spartan life of the parsonage. From his father he inherited a skill in mathematics and a sense of humour that was violent in its imagery and subversive in tone. From his mother came habits of gentleness and piety. In him the parents might recognize a fusion of their individual gifts. He appears in his own writing as a most contented child, the memories of his first home recorded twenty-eight years later, in 'Faces in the Fire',

> An island-farm – mid seas of corn
> Swayed by the wandering breath of morn –
> The happy spot where I was born.

From all the evidence, he was a loving, helpful and considerate child whose world was bounded by the flat horizons of the farmland, by Halton Castle and Keckwick Hill with its long plantations of fir trees. The scene had changed little since the last century or, indeed, the one before. Only in the exposed sandstone of the hillside quarries were the worm-casts and ripples left by prehistoric tides a portent of intellectual dispute in the next generation.

The letters and memories of childhood insist that little Charles Dodgson was loved and indulged. At the age of fifty-seven, when he had not had a home that was truly his own for almost forty years, he dedicated a copy of *Alice in Wonderland* to 'A Nursery Darling',

> Whose dream of Heaven is still to be
> At Home: for Home is Bliss.

The first eleven years among the fields and hills of Daresbury were his true childhood, not his exile at Richmond School nor the far worse turmoil of Rugby, where his possessions were marked with the scornful adolescent tribute 'C. L. Dodgson is a Muff.' To his adolescent contemporaries, unfortunately, he had all the characteristics of a muff, a home-bred child, close to his parents, an easy butt for jokes and aggression. It was of the earlier years at Daresbury that he wrote in his poem 'Solitude',

> I'd give all wealth that years have piled,
>   The slow result of Life's decay,
> To be once more a little child
>   For one bright summer day.

The remarkable thing about those lines is that Dodgson wrote his lament for life's decay when he was only twenty-one years old. He looked back to the innocence of early life in much the same way as William Blake or Thomas Traherne, though as sententiously as Wordsworth. Daresbury parsonage and the glebe farm were the world before the Fall of Richmond and Rugby schools. Within its confines, the Dodgsons and their children acknowledged a God of Love rather than of Retribution, to the extent that their son as a middle-aged clergyman was to reject completely the doctrine of eternal punishment.

It is not without significance that the poem commemorating the Daresbury parsonage should be called 'Solitude'. Those who experienced life in the Georgian remoteness of such homes recalled the silence that lay upon them, summer and winter, 'only broken by the cackling of the poultry or the distant threshing in the barn.' In these surroundings, at first under the supervision of his nurse, 'Dear kind Bun,' as he called her in a note written with adult encouragement, Little Charlie played in the nursery or the garden. His first natural playmates were his two elder sisters, though two more sisters and two brothers were born by the time he was six years old. He also played with the children of the Darbyshire family who lived at Morphany Hall and whose mother, known as 'Aunt Dar' to the young Dodgsons, helped to look after the curate's children when both parents were away. As a rule, it was only his father who travelled, fulfilling his duties as Examining Chaplain to the Bishop of Ripon. Despite such companionship, the impression is still of little Charles Dodgson as a preoccupied and solitary child.[12]

By the time the family left Daresbury in 1843, when he was eleven years old, he had seen little of the world beyond the parsonage and the village. There was one summer holiday at Beaumaris on the island of Angelsey, which involved three days' travelling by coach in order to cover the distance that a steam train would soon pass through in a couple of hours. There was occasion for family visits to the Lutwidge grandparents at Hull. There were trips to Warrington, during one of which the Dodgsons had their silhouette portraits cut at the Warrington Exhibition of Science and Natural History in 1840.

There were a few regular visitors to the parsonage. Frequent among them was Thomas Vere Bayne, a boy three years older than Charles Dodgson. His father, who was Headmaster of Warrington Grammar School, came over on Sundays to assist in the services at All Saints. The son was to precede young Charles Dodgson to Christ Church, where their childhood companionship became a friendship that lasted until Dodgson's death. Among other regular visitors was Richard Durnford of Middleton, a founder of the Oxford Union debating society and its first President in 1823. He was to become Bishop of Chichester and, with Trollopean tenacity, remained in office until his death, at the age of ninety-three.

Despite visits and visitors, it was Daresbury and its environs which wove the fabric of childhood experience reflected in Dodgson's later verse. He had no need to learn the art of the acrostic. There was one example which as a boy he encountered Sunday after Sunday. It was painted in the ringers' chamber of the belfry at All Saints in 1730, its initials spelling out the name of the village. It was a verse form that he was to use frequently in dedications and games with children.

> Dare not to come into this Sacred Place
> All you good Ringers, but in Awfull Grace
> Ring not with Hatt nor Spurs nor Insolence
> Each one that does, for every such offence
> Shall forfeit Hatt or Spurs or Twelve Pence.
> But who disturbs a Peal, the same Offender
> Unto the Box his Sixpence shall down Tender.
> Rules such no doubt in every Church are Used
> You and your Bells that may not be Abused.
> Multa rogare, Togata tenere, Retenta Docere.
> Haec tria Discipulum faciunt superare Magistrum.
> Peter Lowton
> John Okell.   Wardens, 1730.[13]

Family stories told of Charles Dodgson have a predictable tone of affectionate pride in his early intelligence and right mindedness. He set to work gathering rushes from the moat of Morphany Hall and peeling them, under the impression that the pith would be of some use to the poor. He invented 'the strangest diversions for himself,' by choosing pets among 'the most odd and unlikely animals.' Little Charles Dodgson 'numbered certain snails and toads among his intimate friends.' He tried to contrive 'civilised warfare' among earthworms by attempting to encase them in small pieces of piping as body-armour. 'In some things, you know, you can't be quite sure what an insect would like,' says the narrator of *Sylvie and Bruno* more than fifty years later. The tiny Bruno is found trying to take captive a snail, which is quite his own size, by clinging to one of the horns. The rules of the hunt require that the creature shall not be harmed.

The images of this insect world were elaborated in his later fiction. In *Sylvie and Bruno*, where the fairies use a dead mouse as a sofa, he talks of a 'Minimifying glass', to reduce an elephant to the size of a mouse, as well as a 'megaloscope' which will increase a flea to the size of a horse. The creatures of the parsonage garden, like the Cater-pillar with the Hookah and the Wasp in a Wig, are presented as citizens of the world with rights to civilized treatment. And in a sharp aside to subvert the children of the hunting, flesh-eating and landowning bourgeoisie, the author of *Sylvie and Bruno* presents the badger and the herring mourning for their lost children.[14]

The logic of compassion for all creatures reflects the extent to which Little Charlie's early education was essentially from his mother, who superintended his reading. Frances Dodgson kept a record of her son's progress in 'Private' religious reading, religious reading 'With Mama', and 'Useful' daily reading, which he undertook on his own. *Pilgrim's Progress* as well as the fiction of Maria Edgeworth and Mary Martha Sherwood's pietistic novel *The Fairchild Family* were matched by such works of general education as *The Parent's Cabinet of Amusement and Instruction*. There was also Hone's *Everyday Book*, as a source of general and practical knowledge. His first steps in Latin seem to have been taken at about the age of five, under the supervision of his father.

Despite the earnest tone of much of their reading, the Dodgson children were not short of playthings. There was a rocking-horse and dolls, toy animals and homemade puzzles from their Aunt Lucy Lutwidge. The family toys included a model village school of cut-out wooden figures with a teacher, pupils and a dunce. A miniature toolkit survives which the practical young Charles Dodgson made in adoles-cence for his older sister Elizabeth. A curiosity was the wooden nose trick which he had apparently designed himself, a mask that gave the impression that its strings were threaded through his nostrils. Most prescient of all, perhaps, there was a miniature croquet set. They were a genial and sociable family. Even the strictness of their religious instruction was tempered by a sense of intellectual enjoyment, when the Dodgson parents supplemented reading of sacred texts by buying their children a jigsaw puzzle 'Life of Christ'.

As a child in the 1840s, it seems that the young Charles Dodgson read among current publications Halliwell-Phillipps' *Nursery Rhymes of England*, which contained such familiar figures of Wonderland and the Looking-Glass world as the Queen of Hearts, Humpty Dumpty, and Tweedle-Dum and Tweedle-Dee. It seems probable that he read Edward Lear's first *Book of Nonsense* in 1846, since he imitated the limerick form soon afterwards. His childhood parodies of Macaulay, Scott, and medieval ballads also indicate that his reading soon outran the moralizing scope of Hannah More and Maria Edgeworth.

Parental pride in his precocious development underlies family stories of his intellectual curiosity. Long before the age at which it might matter to him, he found a book of logarithms and insisted that his father should explain its tables. Mr Dodgson told his son that he was much too young to understand these things. 'But please explain!' the impatient child persisted.

Young Charles Dodgson was undoubtedly a very clever little boy. He was pious enough to believe in the moral teaching of childhood reading, while finding the teachers themselves hackneyed or trite. Though he had a profound respect for the principles of his Church, a reverence for the Bible, a heightened sensitivity towards whatever was morally suspect, his wit mocked the humourless school-miss morality against which any intelligent child might rebel. He had a quick ear and a sure instinct for parody, often obliterating the original by the verve of his pastiche. Generations remembered 'How doth the little crocodile . . .' or 'You are old, Father William', who neither knew nor cared what the originals might have been. As for the school-room moralists, by the 1840s the evangelicals were apt to seem philistine as well as cliché-mongering. In the name of moral simplicity, they had reduced the Church of England to little more than a hymn-singing preaching-house, shorn of its Elizabethan or Caroline glories in music and liturgy. Though no ritualist, the young Charles Dodgson was to praise the Oxford Movement for bringing back liturgy and formality to Anglicanism.

Not all the prudent moral texts of childhood were derided, and many were quoted with approval in solemn moments. '"Don't care" leads to the gallows' appears in *Sylvie and Bruno*, as does the example of the self-indulgent man who throws away a stale crust and longs for it when poverty overtakes him. Moreover, in his childhood Little Charlie learnt readily the social virtues of punctuality and cleanliness, which he preached to his brothers and sisters in his first poems.

> And when the hour arrives be *there*,
>   Where'er that 'there' may be;
> Uncleanly hands or ruffled hair
>   Let no one ever see.[15]

As an adult he was to be credited with the neatness of the bandbox and the fashion plate, however plain his clothes. He was meticulous to the point of compulsion, whether over clean linen, gloves in summer and winter, or financial matters, and he had a horror of infection. His correspondence was organized by a register of letters sent and received, including a summary of their contents. By his death it contained 98,000 entries of his own correspondence. 'Of no man may it more truly be said that until he was satisfied he was dissatisfied,' remarked the *Academy*'s obituary of 22 January 1898. This degree of correctness and precision in his conduct was to seem obsessive to a later age.

*

Fashionable though it became to see the adult as emotionally crippled by the repressions of childhood, the facts scarcely support that view of the Dodgson family. This was never plainer than in Frances Dodgson's letter to her son, written from Hull, where his parents had gone on the illness of his maternal grandfather, Major Lutwidge. The reference to Will in the letter indicates that it was written after 1838, when the seventh child Wilfred was born and when Charles Dodgson the younger was six years old. He had also started his Latin lessons.

> My dearest Charlie, I have used you rather ill in not having written to you sooner, but I know you will forgive me, as your Grandpapa has liked to have me with him so much, and I could not write and talk to him comfortably . . . It delights me, my darling Charlie, to hear that you are getting on so well with your Latin, and that you make so few mistakes in your exercises . . . I hope my sweetest Will says 'Mama' sometimes, and that precious Tish has not forgotten. Give them and all my other treasures, including yourself, 1,000,000,000 kisses from me, with my most affectionate love. I am sending you a shabby note, but I cannot help it. Give my kindest love to Aunt Dar, and believe me, my own dearest Charlie, to be your sincerely affectionate Mama.[16]

The letter is one of the few direct insights into life at Daresbury. It suggests the boy was in more danger of being spoilt than repressed. He treasured the message and protected it from those younger children who might crumple or tear it, writing on the back, 'No one is to touch this note, for it belongs to C.L.D. Covered with slimy pitch so that it will wet their fingers.'

Charles Dodgson the elder exerted a more instinctive authority than his wife. Yet his feelings for his children appeared as intense and as benign. On 6 January 1840, he wrote to his eight-year-old namesake from Ripon. The boy had given him a commission to buy a file, a screwdriver, and a metal ring. His father's reply was one of wild hilarity, a violent and undisciplined anticipation of his son's later style. He would put Leeds to the sword, if the articles Little Charlie wanted were not forthcoming from the ironmongers. The slaughter would continue until only the last cat was left. In general terror, the inhabitants and animals alike would try to take cover. The Mayor of Leeds would be discovered 'in a soup plate covered up with custard, and stuck full of almonds to make him look like a sponge cake.' The prospect of old women and cows climbing chimneys and ducks hiding in coffee cups is an insight into the family's humour during the younger Charles Dodgson's early childhood.[17]

When his sons went to Christ Church, their father wrote them letters of financial and practical advice. When Skeffington, the second son, failed his degree examinations in 1861 and might have expected a reprimand, his father assured him that the family was disappointed for him and not on its own account. He must not indulge in self-reproach. The conservatism of the High Churchman was tempered by a liberal understanding of the young man's feelings. The only lack of feeling lay in a hint that Skeffington could not be blamed if God had not given him brains enough to confront the Oxford Schools. 'Bravo, old boy!' wrote Dodgson senior when Skeffington passed at a further attempt the following year, 'you are quite the great person here today.'[18]

Happiness, like wealth, is comparative. Such general concepts as happiness in early Victorian childhood are near meaningless when compared with the variety of actual experience. Where in these gradations can life at Daresbury be placed? A decade before Dodgson's infancy, John Ruskin was whipped for falling down stairs and allowed to burn himself on a hot stove that he should learn not to do so again. By contrast with Frances Dodgson's admiration of her six-year-old son, a more vindictive philosophy of upbringing possessed the single-minded women of the 1830s. 'Never let a child think it can deceive you,' wrote Louisa Shipley sternly to her sister-in-law in 1833, 'They are cunning little creatures, and reason before they can speak;

secure this, and the chief part of your work is done . . .' The letter might have come from Dodgson's Duchess.

> I speak severely to my boy,
>   And beat him when he sneezes;
> For he can thoroughly enjoy
>   The pepper when he pleases![19]

The far extreme from Dodgson's early childhood may be represented by the early ordeals of Augustus Hare, whose boyhood was ruled by a demented and sanctimonious matriarchy, the occasional male presence being that of Uncle Julius, summoned from Pevensey Rectory on those occasions when it was decided that the five-year-old should be beaten with a horsewhip for too great attachment to worldly things. His toys were taken from him at five years old and he was permitted none after that time. He was not allowed to play with other children. Grannie superintended his writing lessons, beating his knuckles with a heavy ruler if his pen moved off course. When a woman in the village felt sorry for the child and gave him a toffee-apple, rhubarb and soda were administered with a forcing-spoon, an educational experiment then repeated regularly and which, he believed, did him permanent damage. His last consolation was the cat, Selina, whom he adored and who appeared to be the only creature with affection for him. When this worldly distraction was discovered, a devout supernumerary aunt hanged the animal from a tree in the garden and summoned him to view the result. ('If I don't take this child away,' thought Alice, 'they're sure to kill it in a day or two.') Uncle Julius was the first of this tribe to die. Hare described himself as feeling 'Grief without a pang.'[20]

Of course the moral doctrines of the Daresbury parsonage were inflexible, as they must have been if the world of faith and political hope was to have meaning. That the children found the doctrines oppressive is not substantiated. The enlightened Sabbatarianism of the younger Charles Dodgson, still more his sensitivity to what was profane or improper, seemed to him as rational and enlightened as his moral disbelief in the eternal torment of the wicked or his revulsion at cruelty to animals through vivisection or hunting as a sport. Like Augustus Hare, he was attracted by the idea that Satan might be a candidate for repentance and redemption. He rebelled with equal force in *Sylvie and Bruno* against the performance of religious duty in the hope of divine reward, as though taking a plunge on the stock market. Love was the motive and the reward. On all the evidence, this was the great lesson of his childhood.[21]

*

Despite sixteen years as curate of Daresbury, the elder Charles Dodgson was not without influence in forwarding his career and the interests of his flock. One of his projects was to minister to the itinerant bargemen and navvies who gathered at the canal junction of Preston Brook on the outskirts of Daresbury, where the horses which pulled the narrow-boats were stabled. While walking with the local landowner, Lord Francis Egerton, Mr Dodgson once remarked, 'If I only had a hundred pounds, I would turn one of those barges into a chapel.' Lord Egerton asked him to describe what he had in mind. A few weeks later, Charles Dodgson received a message from Egerton that a barge had been equipped as a chapel and was ready for his use. From then on it was used for Sunday evening services, as well as for baptisms of the bargees' children. If the bargees could not come to All Saints, then All Saints must go to them. It was precisely the attitude required of a modern clergyman in a new industrial age.

The curate of Daresbury was not forgotten at Christ Church. One of his friends was Edward Bouverie Pusey, now Regius Professor of Hebrew, Canon of Christ Church Cathedral, and one of the most prestigious leaders of the Oxford Movement soon after its inception in 1833. When they were young graduates at Oxford, he had presented Charles Dodgson with the manuscript of his prize-winning Latin essay, which he had read aloud in the Sheldonian Theatre in 1824.

More powerful still, in the matter of patronage, was another Christ Church man, Charles Thomas Longley, a future Archbishop of Canterbury. When Longley left Christ Church in 1829, it was to be Headmaster of Harrow. However, his ambition was a bishopric. Lord Melbourne, as Prime Minister, recommended Longley to William IV in 1836 for the new see of Ripon. In the same year, Longley appointed Charles Dodgson as his examining chaplain. In this role, Mr Dodgson supervised the preparation of candidates for confirmation and oversaw religious education in the diocese. It was not a paid post, as Longley made clear, nor was he able to 'reward' him. Charles Dodgson therefore remained curate of Daresbury, though he took on his honorary duties with diligence. The sermon which he preached in Ripon Cathedral at the ordination service in January 1837 was published and in 1839 he issued a series of texts 'for the Instruction of young persons before Confirmation.'

Nor was his ability as a classical scholar overlooked. Dr Pusey had planned a library of translations of the Fathers of the Church, so that Englishmen might debate the religious issues of the day with a clearer idea of traditional doctrine. He invited Charles Dodgson to undertake the translation of the second-century author Tertullian. It was a considerable task, in the light of his other duties, but he had it ready for publication in 1842.

While the years between 1827 and 1836 were something of a fallow period, after the appointment of Longley to Ripon, the young curate began to gain influence in the affairs of the Church. It was unlikely that a man of his abilities would be left to grow old in a remote and scattered Cheshire parish. He had shown what he could do to revive the Church at Daresbury and to extend the ministry of All Saints to the working men of the new age. As for his intellectual position, while Mr Dodgson could not fully align himself with the new fashion of the Oxford Movement, he was High Churchman enough not to seem completely out of step.

In the cliché of the day, he was a sound man and something must be done for him. Longley took up the matter with the Prime Minister early in 1840. Though the young Queen Victoria had by now succeeded the quirky and unpredictable William IV, Lord Melbourne had held on to office. Longley suggested that Charles Dodgson should have the vacant Crown living of Catterick in the North Riding of Yorkshire. It seemed unlikely that there would be another vacancy of this sort in the diocese and recognition of his services was due. Lord Ashley, later and better known as the 7th Earl of Shaftesbury, campaigner for the Factories Acts, wrote in support of the proposal.

Melbourne, to whom many matters of business including government itself were apt to appear 'a great bore', recognized what he called 'the fitness of the candidate and the claims of the Bishop.' But he was in a difficult situation, having been defeated in the House of Commons the previous year. Constitutional convention required that he should give way to Sir Robert Peel, as leader of the Conservative opposition. The young Victoria, however, did not like Sir Robert Peel, while she adored Melbourne as if he was the father she had never known. This dislike was intensified by Peel's demand that she should change her ladies-in-waiting as she changed her prime ministers. She had refused, Peel had withdrawn, and Melbourne remained in office. Patronage was the means of pleasing the friends and allies who would keep him there. Melbourne needed the living of Catterick for this purpose and gave it elsewhere.[22]

The rebuff to Charles Dodgson and his patron was a reminder of how deeply the nation remained divided in its public life between the new earnestness and the old cynicism. There could have been no greater contrast than that between the indolent amateurism of Melbourne and the intense religious and social commitment of Daresbury parsonage. Observing Charles Dodgson's generation with gloom, Melbourne remarked, 'All young people are growing mad about religion.' By 1840, he viewed the young Victoria and Albert with the unhappy prophesy, 'This damned morality will ruin everything!'[23]

But history and youth were on the Dodgsons' side. Voices like theirs, rather than old men like Melbourne, were to dominate the century. By the following year the great amateur was out of office and Peel had replaced him. Sir Robert was Charles Dodgson's type of Conservative, firm in his values but liberal in his determination to improve the lives of ordinary men and women. This Conservative was to become the hero of that labouring class to whom the curate of Daresbury sought to minister at Preston Brook. At Peel's death, Henry Mayhew was told, tears were shed in the hovels of London and a publican whose only customers were 'soldiers, thieves, and prostitutes,' put his very beer machines and gas pipes into mourning for the dead statesman.[24]

On the change of government in 1841, Bishop Longley came forward again. After Melbourne's refusal of Catterick, there was no other living both vacant and suitable in the Ripon diocese. Longley cast a cold eye upon those present incumbents who might be expected to die in the decently close future. The most likely invalid was the Reverend James Dalton, an amiable and elderly botanist at Croft, a little village on the south bank of the Tees, no more than three miles from Darlington. The Tees marked the division of Yorkshire from Durham and of the diocese of Ripon from that of Durham. Mr Dalton was not at all well and seemed unlikely to last much longer. As it happened, the old man put up quite a struggle and managed to impede the Bishop's strategy by living for another two years.

Without waiting for the outcome, Longley wrote to Peel. There was, he admitted, a vacant living of a mere £100 a year, but that was too little for Charles Dodgson. It was impossible to do anything about Croft at the moment but would Sir Robert consent to promise Mr Dodgson that he should have the living when Mr Dalton died? Peel did not respond well to this rather ghoulish form of patronage. He read Bishop Longley a lecture on the folly of 'any assurances calculated to raise expectations' at a time when the appointment could not be made. Bluntly, what the Prime Minister might or might not do in the future was none of the Bishop's business. 'I must reserve to myself the unfettered discretion of dealing as I may think fit with the livings you mention should a vacancy occur in either of them during my tenure of official power.'

It seemed, however, that life at Christ Church, Harrow and Ripon had thickened Bishop Longley's skin. When Mr Dalton breathed his last, a letter was despatched at once to Downing Street from the Bishop's palace. Longley hastened to inform Peel that the living of Croft 'has just become vacant.' In short order, he rehearsed the claims of Charles Dodgson, his career at Christ Church, the hungry mouths of his nine children – the number had actually increased to ten while Longley was arguing his case and an eleventh was yet to come. He urged preferment for 'a Clergyman of high Professional Character, of first rate ability, and of much Theological attainment – one indeed who would adorn the very first Stations in the Church.'

Though there were said by Peel to be 'numberless competitors' for the living of Croft, further letters arrived on Charles Dodgson's behalf from Lord Wharncliffe, who was President of the Council in Peel's government, the Earl of Ripon, Lord Egerton, and the Dodgsons' Member of Parliament. Others were on the way. It must have seemed to Peel that however forward-looking Charles Dodgson might be in some respects, he lacked none of the skills for working the old system of patronage to maximum effect. Indeed, the Prime Minister was considerably annoyed by this attempt to march him in the direction of an inevitable decision. It was Longley who received the first blast. 'Excuse me for saying that I wish I had been left at liberty to make my selection of Mr Dodgson (which I was perfectly prepared to do) on the single ground of his merits and claims – without the intervention of various Colleagues of mine and Members of Parliament who have been urged to address me in favour of Mr Dodgson, necessarily involving me in a very extensive correspondence and not influencing my decision.'

Having relieved his feelings, however, he wrote a graceful and complimentary letter to the Bishop, offering Mr Dodgson the vacant living of Croft. The appointment was made on condition that the new incumbent should live at Croft and carry out the parish duties himself. Gone was the more relaxed system of the 1830s when, for example, the new Bishop of Exeter was allowed to keep a sinecure living in Durham to provide an extra £4,000 a year for his creature comforts without ever having to perform any duties in exchange. Mr Dodgson was to work for his stipend.[25]

The appointment at Croft was a social parable of its time and a lesson that the younger Charles Dodgson learnt with quite as much dexterity as any proposition in Euclid. Despite his rules of behaviour, which to some were prudish and to others priggish, he was to pump the well of patronage throughout his adult life without hesitation. He did not do it for himself, though he did so for his family. The Dodgsons belonged to a class which served its country in the Church, the army and in public life. For the most part, its members did not grow rich. Indeed, as his father had complained, they were introduced to a style of life which they were then denied the income to indulge. They knew however that those who do not ask will not get. Asking and getting were carried out, as by tribal custom, through the system of patronage. It was a matter of influence and prejudices, favours owed and sought. That its use was in any way immoral rarely troubled the strictest conscience at a time when Macaulay in the *Edinburgh Review* in 1833 still defended political corruption as the only way in which eighteenth-century parliamentary government could have survived. So the obligation of the state to Captain Dodgson of the Dragoon Guards or to the Bishop of Ossory and Ferns in his draughty 'palace' was recognized in the person of their descendant.

Those who had sought preferment for the curate of Daresbury must have felt themselves vindicated by the energy and dedication with which he raised himself to become Canon of Ripon in 1852 and Archdeacon of Richmond in 1854. It was said that he later asked to be made Headmaster of Harrow but that was not to be. Instead, he preached and he argued on behalf of his faith. His sermons were printed in Oxford and London. His pronouncements from the pulpits of St Peter's, Croft, and Ripon Cathedral had the same balance of personal belief and social concern that his conduct at Daresbury had shown. It was not religion alone which demanded respect for Holy Writ.

The Bible is the poor man's library – the most indigent strive to possess it; the most careless to retain at least some feeling of reverence for it. In all their doubts and difficulties, an appeal to it is unanswerable; its authority is decisive; and a single text of Scripture will often prove more convincing, than volumes of the most subtle arguments of human wisdom.[26]

It was a precept his son never forgot. As for the young clergymen whose instructor he became, Charles Dodgson senior warned them that the priest had no authority to stray from the path which he had been called to follow.

Let him not exhibit to his flock the picture of one who serveth two masters: the solemn preacher in the pulpit, and the vain trifler in the world ... Let him not appear with words of charity and humility on his lips, and a spirit of selfish pride reigning within his heart: proclaiming a religion of peace, yet encouraging the distractions and fostering the jealousies of religious party.[27]

It was unfortunate for him that as Archdeacon he was too often to be the target of such distractions and jealousies. As a High Churchman, he upset the Evangelicals, taunting them by telling them that to be evangelical meant nothing but preaching the Gospel as interpreted by 'the Catholic Church of Christ.' Much was to be made of the 'honest doubters' of the 1850s who broadened the faith of the Church of England until it seemed to some to be no faith at all. Yet the conflict was no less intense between those who regarded the Established Church as Protestant and those who regarded it as Catholic. In January 1864, Charles Dodgson, as canon in residence, preached in Ripon Cathedral on 'The Sacraments of the Gospel', pointing out that the Articles of Religion of the Church of England laid down that 'the Body of Christ is given, taken, and eaten in the Supper, only after an heavenly and spiritual manner.' The Catechism, however, taught that 'the Body and Blood of Christ are verily and indeed taken and received by the faithful in the Lord's Supper.' Those who denied this were 'in heretical opposition to that Catholic Faith, which the Church believes herself to hold, and binds herself to teach.'[28]

He was asking for trouble, not for the first time, and he got it. The Dean of Ripon, Dr Goode, denounced the sermon in a pamphlet with a prefatory letter to the Archdeacon. He described what Charles

Dodgson thought was heresy. 'It is notorious,' he protested, 'that I maintain both the views here denounced.' The Archdeacon was also attacked in the press, an article in the *Record* containing what he called, 'untruth, uncharitableness, vulgarity . . . Religious party-spirit degraded to a mean and malignant passion.'[29]

The Bishop was dismayed by the virulence of the dispute threatening his diocese. Charles Dodgson made a formal complaint to him of a sermon preached by the Dean in the cathedral on 31 January 1864. Dr Goode trumped that by persuading four of the canons to ask the Archbishop of York to proceed against Archdeacon Dodgson in the ecclesiastical courts. It was the Archbishop's turn to be dismayed. He wrote to the Bishop, and the Bishop wrote to Dr Goode, 'suggesting reasons against any further proceedings whatever.' Dr Goode protested that he was innocent of any part in the design to prosecute the Archdeacon. He had never wished for legal proceedings. All the same, he chided the Archdeacon for making a formal complaint about him, 'a thing which, if the case had been reversed, I would rather have lost my right hand than put my name to.' And he made a final thrust by denouncing again Dodgson's 'solemn *sentences of excommunication* against those who hold different views.'

The threatened prosecution and counter-prosecution came to nothing. With a mental agility worthy of a Student of Christ Church and Lecturer in Mathematics, Charles Dodgson suggested that the bread and wine might not be the Body and Blood of Christ beforehand but became such when taken in Holy Communion.[30]

It was not the first time he had started a public argument. In 1852, Bishop Longley had had to intervene after the Archdeacon preached at Leeds on 'Ritual Worship', remarking in his sermon that 'we do indeed retain, and ever desire to retain, with Rome, every essential element of Catholic Worship: while we denounce as vital corruptions, things which she retains as essential elements.' Yet though his views might not have been welcomed everywhere, there was no doubt that Charles Dodgson could expound them vigorously and hold his own in the consequent row. He was a lively and notable controversialist who had deserved his preferment to the living of Croft in 1843.[31]

The living of Croft was not the only favour sought by the Dodgsons in the 1840s. Pondering the education of his three sons, the Rector wrote to his friend Dr Pusey in 1849, asking him to nominate the eldest for a Studentship at Christ Church. Pusey had not been well placed to assist in procuring the living at Croft. His own alleged

'Roman' sympathies had got him into trouble at Oxford, until in 1845 he was suspended for two years from preaching before the University after a sermon which appeared to commend the 'Romish' doctrine of Transubstantiation. Though his position was now strong again, it seemed he might prove as fastidious in his way as Peel. He replied that he would not nominate his friend's son if it meant passing over a candidate of superior attainments. He need not have troubled himself. By 1849, the eldest son had shown attainments equalled by few other young men in England.

3

Facing the World

I N H I S 1 8 4 1 *Edinburgh Review* essay on Warren Hastings, Macaulay drew a distinction which Georgian England readily understood between the challenge of fame and public life to Hastings and the quiet reclusive piety of his schoolfriend, the poet William Cowper, who knew neither the exhilaration nor the temptations of power. As the early Victorian age developed, however, it became more difficult for members of a family as linked to public life as the Dodgsons had been to avoid its influences and distractions as Cowper had done.[1]

It was a paradox of the younger Charles Dodgson's life that, while sensitive to profanity, lewdness, impropriety, and even indelicacy of any kind, he often lived close to all these things. He seemed like the sleepwalker who must not be woken or the wire-walker who dare not look down. One of the young man's most frequently used criteria was whether some cultural manifestation was 'wholesome' or 'unwholesome'. At eleven years old, in the self-conscious gentility of clerical life, he was closer to the unwholesome life of his contemporaries than William Cowper had ever been.

The village of Croft, to which the family moved in 1843 and which was to be the Reverend Dodgson's home for the remaining twenty-five years of his life, represented a quite different order of existence to the curacy of Daresbury. Croft stood, in a literal sense, at an artery or junction of the nation's history. There was wealth rather than the quaintness of custom on every side. Much of the surrounding countryside might have been mistaken for parkland. With its well-tended paddocks and plain but substantial houses, Croft was an area for breeding hunters and race-horses. Two years after the Dodgsons arrived, the Darlington race meeting was held on the 'new course' at Croft in August 1845. Excursion trains were run from the Bank Top Station in Darlington to Croft at a sixpenny fare. The young Charles Dodgson developed an interest in railway trains and in the mathematics of backing horses to win. He did not, of course, bet on them.

The principal buildings of Croft were far more stylish than those of Daresbury. Apart from the church and the rectory, there was Clervaux Castle, a rich man's folly built for its present occupant, Sir William Chaytor, in a neo-Norman style. The Croft Spa Hotel stood on the road near the rectory, a long, low building with a pillared porch. Croft had been fashionable enough to have a spa in the previous century. 'Croft Sulphur Springs' was represented by a plain but handsome building with an elegant verandah. Most developments were quite recent, dating from the reign of George IV less than twenty years before, though Croft Water had been sold in London in sealed bottles as early as 1713. The hotel had also been one of the principal coaching inns on the road from London to the north until the coming of the railway in the 1830s. By 1843 the spa was going out of fashion, ending Croft as a watering-place. The end of the fashion suited the Dodgsons well. Their parish was unlikely to benefit from a shifting population of tourists and pleasure-seekers.

Croft was a little way north of the mid-point between London and Edinburgh. The road which ran through the village from Northallerton and then turned sharply to cross the river was also a military route in time of war. At the beginning of the sixteenth century a fine stone bridge had been built on seven pointed arches across the width of the Tees, where the river separated the North Riding of Yorkshire from the county of Durham. The bridge was constructed at a time when the Wars of the Roses were a recent memory and invasion by the Scots a constant possibility. It was described in 1531 as 'the most directe and sure way and passage for the Kinge or Soveraigne Lordes armye and ordnance to resort and passe over into the North partes and marches of this realme.'

As with the village, so with the church of which Mr Dodgson was now the rector. St Peter's with its Norman foundations and window arches of the thirteenth century had an air of importance and influence that was quite foreign to All Saints, Daresbury. It boasted traces of Roman workmanship and, inside, a cross-shaft from an Anglo-Saxon tomb, carved with an interweaving of strange animals who might well have earned a place in the 1860s bestiary of Alice Liddell. The traveller crossing the bridge from Durham into North Yorkshire, saw first the low roof-line of the ancient sandstone church and its rather squat tower, separated from the fast flowing current by an uneven little graveyard and the grass of the river bank. In the winter months the Tees was in spate and watermarks in the church bore witness to the floods that had occurred.

Beyond the low door and porch of St Peter's, in the aisle and the north chapel, stood the memorials of those to whom the church and its incumbents owed their privileges. The carved tomb-chests commemorated Sir Richard Clervaux who died in 1490 and two members of the Milbanke family, one of whose younger members, Anne Isabella Milbanke, married Lord Byron in 1815 and separated from him in the following year among rumours of gross sexual misconduct. The Milbanke pew, dominating the interior, was more like a pair of theatrical boxes than a church pew. It was enclosed and roofed, curtained in crimson, raised level with the pulpit on fluted columns, and approached by a wide staircase with a balustrade that might have done for the hall of a manor house. Here, in the brief duration of their marriage, Lord and Lady Byron had attended morning service while staying at the family seat of Halnaby Hall.

Less scandalous but more troublesome in his way, the present congregation included George Hudson, an entrepreneur famous as 'The Railway King'. When the rector's sermon bored him, Hudson would stand up and then sit down again with his back to the pulpit in an attitude of brusque contempt. Mrs Hudson added her protest by raising her parasol, snapping it open and shut as a signal that the homily had gone on too long. The clergy were not to forget that those who paid the preacher called the tune.

The large Georgian rectory, which was to be the Dodgson family home, stood behind the church in extensive grounds. At the rear were kitchen gardens with well-stocked greenhouses and exotic plants, among them the night-blowing cereus whose flowers lasted only a few hours and faded with the setting sun. This was a popular curiosity of the neighbourhood. The lawns of the front garden were those on which the Dodgson children usually played. There was an acacia tree for climbing and a yew tree, known as 'The Umbrella Tree'.

The rectory itself was a solid, old-fashioned home. Even for nine children and two more to come, it seemed ample. The move from Daresbury was delayed until the autumn of 1843 because Frances Dodgson was pregnant with their tenth child, the daughter Henrietta.

An inventory of its rooms listed a drawing-room, dining-room, study, sitting-room, numerous bedrooms, some with dressing-rooms attached. It was a gentleman's house. Below stairs there were two kitchens, a servants' hall, a butler's pantry, a housekeeper's room, a scullery, a laundry, a brewhouse, a larder, and a dairy. The coachhouse had stabling for seven horses. The other outbuildings included a tithe barn, pigsties and a henhouse. There was a three-and-a-half acre field attached to the property and nineteen acres of land at a little distance. It would require two additional servants, another maid indoors and a man for outdoor work.

As was commonly the case in early Victorian England, the rector of Croft was also a gentleman-farmer, running the property to supplement his stipend. The nearby field provided pasture for two cows. Pigs and chickens were kept in the outbuildings. The remaining nineteen acres of land were let to provide part of his income. On this basis, a net income would exceed £850 a year. By way of comparison, when it was necessary to employ a master and mistress for the village school, the rector paid the master £60 a year and the mistress £27. To such people and to those industrial workers and farm labourers who would have been astonished to earn as much as the schoolmaster, Mr Dodgson appeared very well placed. Indeed, when he wrote to his brother Hassard, he sounded like a man who has come into his kingdom at last.

One financial doubt lingered in the rector's mind, concerning the future of the young Charles Dodgson. The eleven year old was clever and precocious, which was gratifying in its way but meant that his education might be all the more expensive. Like most prudent men of his age, the new rector believed that money spent upon a son's education was a far wiser investment than that saved to be bequeathed to him after his father's death. To Hassard Dodgson, the prudent lawyer, his brother suggested that it would be best to forgo £1,000 of capital and take out an insurance policy for the time when Christ Church might open its doors to the boy. Of course, it might be possible to persuade a member of the Chapter at Christ Church to get the young Charles Dodgson a Studentship. But then Mr Dodgson would still have to make him an allowance to live upon and his present income would not bear it. One way or another, he must spend capital.

Though he did not press the subject on his brother, the rector's financial difficulty was compounded by the need to educate two other sons, Skeffington and Wilfred. A fourth boy, Edwin, was to be born in 1846, the last child of Charles and Frances Dodgson. With such responsibilities, it was as well that the father's own career prospered.

If the new rector had done well for himself by his preferment, he did not hesitate to share his good fortune. Both tradition and evidence show the Dodgsons as a benevolent and charitable family. Long after their deaths, those who had been children during the 1840s recalled how the Dodgsons gave milk from their cows to the parishioners as well as apples from the trees in their garden. The young Charles Dodgson was remembered as a tall, thin, serious boy, always pleasant to the villagers. They described him reading or writing, 'sitting or lying full length under the noble acacia tree in the rectory garden.'[2]

Within a few months of his arrival, Mr Dodgson began planning a National School at Croft, where education would be available to all. It was to be under the superintendence of the rector and would train its pupils in the principles of the Established Church. There were, in practice, two schools where boys and girls were separately educated. They would be taught reading, writing, arithmetic and, in the case of the girls, needlework. There were to be sixty children in each school. They would play, as they worked, separately. Payment by the parents was to be twopence a week for one child from each family, threepence for two and fourpence for three or more. A master and mistress from the Training Institution at York were appointed and the total cost of the school was £100 a year.

The payment by the families of pupils totalled £20, the deficit being made up by donations. The sum raised to start the school was £232, of which Dodgson himself subscribed over half, £121. For the year 1845, £75 had been raised for the annual expenses. Mr Dodgson contributed £30 of this and his wife a further £5, while local worthies of far greater wealth than they were content to give a guinea. To judge from such evidence, the generosity of the Dodgsons towards the less fortunate was real enough. Those members of the family who had no money to donate gave their time instead. As years passed, the sons and daughters of the rectory took their part in teaching the village children, as they did in visiting the sick.[3]

Though Croft lay in the mainstream of early Victorian life when compared with the solitude of Daresbury, it still represented a relatively tranquil and agreeable existence. Divided from the industrial north by the Tees, a visitor might find it hard to realize that within three or four miles lay one of the great centres of the industrial revolution. The Stockton to Darlington railway of 1825 had been the first of its kind anywhere. Darlington's population depended upon the iron foundries and railway workshops, the wool mills and the tanneries, the subsidiary trades of heavy industry. Within an afternoon it was possible to walk from the pastures and paddocks of Croft to scenes of fire and din that suggested Dante's *Inferno*, and then walk home again in time for supper. The villas of successful manufacturers began to appear in the clean air of the surrounding fields.

The political culture of the industrial city seemed alien to the Dodgsons' enlightened Conservatism in politics and High Churchmanship in religion. Gaining a parliamentary seat after the Reform Bill of 1832, Darlington was represented by the first Quaker to be admitted to the House of Commons, to be followed in due course by a Liberal. Neither the rector nor his son showed anything but hostility towards the Liberal party.

While the Dodgsons behaved with eighteenth-century village charity in Croft, bearing gifts of food to the deserving poor, the intractable problems of Darlington's slums were beyond them. The younger Charles Dodsgon made no comment on the crowded and insanitary houses of Parkgate, Albert Hill or Bank Top, condemned by an official report in 1850, even though he passed them every time he was driven to the echoing vault of the new Bank Top railway station, where the expresses rattled between London and Edinburgh.

'Never do I walk the streets, but I see wretched ruins of humanity, women trampled and crushed into devils by society,' wrote one of Darlington's most famous sons, 'and my heart has been racked with anguish for these victims of our juggernaut.' W. T. Stead, Dodgson's younger contemporary, and contributor to Darlington's *Northern Echo*, was to be first famous and then notorious as editor of the *Pall Mall Gazette*. His campaign against white slavery in 1885 provoked Dodgson to write to the Prime Minister demanding that Stead should be prosecuted for the indecency of his articles. Better that young men should know nothing of *The Maiden Tribute of Modern Babylon* than that they should risk being excited by what they read. Sure of his moral ground, he denounced those who exposed what would better have remained concealed, as Darlington was from the life of Croft Rectory.[4]

*

In common with most boys of his class, the younger Charles Dodgson was educated at home until he was twelve years old. It was then necessary to find a school where he could board and learn something of the wider society for which he must prepare. He would see comparatively little of family life for the next six years. In August 1844, he was sent as a boarder to Richmond School, ten miles from Croft. It was a sensitive choice for the boy's introduction to the school system. Richmond School was small but distinguished, dating back to the fourteenth century. Its main building was a schoolroom of 1677 in the churchyard, where the boys sat on benches at sloping desks with the headmaster at a rostrum at the far end, assisted in teaching and keeping order by an usher.

The school had 120 boys, divided among the houses where they lived. Charles Dodgson was one of sixteen boys in Swale House, the headmaster's residence which the boarders shared with the family. It was a small enough group to be free of the bullying rabble or personal spite which blemished most public schools of the day. James Tate, the son of a classical scholar who had preceded him in the post, was known as a kind and gentle headmaster, far removed from the sadistic pedagogues of legend. The teaching was principally of Latin and Greek, though such subjects as mathematics could be added for an extra fee.

Richmond was a picturesque little country town, away from the new industries of Yorkshire in the 1840s, with a twelfth-century keep, crumbling castle walls and fine churches. It may have been here that Charles Dodgson saw his first theatre. Richmond's Theatre Royal, built in 1788, was plain but elegant with its boxes on their Tuscan pillars and its graceful proscenium arch.

Unlike the great public schools, Richmond preserved a childish innocence, due in part to the genial character of its headmaster. When the young Charles Dodgson wrote to his two eldest sisters on 5 August 1844, four days after his arrival, the ragging which he had undergone seems hardly more than a child's game.

> They first proposed to play at 'King of the Cobblers' and asked if I would be king, to which I agreed. Then they made me sit down and sat (on the ground) in a circle round me, and told me to say 'Go to work,' which I said, and they immediately began kicking me and knocking me on all sides. The next game they proposed was 'Peter, the red lion,' and they made a mark on a tombstone (for we were playing in the churchyard)

and one of the boys walked with his eyes shut, holding out his finger, trying to touch the mark; then a little boy came forward to lead the rest and led a good many very near the mark; at last it was my turn; they told me to shut my eyes well, and the next minute I had my finger in the mouth of one of the boys, who had stood (I believe) before the tombstone with his mouth open. For 2 nights I slept alone and for the rest of the time with Ned Swire. The boys play me no tricks now.[5]

It seems that Mr Dodgson, keeping moral surveillance from ten miles away, had demanded from his son an account of any faults committed and a list of all the texts upon which he heard sermons preached. The rector need not have worried. The boy's only fault to date had been coming to dinner on one occasion after grace was said. He could only remember the text of one of the Sunday sermons because the other – like the sermon itself – was scarcely audible.

His fifteen months at Richmond School seem to have been happy enough, though he was reputed in the family to have shown that he 'knew well how to use his fists in defence of a righteous cause.' This seems uncharacteristic. He remembered the school and his 'kind old headmaster' with affection. As a pupil, he wrote his first Latin verses on 25 November, in celebration of Phoebus the Sun God descending in splendour and tinged with gold. More enthusiastically, he contributed to the school magazine a story, 'The Unknown One', 'probably of the sensational type in which small boys usually revel.'[6]

Mr Tate's first report on his new pupil, made to the rector of Croft, was filled with praise, except in the matter of scansion or translation from Latin verse, where the boy was inclined to fit the text into the metre and meaning he had already devised. 'I do not hesitate to state my opinion,' wrote James Tate, 'that he possesses, along with other and excellent natural endowments, a very uncommon share of genius.'

Gentle and cheerful in his intercourse with others, playful and ready in conversation, he is capable of acquirements and knowledge far beyond his years, while his reason is so clear and so jealous of error, that he will not rest satisfied without a most exact solution of whatever appears to him obscure. He has passed an excellent examination just now in mathematics, exhibiting at times an illustration of that love of precise argument which seems to him natural.

In the matter of precision, the child was proving father to the man. But Tate was wise enough to add a final piece of advice to Mr Dodgson. 'You must not entrust your son with a full knowledge of his superiority over other boys.' Had there been some hint in the conduct of the twelve year old that suggested priggishness or self-satisfaction?[7]

Any such failing was to be roughly dealt with a few months after Charles Dodgson left Richmond in November 1845 to begin his public-school education in earnest. Though his father had been educated at Westminster, the school now chosen was Rugby, in the wake of Thomas Arnold's much discussed creation of the Christian Gentleman as the pattern to which male adolescence should conform. Rugby's moral and intellectual reputation stood high, while that of Westminster was in decline, and the East Midlands town of Rugby could be reached more or less conveniently by train from Darlington. Though Arnold himself had been dead for four years by this time and the young men who had come under his influence had gone on to the two Universities and to their careers, Rugby's new headmaster seemed intent on preserving his predecessor's reforms. Archibald Campbell Tait had been at Oxford as a Balliol scholar and tutor. In 1841, he had been one of three Oxford tutors who led the attack on John Henry Newman's Roman sympathies in *Tract XC*. After Rugby, he was to become Bishop of London, then Archbishop of Canterbury.

Charles Dodgson arrived at Rugby on his fourteenth birthday, 27 January 1846. He was speedily detected as a muff and the taunt was scrawled on his possessions. To this point in his life he had known little but affection and security. He had been educated by his parents rather than consigned to a tutor or governess. The world of his family was ruled by the certainty that God is Love. Like some of the family's other members, he suffered from a stammer which was sometimes no more than a hesitation and on occasion a complete inability to articulate a word. In his new environment it was a matter for ridicule rather than sympathy. He was, in every way, an admirable target for those already in residence. There was much about him that might recall William Cowper at Westminster half a century earlier, and the poet's subsequent wry suggestions on how a father who was determined on the ruin of his son need do no more than subject him to the expensive privileges of a public-school education.

> Train him in public with a mob of boys,
> Childish in mischief only and in noise,
> Else of a mannish growth, and five in ten
> In infidelity and lewdness men.[8]

Charles Dodgson disliked Rugby, though he kept his feelings from his family until after he left the school. To have done otherwise might seem like ingratitude to his father. Mr Dodgson, as his letters to his second son Skeffington showed, was not averse to giving his children a precise account of how much their education cost him. It was not until 1855, six years after he left Rugby, that the young Charles Dodgson made his feelings plain and only then in his private diary.

> During my stay I made I suppose some progress in learning of various kinds, but none of it was done *con amore*, and I spent an incalculable time in writing out impositions – this last I consider one of the chief faults of Rugby School. I made some friends there, the most intimate being Henry Leigh Bennett (as college acquaintances we find fewer common sympathies, and are consequently less intimate) – but I cannot say that I look back upon my life at a Public School with any sensations of pleasure, or that any earthly considerations would induce me to go through my three years again.[9]

Rugby was far larger than Richmond School – 500 pupils rather than 120. As at Richmond, they were divided among houses in which they lived, most of them in the town. Dodgson was one of those privileged to belong to the School House, which was the headmaster's. Rugby had been founded by Lawrence Sheriffe in 1567. It was rebuilt and reconstituted in the eighteenth century. Much of it was rebuilt again during the Regency period in a Georgian Gothic style which strove to imitate the architecture of the later Plantagenets. Latin, Greek, English grammar and religious knowledge were the basis of its education.

By the time of Thomas Arnold's death, sport in the school was institutionalized as a form of moral and physical training. The school first played cricket against the MCC at Lords in 1840. In 1841–2 'Rugby Football' allowed players to pick up the ball and run with it. This was incorporated in the Rules of 1846. By 1848 there were three 'Fives' courts, against whose buttressed walls two or four players drove a small rubber ball with their hands. Cross-country runs were instituted, 'The Bilton' a mere five miles in length, 'The Crick' twelve and a quarter miles.

If Charles Dodgson felt grateful to the shade of Thomas Arnold it was probably not for the new regime of prefects or praeposters, the power entrusted to the boys of the Sixth Form to govern and punish their juniors. In Dodgson's time there was also the authority of the 'Bigside Levee', when senior members of the school gathered to decide more general matters among themselves. Nor would he have felt much gratitude for the football or cross-country runs. That sport encouraged refinement, let alone punctuation, in the Christian Gentleman might be doubted from such letters as that of Sir Alexander Duff Gordon's ten-year-old son to his parents in 1861. 'Once a fellow took a shot at the ball and caught Freeth such a toe on the ass which made him rub it I can tell you so we all hollowed out how is your ass Freeth which made him fearfully baity.'[10]

As the century wore on and the disciples of Arnold became fewer, it seemed that the great man's most profound influence had been on the curriculum. He had modernized both the subject-matter and the methods of teaching in a manner that offered scope to Dodgson's particular abilities.

George Granville Bradley, an Old Rugboean of the 1830s, recalled this in the *Nineteenth Century* for March 1884. Before Arnold, books were learnt by heart and recited, 'without, so far as I can recall, a word of explanation or illustration. The lists of Kings of England, of the metals, and of the planets were repeated one after the other without interest and without discrimination.' Such unquestioning acceptance of 'factual' learning was to be source material for *Alice in Wonderland*. Arnold, by contrast, had a natural ability for bringing alive Greek and Roman literature in a way that the old system had never attempted. He extended this to other areas, as Bradley recalled.

> Arnold shocked, no doubt, educational Conservatives, much as he shocked the ecclesiastical and political adherents of the past, by some important changes. He did everything that was possible at that day in a school organised as Rugby was, to introduce the teaching of mathematics and modern languages as a regular and essential part of a boy's curriculum. He paved the way for future success.[11]

Dodgson's particular reason for disliking Rugby was never stated. According to the family he was never flogged, but he described school in a poetic warning to his younger brothers as, 'learning lessons in fear of the birch.' When the Prince and Princess of Wales were married in 1863, he drew a pastiche of the 'May they be happy' lettering of the illuminations with a pair of birch-rods and the cryptic comment, 'Certainly not!' Until the first rumours of psychopathology in the late 1880s, Victorian England was apt to regard the stripping and beating of the young with knowing amusement, as a subject far removed from sexual innuendo. 'He never had to enter that dreaded chamber,' wrote Dodgson's nephew and first biographer, 'well known to some Rugboeans, which is approached by a staircase that winds up a little turret, and wherein are enacted scenes better imagined than described.' Nonetheless, childhood brutality was a source of Dodgson's humour, early and late. As a small boy he sent home a jovial message to his infant brother Skeffington, perhaps reprimanding the child for crying, 'Roar not, lest thou be abolished.'[12]

While at Rugby, he clearly suffered and resented the imposition of 'lines' for minor breaches of regulations, having to copy out the same line fifty, a hundred, or several hundred times. In 1857, he also confided to his diary the most tiresome ordeal of his schooldays. 'I can say that if I had been thus secure from annoyance at night, the hardships of the daily life would have been comparative trifles to bear.'[13]

Night was the time when the boys were unsupervised and when the victims of institutional bullying or casual ragging were most at the mercy of their tormentors. Bullying might take as casual a form as snatching the bedclothes from a victim and leaving him to shiver the rest of a winter night so that the stronger boy might sleep more warmly. It might be the more elaborate ritual of tossing him in a blanket to the ceiling of the high communal dormitory. Rowland Williams, a future contributor to theological dissent in *Essays and Reviews*, was tossed so hard at Eton that he hit the rafter and came down with 'the scalp hanging down over the neck and back suspended only by a small piece of skin.' However, as one perpetrator later insisted, 'Bold little fellows liked it.' There is no indication that Charles Dodgson was such a bold little fellow. Other amusements included pillow fights where savage skill might skin an opponent's nose, 'launching' the bed of a sleeping innocent with sudden speed or gently tying wetted whipcord round the toe and waiting for the pain of its tightening to bring him to consciousness. There were also rat hunts which the insanitary buildings made not so much a nightly sport as a necessity.

Far worse than mere bullying to a boy of Dodgson's sensitive moral constitution was the mere sight of anything sexually suggestive or gross. Those who believed that Thomas Arnold had cleansed the Augean stables of Cowper's *Tirocineum* might have pondered his letter of 1840 in which the great headmaster saw the school as prone to good or evil, according to the set of boys who happened to be in residence. To that extent the outcome of individual education was beyond his control. 'I have many delightful proofs that those, who have been here, have found at any rate no such evil as to prevent their serving God in after life; and some, I trust, have derived good from Rugby. But the evil is great and abounding, I well know; and it is very fearful to think that it may to some be irreparable ruin.'[14]

There is no suggestion that young Charles Dodgson was ever subject to such misconduct but he cannot have failed to notice its existence. Augustus Hare's first encounter with school was under the headship of Robert Kilvert, father of the diarist. The 'little flock of lambs in Christ's fold,' as the other boys were advertised, proved to be 'a set of little monsters,' in Hare's experience. 'All infantine immoralities were highly popular, and – in such close quarters – it would have been difficult for the most pure and high-minded boy to escape from them.' In imagery more suggestive than any literal description, Hare adds, 'The first night I was there, at nine years old, I was compelled to eat Eve's apple quite up – indeed, the Tree of the Knowledge of Good and Evil was stripped absolutely bare: there was no fruit left to gather.'[15]

Benjamin Jowett, Dodgson's future adversary at Oxford, was a realist. He had been nicknamed 'Miss Jowett' at St Paul's, as Dean Stanley was called 'Nancy' at Rugby. The names were probably no more than schoolboy derision, though at Harrow the Vaughan scandal of 1859 proved otherwise. The manuscript diaries of John Addington Symonds contain a lurid depiction of sexual violence at Harrow in mid-century. Far from preventing such activities, the headmaster, Dr Charles Vaughan, was a party to them until his resignation was demanded and obtained under threat of a criminal prosecution by Symonds' father and a number of other parents. Jowett wrote to a younger cousin who was being sent away to school, 'Boys about your own age or a little older are sometimes very vicious and indecent both in word and also sometimes in action.'[16]

Yet, for all the moral defects of the Victorian public school, its stereotype ignores one of its most obvious merits. As an institution of learning, it offered its more gifted pupils the foundation of their lives' work. A few years after Dodgson's time at Rugby, Algernon Charles Swinburne discovered at Eton a wealth of Greek and Roman poetry and drama, which fed his imagination for the rest of his life. The same had been true of Henry Fielding at Eton more than a century before. The young Dodgson benefited from this opportunity and, specifically, from Arnold's legacy of encouraging the teaching of mathematics. Arnold had appointed a young mathematician, the Reverend Robert Bickersteth Mayor, as principal master in the subject, and it was he who now taught young Dodgson. 'I have not had a more promising boy at his age since I came to Rugby,' he wrote to the rector of Croft in 1848.[17]

Science was introduced to Rugby in 1849, a little too late for Dodgson. Yet the greatest gift of all, which antedated even Arnold's reforms, was Rugby's gospel of work under his predecessor Dr John Wooll. In 1822, Henry Halford Vaughan wrote to his father, 'I never was so hard worked in my life as I am now, and from a quarter after seven till ten o'clock which is bedtime I literally shall hardly stir off my chair.' In an age of more or less unlimited toil for factory children, it was hardly remarkable that this eleven-year-old schoolboy should work the best part of a fifteen-hour day. Dr Wooll brooked no argument and no indolence, once flogging an entire class of thirty-eight idlers in fifteen minutes.[18]

Raymond Smythies, the second mathematics master and also assistant master of the school, took a benevolent interest in Dodgson's progress. On a spring day in 1849, the boy and a friend called at his house, where Smythies entertained them with wine and figs. 'Well, Dodgson, I suppose you're getting on well with your mathematics?' As Dodgson wrote to his sister, 'He is very clever at them, though not equal to Mr Mayor, as indeed few men are, Papa excepted.' A third teacher of mathematics at Rugby was Bonamy Price, later to be Professor of Political Economy at Oxford, where Dodgson resumed their friendship.[19]

The Reverend Dodgson, who kept a close check on the progress of his sons when they left home for school or Christ Church, was well rewarded by his eldest son's achievements at Rugby. The boy won prizes in almost every subject, including one for mathematics before he reached the Sixth Form, where it was usually competed for. Among the evidence of his early proficiency in Greek had been his annotation of the first seventy-nine lines of the Greek text of the *Prometheus Vinctus* of Aeschylus, which apparently dated from his time at Richmond School, when he was thirteen years old. His earliest known Latin verses, dated 25 November 1844, were composed as a school exercise at Richmond while he was still twelve years old. Such varied ability was essential to his main interest. Before he could proceed to Final Honours in mathematics at Oxford, he would first have to pass degree examinations in classics.

In his letters from Rugby to his elder sister Elizabeth, Dodgson gives the impression of a gifted and strong-minded adolescent. He discusses the books he might choose as prizes and those current publications which had caught his interest, among them *David Copperfield*, 'a poor plot but some of the characters and scenes are good,' and Macaulay's *History of England*, the first volume of which appeared in 1849. Elsewhere, his correspondence suggests the schoolboy rather than the scholar. He writes of his visit from Rugby to the remains of a Roman encampment and enquiries whether his room will be ready by the time he comes home again or whether his younger brother Skeffington still rides the Hendersons' donkey.[20]

On 25 June 1847 his mother wrote to her sister Lucy Lutwidge that he had come home for the holidays. The young Charles Dodgson was delighted with his success at Rugby and with two handsome prize books: Arnold's *Modern History* and Thierry's *Norman Conquest*. These volumes were his prize for Composition in Latin and English. He would have won another prize for coming second out of the fifty-three boys in his form but the rules allowed only one prize per pupil.

In the autumn of 1847 he entered the Lower Middle school and eighteen months later the Upper Middle school. During this time there were more prizes for mathematics but also for classics as well as history and divinity. For the most part, the books he chose as prizes were history and biography, including Middleton's *Life of Cicero*, Roscoe's *Life of Lorenzo de Medici* and Ranke's *History of the Popes*.

Dr Tait was impressed by the variety of his pupil's abilities, as he wrote to Mr Dodgson when Charles left Rugby for the last time.

> I fully coincide in Mr Cotton's estimate both of his abilities and upright conduct. His mathematical knowledge is great for his age, and I doubt not he will do himself credit in classics. As I believe I mentioned to you before, his examination for the Divinity prize was one of the most creditable exhibitions I have ever seen.[21]

When he left Rugby in December 1849, a month before his eighteenth birthday, it might have seemed that he had taken all that the school had to offer him. By this time, his father had written to Dr Pusey and obtained the conditional premise that Pusey would nominate his son for an undergraduate studentship at Christ Church, provided that no other candidate of obvious superiority presented himself. The list of prizes he had won at Rugby suggested that this was unlikely.

His departure from Rugby may have been caused by something as simple as the insanitary conditions of communal living in the 1840s. Apart from the intellectual decline of Westminster School, it had also suffered from the cholera and typhoid which were common in the crowded conditions of London. Schools like Rugby were more healthily situated, though the diseases of childhood were still rife. In his last eighteen months at Rugby, the young Dodgson suffered both whooping-cough and mumps. In the summer holidays of 1847, he had nursed and played with the other children at Croft as whooping-cough went through the family, though he managed to avoid it himself. When he caught it at school in March 1848, its effects persisted for three months.

In November 1849 he had a bad attack of mumps and it seems that he was afterwards permanently deaf in his right ear. Whether this was caused in the first place by the present infection or by an earlier attack of 'infantile fever', his parents' concern over the uncertain quality of medical care at the school led to Charles Dodgson leaving Rugby very soon afterwards.

*

Though most of his life between the ages of eleven and eighteen had been spent away from home, the rectory at Croft remained the focus of his affections and interest. Indeed, the move to the Teeside parish spurred the inventive talents of the eldest boy as the leader of the children, who entertained the others. At sixteen or seventeen he was the gifted boy who could win prizes and indulge himself with Ranke's *History of the Popes*, yet also play the games of younger children throughout the summer without impatience. It was a combination of qualities that he was never to lose.

Of all the industrial wonders of the new age, none beguiled the childish imagination more surely than the railway train. Family journeys were from Darlington down to Hull or Rugby, with a change of trains at Birmingham and scope for the loss of luggage in the latter case. Yet to a child's eye these were encounters with a creature of technology that had the ungainly air of a fire-breathing monster from a medieval legend. It might almost have been the Jabberwock with eyes aflame. Even without boarding a train, a short walk from the rectory brought the children to the bridge where the line from London to Darlington crossed the Tees. Croft, like so many villages, also had its own station. A few miles away, Darlington boasted a major railway works, as well as the temple of industrial brick on Bank Top, a principal junction on the London to Edinburgh line.

As if in homage to this, the young Charles Dodgson began to build a railway train for the other children. The geometrically ordered paths of the kitchen-garden were to be the railway system. The stations were canvas booths the size of a bathing tent with a name hung on each. 'At each of these stations,' as his brothers and sisters recalled, 'there was a refreshment room, and the passengers had to purchase tickets from him before they could enjoy the ride.' The train consisted of an 'engine' attached to a roughly made little cart, constructed from wooden boxes. The engine was a wheelbarrow containing a barrel laid on its side to resemble a boiler. The date of the kitchen-garden railway's construction is not certain but Mrs Dodgson referred to it as still being in operation, propelled by her eldest son, when she wrote to her sister Lucy Lutwidge on 5 July 1848. At sixteen he remained willing to play with the younger children, including three-year-old Edwin, who joined in the game on the wooden horse which had been a present from Aunt Lucy.[22]

In reality, at the beginning of the 1840s, third-class carriages were little better than the open cart in the garden at Croft. The passengers were subjected to appalling grime and the risk of suffocation every time the engine entered a tunnel. When it rained, the only protection was the passengers' umbrellas which dripped into a growing puddle on the floor. By 1845, the New Railway Regulations required that 'The carriages in which passengers shall be conveyed by such trains shall be provided with seats and shall be protected from the weather in a manner satisfactory to the Lords of the Committee of the Privy Council for Trade and Plantations.'

The archaic style of the Privy Council decree evidently caught the eye of the young Charles Dodgson who dashed off his own 'Rules' for the Croft kitchen-garden, in imitation of the council and its dependent railway companies. Passengers who fell out of the train when it was upset were 'requested to lie still until picked up – as it is requisite that at least 3 trains should go over them, to entitle them to the attention of the doctor and assistants.' Those who missed a train were not to run after it but wait for the next. In fact, some trains were so slow that they might almost have been overtaken at a sprint. Passengers without money at the kitchen-garden stations were required to earn the price of a ticket by making tea for the station master and grinding sand for undisclosed purposes.[23]

The railway was a success with the other children. When Charles Dodgson wrote for the marionette theatre which he had built, George Bradshaw's famous railway guide was burlesqued in his mock-heroic ballad-opera *La Guida di Bragia*. *Bradshaw's Guide* had first appeared in 1839–41, and with its comprehensive timetables became the railway traveller's bible for the next century, known simply as a Bradshaw. The lyrics of *La Guida di Bragia* were often parodies of well-known songs, so that 'Auld Lang Syne' became 'Should all my luggage be forgot/And never come to hand.' The action involves two incompetent employees of the railway, Spooney and Mooney, and a good deal of Dickensian working-class English, which echoes the schoolboy Dodgson's enthusiasm for Mrs Gummidge in *David Copperfield*, in his letter to his sister Elizabeth. Bradshaw himself appears, having taken his revenge on servants who refused to sing at their work. He has thrown all England into confusion as, 'I altered all the train times in my book.'[24]

The Croft railway was a game for summer in the garden, while in the winter Charles entertained the others by tracing a maze in the snow, 'of such hopeless intricacy as almost to put its famous rival at Hampton Court in the shade.' For winter too there was the marionette theatre, perhaps inspired by a glimpse of the Theatre Royal at Richmond. The young Charles Dodgson built and furnished the model, assisted by the other children and the village carpenter.

Model theatres remained an enthusiasm throughout his life. He later adapted a German model of the 1880s, the figures of the drama mounted on metal slides. The theatre which he built as a boy was remembered as being far more sophisticated in design, with marionettes operated by threads down through the flies. He was nimble-fingered enough to manage the figures proficiently. The greater difficulty, as he recalled in 1853, was in finding suitable material to perform. Plays from the theatre were unsuitable for children, in his view, while those written for puppets were extremely dull. In the end, he wrote all the plays that were performed on the model stage, including *The Tragedy of King John*, himself. In such pieces as *La Guida di Bragia*, he added to the other children's amusement by including topical and family references. Even at this age, he showed a character- istic distaste for realism and a belief that the example of purity was more worthy than a depiction of the world as it was. This rule governed his model stage, as he insisted in *La Guida di Bragia*.

> Why can't we have, in theatres ideal,
> The good, without the evil of the real?[25]

His sleight of hand made him a natural magician, and, in a brown wig and white robe, he caused 'no little wonder to his audience' at the rectory. The craft of simple magic was one that he used to entertain children for the rest of his life. Some tricks were simple and could be produced in later years to make the acquaintance of little girls on wearisome railway journeys. A clean handkerchief would be unfolded, a match placed upon it, and the linen then folded up. The watching child would be invited to feel the match through the thin cloth and snap it. This was easily done and there was no doubt that the match was in two pieces. He would then open the handkerchief and reveal the match still intact. It was sometimes marked beforehand to show that it must be the same one. The explanation lay in the hem of the handkerchief which was left open at one end by the manufacturer. Into this opening a second match could be slid, with no risk that it would fall out when the handkerchief was opened in a flourish.

*

The most impressive and durable of the memorials of Croft was the succession of magazines for the younger children which Charles Dodgson wrote, edited and produced. The first of these, ironically entitled *Useful and Instructive Poetry*, was written for Wilfred and Louisa in about 1845. They would have been seven and five respectively at that date but there is some reason to think that, though begun in 1845, some of the poems may have been written a little later. He enquires in a letter to his sister Elizabeth on 9 October 1848 whether the copies of the collection for Wilfred and Louisa have finished binding yet. Moreover, the poems include limericks in the manner of Edward Lear. Lear's *Book of Nonsense* appeared in 1846 and it seems likely that the young Dodgson had read it before he completed his own collection.

During an Oxford vacation at Croft in 1855, the twenty-three-year-old Charles Dodgson recalled the successive magazines produced at the rectory in his teens. Apart from *Useful and Instructive Poetry*, there was the *Rectory Magazine*; before 1848, 'most of the family contributed one or more articles to it.' The *Comet* of 1848 ran for only six numbers and the *Rosebud* for only two. Neither the *Star* nor *The Will o' the Wisp* lasted long. The *Rectory Umbrella*, named after the yew tree in the front garden, ran for a year and a half in 1849–50, but only because Charles Dodgson himself wrote and illustrated the whole of it. To begin with, the magazines had been a collective production but as time went by the rest of the family had given up.[26]

A number of the sixteen short poems in *Useful and Instructive Poetry* are clever schoolboy parodies of the exemplary verses for children which had been in vogue for the past twenty years with evangelical authors of children's reading. Indeed, their sententious style as a means of directing the young had been popular as far back as Isaac Watts in the early eighteenth century. All but four of the schoolboy poems in the first collection at Croft end with a separate line, for the moral instruction: 'You mustn't', 'Don't get drunk', 'Pay the costs', 'Don't dream', 'Change your conduct', or, more simply, 'Behave'. Those whose earnest style the adolescent Dodgson subverted believed that their moral lesson alone would win the child's attention. Dodgson believed all his life that the child must first be attracted and then taught. He demolished pomposity and earnestness only to teach their lessons through charm and laughter.

Occasionally in *Useful and Instructive Poetry*, as when preaching the virtues of punctuality and tidiness, the tone is more earnest than ironic, as if assisting Frances Dodgson in the management of the rectory. Elsewhere the irony points a moral of his own. In his manhood, for example, Charles Dodgson was to regard charity with ambivalence. It was not the duty of a Christian to support idleness nor to fall prey to trickery. Beggars, especially of the young female kind, may have an emotional as well as moral charm, the more dangerous for that. The schoolboy poem 'Charity' anticipates his photograph of Alice Liddell in tatters as a coy beggar-maid. The heroine of the poem is found in the muddy street begging for food. The poet is moved, sufficiently so to buy her bread and 'strengthening beer.' The laconic view of charity which results is a welcome corrective to the image of the child-saint of Daresbury peeling rushes for the poor.

> In my left pocket did I seek,
>   To see how time went on,
> Then grief and tears bedewed *my* cheek,
>   For, oh! my watch was gone!

Moral: 'Keep your wits about you.'

Even as the productions of his adolescence, the pieces in the collection are linked by a clear and idiosyncratic tone. There is comic menace in the voice of authority, as strident and sometimes as irrational as it was to be twenty years later in his most famous work. The voice of command is strong in poems like 'Rules and Regulations', where even the Dodgsons' speech defect is not spared.

> Learn well your grammar,
> And never stammer,
> Write well and neatly,
> And sing most sweetly . . .

> Drink tea not coffee;
> Never eat toffy.
> Eat bread with butter.
> Once more, don't stutter . . .

Many of the poems derive their energy from verbal threat or physical violence, and a good many of their characters come to harm. The Headstrong Man falls from a tree, from a wall, and is then knocked down by the sandman's fist. A brother after an argument with his sister – 'Do you want a battered hide or scratches to your face applied?' – 'I'd make you into mutton broth as easily as kill a moth' – decides to kill and cook the little girl. The plan is frustrated by the cook, who refuses to lend him a frying-pan, and the obvious moral is: 'Never stew your sister.' 'The Trial of a Traitor' was the boy's first venture into courtroom drama. Elsewhere, in 'A Tale of a Tail', a dog twists its tail round the drunken gardener's legs and has it chopped off as part of the undergrowth, a joke at the animal's expense and an amusement to the gardener.

When this was done, with mirth he bowed,
  Till he was black and blue,
The dog it barked both long and loud
  And with good reason too.

These family magazines were his apprenticeship in parody and pastiche for the pieces which he later contributed to *College Rhymes* and the *Comic Times*. By 1850, the style was fully developed in the *Rectory Umbrella*. 'Ye Fattale Cheyse' is a characteristic Dodgson lampoon of medievalism and 'Lays of Sorrow No. 2', imitating Macaulay's *Lays of Ancient Rome*, describes the Dodgson sons trying to get the better of a donkey by riding it through the village. A good many of the pieces elevate the incidents of life at the rectory to the status of mock-heroic dramas. The first 'Lay of Sorrow' describes an inquest on a dead chick, an inquiry as to whether the mother was guilty of infanticide. The acquittal of the bird is followed by one of the Dodgson children bursting upon the throng with dramatic news.

'The sight that I have come upon
  The stoutest heart would sicken,
That nasty hen has been and gone
  And killed another chicken!'

These mock-heroic verses counterpointed the comfortable and affectionate family life at Croft. They continued for some years after Charles Dodgson had become a Christ Church undergraduate. 'Two Brothers', written in 1853, described Skeffington and Wilfred fishing from the bridge over the Tees, just beyond the churchyard. Skeffington uses his younger brother as bait, despite the despairing cries from the river beneath.

The wind to his ear brought a voice,
  'My brother you didn't have ought ter!
And what have I done that you think it such fun
  To indulge in the pleasure of slaughter?'

Slaughter is the inevitable result of the experiment. The younger brother may struggle for ten minutes in the water when the pike is hooked. Drowning is an odds-on chance, as the exchange between them makes clear.

'But in those ten minutes to desolate Fate
   Your brother a victim may fall!'
'I'll reduce it to five, so *perhaps* you'll survive,
   But the chance is exceedingly small.'

Parallel to this taste for the macabre, the humour of dreams and nightmares was richly appealing to him. In 1868, writing to the Senior Censor of Christ Church, Dodgson equated lobster sauce at dinner with 'possible nightmare.' In the *Rectory Umbrella*, monsters haunt the dreaming mind until the cheerful voice of morning breaks their spell.

'Wake! Mr Jones,
You're screaming in your sleep!'

The degree of threat and casual violence in these early poems, as in his later writing, might have caused unease to the educators of a post-Freudian child. However this child was neither post-Freudian nor, in one sense, Victorian. He had been born into that late Georgian world whose robustness and slangy self-confidence overran the early years of Victoria's own reign.

Playful menace and sardonic injury, the stock in trade of his fantasies, were less a symptom of psychic trauma than a sign of being a child of his time. Victor Hugo had offered a definition of modern culture in 1827 in a famous passage from the preface to his play *Cromwell.* The great subject of the moderns was the grotesque, as a rival to the sublime. Hugo might almost have had the young Dodgson in mind. Indeed, the grotesque was to be Hugo's necessary complement to the beautiful in modern art. 'Everything tends to show its close creative alliance with the beautiful in the so-called "romantic" age,' Hugo wrote. 'Antiquity could not have produced *Beauty and the Beast.*' As Browning wrote half a century later in 'A Forgiveness',

I think there never was such – how express? –
Horror coquetting with voluptuousness . . .

The nineteenth century was not, perhaps, the most illustrious in the history of European culture. Yet, morally and aesthetically, it had become the most uneasy. In 1843, in the *Revue des Deux Mondes*, Sainte-Beuve identified Byron and Sade as 'the two great inspirations of the moderns. One of them is well-advertised and visible, the other is hidden – but not too hidden.' Few people in England had heard of Sade, much less read him, though the indictments of the Court of King's Bench show that editions of his work were available in England, where George Cannon was prosecuted for publishing *Juliette* in 1830.[27]

The young Charles Dodgson did not need the neurosis of sexual repression or the trauma of public-school brutality to write as he did. While his macabre vision did not coquette with voluptuousness, it was nonetheless a match for the style of the time. The example of the Regency was one of self-confident animal spirits, characterized by a section of English society that was sporting, patrician, gallant and military. Its romanticism had also grown macabre. Thomas Hood exploited this in his epic-length poem of social comedy 'Miss Kilmansegg and her Precious Leg' the story of a rich young lady who loses a leg and has a gold one fitted. Courted for the wealth of this artificial limb, Miss Kilmansegg marries a foreign nobleman who at last beats her to death with it. The verdict is suicide because her own leg had killed her. It might have been a tale from the young Charles Dodgson, who had a copy of Hood's poem on his bookshelves. More popular still was Hood's *Comic Annual* and its verses, comic and macabre, like 'Mary's Ghost', the apparition of a girl whose fresh corpse has been dug up by body-snatchers for an anatomy class. Eager children opened the *Annual* on Christmas morning and chuckled over its dark humour.

> You thought that I was buried deep,
>   Quite decent like and chary,
> But from her grave in Mary-bone
>   They've come and bon'd your Mary.

For children and adults few collections rivalled R. H. Barham's *Ingoldsby Legends* with comic poems like 'The Execution. A Sporting Anecdote', in which a group of swells make an all-night party to see a man hanged in the morning. Even after the publication of *Alice in Wonderland*, men, women and children packed Snow Hill on Monday mornings for the free entertainment of other men and women being put to death outside Newgate gaol.

> My Lord Tomnoddy jump'd up at the news,
>   'Run to M'Fuse. And Lieutenant Tregooze,
> And run to Sir Carnaby Jenks of the Blues.
>   Rope-dancers a score I've seen before –
> Madame Sacchi, Antonio, and Master Black-more;

> But to see a man swing   At the end of a string,
> With his neck in a noose, will be quite a new thing.'

Hood, Barham and their kind exemplified the energy of English verse-writing in the raffish and turbulent period of the 1830s and early 1840s, as the young Charles Dickens was demonstrating a parallel vivacity in prose. Public life as well as literature, in Dodgson's childhood, lacked those self-conscious decencies which would have stamped them as 'Victorian' forty years later. On 22 July 1885, in the *St James's Gazette*, Dodgson deplored the modern style of journalism which detailed sins or crimes that in earlier decades would have been omitted by the press with the comment, 'the evidence was unfit for publication.' His memory was evidently failing. Anyone who opened a newspaper in the 1840s, when female susceptibilities or childish innocence were not allowed to stand in the way of a good story, knew otherwise. When the Duke of Brunswick attacked the *Age* for calling him a sodomite, the paper replied in verse on 6 February 1842.

> To do so he courage or prudence must lack,
> Yet it sometimes *is* the case,
> That men will do behind your back,
> What they will not do to your face.

Next year, when the Earl of Cardigan had intercourse with Lady Frances Paget on the sofa of her Mayfair drawing-room, the entire incident appeared in detail in the columns of *The Times* on 23 December, thanks to the solicitor's clerk who had been installed under the sofa with a bottle of sherry by the suspicious husband. The English middle class of the 1840s read without protest of the creaking of sofa springs and cracking of military boots, the kisses loud enough to be heard in the next room, the fact that the seducer managed to retain the spurs of his regimental uniform during the encounter, and that 'The breathing was hard like persons distressed for breath after running.'

In private, survivors of the Regency spoke their minds with immodest bluntness, even at the level of the Privy Council. On witnessing young Lord Durham's impudence to Lord Grey, Melbourne commented, 'If I had been Lord Grey, I would have knocked him arse over head.' Of course, there was not to be reading aloud of such court cases or conversations in the family circle at Croft. A growing gentility in this bourgeois culture purged it of sexual innuendo while nourishing the macabre and the violent as a harmless and even moralistic diversion. Dodgson himself, talking of railway literature in *Sylvie and Bruno*, objected only to the feebleness of its midnight murders and ghosts. His childhood had seen stronger stuff.[28]

*

The translation from Rugby to Christ Church was neither sudden nor easy. Dodgson matriculated on 23 May 1850, six months after leaving school. It was not until January 1851 that he went into residence at Oxford. Possibly he wanted to prepare himself by further reading for the double degree upon which he was to embark, having to take classics as well as mathematics. If he lacked the tuition that Oxford might have given, he had the assistance of his father, himself a Student of Christ Church and Lecturer in Mathematics until 1827. A more mundane reason for delay was that Christ Church was usually short of accommodation and those who had matriculated might still have to wait until rooms fell vacant. So far as the date of his residence was concerned, it was entirely normal for men to begin their first year in January.

Dodgson left Croft and went into residence on 24 January 1851. It seemed at first that he might have to take lodgings in the town because the College rooms were still full. However, it was arranged that he should use a room at Christ Church belonging to his father's friend, the Reverend Jacob Ley, who was also to be his tutor in classics. On his arrival at the College he scarcely had time to unpack before he was urgently summoned back to Croft two days later. His mother had died, unexpectedly and inexplicably, beyond a diagnosis of inflammation of the brain. Her death occurred so soon after his arrival in Oxford that it seems probable she must have been ailing when he left home. Perhaps Frances Dodgson had succumbed to one of the many contagions such as cholera and typhoid which thrived in towns like Darlington. In an age when the practice of hygiene was erratic and remedies few, the possible causes might be innumerable. One thing is certain, however. For the rest of his life Charles Dodgson had a horror of infection that might seem excessive even in the circumstances of the age. Perhaps this was its origin.

Deaths from diseases almost unknown in England a century later were commonplace enough to have occurred among most families.

An Oxford college, despite its relative seclusion, was an uneasy lodging for a young man with a phobia about infection. Oxford was swept by the cholera of 1849. In 1854, Dodgson's last year as an undergraduate, cholera became an epidemic, coinciding with smallpox and typhoid. It was no wonder that he used such scenes many years later in *Sylvie and Bruno*. There was a cholera 'camp' at Oxford in 1854 to house the dying and the convalescent, and a home for the orphans. At one church, three-quarters of the congregation were in mourning. Cholera was the major scourge, its victims often dying within hours of the first symptoms and being buried hastily next day, but in a city population of some 25,000, there were also a thousand cases of smallpox. Public hygiene was to improve beyond measure in the next decades, but Charles Dodgson had reason to recall his early experiences.[29]

Frances Dodgson's death left little in the way of eulogy, except from the family and intimate friends who had known her as an anxious and loving mother. Dr Pusey wrote to his friend, the rector of Croft, but the letter was full of the promise of reunion in heaven, rather than of the dead wife's qualities in her mortal life. 'One cannot think that any holy earthly love will cease, when we shall "be like the Angels of God in Heaven." '[30]

As a more practical step, Mrs Dodgson's unmarried younger sister, Aunt Lucy, became housekeeper to the rectory family for the rest of the widower's life. Thereafter, she and the unmarried daughters formed a new household in Guildford. For the most famous son of Croft rectory, there was always a family home. A younger generation gradually supplied the places left empty by the death of elders. He himself became increasingly a visitor rather than a resident. Yet it was to remain the only home that he had.

After the sad return to Croft and his mother's burial in the little churchyard beside the Tees, he set out once more for Oxford. A man might be affected in many ways by such an event. In Dodgson's case, the grief that he felt was kept in check, subsisting at a level of chronic depression, while he trained himself to the ideals of moral excellence and academic distinction.

4

Shooting the Dean

'IF I HAD shot the Dean, I could hardly have had more said about it,' Charles Dodgson wrote to his sister Elizabeth from Christ Church on 9 December 1852. The occasion was one of a succession of examination triumphs which, two years short of graduation, brought him a Studentship at the College and security for the rest of his life. Under an old and embattled system of privilege, his residence ended only with his death, forty-seven years after he first took rooms in Peckwater Quadrangle as a youth of nineteen. The span of time was impressive but not exceptional. His childhood friend, Thomas Vere Bayne of Warrington, outlasted him and lived for sixty years in the College. He was outlived, in turn, by Thomas James Prout, who came to Christ Church as a fine young athlete in 1842 and was borne out in his coffin, having died as a deaf and enfeebled old man in 1909.[1]

It seemed a curiosity, at the end of his life, that Dodgson should have been regarded as belonging to the 'old order' of pre-Victorian Oxford, hopelessly outdated, obscurantist and reactionary. With his enthusiasms for mathematics and medicine, photography and railways, his humane views on vivisection and blood sports, his disbelief in the Christian doctrine of eternal damnation and bodily resurrection, he might have seemed in advance of much contemporary opinion. In a riposte to orthodoxy which combined Carrolingian paradox with a Victorian image of the missionary in the cooking-pot, he insisted that bodily resurrection was incompatible with cannibalism. If one man eats another, how can both bodies rise from a single cadaver?

Yet the reputation of old-fashioned Dodgson stuck to him. An obituary in the *Academy* of 22 January 1898 described him at Oxford as 'the most old world of all the elements in that place.' Younger than Newman, Matthew Arnold or the honest doubters, he seemed to belong to 'an earlier and quieter' existence. Even his Alice was 'the property of an elder and vanishing world.' A Christ Church colleague, T. B. Strong, remembered him as 'the product of the old order of things at Oxford.' Henry Scott Holland always thought that 'Dodgson had to a certain extent missed his age: that he ought to have lived in the Middle Ages in the palmy days of Scholasticism.'[2]

It was true from the start that ingenuity and invention were tempered by his moral conservatism. Moreover, as his birth was pre-Victorian, his first years at Christ Church were passed in a university still governed under statutes given it by Archbishop Laud in 1636. When Dodgson came into residence in 1851, as a later Warden of Merton described it, Oxford lay in 'organised torpor,' under Laud's collegiate rules. All this was to change, as men of modern views brought the ancient universities under political control. In 1898, Warden Brodrick looked back scornfully to that time half a century before when 'Colleges sheltered many an eccentric recluse, of a type now obsolete, who had perhaps never entered a London club or drawing-room.'[3]

This last comment might have been made to fit Dodgson, though not as the young man who moved into rooms in Peckwater in January 1851. There was a good deal of interest in his character while he was still an undergraduate. On one occasion he was submitted to the fashionable phrenological examination of his 'bumps'. A year after his arrival at Christ Church, his head was read by an Edinburgh phrenologist, Edward Hamilton, who identified among the young man's other traits a love of friends and children, as well as power of reasoning by analogy and an instinct for precision and elegance. Phrenology, a craze of the 1830s, had not yet become the fairground entertainment or subject for ridicule that it was later to be.

Soon after 1853, a clairvoyante, Minnie Anderson, whose skill was in tracing character from handwriting, described him with an accuracy which seemed remarkable to his family.

> Very clever head; a great deal of number; a great deal of imitation; he would make a good actor; diffident; rather shy in general society; comes out in the home circle; rather obstinate; very clever, a great deal of concentration; very affectionate; a great deal of wit and humour; not much eventuality (of memory of events); fond of deep reading; imaginative; fond of reading poetry; *may* compose.[4]

Allowing for information being casually acquired by the phrenologist or clairvoyante and for the natural impulse to flatter a client,
the bumps and the graphology suggest an early formation of that
character which Dodgson was to show in his youthful dealings with
others, as well as in his diaries and letters. That he could also be
petulant, reactionary, unpredictable, and 'the most prolific malcontent,' appears as a development of his middle years. The humorous
cruelty of light verse and facetious letters was sufficient outlet for
present frustrations.

In his early twenties, photographs show that 'dignified calm' with
which his family recalled him navigating the awkward years of adolescence. The face is firm, bland, androgynous, thin-lipped, the blue eyes
not quite aligned. The 'bandbox' neatness is evident in frock-coat and
tie, the hair immaculately parted. The slimness of his build led friends
to think of him as quite tall, though his height was only five feet
and nine inches. During his years as an undergraduate he wore his
commoner's cap and gown during the mornings. 'When you turned
out at two o'clock for your walk or ride, the black coat and regulation
hat were as indispensable as in the streets of London.' As a matter
of habit, Dodgson wore grey and black cotton gloves all year round
but never a top coat, even in winter.[5]

Peckwater Quadrangle, in which he had his first rooms at Christ
Church, had been built in the Palladian style under Dean Aldrich.
Three sides were completed by 1713; the fourth side, occupied by
the Italianate elegance of the New Library, was finished in 1772. A
few years before Dodgson, John Ruskin had looked out on 'the
smooth gravelled square' of the spacious quadrangle from similar
rooms, while he yearned for an oriel window and a Gothic view or
deplored 'the modern vulgar upholstery' of the college furniture.[6]

For such newcomers as Ruskin and Dodgson, college custom and
history were apt to seem complex, if not oppressive. Instituted by
Cardinal Wolsey in 1525 as Cardinal College, the foundation had been
reconstituted in 1546, when Henry VIII combined Osney Abbey and
Cardinal College into Christ Church, containing both a college and
the cathedral church of Oxford. Part of the Great Quadrangle, including the dark panelled Hall and much of the west front on St Aldate's,
dated from Wolsey's time. Demolition, rebuilding and expansion had
accounted for the rest over four centuries. Christopher Wren added
a fine, domed bell tower – Tom Tower – above the main gate of the
St Aldate's front in 1682, housing 'Great Tom', the bell of Osney

Abbey. The eighteenth-century grandeur of Peckwater and the New Library, though it had irritated Ruskin, was later regarded as one of the splendours of this largest of the Oxford colleges. There was variety enough at Christ Church to please and offend almost every architectural taste. The extent of the College was such that some of its backwaters were said to be like the quietest streets in London. In time there was decay as well as magnificence. By the Victorian period, areas like Fell's Buildings and Chaplains' Quadrangle were in rat-ridden shabbiness. Frederick Oakley, a Tractarian who became Chaplain of Balliol and a convert to Rome, used to cry every time he returned as an undergraduate to his seventeenth-century rooms in Fell's Buildings.

As a royal foundation, Christ Church, under the rule of its successive Deans appointed by the Crown, had been in the mainstream of English history. In 1561 Queen Elizabeth established the link by which certain Studentships at Christ Church were reserved for boys from Westminster School. The College drew most of its undergraduates from Westminster, Eton, and Harrow. Rugby was something of a rarity, though the future Dean Liddell when still a tutor preferred undergraduates from Rugby because they had been taught to write a good English style. Among the earlier royal patrons of Christ Church, Charles I and his Queen Henrietta Maria had been guests in 1636 when the first English play to have scenery and stage machinery, *Passions Calmed*, was performed in Christ Church Hall. In the Civil War, the College was both the headquarters and drilling ground for royalist Oxford. Under the later Stuarts, two of its most famous sons were expelled for unorthodoxy: John Locke, the philosopher, and William Penn, founder of Pennsylvania.

The eighteenth century had seen the Palladian developments of Dean Aldrich and his successors, as well as a certain slackening of intellectual endeavour. A sporting young squire was advised to choose Christ Church as his college, being promised that he could get through two years without reading anything apart from the *Stud Book* and the *Racing Calendar*. Noblemen lived on a grander scale than their contemporaries. Even as late as 1815, it was usual for a young nobleman, recognized by the gold-tasselled cap of his academic dress, to have his own retinue of servants and his own stable of horses.

Earnest Victorians, like the reformer Goldwin Smith, later protested that the eighteenth century had been 'a blank, or worse than a blank' in the history of such colleges. In the days before examinations were written, Lord Chancellor Eldon recalled getting his degree by answering two questions viva voce: 'What is the meaning of Golgotha?' and 'Who founded University College?' Sometimes a kindly examiner would prompt a candidate's knowledge of such subjects as ancient history. Dr Barnes of Christ Church saw one candidate safe home by asking helpfully, 'Who dragged whom how many times round the walls of what?' More accommodating still, the University allowed a man to choose his own examiner upon payment of a fee to the University Officer, and upon agreeing to 'treat' the examiner afterwards. Dodgson himself managed to triumph at Classical Moderations by recalling, when asked to cite something from Herodotus, a tribe that painted itself red and ate apes.

Yet, as Macaulay remarked of eighteenth-century Christ Church in his 1838 essay on Sir William Temple, 'Though that college seems then to have been almost destitute of severe and accurate learning, no academical society could show a greater array of orators, wits, politicians, bustling adventurers who united the superficial accomplishments of the scholar with the manners and arts of the man of the world.' What had been true in the eighteenth century remained so in the decades that followed. Among the most famous of Christ Church graduates to hold high public office were no less than three successive Governor-Generals of India and four Victorian prime ministers, Sir Robert Peel, Gladstone, Salisbury, and Rosebery. Even the 'blank' eighteenth century had seen such Christ Church graduates as John Wesley, William Murray, who as Lord Chief Justice Mansfield was to be one of the great jurists of the age, and George Canning, one of the nation's most accomplished Foreign Secretaries. In the new sciences, the bequest of Matthew Lee, physician to Frederick, Prince of Wales, had endowed an Anatomy Theatre at Christ Church and a lectureship to go with it.[7]

*

Of course the old system would not do for the high seriousness which Thomas Arnold and his kind had bequeathed to the 1850s. Yet Christ Church and Oxford before reform were the destination of young Charles Dodgson in 1851. A good deal of *Alice in Wonderland* was to depend on the caricature of a grotesque and doomed authoritarianism. In that respect, it might seem that he passed through the gate of Christ Church to be confronted by figures who would not have been out of place in his child heroine's underworld.

Authority lay with Thomas Gaisford, Professor of Greek, Dean of Christ Church since 1831, determined opponent of what he called the 'serious evils' of university reform. Gaisford never gave lectures. He had come early to that truth to which most come late. Learning is everything and teaching very little. He was redoubtable, efficient but hardly in the vanguard of intellectual fashion. His most famous sermon in Christ Church Cathedral concluded with an exhortation to the study of Greek, 'which not only elevates above the vulgar herd, but leads not infrequently to positions of considerable emolument.'

Not for Gaisford any nonsense about 'honest doubt' in religion. A young undergraduate with misgivings at signing the Thirty-Nine Articles of Religion of the Church of England sought the Dean's spiritual counsel. Gaisford demanded to know precisely how much the young man weighed, his height to the half inch, his age to the hour. The doubter was unable to answer with such precision. 'Yet,' said Gaisford, 'you walk about saying "I am twenty years old, I weigh ten stone, and am five feet eight inches high." Go, sign the articles: It will be a long time before you find anything that you can have *no* doubts about.' By the same forthright theology, Gaisford had little patience with Pusey's enthusiasm for the Fathers of the Church, whose works the Dean summed up briskly as 'sad rubbish.'[8]

Gaisford's reforming antagonist in the college, the future Dean Liddell, thought of him as 'that Siberian monster our Bear of Christ Church.' Ruskin saw him exuding 'real power of a rough kind' and looking like a 'sign of the Red Pig which I afterwards saw set up in pudding raisins with black currants for eyes by an imaginative grocer.' The Dean's presence was that of 'a rotundly progressive terror' and, more alarmingly, of 'a semi-maniac.'[9]

True to his belief in the values of classicism, however, Gaisford had made formal examinations the core of college teaching. 'Collections' as they were called had been instituted in the seventeenth century. It was Gaisford in 1831 who insisted that these examinations must be written rather than oral and that there should be no escape from them. They were, in his view, of far greater significance than the university examinations. Collections were written in Christ Church Hall, under the gaze of portraits by Holbein and Kneller, Romney and Lawrence, and, rather more intimidatingly, under that of Gaisford in the flesh. The ordeal remained vivid in Ruskin's mind half a century later, dominated by Gaisford's image. 'Scornful at once, and vindictive, thunderous always, more sullen and threatening as the day went on, he stalked with baleful emanation of Gorgonian cold from dais to door, and door to dais, of the majestic torture chamber, – vast as the great council hall of Venice . . .'[10]

Whether or not these papers were more important than the Oxford degree exams, they were certainly more exacting. After Charles Dodgson had distinguished himself in the university Moderations papers, he wrote to his sister Elizabeth that he thought it very unlikely he would gather any honours at Gaisford's Collections. He was allowed a single day in which to prepare the Acts of the Apostles, two Greek plays and the entire *Satires* of Horace.

Despite these misgivings, he was about to get his Studentship, on Dr Pusey's nomination. Undergraduate scholars and senior members of Christ Church were known as Students. A Studentship was awarded for life, even though the recipient was still an undergraduate. Some were reserved to those who had been boys at Westminster School. Students could not marry and were expected to take Holy Orders. Members of the cathedral Chapter took turns to nominate their chosen candidate to a Studentship. There was no competition and no examination. Gaisford was irritated by the government's proposal that Studentships should be competed for or that they should go to the most able candidates. He warned Palmerston sharply that Studentships were not intended as what he disparagingly termed 'prizes'. They were created to aid those known to the College who could not otherwise afford to pursue a career, if not of scholarship, at least of residence at Christ Church.

It was certainly absurd to complain of nepotism as corrupting the system, since the system depended entirely upon it. Dr Frederick Barnes of the cathedral Chapter remarked sadly, 'I've given Studentships to my sons, and to my nephews, and to my nephews' children, and there are no more of my family left. I shall have to give them by merit one of these days.' In such voices there rises an anticipation of the Wonderland caucus race, where merit is superfluous.[11]

The morally grotesque did not lack a zoological counterpart, in Christ Church as well as Wonderland. Charles Dodgson came into residence while Frank Buckland was still a Student. Buckland and his father, Professor William Buckland, had filled their college quarters with animals seldom encountered outside a circus or a zoo. William

Buckland, as Professor of Geology and a Canon of the cathedral, was permitted to marry. His family lived in a corner of the Great Quadrangle. So did his menagerie. William Tuckwell recalled a childhood visit and the 'grinning monsters' on the stairs, waiting to pounce. The children played with dead crocodiles, sent to Buckland from abroad, which had been first floated in the Great Quadrangle's central pool, Mercury, in hopes of revival. Frank was allowed a ride in the pool on the back of a tethered giant turtle, before the creature was taken as a culinary item to the kitchens, where its head was first severed and then bit the cook.

The talking point of the Buckland dining-room was a table constructed of fossilized saurian faeces. Guests were 'waited upon,' as Ruskin called it, by lizards who caught the flies on summer days. The menu was adventurous. Tuckwell recalled, 'horseflesh I remember more than once, crocodile another day, mice baked in batter on a third day – while the guinea-pig under the table inquiringly nibbled at your infantine toes, the bear walked round your chair and rasped your hand with file-like tongue, the jackal's fiendish yell close by came through the open window.' Small wonder that Dodgson twenty years later was still teasing little girls with such dishes as rat-tail jelly and buttered mice for breakfast.[12]

It might be wondered whether Alice encountered anything more macabre than certain aspects of Gaisford's unreformed Christ Church. William Buckland endeavoured to eat his way through the animal kingdom. Moles tasted very unpleasant and bluebottle flies were worse but he persisted. Who better than he to make the butterflies of Dodgson's poem into mutton pies? He stopped short of cannibalism, except when shown the heart of a French king preserved as a relic in a snuff-box. 'I have eaten some strange things,' Buckland said wistfully and, to the dismay of his hosts at Nuneham, he gobbled it up. In a spirit of scientific inquiry, he installed a dead giraffe in Dr Pusey's stable until he should have time to dissect it. Before long, its presence was unpleasantly evident to those who lived in that area of the College.

Yet he was no mere eccentric. Before Darwin, William Buckland had established evidence of pre-history that antedated Creation as calculated by Genesis. Baron Bunsen denounced the persecution of Buckland by 'bigots' in 1839 for 'having asserted that among the fossils there may be a pre-Adamite species.' Though a Canon of Christ Church and later Dean of Westminster, Buckland was capable

of trenchant scepticism. On his wedding tour, he had caused outrage
when shown at Palermo the bones of St Rosalia. 'They are the bones
of a goat!' he cried. When saintly blood liquefied before him, he
dabbed his finger in a fallen drop and announced, 'I can tell you what
it is. It is bat's urine!'[13]

After William Buckland, his son Frank became a Student of Christ
Church and created his own menagerie in Fell's Buildings. Jacko the
monkey, Tig the bear and their companions escaped at will to roam
the College and the cathedral precincts. Visitors to the rooms in Fell's
Buildings heard the crunch of the jackal eating live guinea pigs under
the sofa. William Buckland had once bought a dead bear, displayed
as an advertisement for hair-grease outside an Oxford barber's, so
that he could cook and eat it. His son, hearing of the death of a
panther in London, had the chops exhumed and sent down for his
dinner-table. The more fortunate bear, Tig, appeared in the undergraduate chorus of a Sophocles play and was introduced to distinguished guests at the Oxford meeting of the British Association in
1847, anticipating the Baker in *The Hunting of the Snark*, who 'once
went a walk, paw-in-paw, with a bear.'

It could not last. Jacko the monkey was escorted out through the
main gate of Christ Church on the Dean's instructions. An eagle flew
into a cathedral service and the bear attended chapel. 'Mr Buckland,'
said Gaisford sternly, 'I hear you keep a bear in college. Well, either
you or your bear must go.'[14]

Few eccentrics are as eccentric as reputation would suggest. Yet
Gaisford's Christ Church was rich in a type that would never recur.
Strange creatures and pre-history, eccentric authoritarianism, anti-
quated ritual divorced from reality, wove the legends of Charles Dodg-
son's new home. If he sought an entrance to the underworld of
Wonderland, it seemed he need look no further.

*

Dodgson's own life as an undergraduate was more mundane and
regimented. In his daily routine, he was called by his scout at 6.15 in
time to be down from his room at 7. Compulsory morning chapel,
still in Latin, was held in the cathedral at 8, followed by a hasty lecture
in divinity before breakfast. He was punctilious over attending chapel,
writing home contritely on the occasion when he went back to sleep

after his scout had called him and woke again to find it was ten past eight. No one had missed him, though undergraduates acting as 'prickbills' were supposed to check attendance at chapel.

After breakfast, the morning was spent attending either the Mathematical Lecturer at Christ Church, Robert Faussett, or his Classics tutor, Jacob Ley, a Student of the college and also Vicar of St Mary Magdalen, Oxford. There were some one hundred and eighty undergraduates with six tutors in classics and one lecturer in mathematics. Most teaching was in tutorials or small classes, though college lectures were given by the Readers in Greek and Rhetoric.

The tutorial system in the early 1850s was vestigial. Senior members of colleges had little obligation to teach and junior members even less obligation to learn. Tutors customarily had few pupils. At Christ Church in 1831, Charles Wordsworth had had four and the future Dean Liddell only a dozen. On the other hand, a tutorial was not limited to any length of time. Early in his career as a tutor, in January 1855, Dodgson himself records giving an undergraduate a long lecture in oblique coordination, which seems to have lasted most of the morning. It was possible for undergraduates to attend the classes of other tutors in addition to their own but these provisions were not intended to supply all the instruction needed.

The deficiency was made up by private tutors, either college tutors working privately or recent graduates who had remained in residence. Customarily, it had been expected that undergraduates should make their own arrangements for such tuition, as they negotiated with servants over the purchase of dinner in Hall. Tuition apart, it was assumed that they would read together in groups without any form of supervision. There were misgivings over the private tutor system and Gaisford opposed it. He particularly disliked the possibility that his undergraduates should be privately tutored by anyone who was not himself a Christ Church man, though if the system was banned in Christ Church men would seek tutors elsewhere.

At the end of Dodgson's second term, in June 1851, he was required to pass Responsions. This examination involved papers in arithmetic, the first two books of Euclid, divinity, Latin and Greek texts. He wrote a brief but facetious account of it for his sisters in the high-flown style of a popular contemporary novelist, G. P. R. James. Responsions represented little more than a general test of the candidate's suitability to read for a degree. Dodgson, in formal dress with white neck-cloth and clerical bands, entered the examination schools. There was a long table with books upon it and two examiners sitting behind it, confronting twelve pale-faced youths. Tiers of seats rose either side for the spectators. When his turn came, he was handed a copy of Sophocles and instructed to translate from line four hundred and fifty onwards. After two pages they stopped him and he was told to go. The examination in Greek texts was over and he had passed.

At the end of his second year came the First Public Examination, known as Moderations and divided into classes. He was a classman rather than a passman and therefore a candidate for honours. The two subjects were Classics and Mathematics. When the time came, he got a Second in Classics and a First in Mathematics.

In the evenings of his four years as an undergraduate he worked in his room until midnight and beyond but the afternoons were devoted to leisurely exercise. At two o'clock, undergraduates emerged from their college gates, walking or riding according to taste and income. The long walks of fifteen or twenty miles which Dodgson took in later years originated in this habit. As yet, however, there was too little time for walks of that length. Oxford and England still dined early and at leisure. College dinner was at 5 p.m. followed by evening chapel at 7 p.m.

In the dark panelled Hall, lit by triple-branched brass candlesticks, 'Wolsey's dining-room' as Ruskin called it, the social distinctions of the College were plain. Undergraduates of noble family, wearers of the gold-tasselled cap and gown, sat at the doctors' table on the dais. The senior Masters of Arts sat just above the main fireplace on the north side and the junior ones just above the fireplace on the south. Below them on the north side were the chaplains and on the other side the Bachelors of Arts. Below all these sat the gentlemen commoners, Charles Dodgson among them. There was one chair, for the Dean, benches for all others. Around the 'doctors' and the young noblemen stood servitors who received a college education in return for waiting at table and attending to the needs of their social superiors. The practice died hard at Christ Church, revealing how distinctive the characters of individual colleges were.

Each commoner in Hall belonged to a mess of half a dozen undergraduates who sat together at one of the tables, where the tableware was pewter and the silver cutlery past its best. The food was not supplied by the College but by certain of its servants who enjoyed a monopoly and charged their own prices. It was their livelihood. The manciple provided dinner and the cook such meat as was needed on other occasions. The butler supplied bread, butter, cheese and beer. In January 1855, after he had graduated and moved up to the Bachelors' table, Charles Dodgson became 'caterer' for his mess. He was to manage the accounts and order the dinners. In the box belonging to his table were account books going back to 1812, including some with entries in his father's handwriting. His experience as caterer left him strongly opposed to this monopoly system. As soon as he was in a position to do so, after the so-called 'Bread and Butter' dispute at the College in 1865, he advocated the abolition of the monopoly supply system and the institution of salaries for these college servants instead.

G. J. Cowley-Brown recalled his dinners as a member of Dodgson's mess, writing his friend's obituary in the *Scottish Guardian* on 22 January 1898. 'The joint was pushed from side to side, each man hacking off his own portion, and rising from the table without waiting for one another.' Nor did they wait for Latin grace to be said by a junior Student, despite the reproof of the senior scout, a fat man with a squeaky voice, 'Gra-ace, Gen-tlemen, ple-ease!' Cowley-Brown and most of the others at first regarded Dodgson as poor company. He was not termed a 'muff', as he had been at Rugby, but it amounted to much the same thing.

> We all, however, I may safely say, sat in the same hall and some of us even at the same table as Dodgson without discovering (perhaps from our want of it) the wit, the peculiar humour that was in him. We looked upon him as a rising mathematician, nothing more. He seldom spoke, and the slight impediment in his speech was not conducive to conversation.

Among other members of the mess, at least four of whom were to become clergymen, was Philip Pusey, the son of Dr Pusey, and George Woodhouse, who befriended Dodgson and with whom he exchanged family visits in the vacations. Almost a lifetime later, Dodgson wrote to this friend's widow at the time of her bereavement, 'Of all the friends I made at Ch. Ch., your husband was the *first* who ever spoke to me – across the dinner-table in Hall ... I remember, as if it were only yesterday, the kindly smile with which he spoke.' The tone of the comment perhaps reveals less of the kindness of Woodhouse than of the loneliness of the young Charles Dodgson.[15]

Dean Gaisford on his dais ruled his undergraduates with an array of penalties. Despite their privileges, they were still treated much like schoolboys. Corporal punishment, which Wolsey's statutes had prescribed, had fallen into disuse but lines and impositions remained, as well as gating for a period within the college, rustication from Oxford for a while, or the final decree of sending down. The writing of lines as a punishment had led to a thriving little industry in Oriel Lane, where an old man named Boddington and his stable of hungry scribblers would produce them by the yard for any undergraduate with money in his pocket who had fallen foul of his tutor. The last senior member of Christ Church who persisted in punishing his young men by setting them lines, as if they were schoolboys, was Charles Dodgson himself. On one occasion, when an imposition was not in the handwriting of the culprit, Dodgson went straight to the Dean and reported the matter.

His own success in his degree examinations never seemed to be in doubt. On 1 November 1851, almost at the end of his first year, he had shown sufficient promise to be awarded the College's Boulter Scholarship, which was worth twenty pounds a year. The reasonable costs of a degree at Oxford were thought to be between eighty and a hundred and fifty pounds a year.

A year later, following his success in Moderations, Dr Pusey nominated him to a Studentship on Christmas Eve 1852. Though his final degree examinations were still two years away, the award made him a member of the foundation with an annual income of twenty pounds and the right of residence at Christ Church for the rest of his life, provided that he remained a bachelor, proceeded to Holy Orders, and was not guilty of 'gross immorality.'

Dr Pusey wrote to his old friend, Archdeacon Dodgson, sending him the good news about his son. There had been another candidate on his list of greater elegance as a scholar, but lacking young Dodgson's solid qualities and more cultivated intellect. 'One of the Censors brought to me today five names; but in their minds it was plain that they thought your son on the whole the most eligible for the College.' The Archdeacon was able to assure his son that there was no question of personal favouritism in Pusey's choice but that, 'you have *won*, and well won, this honour for *yourself*, and that it is bestowed as a matter of *justice* to *you*, and not of *kindness* to *me*.'[16]

The next two years showed that the Studentship, by whatever system it had been awarded, was not unmerited. In the summer of 1854, Charles Dodgson got a Third in Classics, enabling him to take a First in Mathematics that autumn, after studying with Bartholomew

Price during the long vacation. On 13 December 1854, in what he described as 'a very boastful letter' to his sister Mary, he added that he had the highest marks of the five Christ Church men who had been awarded First Class Honours. Five days later he took the degree of Bachelor of Arts.

Such leisure as the undergraduate Dodgson had during these Oxford terms, which occupied almost half the year, was spent in his afternoon walks with friends like Richard Colley, whom he had met at tea in the rooms of their Classics tutor, Jacob Ley. The young men also went to the assize court to listen to the cases, though arriving too late on the first occasion. A good deal of Charles Dodgson's own writing already showed his interest in the law and legalistic device. He later went to hear cases in court with Robert Faussett, who had been his mathematics tutor.

His letters to his sisters and family suggest a conventional life of conscientious hard work, a young man loyal to his college crew on the river but taking no part himself, playing cricket once and being no good at it, and skating in the winter. Outside the window of his room, the dogs of the undergraduates fought in Peckwater Quadrangle while their masters strove to control them. There was an inept conjuring performance in the town before an audience of sceptical and rowdy undergraduates. His life was dutiful but less than exciting.

As an undergraduate, he attended the annual Commemoration, pushing his way up the crowded spiral staircase to the packed top gallery of the Sheldonian Theatre. Honorary degrees were conferred on important people, prize poems and essays were read, including Edwin Arnold's Newdigate poem 'The Feast of Belshazzar'. The undergraduates cheered the ladies in blue and the ladies in white among the elegantly dressed visitors. When there was a pause in the proceedings, they hissed the Junior Proctor as the representative of university discipline. Following this there was the butterfly elegance of 'Show Sunday' when the fashionable and the famous paraded in Christ Church meadow.

Dr Pusey wrote of the younger Dodgson's 'uniform, steady and good conduct.' He had learnt of this from young men of the candidate's own age, which suggests that the source might have been his son, Philip, who was in Dodgson's mess at Hall. Archdeacon Dodgson passed the comment on to his son, adding, 'what I have so often inculcated, that it is the "steady, painstaking, likely-to-do-good" man, who in the long run wins the race against those who now and then give a brilliant flash and, as Shakespeare says, "straight are cold again.""[17]

Steady, quiet and likely to do good was how the world saw him. There was nothing flashy or vainglorious. Years later, in an article on the mathematical paradox of Achilles and the Tortoise, it seemed that he echoed this parental judgement when he allowed the worthy and persistent reptile a good deal of fun at the expense of the braggart warrior.

*

The new year of 1855 brought further rewards. As a Bachelor of Arts, he was made Sub-Librarian of Christ Church with an annual salary of thirty-five pounds. In May, he wrote, 'The Dean and Canons have been pleased to give me one of the Bostock Scholarships, said to be worth £20 a year – this very nearly raises my income this year to independence. Courage!' He also began private tutoring of undergraduates and by April had fourteen pupils. Towards the end of the year, he was appointed Mathematical Lecturer, in effect an official tutor, in place of his own tutor Faussett. War with Russia had broken out in 1854. As the conflict in the Crimea intensified, Faussett had taken a commission in the Commissariat and was on his way to the front. Gaisford hesitated until the autumn before appointing Dodgson as his successor because, Dodgson thought privately, the Dean was reluctant to have a lecturer who had not yet served his time as a 'bachelor' and taken his degree as Master of Arts.[18]

The Lectureship and his income from tutoring made him independent. His father, now a Canon of Ripon cathedral, wrote him a letter of advice on his finances, a 'supposed case' of a young man of twenty-three who could save one hundred and fifty pounds a year. One hundred pounds should be invested at four per cent. Twenty-nine pounds and fifteen shillings should be used to insure his life for fifteen hundred pounds. The balance of twenty pounds and five shillings should be invested each year in books. At the end of ten years there would be 'A nest egg of £1,220 ready money,' a sum of fifteen hundred pounds secured upon death and a library worth two hundred pounds. As it happened, Charles Dodgson was not to be a nest-builder. On the other hand he was to prove careful, if not tight-fisted, in financial matters and the advice must have appealed to him. His was a family which combined moral diligence and financial self-interest without the least unease.[19]

His life at Christ Church, comfortably provided for as long as he cared to remain, seemed agreeable in every way. He had a good many friends, made during his undergraduate career. Vere Bayne was to remain in residence even longer than he; Henry Liddon, a popular preacher and leader of the High Church faction, became a lifelong friend and Dodgson's companion on his only journey abroad; Faussett returned to Christ Church after his service in the Crimea, as his Studentship entitled him to do. Among friends who had moved to other colleges was Robinson Duckworth, destined to be his companion on the most celebrated river outing in English literature.

It was a time when public interest had turned to the military deadlock in the Crimea and the question of whether or not the British and French could take Sebastopol. On 16 March even Dodgson, who seldom recorded comments on public affairs that did not directly concern him, went to hear a lecture by a Christ Church man on the defences of the Russian city. War and politics might have seemed far away from the secluded life of an Oxford college, where Dodgson now had rooms in Chaplains' Quadrangle.

As it happened, the storm which overtook Christ Church came not from the Crimea but from London and Oxford. The old collegiate system, seen at its most bizarre in institutions like Christ Church, had become intolerable to the new puritanism, as Charles Greville called it, of the 1850s. There must be an end to nepotism, self-indulgence, the amateurism of the tutorial system, and the medieval eccentricities of collegiate idleness. Dodgson's Oxford, with its lifelong Studentships by nomination of family friends and its ancient learning which 'elevates above the vulgar herd,' continued to live as though it were 1636 and Archbishop Laud was still Chancellor. Dr Barnes made no secret of having distributed the good things of the college to his nearest male relatives. Dr Bull, to whom Charles Dodgson senior had written about his financial difficulties in 1832, was a byword for men who held one post and were paid for several.

There was a set of verses in circulation about a man who travelled to London by coach. He was accompanied by a Canon of Christ Church, a Canon of Exeter, a Prebendary of York, and a parson 'With a Vicarage fat and four hundred a year.' But there were only two men in the coach, since all these other appointments and incomes were held simultaneously by one man, Dr John Bull, Treasurer of

Christ Church. Aptly named, John Bull, the friend of Charles Dodgson senior, represented just the sort of abuses of which the reformers complained. Yet he survived as Treasurer of Christ Church from 1832 to 1857. No one doubted that he deserved some form of preferment, having been King's Scholar at Westminster and a Double First at Oxford. The question was whether he should have had all four.[20]

Dr Bull was one of two colleagues of the young Charles Dodgson who attracted most of the reformers' hostility. Gaisford was more apt to frighten them speechless. The other was Dr Frederick Barnes, ironically nicknamed 'Brains' by the Christ Church undergraduates. He was often known as Major Barnes, in tribute to his period as an officer in the Oxford Volunteer Corps during the Napoleonic Wars. He believed strongly in the importance of nepotism as a principle of Oxford life and he died at Christ Church in the fiftieth year of his residence as a senior member in 1859, at the age of eighty-eight. But for a break of five years, he had lived there since 1790, most of them in the splendour of canonical apartments in Peckwater.

Among the aims of the reformers were the opening of all college fellowships and studentships to competitive examination; the separation of the University from the Established Church, ending the ecclesiastical character of Oxford life; the consequent abolition of the obligations to celibacy and Holy Orders; the transfer of power from colleges to an enlarged university professoriate, governing through faculties rather than by colleges. In 1850 the government of Lord John Russell appointed Commissioners to investigate and report back. Dean Gaisford was appalled and, for as long as possible, kept the enemy at bay by simply ignoring all correspondence on the matter. Later he wrote to Palmerston, deploring election to Studentships and Fellowships on 'mere intellectual merit,' but by then the battle was lost.[21]

Oxford was, of course, still restricted at the time to men who were members of the Church of England. Yet even within that restriction the advocates of open competition for fellowships and studentships, like Goldwin Smith, Joint Secretary of the Commission, pointed to Balliol and Oriel, which had already made their fellowships competitive and had gained a start on all other colleges in 'the race of regeneration.' Dodgson was unimpressed. He supported Dean Gaisford and the existing system, which had made him what he was. Distrusting 'mere intellectual merit' as much as Gaisford had done, he saw in open competition an invitation to moral indifference, if not to villainy and vice, described in his satire on 'The Elections to the Hebdomadal Council'.

> And then our Fellowships shall open be
> To Intellect, no meaner quality!
> No moral excellence, no social fitness
> Shall ever be admissible as witness.
> 'Avaunt, dull Virtue!' is Oxonia's cry:
> 'Come to my arms, ingenious Villainy!'
>   For Classic Fellowships, an honour high,
> Simonides and Co. will then apply –
> Our Mathematics will to Oxford bring
> The 'cutest members of the betting-ring –
> Law Fellowships will start upon their journeys
> A myriad of unscrupulous attorneys –
> While poisoners, doomed till now to toil unknown,
> Shall mount the Physical Professor's throne![22]

The Commission made its report. The decline of Christ Church was singled out and attributed to the awarding of Studentships as though they were a form of ecclesiastical patronage. Henceforth, Studentships must be competitive. They must not be awarded to undergraduates unless they were undergraduate Studentships only. There were to be no more Dodgsons passing through the system to lifelong tenure without a check. The Commission also proposed to transfer power from the colleges to the University. The Oxford Act of 1854 created a Hebdomadal Council on which the professoriate was amply represented. It also appointed executive commissioners to superintend the running of the University and the revision of individual college statutes. What was later to be called accountability was imposed on Oxford wholesale, or so it seemed.

Oddly enough, though Christ Church was in the eye of the storm, its particular anomaly remained unresolved. It was unique in being both a college and a cathedral. The governing body consisted of the Dean and Chapter, not the Students. Other colleges had fellows who might govern them. Christ Church Students performed the same teaching functions as fellows but were subordinate to the Dean and Canons of the Cathedral. Some Canons were professors and some were not but they had no other necessary connection with Christ Church as a college. They presided over an institution in which they had far less interest than those who had no say in their own government. Of course it would have been far better had the College and the cathedral been separately constituted in 1546 but that had not happened.

The anomaly remained for the time being, though it was soon to absorb a good deal of Dodgson's energy. In the University as a whole, thanks to what was called the 'conservative reform' of the Oxford Act which Gladstone saw through parliament in 1854, the most radical reformers got a good deal less than they wanted while their opponents lost less than they had feared. Yet the new institutions and regulations dictated that Charles Dodgson at twenty-two belonged already to that old order in which he was placed by writers of his obituary more than forty years later. Mark Pattison, contrasting the professorial and tutorial systems, described the first as consisting of 'accomplishment and current information.' The Oxford tutorial tradition he called 'disciplining the faculties, and basing ideas on the thought proper to the human reason.' It did not progress but remained sure of the ground on which it stood.[23]

That was precisely Dodgson's position. He preferred Euclid to the new mathematics of Riemann and his contemporaries, in which he showed virtually no interest. Indeed one of his major publications as a mathematician, paradoxical rather than mathematical, was to show the superiority of Euclid to his modern rivals. The modern rivals he chose were almost all the writers of educational textbooks. It was to be said of Dodgson that, for all his genius, he made no showing as a major mathematician. Yet, so far as Oxford was concerned, he had been trained in a world which did not require him to do so. He himself advised a friend that Cambridge would be preferable to Oxford for anyone with a serious interest in the subject. Time and reform had overturned the comfortable world with which he had been content, almost before he had time to explore it. Of course, his Studentship was safe, since the Oxford Act did not deprive present incumbents. He might live in Christ Church for the rest of his life, doing as much or as little as he chose. He was one of the last men to be awarded that privilege by nomination and favouritism. So far as his contemporaries in the University were concerned, the type he represented was soon destined to be, not inappropriately, dead as the dodo.

5

An Oxford Chiel

FOR CHARLES DODGSON there was a change in his circumstances during 1855 far more significant in its way than the agitation for university reform or the Oxford Act. On Saturday 26 May 1855, Osborne Gordon, a Classics tutor, Dodgson and Dean Gaisford were putting away new books on the library shelves. On these afternoons which were occupied by the duties of Sub-Librarian, Dodgson worked in surroundings that might have beguiled a Renaissance prince.

The New Library, completed in 1772, with tall Corinthian columns and balustrading along its roof-line, was as great a treasure as its splendid collection of books, manuscripts and prints, dating back to Tudor legacies. The ground floor of the building had been intended as an arched piazza, until a bequest of Italian Old Masters by General John Guise in the 1760s required the transformation of the arches into windows so that the space might become a picture gallery. The upper floor, with its galleried shelves of polished wood and ornate ceiling was the library proper. Thomas Gaisford at seventy-five, not a great age for a Christ Church incumbent, was content to spend his time among its treasures. Though the Oxford Act had received the royal assent in the previous August, its 'serious evils', as he termed them, had not yet become apparent in the College.

A week later, early on 2 June, it was announced that the Dean was suddenly and gravely ill. One bulletin followed another with ominous rapidity, until at half past eleven that morning the notice of his death was posted. The shock was the greater for his appearance of perfect health, as Dodgson described it, a week before. Moreover, Gaisford had seemed to Dr Pusey and the traditionalists to be all that remained between the College and the triumph of reform. 'I think it is not merely inexpedient but unjust and tyrannical!' he had insisted defiantly as the reformers appeared to be winning at Westminster and Oxford.

No one felt the loss of the late Dean of Christ Church more than Dodgson's patron. Pusey paid tribute to Thomas Gaisford as 'a representative of the best in the past which has been passing away, and respect for him was a check to revolution in many institutions.' Privately, Pusey expressed apprehension more strongly than grief. What, or who, would follow the Dean? 'Now nothing but what is evil is threatened as his successor,' he said gloomily. 'They imagine Liddell.'[1]

Henry George Liddell, Headmaster of Westminster, Chaplain to Prince Albert, had been a commoner in 1830, then a Student and tutor at Christ Church until 1846. Forty-four years of age, handsome, married to a wife of Hispanic beauty, he had a young family of a son and three daughters. This would have disqualified him as a Student but not as Dean. Far worse, to Pusey, Liddell was a member of the infamous Commission of 1850, a rabid reformer. Indeed, he had turned upon Gladstone and denounced the 1854 legislation as worse than no reform at all. He was the worst kind of reformer, because he was also patrician and authoritarian. Frank Markham, as a schoolboy, remembered him clouting boys round the head at arm's length in the yard at Westminster, 'handing' as it was called, a self-assured but scornful figure. 'Inferior to his parents in natural charm of character,' wrote Augustus Hare fastidiously. As a scholar, however, Liddell had a formidable reputation as partner with the Master of Balliol in Liddell and Scott's *Greek-English Lexicon*. This gave rise to an epigram which circulated with variations. Hare, a distant cousin of Liddell, wrote it down as he heard it from Westminster.

> Two men wrote a Lexicon,
>   Liddell and Scott;
> One half was clever,
>   And one half was not.
> Give me the answer, boys,
>   Quick to this riddle,
> Which was by Scott
> And which was by Liddell?[2]

There were no grounds on which Christ Church might object to his appointment. Had the Students been allowed to vote, they would not have chosen Liddell. But Deans were appointed by the college Visitor, and the Visitor at Christ Church was the Queen. Victoria would make the appointment according to constitutional convention, on the advice of her Prime Minister. Gaisford had died on Saturday morning and for Palmerston to have acted over the weekend might have seemed indecorous. On Monday, however, he submitted Liddell's name and by Wednesday the appointment was confirmed. For good measure, Palmerston advised Her Majesty to appoint another reformer and modern churchman, Benjamin Jowett of Balliol, as Regius Professor of Greek in Gaisford's place.

Christ Church undergraduates had their fair share of a reputation for loutish behaviour at Oxford, no doubt fostered by those who regarded the College as a byword for snobbery tempered by mediocrity. There were indeed spectacular disturbances under both Gaisford and Liddell. Dr Jelf of Christ Church was one of the most unpopular proctors in living memory and his pupils had howled him down during the solemnity of the degree ceremony of Encaenia in 1843, urged on by High Church friends who wanted to disrupt the conferring of an honorary doctorate on an American Unitarian.

Fifteen years after his arrival at the Deanery, Liddell described for the first time how he was received by Christ Church undergraduates.

> When I first came, I confess my heart often sank; it is hardly too much to say that hardly a week passed without some disturbance. Gunpowder was freely used in such a way as to terrify not only the inmates of the House, but all the neighbourhood. One night, not very long after I took possession, a kettle charged with gunpowder was found fastened to the handle of my front door with a match inserted by the spout; and had the match taken effect, probably the door would have been blown in and immense injury done. About the same time, I forget whether before or after, Mrs Liddell received an anonymous letter, in which she was advised to quit the house with her young family, because in the course of a few nights it was to be blown up.[3]

None the less, two of the most active reformers, one overt and the other more subtle, were now installed in high places. The last chance of resistance from Christ Church men like Pusey had vanished as the enemy entered the gate. The Act of 1854, combined with Liddell's arrival, brought changes of a kind to Oxford that Dodgson could either have accepted or secluded himself from. As time went on, his contemporaries found that he chose increasing seclusion, constructing a world of his own certainties. In his middle years, he became a recluse.

The certainties of childhood, memories of early years at Daresbury, were part of his private world. Yet the advent of the Liddells was no less significant to that inner vision. He was not to meet the Dean's children for another year and his first specific reference to Alice Liddell came in 1857. At the time of their arrival in Oxford, the eldest child, Edward Henry, known as 'Harry', was nine years old. Of the girls, Lorina was six, Alice three and Edith a year old. Not since the days of Professor Buckland had children of this age been a feature of college life. To be the young father of young children gave the new broom a certain moral force.

Despite shyness and reserve, perhaps in part the result of his stammer, Dodgson was neither inhospitable nor inconsiderate towards his pupils. In one act of self-conscious kindness, he summoned a servitor, one of the poor scholars who worked their way to a degree by waiting on their superiors. The young man could not afford the private tuition which others enjoyed. 'If you are intending to read mathematics,' Dodgson said, 'I shall be glad to give you any help you need.' As a sociable newcomer, he gave a 'wine' on the evening of 2 March 1855 to all he knew in Christ Church. Forty people, a quarter of the college, attended. Ruskin held a similar wine as an undergraduate and assisted in carrying Dean Gaisford's son downstairs after it.[4]

For his own intellectual development, Dodgson set himself lists of reading, including volumes of history, the novels of Scott, the plays of Shakespeare, the poetry of Milton, Wordsworth, Coleridge and Byron. The great English poets might help to crowd out troubled thoughts and idle moments. There was also to be philosophy, divinity and a possible encounter with Aeschylus, in the plan that he drew up on 13 March 1855.

In his first term as a graduate he sat for a Senior Mathematical Scholarship, only to lose it to Samuel Bosanquet, who had come second to him in the final Honours list the previous autumn. Dodgson did only two questions in the paper on the morning of the second day. He decided to miss the afternoon paper, abandon the scholarship, and instead go for a long walk to Kidlington and back with his friend Robert Mayo. He repeatedly rebuked himself in his diary for not getting the scholarship, which was easily within his grasp, and for failure to work properly in the term he had wasted.

That term began with the novelty of being a tutor. In January 1855, he explained it to his younger sister Henrietta and his youngest brother Edwin in a whimsical letter. The tutor sat in his room with the pupil in the 'yard', so that the one should be 'dignified' and the other 'degraded'. At intervals between them stood a scout outside the first door, a sub-scout outside the second and a sub-sub scout half-way down the stairs. These servants echoed the questions of the tutor, misunderstanding them a little more at each stage. 'What is twice three? . . .', 'What's a rice tree? . . .', 'When is ice free? . . .', 'What's a nice fee? . . .' The bewildered pupil suggested, 'Half a guinea!' Back came the answer, 'Can't forge any . . .', 'Ho for Jinny . . .', 'Don't be a ninny . . .'. 'And so,' wrote Dodgson, 'the lecture proceeds. Such is Life.'[5]

This whimsy soon yielded to the less agreeable reality of teaching idle or indifferent young men. Dodgson gave his first lectures on Euclid and algebra on 28 January 1856 and was irritated that only nine men attended Euclid and eleven algebra, of the twelve who should have been at each. He taught for a while in his spare time at St Aldate's School, restricting himself to the boys because he thought boys and girls would not mix. His idea was to combine each lesson with a story. He began on 29 January 1856, found the children noisy and inattentive, and withdrew exactly a month later.

It was impossible to keep to his reading scheme and he soon abandoned that as well. By the end of the following year he had decided on setting himself tasks to be learnt by heart. Poetry, geometrical problems, formulae might be recited or pondered on railway journeys and at other times of mental idleness throughout his life. He did some reading, none the less, even if it was not of the solid and systematic kind that he envisaged. Among the new books of the decade, he chose Elizabeth Barrett Browning's *Aurora Leigh* and George Eliot's first fiction in *Scenes from Clerical Life*.

When the Easter Term began in April 1855, he had fourteen private pupils who were to come to him by arrangement with the Mathematical Examiner at Christ Church, Dr G. W. Kitchin. It was not an official appointment but a private agreement between the two men, Kitchin having more pupils than he could manage. Predictably, Dodgson found himself with the less able, whose only interest in mathematics was in clearing the first hurdle of Responsions in arithmetic and Euclid, so that they might go on to other subjects.

Was he happy? His diary entry at the end of 1855, his first full year as a tutor, is a lament for great gifts bestowed and thrown away. He sounds like a young man ill at ease with himself, writing philosophically but without hope.

> I am sitting alone in my bedroom this last night of the old year, waiting for midnight. It has been the most eventful year of my life: I began it a poor bachelor student, with no definite plans or expectations; I end it a master and tutor in Ch. Ch., with an income of more than £300 a year, and the course of mathematical tuition marked out by God's providence for at least some years to come. Great mercies, great failings, time lost, talents misapplied – such has been the past year.[6]

*

The months that followed did little to cheer him. On 26 November 1856, less than two years after he had begun, he confessed himself weary of teaching. He had examined a number of his candidates for Responsions that day and not one was fit to enter even this preliminary examination. They had no taste for the work. It was drudgery on both sides, added to idleness and stupidity on theirs. Men like Baldwin Leighton, a classicist, only got a Fourth in his own subject. A fortnight earlier Dodgson had noted that he was teaching for seven hours a day, and that he had neither the time nor the mental alertness for reading, let alone for studying divinity as a step to ordination. He feared that he might have a complete breakdown. It was far removed from the comic letter with which he had greeted his new life two years before.

Unsympathetic colleagues might think the problem was not in the work of the Mathematical Lectureship but in Dodgson's personality. T. B. Strong, his Christ Church colleague, remarked that 'This office was in no way an arduous one and he had plenty of time left to him in which to pursue his own studies.' It was Dodgson who chose to keep his mind busy every moment of his waking life and who ran the consequent risks. 'He was a laborious worker, always disliking to break off from the pursuit of any subject which interested him; apt to forget his meals, and toil on for the best part of the night, rather than stop short of the object which he had in view.'

Strong's opinion was that the mental collapse Dodgson himself feared was averted by these 'paroxysms' of work being frequent but not continuous. 'No man could have held out for very long under such a *régime* as his when the fever of work came upon him.' He insisted on the importance of going to bed each night physically exhausted. A later age might see this as the muscular Christian's attempt to blunt sexual desire. A crowded and active mind was a healthy mind, as important to the religious conscience as to curbing the libido. In the introduction to *Pillow Problems* (1893), itself a title of some resonance, the book's mathematical puzzles are prescribed by Dodgson as an insomniac's palliative for 'mental troubles, much worse than mere worry.' These are the torments of the bedroom, taunts of profanity or impurity. There seems no doubt as to what impurity he had in mind, writing elsewhere of sexual relationships, 'without which purity and impurity would be unmeaning words.'

> There are sceptical thoughts, which seem for a moment to uproot the firmest faith; there are blasphemous thoughts which dart unbidden into the most reverent souls; there are unholy thoughts, which torture with their hateful presence the fancy that would fain be pure. Against all these some real mental *work* is a most helpful ally. That 'unclean spirit' of the parable, who brought back with him seven others more wicked than himself, only did so because he found the chamber 'swept and garnished,' and its owner sitting with folded hands: had he found it all alive with the 'busy hum' of active *work*, there would have been scant welcome for him and his seven!

It might seem like the logic of Wonderland to believe that insomnia would be averted or placated – rather than induced – by the patient being required to 'find a general formula for two squares whose sum = 2,' or placing in a triangle 'a line parallel to the base, such that the portions of sides intercepted between it and the base, shall be together equal to the base.'[7]

In life's other psychic terrors, he was not in the least squeamish. Having seen a man in an epileptic fit, he determined to learn first aid. He took an interest in medicine and acquired a collection of medical books that would have done credit to a physician. It was then that he put himself to the test by watching the amputation of a man's leg under chloroform in 1857 and was pleased to find that he did not feel in the least sick or faint during the hour of the operation.

In his twenties the 'busy hum' of self-imposed reading, the committal to memory of poetry and formulae, the seven hours of tutoring every day, the puzzling and contriving of Memoria Technica, became as essential to this celibate destined to Holy Orders as were the walks of ten, fifteen, or twenty miles which brought him easier sleep. 'His brain seemed to give him no peace,' wrote A. S. Russell of him, as tutor and mathematician, 'it was everlastingly multiplying, or dividing, or calculating probabilities.'

'In the small world of elementary geometry, arithmetic and algebra, he was a supreme master,' Russell added. In 1860, reflecting this conservatism and traditionalist frame of mind, Dodgson published his *Syllabus of Plane Algebraical Geometry* and *Notes on the First Two Books of Euclid*. These owed more to Rugby and Responsions than to any sense of intellectual adventure on the frontiers of the subject. His lectures were what one undergraduate called 'dull as ditchwater', and his pupils collectively wrote a letter to Dean Liddell asking to be transferred to another tutor. A more humane twentieth-century assessment came from Sir Herbert Maxwell, biographer of Wellington and editor of Thomas Creevey's diaries, who recalled, 'The lean dark-haired person of Charles Lutwidge Dodgson, before whom as Mathematical Lecturer we undergraduates of Christ Church used to assemble.'

> Very few, if any, of my contemporaries survive to confirm my impression of the singularly dry and perfunctory manner in which he imparted instruction to us, never betraying the slightest personal interest in matters that were of deep concern to us. Yet this must have been the very time when he was framing the immortal fantasia of Alice.[8]

Self-assurance and fame made him more agreeable as a tutor, if increasingly petulant and unpredictable among his colleagues. Neat, fussy, pedantic, from time to time he showed a quaintness of humour, unpredictable as his rebuffs. Watkin Williams recalled being asked by Dodgson at his first tutorial to define a corollary. He stood in silence, unable to do it. 'Do you ever play billiards?' Dodgson asked. 'Sometimes,' the young man said. 'If you attempted a cannon, missed, and holed your own and the red ball, what would you call it?' 'A fluke.' 'Exactly. A corollary is a fluke in Euclid. Good morning.' The advice proved more memorable than useful.[9]

When he was not teaching, he made the curiosities of mathematics amusing. The years 1855 and 1856 had been a time of depression for him. His mood, however, lightened and on 5 May 1857 he wrote to *Bell's Life* in London, explaining how to construct a winning system for betting on the Derby and similar races. It was necessary to bet in favour of every horse or against every horse, according to a compilation of the odds. He was quite right. Unfortunately, the following issue of the paper contained a letter explaining that the system would fail for non-mathematical reasons. No bookmaker would accept such a combination of bets. Mr Dodgson might try to organize a 'betting round' on the turf, but the moment it was discovered he would find it impossible to get his bets on. Even if it worked, the profit would be so small that the whole scheme was not worth the risk.

The greatest curiosity of this incident is that he should have wanted to see his name in this particular paper. *Bell's Life* was regarded as flashy, sporting, and less than respectable. Rebecca Solomon's painting of the 1850s, *The Dissolute Undergraduate* – a pair to *The Virtuous Undergraduate* – showed the young wastrel lounging with a copy of the paper.

In November 1866 Dodgson tried again, when an advertisement appeared in the *Pall Mall Gazette* offering £500 for a betting system that would work. His letter was published on 19 November and reprinted in *The Times* next day but his mathematical example contained an error, noticed by his friend Bayne. The principle remained valid mathematically but again unworkable on the race course.

Write all the possible events in a column, placing opposite to each the odds offered against it: this will give two columns of figures. For the third column add together the numbers in each case, and find the least common multiple of all the numbers in this column. For the fifth and sixth columns multiply the original odds by the several numbers in the fourth column. These odds are to be given, or taken, according as the sum total of the sixth column is greater or less than the least common multiple. The last two columns give the *relative amounts* to be invested in each bet.

Dodgson's other early contribution to the press was a re-working of 'When Does the Day Begin?' given as a lecture to the Ashmolean Society at Oxford and then published as a contribution to the *Illustrated London News* on 18 April 1857.

Suppose yourself to start from London at midday on Tuesday and to travel with the sun, thus reaching London at midday on Wednesday. If at the end of every hour you ask the English residents in the place you have reached the name of the day, you must at last reach some place where the answer changes to Wednesday. But at that moment it is still Tuesday (1pm) at the place you left an hour before. Thus you find two places within an hour in time of each other using different names for the same day ... I shall be glad to see any rational solution for the difficulty as I have put it.

The peremptory answer was to be the International Date Line.

*

Dodgson's career was now marked by those formal steps which led to his ordination as deacon in December 1861. When Liddell was appointed Dean in 1855, general honours had been bestowed and in Dodgson's case he was made a Master of the House, which gave him the privileges of a Master of Arts within Christ Church, though he could not qualify for these in the University until 1857. With his residence and income secure, he was well placed to follow his father's advice of investing a hundred pounds a year, insuring his life, and buying a library, all with a view to being comfortably off by his early thirties.

Indeed, there was new comfort for his innate conservatism. The victory of the modern men at Christ Church was of less consequence than the traditionalists feared. When Liddell saw how he and radical proponents of change had been betrayed by Gladstone's smooth tongue and deftly drawn legislation, he prophesied that college tutors would find means to block reform. The truth was that Liddell, A. P. Stanley and their supporters were energetic but amateur politicians. They had been outclassed by the professionals. Liddell narrowed his aims to the abolition of celibacy for college fellowships and an extension of the professoriate. In the first he failed for the moment but in the second he had some success. Unfortunately, just as he mastered the rules of political brokering, he was removed from the game.

At a most critical moment, a year after the new Dean's appointment, Fortune spun her wheel. Liddell, the handsome and vigorous Dean in his early forties, fell ill with bronchopneumonia, so ill that it was necessary for him to embark on a voyage to Madeira and spend two winters there in 1856–8. Without him, the college reformers seemed unable to press home such advantages as they had gained. Christ Church avoided the worst, so far as its tutors were concerned. Older men died hard and in harness. As Liddell departed, he left behind the pluralist Dr Bull and the nepotist Dr Barnes still in office, Canons of the cathedral still governing the College. Of course, by statute, the Studentships now had to be open to competition but it was possible to qualify this by restricting it to those who had already spent a year in residence and who could be judged to show 'exemplary' moral character. In other words, those who took the fancy of men like Bull and Barnes. There had to be an examination, but it might consist of a private interview without anyone being held accountable for the outcome.

By the time Liddell returned to the full-time occupancy of his appointment, two years of ill-health had tempered his combative energy. In June 1857, before setting out for Madeira a second time, he had warned the Commissioners appointed by the Oxford Act that '*Any* change from existing rules which is not positively required will give offence here.' When he was well again, the practical difficulties of college administration absorbed him. Reform of quite a different kind was now being demanded by his colleagues. The Students of Christ Church would have been called fellows in any other college. As such they would have taken a major part in college government. But Christ Church, despite the 1854 statute, remained under the Dean and the Chapter of the cathedral. The Censors, as senior Students, acted as go-betweens and purveyors of opinion but neither they nor their colleagues had any power of college government. It was plainly unjust by the standards of other Oxford colleges and not to be tolerated. If Dean Liddell truly believed in reform, let him put his own house in order. Even Charles Dodgson was prepared to take part in this campaign, protracted though it proved to be.[10]

After the first two years of depression and self-doubt, it seemed that by 1857 Dodgson had made a life for himself in the College. His brothers Skeffington and Wilfred matriculated in May 1856 and came into residence at Christ Church that autumn, under his supervision. His cousin Frank, son of Hassard Dodgson, was also there. His friend from Daresbury days, Thomas Vere Bayne, remained a companion and was appointed Greek Reader at Christ Church in 1861. Charles Dodgson's leisure was divided between riverside walks with his friends to Iffley, Godstow and Radley, whose school he found superior to Rugby, and his attraction to the river itself. He rowed upstream to Godstow or down to Nuneham with his High Church friend Henry Liddon, his brothers, his cousin Frank, and

Robinson Duckworth of Trinity, whose singing voice was in demand for walks, boat-trips, and university recitals.

With Frank, Dodgson watched torpids, the college boat races of the early year which were still an innovation, and the summer eights in May. The cousins also watched the 1856 Oxford and Cambridge boat race from a steamer on the Thames. Dodgson never took part in such races himself nor did he attempt to play cricket again after the match in which he was taken off as bowler after a single over. Someone unkindly informed him that his deliveries would have been wides, if they had gone far enough. All the same, he felt a natural allegiance to the College on the cricket pitch and the river. He went with Frank on 17 May 1856 to the match on the college ground between Christ Church and All England, which not surprisingly Christ Church lost by an innings and some fifty runs.

Although Frank was a congenial companion Dodgson found most undergraduates, including his younger brothers, tiresome. Christ Church had its reading sets and its rowdy sets. The noise in Hall at dinner was sometimes so insufferable that tutors like Osborne Gordon would turn men out if they appeared to be the source of the trouble. On 2 February, in his brothers' first year at Christ Church, Charles Dodgson had a row with Wilfred over the importance of keeping college rules and came away from it depressed by his failure to win the argument. He now felt uneasy about his value as a clergyman, if he could not hold his own in argument against unbelievers. The problem lay in such unforeseen arguments, made all the worse by the disadvantage of his stammer. With the prospect of ordination and parish work before him, he had begun to seek advice from friends such as Henry Parry Liddon and he attempted to cure the stammer by reading aloud a scene from a Shakespeare play every day.

*

During these first years at Christ Church, Dodgson still regarded himself as a High Church traditionalist of the conservative kind, though still with no taste for the ritualism or the Romanism which had grown out of the later stages of the Oxford Movement. In his moral attitudes, he seemed to reconcile this with what might have been taken for a pattern of Low Church evangelical piety.

As he prepared himself for a life of clerical duty, the theological battles of faith and doubt that ruffled mid-Victorian England were being fought in Oxford with unfraternal intensity. In 1860, the year before Dodgson's ordination, there appeared *Essays and Reviews*, the work of seven contributors, including Frederick Temple, Headmaster of Rugby and future Archbishop of Canterbury, and Benjamin Jowett, Professor of Greek and future Master of Balliol. Among other heresies, the contributors challenged the authority of the Bible to be regarded as greater than that of any other historical document. On another front, H. B. Wilson, who had previously taught at Oxford for twenty-five years and had led the attack on Newman's *Tract XC*, suggested that if the Church of England abandoned subscription to the Thirty-Nine Articles, it might become a truly national church.

The comfortable cliché of honest and progressive men under attack by traditionalists and obscurantists was less than a half truth, however. Catholic and traditionalist beliefs were just as much targets for the evangelical and progressive wing. Henry Parry Liddon had become vice-principal of Bishop Wilberforce's Theological College at Cuddesdon, within walking distance of Christ Church, when it was founded in 1854. It was High Church, though not too High for Dodgson. At a later date, however, Liddon and his colleagues at Cuddesdon might have been termed Anglo-Catholic. In the circumstances of 1859, they were denounced for 'Romanising' the Church of England and permitting 'Romish' adornments and ceremonies. Liddon was forced from his post that year and became vice-principal of St Edmund Hall. He was Bampton Lecturer in 1866 and Ireland Professor of Exegesis in 1870–82, ending his life as Canon and Chancellor of St Paul's Cathedral. He was known as the Tractarian Gamaliel, a fine preacher and an inspiration to his followers, bearing the torch lit by Keble and Pusey. As surely as Jowett, Liddon in the sights of clergy like G. P. Golightly was a target for what Jowett himself called ecclesiastical 'terrorism.'[11]

The foundations of the traditional beliefs in which Dodgson had been educated were under direct attack from *Essays and Reviews*. Indignation at the assailants, the 'Septem contra Christum' as they were dubbed, was at its most intense in Oxford. Two of the seven, H. B. Wilson and Rowland Williams, the former Rawlinsonian Professor of Anglo-Saxon at Oxford in 1839–44, were charged with heresy and convicted in a trial before the ecclesiastical Court of Arches. In one respect their heresies anticipated Dodgson's own, by denying the doctrine of eternal punishment. Williams and Wilson appealed to the

Privy Council. Lord Westbury overturned their conviction by the lower court. His lordship, wrote Sir William Hardman laconically, 'dismissed Hell with costs, thus depriving the Clergy of their last hope of eternal damnation.'[12]

After Williams and Wilson were convicted by the Court of Arches in 1862 but before their convictions were quashed, Pusey made his move against Jowett. With a legal opinion from the Queen's Proctor, Dr Phillimore, Pusey brought a prosecution against Jowett before the Vice-Chancellor's court. He was supported by the Regius Professor of Pastoral Theology and the Lady Margaret Professor of Divinity. The charge was 'infringing the Statutes and privileges of the University' by publishing his commentary *The Epistles of St Paul* and his contribution to *Essays and Reviews*, 'On the Interpretation of Scripture.' When the case opened, on 13 February 1863, Jowett announced through his proctor his intention of 'entering a protest against the jurisdiction of the Court.'[13]

The following day *The Times* attacked the trial as the work of a 'rusty engine of intolerance.' On 19 February, Pusey wrote to the paper, praising the court's 'majesty of Justice,' which was to give Dodgson the title of a poem on the subject. Indeed, Pusey argued his case in the newspaper even before the court had heard it and while the issue was still sub judice. Next day the assessor, a legal adviser appointed by the Vice-Chancellor, doubted whether he had jurisdiction in the case. Even if he had, he insisted that he was not going to exercise it. Jowett was not summoned to appear and Pusey's case was dismissed. Though the prosecutors thought of appealing to Queen's Bench, both Dr Phillimore and John Duke Coleridge, future Lord Chief Justice, advised them that they would lose. There the matter ended.

As the case against Jowett collapsed, Dodgson wrote, 'The Majesty of Justice: An Oxford Idyll', which appeared in *College Rhymes* for Lent Term.

> 'A Court obscure, so rumour states,
>   'There is, called 'Vice-Cancellarii,'
> 'Which keeps on Undergraduates,
>   'Who do not pay their bills, a wary eye.'

It seemed absurd that a court intended for such trivialities should presume to dictate to the world on the great issues of conscience and belief. Indeed, that had been more or less the assessor's view. Justice, wrote Dodgson in his poem, may reign in dignity in other courts but, 'She's not majestic *here*.' The undergraduate in the poem suggests that perhaps the court is merely too small to be the arena of justice but the don assures him that size has nothing to do with it.

> 'Nay, nay!' the Don replied, amused,
> 'You're talking nonsense, sir! You know it!
> 'Such arguments were never used
> 'By any friend of Jowett.'

Their conclusion is that the world and its newspapers cannot take such a court seriously unless judges and counsel are wigged and gowned, unless the curious can see 'The horsehair wig upon her brow.' For so fundamental a reason was justice denied and Jowett allowed to escape.[14]

Within the confines of Oxford in the 1850s and 1860s, Dodgson and Jowett might almost have assumed the roles of Tweedledum and Tweedledee. The manner of their lives had much in common. Both were bachelor dons who lent themselves easily to caricature. Both became legends in their lifetimes. Their tutorial ripostes were in much the same style and they shared a passion for exact learning. They were equally concerned with the direction and doctrines of the Church of England. Both enjoyed a good deal of worldly success, Dodgson through his writing and Jowett as Master of Balliol, while at the same time both lived in well-protected privacy. The most profound difference between them was not so much over Jowett's beliefs, Dodgson himself came to accept such Broad Church variations as a disbelief in eternal punishment. It was in their backgrounds: Dodgson the well-connected son of a successful professional class; Jowett, whose father was a failed furrier and whose mother had withdrawn to Bath, lived alone in shabby city lodgings at eleven years old while attending St Paul's School and sharpening a formidable intellect. Dodgson's family upbringing had been comfortable and reassuring. The boy Jowett faced privations that had more in common with the eighteenth century.

That they disagreed as vigorously as the two famous twins of the nursery rhyme was evident from Dodgson's own writings. In his Oxford satires, he dealt more often with Jowett than with any other adversary, even Dean Liddell. His satire had begun early with such laboured and unpublished parodies as *The Ligniad*, which he composed for his friend George Woodhouse when they were still undergraduates in 1853. The more important of his Oxford pieces were collected in *Notes by an Oxford Chiel* in 1874, with the sardonic epigraph,

> A Chiel's among ye takin' notes,
> And, faith, he'll prent it.

Jowett had been Professor of Greek since Gaisford's death in 1855. The stipend had been fixed in the sixteenth century at £40 a year. It was a paltry income, which had not mattered much to Gaisford who was also Dean of Christ Church. To Jowett and his sympathizers it was a disgrace. A campaign was begun to have the stipend increased. Though Jowett was a Fellow of Balliol, his professorial post was a matter for the Dean and Chapter of Christ Church.

Unfortunately the question of the stipend, first raised in 1858, was soon to be complicated by Jowett's heretical opinions. A considerable number of those who voted in Congregation and elsewhere did so according to whether or not they approved of Jowett, rather than on the merits of the case. Dodgson, according to his diary entry for 20 November 1861, seems privately to have been one of them, while insisting publicly that they were separate issues.

> Promulgation, in Congregation, of the new statute to endow Jowett. The speaking took up the whole afternoon, and the two points at issue, the endowing a *Regius* Professorship, and the countenancing Jowett's theological opinions, got so inextricably mixed up that I rose to beg that they might be kept separate. Once on my feet, I said more than I at first meant, and defied them ever to tire out the opposition by perpetually bringing the question on (*Mem:* if I ever speak again, I will try to say no more than I had resolved before rising). This was my first speech in Congregation.'[15]

It was not the speech on this subject by which he was to be remembered but by his satire *The New Method of Evaluation as Applied to π*, written and published in March 1865. Liddell had written to the Vice-Chancellor on 17 February, informing him that the Dean and Chapter had agreed to raise Jowett's stipend from £40 to £500, though they were neither legally nor morally obliged to do so, since it was a matter for the Crown. Dodgson's pamphlet appeared early in March, its epigraph comparing Jowett to Jack Horner and the Greek letter π to the Professor's Christmas Pie.[16]

The following are the main data of the problem:

Let U = the University, G = Greek, and P = Professor. Then GP = Greek Professor; let this be reduced to its lowest terms, and call the result J.

Also let W = the work done, T = the *Times*, p = the given payment according to T, π = the payment according to T, and S = the sum required; so that π = S.

Though topical satires of this kind are doomed to grow cold rapidly, it was the best of Dodgson's Oxford pamphlets. He had fun at Jowett's expense, not too kindly, and also found space for *Essays and Reviews*.

Let E = Essays, and R = Reviews: then the locus of (E + R), referred to multilinear coordinates, will be found to be a superficies (*i.e.*, a locus possessing length and breadth, but no depth). Let v = novelty, and assume E + R as a function of v.

As might be expected, it is discovered that the element of novelty 'did not even enter into the function' of *Essays and Reviews*. The other possible calculation involves 'The Elimination of J', as the founders of Christ Church might have contrived it.

It has long been perceived that the chief obstacle to the evaluation of π was the presence of J, and in an earlier age of mathematics J would probably have been referred to rectangular axes, and divided into two unequal parts – a process of arbitrary elimination which is now considered not strictly legitimate.

The wit was neatly pointed and the manner droll as well as learned. Though of a lesser order, it shares with the satire of Dryden and Pope the ability to amuse the reader long after the events to which it refers have ceased to be generally known. Perhaps it is not without significance that Dodgson should have written it in the same spring as he was finishing *Alice in Wonderland*.

By this time, he was in Holy Orders. His ordination as deacon took place in December 1861 while assertion and indignation still marked the religious life of the University. His doubts, so far as he had any at the time, were not over matters of doctrine but over his difference of opinion with the Bishop of Oxford, Samuel Wilberforce, as to whether it was proper for a clergyman to be a theatregoer. Compared to the great issues of the day, it appeared a frivolous point. However, Wilberforce believed that attendance at the theatre or the opera was 'an absolute disqualification for Holy Orders.' Fortunately this applied to parochial clergy rather than to fellows of colleges. Dodgson's dilemma, as his nephew recorded it, was that ordination as a deacon, if not as priest, was 'necessary if he wished to retain his Studentship.' He made no secret that 'he was not prepared to live the life of almost puritanical strictness which was then considered essential for a clergyman.'[17]

The consequent question was whether a Student of Christ Church might be ordained deacon without ever intending to be ordained a priest or undertake parish work. Dodgson discussed his position with both Dr Pusey and his friend Liddon. Liddon, at least, assured him that a deacon might 'abstain from direct ministerial duty,' if he thought himself unfit for it. A stammer might be enough to disqualify him. Dodgson was reassured and was ordained deacon. As time went by, he assisted in a number of parishes, preaching at St Mary Magdalen, Oxford, at the University Church of St Mary's, at Guildford, and at Christ Church, Eastbourne during the vacations.

He was not yet the recluse that he became in his later years. Christ Church might be secluded, yet Dodgson was well aware that he and it were at the centre of influence in the England of the 1850s. In January 1857, Gladstone dined in Hall as a member of the College and afterwards retired with Dodgson and other senior members to the Common Room for dessert, coffee, and a discussion of the issues of the day round their communal table. The Prince of Wales became a Christ Church undergraduate, though he and his retinue lived at Frewen Hall, some five minutes' walk distant, off the Cornmarket. The Prince came into residence in October 1859. On 12 December 1860 Queen Victoria and Prince Albert arrived unannounced to visit the scene of their son's education. It was the end of term and Liddell was in the Hall where Collections were in progress, a dozen young men being examined as the Queen entered. There was an evening entertainment at the Deanery, where Dodgson was introduced to the Prince of Wales, whose photograph he hoped to take. The Prince had just returned from his visit to the United States and Canada, the first British monarch who, even before accession, had ever crossed the Atlantic. Dodgson recorded the meeting in his diary with some excitement.

> He shook hands very graciously, and I began with a sort of apology for having been so importunate about the photograph. He said something of the weather being against it, and I asked if the Americans had victimised him much as a sitter; he said they had, but he did not think they had succeeded well, and I told him of the new American process of taking twelve thousand photographs in an hour. Edith Liddell coming by at the moment, I remarked on the beautiful *tableau* which the children might make: he assented, and also said, in answer to my question, that he had seen and admired my photographs of them.[18]

There was not to be a sitting by the Prince but he presented Dodgson with his autograph and chose a dozen or so of the photographs for his collection.

Despite Dodgson's self-doubt and depression, weariness at his pupils, forebodings over reform and religious scepticism, he had found a doorway into another world, even within the walls of Christ Church. Twice in the warm June weather of 1856, he and Frank Dodgson rowed down the river to Sandford. On the first occasion, they took the ten-year-old Harry Liddell with them. Next time seven-year-old 'Ina', the elder Liddell daughter, came with them as well. There was an impromptu picnic of biscuits, ginger beer and lemonade. The children were in wild spirits with the excitement of the river outing and the boatload was the focus of attention on the river that afternoon. Dodgson confessed his surprise that Ina was allowed to come unchaperoned. In tribute to the Roman custom of marking good days on the calendar with white chalk and bad days with black charcoal, Dodgson was apt to mark certain days in his diary figuratively with a white stone. He marked this day's happiness not only with a white stone but as a 'Dies Mirabilis.' The tone of the diaries changed. At last, it seemed, his life's adventure had truly begun.

6

The Lion Hunter

DESPITE THE EASE with which his schoolboy cleverness was rewarded, Dodgson's first years at Christ Church were a time of self-questioning and gloom by contrast with the contentment of life at Croft. Yet Christ Church was only half his life, university vacations making up seven months of the year. In those months, a good deal of his early twenties seemed like an extended childhood of home life, leisure and self-indulgence.

Until the long seaside summers of his later years, he was apt to leave his work behind him each time he broke off his residence in Oxford. An exception had been the last undergraduate summer of 1854, which he spent 'coaching' at Whitby with the Oxford mathematics tutor, Bartholomew Price. Whitby, scene of the Dodgsons' summer holidays, was a fishing port rather than a resort. Even while being coached for his final degree examination, he found time to write some of his first published work, which he contributed to the *Whitby Gazette* during his stay. The paper accepted his story, 'Wilhelm von Schmitz', and a poem, 'The Lady of the Ladle'. In common with many contemporaries, Dodgson wrote of sexual attraction as comic and therefore unobjectionable. His verses describe a 'heavy swell' in love with a cook, she having sailed from Whitby and he having missed the boat by running back to fetch his gold tie-pin.

> Rich dresser of suet!
>   Prime hand at a sausage!
> I have lost thee, I rue it,
>   And my fare for the passage!
> Perhaps *she* thinks it funny,

> Aboard of the Hilda,
> But I've lost purse and money,
> And thee, oh, my 'Tilda!

In defence of such laboured facetiousness, it can only be said that Dodgson was working out his apprenticeship in the style of the day. His mentors Thomas Hood and Winthrop Mackworth Praed produced better results but they had worked with much the same literary devices. By 1850 subtlety in humour remained at a discount. It was a time when, as a visitor to Buckingham Palace remarked, the most likely way of making Victoria and Albert laugh was by catching one's finger in the door.

The image of Dodgson at Whitby which proved more significant for the future appeared in a memoir by his lifelong friend Thomas Fowler in the *St James's Gazette* in 1898. Fowler, later a Fellow of Lincoln, was another member of the reading party. He recalled Dodgson spending his leisure sitting on a rock, telling stories to an eager young audience of both boys and girls.

After his final degree examinations, the months of the Oxford vacations were holidays, if he chose to make them such. In the New Year of 1855, Canon Dodgson was in residence at Ripon with his family. His son's diary entries are a catalogue of failure to work. The result of six weeks vacation was nil. This, presumably, was what made him abandon the examination for the Senior Mathematical Scholarship in March. He sketched a little and some of his reading reflected an interest in art, including the autobiography of the painter Benjamin Robert Haydon and M. E. Chevreul's *Principles of Harmony and Contrast of Colours*. Literary romanticism was his other reading, represented by Thomas Gray, Coleridge and Monckton Milnes' revival of a neglected genius in his *Life, Letters and Literary Remains of John Keats*. As term began in mid-January, such reading stopped, though a grateful pupil seems to have identified a darker source of Dodgson's taste by presenting him with the poems of the master of the macabre, Thomas Hood.

Most of his reading was done during the vacations until, by February 1858, he found time for it in term as well. His comments on contemporaries suggest a rather evangelical sensibility in the judgement of authors. In novels, he was apt to look for loveable characters and a healthy moral tone. In the summer of 1855, for example, he found that Marmion Savage's *Bachelor of the Albany* lacked both. It was not a book for right-minded readers. Dinah Mulock's *The Ogilvies* also lacked loveable characters but passed the moral fitness test. When he read *Shadows of the Clouds* by J. A. Froude, author of a novel about the loss of Christian belief in *The Nemesis of Faith*, Dodgson compromised. He cut out the pages on which he considered there was anything objectionable to his religious belief and had the remains of the novel rebound.

As for the major novelists of mid-century, Mrs Gaskell's story of industrial Manchester, *North and South*, impressed him by its realism. However, he distrusted all her work because she had written *Ruth*, unacceptable to him because its heroine has a child out of wedlock. Despite this reservation, his curiosity over legal matters led him to read her *Life of Charlotte Brontë* in the long vacation of 1857. The book had been lent to him by Mrs Longley, wife of the Bishop of Ripon, in its first edition, containing libellous passages which were subsequently deleted. Perhaps he felt that it would have been tactless to refuse the loan. Once borrowed, the book must be read. He concluded that Charlotte Brontë's talents as a novelist fed on solitude and depression, the latter diseased, while he thought her sister Emily's *Wuthering Heights* was not a credible story. In the same long vacation he expressed a general weariness for fiction which described the sorrows or ordeals of romantic sensibilities. There were too many victims. Not only must his fictional heroes and heroines be healthy and loveable, they were also required to display strength and stoicism.

Predictably, he admired the more pious of popular novelists, including the American 'Elizabeth Wetherell', the pen name of Susan Bogert Warner, whose sentimental novels included such tales as *Queechy*, in which a little girl loves a man old enough to be her father but who becomes her husband instead. Dodgson presented his younger sister, Henrietta, with Mrs Wetherell's fiction on her twelfth birthday.

If his response to literature held a mirror to his nature, the image of Dodgson in his early twenties is that of a prig. The truth of life beyond his tranquil world of Christ Church and Croft seemed unwelcome. Small wonder that he disliked the realism of *Oliver Twist* but was moved by the pathos of little Paul's death in *Dombey and Son*. Those who labelled him a muff might have felt their judgement confirmed by his thoughts on *Alton Locke*, Charles Kingsley's novel of urban social problems. 'If the book were but a little more definite, it might stir up many fellow-workers in the same good field of social improvement. Oh that God, in His good providence, may make me hereafter such a worker!'[1]

The mood did not last. The prospect of Dodgson entering public life as a crusader to improve the position of the urban working-class was improbable. He was, as he said, first an Englishman, then a Conservative. When he saw men demonstrating for the right to vote at the time of the 1868 Reform Bill, he knew instinctively that they were 'roughs'. So far from improving working conditions, he wrote to his friend, the Prime Minister Lord Salisbury, whom he met in 1870, that employees should be paid strictly by the hour for the work that they did. He was also concerned that charity or remuneration might go to the undeserving poor. When hiring a cab, he calculated to which lamp post in front of which house he might go without an increase in the fare. At a time when railway porters ran after cabs to their destinations, hoping to get a tip for unloading the luggage, Dodgson was full of advice on how to avoid such importunities by having one's luggage fitted with wheels. When he paid for service he demanded not just satisfaction but obedience. After almost ten years of spending a couple of months each summer in the same house at Eastbourne, he sent to his landlady an ultimatum without preamble telling her that unless an engineer inspected her drains and they were made good as necessary, he would move elsewhere.[2]

Dodgson had neither the talents nor the true inclination to be a social reformer but he had the honesty to see that this was so. Indeed, two lines further on in his diary beyond the comments on Kingsley, he adds that there are no means available to him for such social improvement and that his prayer to be of service is strictly conditional on God providing the opportunity. He had no intention of being involved unless 'I were sure of really effecting something by the sacrifice, and not merely lying down under the wheels of some irresistible Juggernaut.'[3]

In the aftermath of his death, the quotation from the diary stopped at this point in his nephew's biography of 1898. What followed was the young Dodgson's unappealing view of human nature as, 'merely refined animal.' Men and women sought only 'βίος ἀπολαυστικός,' as he termed it, the life of pleasure. Such a philosophy perhaps excused the young Student of Christ Church from launching himself into public philanthropy.[4]

Perhaps the greatest disqualification was that for too long he had matured little beyond the clever schoolboy who ten years earlier bore his first prizes home from Rugby. Death had touched him once. His mother was gone, the most loving figure of his life. Yet the strong-minded genial father and the bevy of admiring sisters and aunts maintained a life at Croft Rectory that was remarkably unchanging. Dodgson at twenty-three was still working on the family magazines, even pasting in the items that had appeared in the *Whitby Gazette* or elsewhere. He was still pondering the problems of marionettes and presenting his *Tragedy of King John* on the toy stage. As a Christ Church tutor, he still planned to write *Alfred the Great* to be staged with the family puppets at Croft.

The future seemed far from clear as the Great Northern Railway carried him back to London or to Bletchley and Oxford. He came home in the summer of 1857 and finally rejected the financial advice which his father had given him two years earlier. Like the other members of his family, he was not short of money and his plan now was simply to save as much as he could. As for the insurance policy on his life, he had decided against it. The scheme would only be of use to protect his wife, if he were to marry. Marriage was something of which, at twenty-five, he saw 'no present likelihood.'[5]

The more immediate likelihood was Christmas at Croft and family summers at Whitby, varied by visits to his Lutwidge aunts at Hastings, where he sought treatment for his stammer from James Hunt, an eminent speech therapist who lived nearby at Ore. A fortnight's walking in the Lake District in August 1856 was in the company of his two younger brothers, Skeffington and Wilfred. They followed it in 1857 with a holiday in Edinburgh and the Scottish lowlands.

Oxford apart, Dodgson still resembled Macaulay's description of Cowper in his 1841 essay, the reclusive figure of devout ambition and poetic dreams, untroubled but also unrewarded by the ambivalent lure of public life. It was easy to imagine him slipping into an existence of retired scholastic piety, a man among children but a child among men.

Had he known it, he lived next to one of the most brash and bohemian figures of Victorian life, a brief walk from the placid world of Croft.

Across the Tees was the parish of St Cuthbert's, Darlington, whose incumbent was Alexander James Howell. The Reverend Howell's nephew lived with him for some time in the 1850s, a striking youth of top-boots and swashbuckling manner, seven years Dodgson's junior but looking more than his age. Like Dodgson, Charles Augustus Howell mixed with the local clergy; unlike Dodgson he made fun of them behind their backs. Young Howell became a leading figure in the Darlington and Literary Philosophical Society in 1856–7 with interests in art and invention to match Dodgson's own. Dodgson's interest in Darlington Polytechnic is mentioned twice in his journals for September 1855. Elizabeth Melland recalled Howell, almost sixty years later, as the leader of young men and women in Darlington, 'a very interesting and stimulating friend, well read even then, and he gave us ideas on books and art.' Like Dodgson, he made the journey to the Manchester Fine Arts Exhibition in 1857. He came back and astonished the other young people by sketching every picture from memory.[6]

It would have been difficult for Dodgson to escape Howell in the thinly populated world of Darlington's civic culture, or in its ecclesiastical society which Howell lampooned by descriptions of after-dinner drunkenness. Their lives touched later when Howell was Ruskin's assistant and Dante Gabriel Rossetti's agent at the time of Dodgson's friendship with both. Dodgson and Howell were Rossetti's dinner guests. By then, Howell had been abroad, living by his own account as a diver for treasure and then sheikh of a Moroccan tribe. He was reputed to have forged Rossetti's paintings, and was dismissed by Ruskin in 1870 for embezzlement. He was the blackmailer of the Swinburne family over the poet's sexual eccentricities, a thief who stole from Whistler, an unconvicted criminal whom Conan Doyle transformed into 'Charles Augustus Milverton', 'the worst man in London' in *The Return of Sherlock Holmes*. Anglo-Portuguese by birth, he lived with his uncle at Darlington because his activities as a gambler and cheat had made it too dangerous for him to remain in Oporto by the age of sixteen. His employment at Darlington was vaguely described but he worked at some point for the Stephenson family, the first locomotive builders. Of his English relatives, one female cousin at Darlington 'went on the streets' and another died in the workhouse. Both Oscar Wilde and Thomas James Wise claimed that Howell's own death from 'pneumonia' in 1890 actually occurred when he was found in the gutter outside a Chelsea public house, his throat cut and a half sovereign wedged between his teeth.[7]

Dodgson's sensitivity over his own image of absolute propriety led him to avoid all those who might in any way compromise him. It would hardly have reassured him to discover that he had unwittingly come close to a dangerous association with a man whose death was celebrated in Swinburne's crisp epitaph:

> The foulest soul that lived stinks here no more,
> The stench of Hell is fouler than before.

The elusive threads of Victorian acquaintanceship wove themselves about Dodgson's personal history. The paths of the two men not so much crossed as intertwined. Yet Dodgson came no closer to him. A sententious view might see the son of Croft Rectory as guarded by angels against association with the world and the flesh. A fastidious nose for the morally suspect, whether in life or contemporary fiction, served him equally well.

*

The complex network of the Dodgson and Lutwidge families soon led him beyond Croft and Oxford. At the Great Exhibition of 1851, the freshman had discovered how easily the excitements of London might be reached from Oxford in the railway age. He had the advantage of two London houses which were always open to him, those of his lawyer uncles, Skeffington Lutwidge and Hassard Dodgson. Skeffington, barrister and Commissioner in Lunacy, lived a bachelor life of gadgets and enthusiasms in Alfred Place, Brompton. Hassard, later Master of the Court of Common Pleas, lived with his wife and children at Park Lodge, Putney.

Skeffington seemed more akin to his nephew, not least in his curiosity about photography. On an undergraduate visit in June 1852, Dodgson discovered the riches of his uncle's collection. These included a telescope, a microscope, a lathe, an instrument for measuring distances on a map, and an early Victorian refrigerator. Appropriately for a Commissioner in Lunacy, the items were known as 'oddities'. Uncle and nephew spent the evening studying the heavens through the telescope, then using the microscope to watch the movements of organs in the bodies of transparent animalcule.

With the curiosities of his collection and the lunacies of his professional life, Skeffington Lutwidge's was a more dangerous career than that of the self-assured Hassard Dodgson. Indeed, Skeffington was curiously prone to injury and was to die from wounds inflicted by a lunatic. Whether from heredity or example, there were intellectual enthusiasms which Dodgson and Uncle Skeffington shared, not least the worlds of madness and the law. By September 1855, when Uncle Skeffington paid a visit to Croft, Dodgson was his companion on a photographic tour of the village and a visit to Richmond, ten miles away, during which the nephew tried his own skill at taking pictures.

Hassard Dodgson was the man of business. Family gatherings were held at Park Lodge, rather than at Skeffington's bachelor home. Uncle Hassard's chambers in the Temple were also one of his nephew's London haunts. Hassard was a member of the evening parties in which Dodgson went to the Princess's Theatre, the Haymarket, and farces at the Olympic. When Dodgson and his friend Henry Liddon of Christ Church stayed at the Northumberland Hotel in 1856 and found it too like a public house, it was Uncle Hassard who got them out and installed them at the Golden Cross instead.

Within a few years, the nephew made his own arrangements for accommodation. He preferred the Old Hummums Hotel in Covent Garden and made use of it at first on his visits from Oxford. Once a Turkish Bath and a place of raffish reputation, it was now a venue for artistic life in mid-Victorian London. His choice of Old Hummums suggested that by his mid-twenties Dodgson saw himself as a scholar in Oxford and an artist in town.

He fell upon London like a boy let out of school. On saints days, whose observance was not a matter of religious obligation to him, he gave no lectures. This allowed him a free day and an extra night in town. London was the Princess's Theatre in Oxford Street, the Olympic for popular farces, and the Lyceum for drama. Dodgson gorged himself on entertainments like a child on sweets, two nights at the opera and a third at the theatre in his first four days in London. As though it was a child's reward, he called it a 'treat'. He also showed a child's rejection of what he thought coarse or profane. Yet he gobbled up the delights of Shakespeare and performing dogs, Olympic farces and the Drury Lane Circus, pantomimes and the Royal Academy, photographic exhibitions and the zoo.

His taste in drama was no more adventurous than in fiction. He enjoyed the music of Bellini's *Norma* but disliked the Drury Lane production. He found Covent Garden's *Barber of Seville* tedious. He liked a good tune and soon added Donizetti to his list, *The Daughter of the Regiment* and *Don Pasquale*. Ballet, however, distorted the natural grace of children. It was ugly, he decided, after seeing one example in 1855, and he had no wish to repeat the experience. Within two years he had repeated it none the less, and enjoyed it, although the performers were adults rather than children.

His fastidious taste found a growing proportion of entertainments morally questionable. Perhaps he was uneasy at spending so much time in the stalls or the circle, as if reading idle fiction. He patronized Thomas German Reed and his wife Priscilla Horton, who gave recitals of dramatic pieces for those who felt theatres were not places they should frequent. But then it sometimes seemed that Dodgson liked the world of the theatre, the excitement of the players and their stage, more than the plays that were being performed. A clear exception to this was the Shakespearean repertoire at the Princess's Theatre in Oxford Street, managed by Charles Kean.

In June 1855 he first went to the Princess's Theatre and saw Shakespeare's *Henry VIII*, 'the greatest theatrical treat I ever had or ever expect to have.' The grandeur of the setting and the acting was beyond all he had imagined. When he went back a year later, there was a greater treat still. He thought *The Winter's Tale* not as good a play but was enchanted by 'the acting of the little Mamillius, Ellen Terry, a beautiful little creature,' just eight years old. In December he admired her as Puck. He went back a month later to see her again, and also thought her sister Kate a beautiful Titania, as she was to be a beautiful Ariel in July. He went to see Kate as Ariel a second time, mentioning the sisters with more enthusiasm than Shakespeare.[8]

Among plays that he found objectionable, he thought Goethe's *Faust* profane, with Mephistopheles carrying off the hero and angels bearing away Marguerite, a judgement logically applied to Mozart's *Don Giovanni* as well. Profanity of any degree on the stage was a fault to which he was constantly alert.

At the Haymarket Theatre in 1856, he felt intuitively that *The Little Treasure* by Augustus Glossop Harris was insulting to the finest human passions. Perhaps the fastidious nose detected the playwright's moral flaw. Augustus Harris soon became manager of the Covent Garden Opera. A frequent traveller to Europe, he was the secret assistant of a former royal page and guards officer, Frederick Hankey, son of a Governor of Malta and self-confessed disciple of the Marquis de Sade. Hankey was a purveyor of obscene books and works of art to the Conservative parliamentarian and patron, Richard Monckton Milnes, whose *Life, Letters, and Literary Remains of John Keats* had distracted Dodgson from mathematics in January 1855. Augustus Harris was employed to smuggle books and statuary past Her Majesty's Customs. He had a curiously shaped back and was able to carry quarto volumes and porcelain figures by this method. 'He is not only most devoted to me,' wrote Hankey, 'but a very good hand at passing quarto volumes as he has done *several* times for me in the *bend* of his back.'[9]

*

On 22 January 1856, Dodgson despatched a letter to his Uncle Skeffington which was to have more profound consequences than almost any other that he wrote. After all that had been done for him by his family and its friends, and all that he had done himself, it suggested a weariness of Christ Church and its routine. There was a sense that the world was passing him by. Arriving in London the previous week, at the end of the Christmas vacation, he had spent four days with Uncle Skeffington, going to the theatre twice, seeing one of his first pantomimes, visiting Skeffington's friend Dr Diamond at the Surrey Lunatic Asylum, and going twice to the annual exhibition of the London Photographic Society. The contrast of life at Christ Church the following week had made him take stock. There was no doubt that he was clever at playing the mathematical don. But was he happy? He wrote to Uncle Skeffington, complaining that there must be more to life than 'mere reading and writing.' He had decided to acquire a camera and asked for his uncle's assistance in getting one.[10]

The 1850s called photography the 'black art' because its practitioners were apt to appear with fingers – and even clothes – stained black from silver nitrate. To Dodgson, it was a magic world of illusion, beauty preserved and the past recalled. It also incorporated his enthusiasm for gadgets and experiment. He had little talent with pencil or brush but the camera offered a new dimension in visual creativity. It was also an entry to society, a direct route to men and women of fame and charm. The photographer possessed an authority over his subjects, establishing a familiarity, if not an intimacy, where none had existed before. This was to prove particularly significant where the photographer was suited and male, and the model was female and naked. Dodgson, in private, was apt to refer to his subjects, however innocently, as 'my victims' and 'little nudities'.

His first practical experience of a camera seems to have been when he accompanied his uncle to Richmond in 1855. This is the first reference connecting either of them with photography, which is not in itself surprising. It was only at this time that the art passed from the world of the professional into the hands of a host of amateur cameramen. Until 1855 the amateurs had been held in check by doubts over the legality of their hobby.

The problem was at length resolved after a technically difficult legal action. Henry Fox Talbot claimed to have made the first photographic prints as early as 1833, though photographic images had been produced in France in the previous decade. By 1840 the French daguerreotype process gave clear portrait images on copper plate but could not produce further copies. Fox Talbot's calotype process, which he patented in 1841, gave an indefinite number of prints on paper. All the same, the process was not an easy one for the beginner.

The popularization of photography among amateurs like Dodgson and his uncle resulted from the introduction of the wet collodion process in 1851. It was the method which Dodgson himself was to use for the next twenty-five years, during which he produced a remarkable total of some 2,700 photographs. The theory of the wet collodion plate had been devised by Gustav Le Grey in Paris early in 1850 and was then proved in practice by Frederick Scott Archer in London during the autumn of the same year. It was still far from simple, requiring the photographer to carry a chemical chest and a dark tent, as well as a camera. In brief, a glass plate was coated with wet collodion, which Dodgson's Oxford contemporary Nevil Story Maskelyne described as looking rather like sherry. The plate was then placed in the camera to be exposed for a minute or so while still wet. It was taken out of the camera after exposure and developed in pyrogallic acid, rather than the gallic acid of Fox Talbot's calotype process.

At that point, the success or failure of the individual photograph had been determined. A photographer of Dodgson's means could afford to send the glass negatives to be printed by a firm of professional photographers of a kind which he found in Oxford, London, and Tunbridge Wells for his Eastbourne holidays. Where the subject-matter of the photograph was at all delicate or compromising, he could still make prints himself. In the case of his little nudities, he also preferred to have them hand-tinted by professional photographic colourists like Anne Bond of Southsea, who added skin tones and background hues.

Dodgson, like most amateurs, preferred to buy collodion ready made. Otherwise, he was obliged to make it up by dissolving gun-cotton in sulphuric ether, with the addition of potassium iodide in alcohol. The glass-plate negative was then prepared by pouring the mixture on to it and tilting the glass until its surface was covered.

Though Dodgson was to be the most famous of Oxford photographers, he was by no means the first. Archer published his account of the wet collodion process in March 1851, though he took out no patent. Within a month it was being used by Nevil Story Maskelyne, Deputy Professor of Mineralogy during the absence of William Buckland. There was a good deal of interest in alternative techniques at Oxford. Maskelyne succeeded in producing negatives on thin mica rather than glass. He also made direct positives by adding nitric acid to the pyrogallic acid. By painting black varnish on the back of the transparent print, he heightened the contrast of light and shade, the so-called ambrotype. The disadvantage of mica was that it was apt to become brittle. With collodion, Dodgson had the further advantage that he could rinse off his negative images in a solution of washing soda and use the glass plate again.

Fox Talbot, however, insisted that the wet collodion process was covered by his patent of 1841. Professional photographers would require his permission to use it and, though amateurs might use it to make photographs for themselves, he could not allow them to give prints to others. Indeed, his original patent actually gave him rights over all prints on paper. Such restrictions were plainly unrealistic and he soon found himself obliged to take legal action against Martin Laroche, a Camberwell photographer who challenged Fox Talbot's rights in the new process.

Amateur photographers like Skeffington Lutwidge and his friend Dr Diamond of the Surrey Lunatic Asylum remained in limbo until Laroche's case was decided in 1854. Fox Talbot's patent recognized his rights in the use of gallic acid with a silver solution to make paper more sensitive to light. The question for the court was whether gallic acid in the calotype process was the same as the pyrogallic acid used in the new wet collodion method. Pyrogallic acid could certainly be made by distilling either gallic or tannic acid. Maskelyne, as a chemist, was invited by Fox Talbot to demonstrate that these two acids had a radicle in common. However, the investigation was overtaken by the defendant's further argument that Fox Talbot had no right to the patent of 1841 at all. He was not the first person to have used gallic acid. The Reverend J. B. Reade had not only used it earlier but had discussed it in a lecture of 1839. Sir John Herschel had used it even before that.

The jury found for Martin Laroche and Fox Talbot lost his claim to the wet collodion process. By 1855 it was in the hands of amateurs and professionals alike.[11]

The camera which was to effect this change in Dodgson's life was purchased on 18 March 1856, no doubt because Hilary Term was then coming to an end and he saw greater prospect of leisure. With his friend and fellow-enthusiast Reginald Southey of Christ Church, he travelled to London and paid £15 for an Ottewill camera and lens from its manufacturer, off the Caledonian Road. The camera would not arrive in Oxford for a few weeks, however, and Dodgson still had to buy the chemical chest and dark-room tent, destined to travel all over England with him during the next twenty-five years.

It was May before the Ottewill camera was delivered at Christ Church. In the sunshine of Oxford's summer term, Southey instructed his friend in the 'black art'. Attempts to photograph Christ Church cathedral were a failure and so they tried photographing their friends and one another with mixed success. They called on the Dean's son Harry and asked him to sit for them in Southey's room. The child fidgeted during the long exposure and the images on the plates were blurred. At least it was possible to wash the glass plates off and use them again. They sat the boy in the strong afternoon light and managed to get his profile.

When the long vacation of 1856 began, Dodgson was confident enough in the techniques of photography to begin portraiture in earnest. While staying at Putney with Uncle Hassard, he went to visit a family friend and future cousin by marriage, Charles Pollock, the son of another legal family whose father, Sir Jonathan Frederick Pollock, was both Lord Chief Baron of the Court of Exchequer and President of the Photographic Society of London. The visit provided Dodgson with a child to photograph, Alice Murdoch. One of his first portraits, it was competent enough, though the requirement of keeping absolutely still for a minute or so left the subject looking more like a porcelain figurine than a child. He wrote her a little poem of appreciation saying that she had inspired in him a bold adventurous thought, though he did not reveal what it was.

When Dodgson's interest was taken by a family or its children, his approach was to suggest that he might send an album of his prints so that they could decide whether or not they wished to be his subjects. Almost without exception they agreed. Photography remained a novelty to them, capturing a moment for all time. It also played upon sentiment and nostalgia. In the decade of Tennyson's *In Memoriam*, it immortalized for the fading memory of the survivors a reality of those who in the relatively short span of mid-Victorian lives might soon be known no more, as Dodgson put it.

In the months after his acquisition of the camera, he tried his skill on sitters at Croft and Oxford who had the patience and time for it. Aunts or sisters were readily available. From time to time he wrote a facetious little piece that remained funny only so long as popular photography was a new and frustrating art. The humour was dead within ten years. A few weeks after his visit to Richmond with Uncle Skeffington, he devised literary criticism for the rectory magazine in 'Photography Extraordinary'. He shows how the novelist need only put the feeblest ideas and characters on to 'developing paper' and let the chemicals bring them 'up to any required degree of intensity.' The same specimen of Dodgson's pastiche of contemporary fiction is 'developed' in density to the faint figures and outlines of the Milk and Water School of novels, to the Matter of Fact School, and finally to the unbearable density of the Spasmodic or German School.

In similar vein, he sent 'A Photographer's Day Out' to the *South Shields Amateur Magazine*, which was published to raise funds for the local Mechanics' Literary Institute. Again, its humour is strictly topical. It turns upon the photographer's dream of taking the picture of a beautiful girl, Amelia, who is all the time setting a trap to get him beaten senseless by an angry farmer who finds him trespassing. A third such piece was Dodgson's verse parody, 'Hiawatha's Photographing', in the style and metre of Longfellow's poem, describing the equipment and procedure required for photographing an entire family. It was one of his first pieces to be commercially published, appearing in Edmund Yates's humorous magazine the *Train* for December 1857. Within a very few years these too were faded flowers.

Dodgson was, in his quiet way, an ambitious young man, sufficiently well-born to be acceptable to the leaders of society now that Christ Church had set its seal upon that acceptability. In the years of his fame, he abhorred 'lion-hunters', who pestered him for an autograph as 'Lewis Carroll', or worse still contrived to interview him, or ask him about the meaning of his work. Yet as a young man in search of the famous he saw these things differently. By the summer of

1855, when he went to London with Vere Bayne and his friend William Ranken, he wrote candidly that they were to view the famous and had made arrangements to go lion-hunting. Two months later, he had his first practical experience of photography, and saw how a camera might open his way to reclusive public figures as easily as its mysterious and magical operation fascinated his child-friends.

*

Thackeray, Ruskin and Tennyson were the major targets in his sights during the next ten years. With Thackeray he was unlucky. In the summer term of 1857, the novelist visited Oxford to give his lecture on George III, part of *The Four Georges*. On the follow morning, his friend Fowler of Lincoln College invited Dodgson to breakfast to meet the celebrity. Dodgson took to Thackeray. 'I was much pleased with what I saw of him; his manner is simple and unaffected; he shows no desire to shine in conversation, though full of fun and anecdote.' What about a photograph? The novelist's cousin was another Fellow of Lincoln and promised Dodgson to ask the author to sit for his portrait. Thackeray politely agreed but just as politely never found the time for the sitting.

Ruskin escaped Dodgson's camera for some years but was caught at last. As early as August 1855, Dodgson had been reading *The Stones of Venice*, on which he recorded no comment, and first met Ruskin at Common Room breakfast in Christ Church on 27 October 1857. He confessed in his diary that evening that Ruskin had been a disappointment. Yet their familiarity – if not friendship – developed over the next twenty years, until in 1875 Ruskin ceased his resistance and sat for Dodgson's camera. Long before that, however, he looked at Dodgson's sketches and confirmed what the young man himself must have felt, that 'he had not enough talent to make it worth his while to devote much time to sketching, but every one who saw his photographs admired them.'[12]

Celebrities did not come easily before his camera but little more than a year after buying his Ottewill, Dodgson caught his first and most important lion. It was a tortuous hunt. In August 1857, he and his family were staying at Bishop Auckland as guests of Charles Longley, formerly Bishop of Ripon and now Bishop of Durham, where he and his clergy were the object of a sardonic lampoon by

Charles Augustus Howell. Not surprisingly, Dodgson's photography was of great interest to the Longley family and its guests, during the Trollopean leisure of the summer days. He took a good many portraits, including one of Bishop Longley himself. Among the guests who came to be photographed were Mrs Weld and her little girl, Agnes Grace. In the course of the sitting, Dodgson discovered that Mrs Weld's sister, Emily, was married to Alfred Tennyson, Poet Laureate.

As Dodgson admitted, Agnes Grace was not a strikingly attractive child, though F. T. Palgrave, who was to be famous as the editor of the *Golden Treasury* four years later, had written a sonnet on her. Dodgson dressed her up in a cloak, put a basket in her hand, stood her in front of an ivy hedge and photographed her as a rather glum Red Riding Hood. When he gave Mrs Weld copies of the photographs, he included another set for Uncle Tennyson's 'acceptance'. Agnes Grace as Little Red Riding Hood had a pathos to pierce the mid-Victorian heart. A fortnight later, he was told that the Poet Laureate thought the photograph a gem. The child's mother was delighted. Palgrave was invited by Mrs Weld to write another sonnet on her daughter but declined.

Packing up his camera and equipment, Dodgson set off for Scotland on 3 September, making his way back through the Lake District, where Tennyson was staying at Tent Lodge, near Coniston Water. He called at the house and handed in his card, on which he wrote a line describing himself as the 'artist' of Agnes Grey and Little Red Riding Hood. Tennyson was not at home but Dodgson was received by Mrs Tennyson and met her two sons, Lionel and Hallam. Dodgson moved into a hotel nearby and called at Tent Lodge four days later. At the door, he explained that he wanted to take photographs of the two boys. He was shown to the drawing-room while his request was conveyed to Mrs Tennyson. He was left to his own devices for some time. Then the door opened and a curious figure confronted him.

A strange shaggy-looking man; his hair, moustache, and beard looked wild and neglected; these very much hid the character of his face. He was dressed in a loosely fitting morning coat, common grey flannel waistcoat and trousers, and a carelessly tied black silk neckerchief. His hair is black; I think the eyes too; they are keen and restless – nose aquiline – forehead high and broad – both face and head are fine and manly. His manner was kind and friendly from the first; there is a dry lurking humour in his style of talking.[13]

Such was his first sight of Alfred Tennyson. The Laureate agreed to the taking of his sons' photographs but arranged that it should be done in a friend's house nearby. As they walked over, Dodgson did what would have infuriated him a few years later in his own case by asking Tennyson the meaning of various lines in his work. In the end, Tennyson said brusquely that a passage 'should bear any meaning the words would fairly bear.' Dodgson was invited to dinner that evening with his album of samples. Tennyson studied the photographs and seemed most taken by one of a monkey's skull, its similarity to that of a man and its aptitude for degenerating in the same way. Darwin's *Origin of Species* was just eighteen months away.

Four days later, Dodgson, his camera, black tent and chemical chest were back at Coniston, staying with the Tennysons' hosts. He took photographs of Tennyson and his wife, of the two sons, and of the Tennysons' friends. Before he left, three days later, he had photographed the Laureate's family again.

In the Easter vacation of 1859, Dodgson found himself staying with a friend on the Isle of Wight, at Freshwater. With what he called 'the inalienable right of a free-born Briton,' he went across to Farringford where the Tennysons then lived and found the Laureate mowing his lawn in a wide-awake hat and spectacles. He evidently had to be reminded who Dodgson was. Mrs Tennyson was unwell but Tennyson invited the visitor to dinner the next day. In the days of Dodgson's own fame, any such 'free-born Briton' would have found himself escorted from Christ Church by the porter.

During the next two evenings Dodgson curbed all his sensitivities and sat amiably through moments that might elsewhere have been the occasions for affront. Tennyson was in thunderous mood, proclaiming that 'clergymen as a body don't do half the good they might if they were less stuck-up and showed a little more sympathy with their people.' He marched his two guests up to the smoking-room and offered Dodgson a pipe. Dodgson, who was known for refusing to sit in the same room as a smoker, declined the offer. But he inhaled the smoke from the two other men as if it had been the breath of life. Nothing seemed unwholesome or objectionable here. 'Up in the smoking-room the conversation turned upon murders, and Tennyson told us several horrible stories from his own experience: he seems rather to revel in such descriptions – one would not guess it from his poetry.'

When the two visitors left, his companion asked if Dodgson would object to the smoking of a cigar in the carriage. 'He didn't object to *two pipes* in that little den upstairs,' said Tennyson gruffly, 'and *a feebliori* he's no business to object to one cigar in a carriage.'

Dodgson was meekness itself in the face of the cigar. It was, he wrote, 'one of the most delightful evenings I have spent for many a long day.' He was intrigued when Tennyson described how he dreamed long passages of poetry – 'You, I suppose, dream photographs,' he said to Dodgson. When he woke, all memory of the poems was erased except in the case of one, which as Dodgson said, failed to appear in the Laureate's collected works.

> May a cock sparrow
> Write to barrow?
> I hope you'll excuse
> My infantine muse.

There was also a dream poem of Tennyson's, 'where the lines from being very long at first gradually got shorter and shorter, till it ended with fifty or sixty lines of two syllables each!' As Tennyson's grandson remarked, it was the pattern Dodgson gave to 'The Mouse's Tale' in *Alice in Wonderland*.

Dodgson and Tennyson parted, their brief association commemorated lastingly by the photographs Dodgson had taken. The grumpy sidelong glance at Coniston was not the best photograph of Tennyson and nowhere near the best of Dodgson's work. All the same, it marked his arrival as a memorialist of great contemporaries.[14]

Dodgson admired *Maud* for its powerful sense of love betrayed, and revered *In Memoriam* sufficiently to punish his sisters by making them compile a 3,000 entry index to it, each clause of each sentence by the most important noun or verb. When he became editor of *College Rhymes*, the third volume of 1862–3 was dedicated 'by permission' to Tennyson, 'by his obedient servant, the Editor.' Even in the formal courtesy of mid-century, 'obedient servant' had a curious ring of flattery in such a context.

*

Yet Dodgson and Tennyson had affinities characteristic of their age in their attraction to dreams, madness and the macabre. Tennyson might tell grisly murder tales but laws, trials, pain and executions had their part in Dodgson's humour, not least in connection with children. By 1862 he was not above sending Hallam Tennyson a knife for his birthday and suggesting laconically that the child should try cutting himself with it regularly, doing so with particular severity on his birthday. Perhaps his brother Lionel would like to be cut as well. In that case, Hallam was to oblige him. He sent a similar knife to ten-year-old Kathleen Tidy, whom he photographed at Ripon in 1858, explaining its use in punishing her brothers, concentrating on their hands and faces. The emergent science of psychopathology might have read more than adult fun into this advice. To the age of Thomas Hood and 'Mary's Ghost', it was mere macabre whimsy.[15]

So far as a shared interest in madness and unreality went, *In Memoriam* contained a fine lament for a mind at the end of its tether. In the fiftieth section and following verses, faith is overwhelmed by the fear and sorrow of a desolate interior landscape, a sleepless world of neurasthenic torment,

> When the blood creeps and the nerves prick
> And tingle; and the heart is sick . . .

Maud, too, had the lunatic vacancy of the hero in his asylum, the image of burial alive.

> For I thought the dead had peace, but it is not so;
> To have no peace in the grave, is that not sad?

In Dodgson's twenties, Dr Diamond of the Surrey Lunatic Asylum, a friend of his Uncle Skeffington, was valued for his knowledge of madness as well as his enthusiasm for photography. After one meeting with Diamond in 1856, Dodgson noted in his diary a question which informed his most famous writing. He remarked that people who dream sometimes have a consciousness that they are dreaming and that their words or actions would be judged insane by the rules of conscious life. 'May we not then sometimes define insanity as an inability to distinguish which is the waking and which the sleeping life?' Francis Kilvert describes in his diary a Victorian double nightmare, dreaming of the death of a friend, then dreaming of waking and describing that first dream without being aware that he was still asleep.[16]

It would have been remarkable if Dodgson had shown only a

passing interest in the world of madness which plays a defining part in his greatest creation. Skeffington Lutwidge, as a Commissioner in Lunacy, spent his life in the company of lawyers and medical men, inspecting asylums and examining their inmates. Among Hassard Dodgson's circle and his nephew's friends was the Pollock family. Hassard Dodgson's third daughter Amy married into it in 1865. Her father-in-law was thus Hassard's friend Jonathan Frederick Pollock, the Lord Chief Baron of the Court of Exchequer, perhaps the closest thing to a court of appeal. Amy's husband Charles was himself to become a Baron of the Exchequer. In 1849–50, Jonathan Frederick Pollock was in the thick of the dispute as to what constituted madness. He presided over the case of Nottidge v. Ripley, concerning Miss Nottidge who was alleged to have been improperly confined in a private asylum. Pollock expressed the view that no person ought to be so confined who was neither suicidal nor a danger to others. His remarks created an impressive storm, the Commissioners in Lunacy writing a letter to the Lord Chancellor to describe Pollock's finding as 'likely seriously to mislead the medical profession and the public.' The debate continued into the 1850s, during which some medical opinion continued to support the view that a single constitutional moral defect amounted to insanity, while juries at commissions of lunacy were more apt to set the patient free.[17]

Nor was it just a matter of Dodgson's family associations that drew his interest to madness and its treatment. Lunacy was a public issue of the day. Dodgson lists relatively few contemporary novels in his first extant diaries, apart from the work of major authors, yet early in 1855 he notes the work of Dinah Mulock, whose father's wrongful confinement in an asylum had been a *cause célèbre*. She and her future husband were well-known to Dodgson. He had read Henry Cockton's novel *Valentine Vox* on the same topic. The number of lunatics confined in asylums rose from 11,000 in 1844 to over 30,000 by 1866. One signature would commit a pauper and two a private patient. There were scandals, protests and actions for false imprisonment, while the abuses of the private asylums and their owners continued to be the stuff of fiction, culminating in Charles Reade's masterpiece *Hard Cash* in 1863. Hearings of cases by juries before Masters in Lunacy were extensively reported in the press with sufficient misgivings to lead to the appointment of the Parliamentary Select Committee on the Treatment and Care of Lunatics in 1859.

Dodgson's interest was less in fiction than in psychopathology. He was familiar with such texts as Henry Maudsley's *Responsibility in Mental Disease* (1874), which he quoted to Lord Denman two years later with reference to a murder trial over which Denman himself had just presided. It is unlikely that he read Krafft-Ebing's *Psychopathia Sexualis* when it first appeared in English in 1894, but he may have known of it through his Christ Church colleague Max Müller, whom Krafft-Ebing acknowledges as having given him the term 'fetishism'. Dodgson's diaries record that he and Müller were one another's guests and met at Liddell's Deanery dinners. On 30 May 1867, the Müllers and their two daughters posed for Dodgson's camera, as they continued to do over the next three years. Dodgson commented on the loveliness of the two girls, Ada and Mary.

In the 1850s, a sinister aspect of the asylum system was the extent to which sexual aberrance or even mere oddity was deemed proof of insanity. Oddity was a chief characteristic of Alice's world and, indeed, of Dodgson's own behaviour. He was told to his face, by those unaware of his *alter ego*, that the famous Lewis Carroll had gone mad. Sexual frailty was a sign of madness in his poem 'Stolen Waters'. 'They call me mad . . .' The area of madness in contemporary life had increased. 'Moral insanity' had been in vogue since the 1830s, recognizing, as Dr James Prichard put it, a lunatic's incapacity 'of conducting himself with decency and propriety in the business of life.' It was by no means clear that certain forms of eccentricity or failure to conform were not madness. As late as 1870, Dr Henry Maudsley still insisted that 'moral peculiarities' were constitutional and evidence of the 'insane temperament.'[18]

Dodgson also saw madness through the experience of a family of lawyers. In 1862, less than six months before he first told the story of Alice, the self-assurance of the 'mad doctors' had been badly bruised by the hearing before a commission of lunacy of the case of William Frederick Windham, then the longest and costliest hearing in legal history. As heir to the estates, he was known as 'Mad' Windham at Eton. His later frolics included dressing in railway livery, persuading officials to let him drive express trains, and wearing police uniform to 'arrest' prostitutes in the West End. To the dismay of his family, Windham announced that he proposed to marry one of these girls, Agnes Willoughby, alias Rogers, whom he had apparently acquired from her keeper 'Bawdyhouse Bob' Roberts in exchange for rights to timber on the family estate.

Windham's uncles, including General Windham of the Redan,

brought him before the commission after he had married Miss Willoughby and given her the money, she deserting him soon afterwards.
The commission and the press were regaled with denunciations of
Windham's madcap behaviour, addiction to masturbation, and glut-
tony to the point of vomiting. The jury at last found in Windham's
favour, among what *The Times* called cheers that suggested an alehouse.
He died four years later, the remainder of the estate passing to young
Mrs Windham. Sir William Hardman speculated that the jurors were
swayed by the revelation that General Windham dared not testify,
having once been arrested for indecent exposure in Hyde Park, excul-
pating himself by pleading his own insanity. To the more sinister facets
of madness was added a jocularity that anticipated the philosophy of
the Cheshire Cat. When Dodgson told his famous story madness was
no mere trick of facile humour. Other men and women had cried
with greater urgency than Alice, 'How do you know I'm mad?' and
had heard the Cat's words in the keeper's cold reply, 'You must be
or you wouldn't have come here.'

*

On the evidence of the eight years which followed his graduation, it
might have seemed that Dodgson was destined to be remembered as
a photographer rather than a poet or story teller. Yet his writing was
as much in tune with the age as his photography was with the adventure of a new science. These were the years in which he emerged
from the rectory magazines and found that the mid-Victorian readers
of periodicals wanted to read his work.

If, as Hugo predicted in his preface to *Cromwell* in 1827, classicism
and romantic medievalism were to be followed by a post-romantic
age characterized by a macabre balance of beauty and the grotesque,
Dodgson like Browning seemed to fit it well. In 1860 he wrote to
his sister Mary from St Leonard's about a boy seen in a concert room:
'He really was, I think, the ugliest boy I ever saw. I wish I could get
an opportunity of photographing him.' In choice of subjects, the
deformed or aberrant held an interest to rival the beautiful, as surely
as Dr Diamond's patients at Surrey Asylum made subjects for their
keeper's camera.[19]

During these years, Dodgson contributed poems and short pieces
to the *Comic Times* in 1855 and to its successor the *Train* in 1856–7.

Other poems and stories went into the last of the rectory magazines, *Misch-Masch*, in 1855. The *Comic Times* and the *Train* were edited by Edmund Yates, Dodgson's junior by a year, who held a civil service appointment in the post office and was apt to antagonize the eminent. Known to the *Pall Mall Gazette* as Neddy Yapp, he was expelled from the Garrick Club for offending Thackeray in 1861 and in 1883 was sent to prison for four months after publishing an account in the *World* of the elopement of Hugh Cecil, Earl of Lonsdale, with a young girl. Lord Lonsdale was already married and Yates was sued for libel. Yet as editor of what he hoped would be a rival to *Punch*, Yates gave Dodgson his first public platform. Between 1860 and 1863, Dodgson also contributed to *College Rhymes*, of which Yates was editor from July 1862 until March 1863.[20]

While he was still contributing to the *Train*, Dodgson and Yates agreed on the need for a pseudonym. Dodgson's first suggestion was 'Dares', taken from the name of his birthplace. Yates wrote back in February 1856 and told him it was too much like a newspaper signature. Dodgson wrote again and gave him a choice of pseudonyms, which were either anagrams or latinisations of his first two names. There were four choices: Edgar Cuthwellis, Edgar U. C. Westhill, Louis Carroll and Lewis Carroll. Yates must have looked at the first three in dismay. He chose the last.

Dodgson's contributions to the magazines were uneven in quality. The facetiousness of some was embarrassingly flat. Others, once read, were never forgotten. His contributions might be divided into parodies, the grotesque, and the wistfully sentimental. He parodied Tennyson's poem 'The Two Voices' in 'The Three Voices', Longfellow in 'Hiawatha's Photographing', and Thomas Moore in 'My Dear Gazelle'. The best, however, is his assault on the leech-gatherer in a splendid pastiche of Wordsworth's 'Resolution and Independence', entitled 'Upon the Lonely Moor'.

> I met an aged, aged man
>   Upon the lonely moor:
> I knew I was a gentleman,
>   And he was but a boor . . .
>
> I gave his ear a sudden box,
>   And questioned him again,
> And tweaked his grey and reverend locks,
>   And put him into pain . . .

And now if e'er by chance I put
  My fingers into glue,
Or madly squeeze a right-hand foot
  Into a left-hand shoe;
Or if a statement I aver
  Of which I am not sure,
I think of that strange wanderer
  Upon that lonely moor.

The middle-class pretentiousness of Wordsworth's verses, with their moralistic patronizing of the peasant, was exquisitely pierced by Dodgson's wit. The poem was revised and given to the White Knight in *Through the Looking-Glass*, where, as if in homage to William Buckland's culinary experiments, the singer looks for butterflies and makes them into mutton pies.

Among Dodgson's earlier triumphs of the grotesque is 'My Fancy', whose tone and rhythm were copied for 'She's All My Fancy Painted Him', revised in turn as the White Rabbit's evidence in *Alice in Wonderland*. The gullible swain discovers that his Pre-Raphaelite beauty has a temper far removed from the 'stunners' of whom Dante Gabriel Rossetti's young followers, like Edward Burne-Jones and William Morris, dreamed in late 1850s Oxford.

I painted her a gushing thing,
  With years perhaps a score;
I little thought to find they were
  At least a dozen more;
My fancy gave her eyes of blue,
  A curly auburn head;
I came to find the blue a green,
  The auburn turned to red.

She boxed my ears this morning,
  They tingled very much;
I own that I could wish her
  A somewhat lighter touch;
And if you were to ask me how
  Her charms might be improved,
I would not have them *added to*,
  But just a few *removed*!

She has the bear's ethereal grace,
  The bland hyena's laugh,

The footstep of the elephant,
   The neck of the giraffe;
I love her still, believe me,
   Though my heart its passion hides;
'She's all my fancy painted her,'
   But oh! *how much besides!*

In such pieces, the fulfilment of Dodgson's subversive genius was already at hand. When he turned to subjects for his early verse that were wistful or solemn, he showed little genius and barely more than facility. He rarely responded in any form to the public events of his age but 'The Path of Roses' in 1856 was an attempt to discuss in verse the example of Florence Nightingale and the role of women in war. This and others, like 'The Willow Tree' and 'The Sailor's Wife', might have been the work of any third-rate poet of the day.

The more personal poems reflect something of his own state of mind in his twenties. 'Solitude', written while he was still an undergraduate, is a lament for lost childhood and maternal love. 'Faces in the Fire', dating from 1860, recalls the Daresbury parsonage where he had been born. 'Three Sunsets' is a poem with echoes of *Maud* and *Enoch Arden* in the misery of the 'lonely man' parted from the girl he had loved in 'A moment's glance of meeting eyes.' A good deal of this last poem is self-indulgent reverie but there is a striking image that must be one of the first suggestions in Victorian poetry of suicide by gas.

As when the wretch, in lonely room,
   To selfish death is madly hurled,
The glamour of that fatal fume
   Shuts out the wholesome living world . . .

In his poem of 1862, 'Stolen Waters', moral weakness in the face of seduction, and physical repulsion in the aftermath, lead to the poet's madness. He is seduced by a beautiful woman, 'the witchery/ Within her smile that lay,' and then by consuming the juice of the 'rarest fruitage' which she plucks from a branch overhead.

And unawares, I knew not how.
   I kissed her dainty finger-tips,
I kissed her on the lily brow,

> I kissed her on the false, false lips –
> That burning kiss I feel it now.

Yet the physical reality of the woman is repellent to him, as the enchanted dream of kisses dies in the dawn,

> In the gray light I saw her face,
> And it was withered, old, and gray . . .

The poet's refuge from this revelation is in a comforting world of madness, where voices and images of children in a song teach him the way to heaven.

> If this be madness, better so,
> Far better to be mad,
> Weeping or smiling as I go.

Dodgson wrote comparatively little poetry of this sort and his reading of Tennyson certainly left its mark upon the treatment of subject-matter as much as upon rhyme and rhythm. Yet perhaps his greater affinity is with the Pre-Raphaelites. 'Beatrice', written at the end of 1862, mingles images of Dante's mistress with the reality of a Victorian child of the same name. The enchantress of 'Stolen Waters', who combines the legend of Lilith with that of Eve, is an anticipation rather than a copy of Rossetti's 'Lilith' in painting and poetry during the 1860s. Dodgson's religious sensibilities sometimes relate directly to the Pre-Raphaelite Brotherhood in such poems as 'After Three Days', a tribute to William Holman Hunt's painting *The Finding of Christ in the Temple*, or obliquely in the Victorian medievalism of 'The Willow-Tree':

> The morn was bright, the steeds were light,
> The wedding guests were gay . . .

or graphically in the successive images of 'Only a Woman's Hair', culminating in the word-painting of St Mary Magdalene.

> I see the feast – the purple and the gold;
> The gathering crowd of Pharisees,
> Whose scornful eyes are centred to behold
> Yon woman on her knees.

The quasi-religious dedication to painting adopted by the original Brotherhood in 1848 was a parallel to Dodgson's own view of his art. The Rossetti brothers and their sister Christina, as well as Holman Hunt and Millais, were among his conquests of the 1860s, while of the younger followers Arthur Hughes was a friend for many years. Dodgson was no match for the new generation in either verse or drawing but he had one gift that led him straight to the centre of the Pre-Raphaelite circle, his patient genius for photography.

On the evidence of his writing, his twenties might seem a curious age of scattered achievement and talent misapplied. Little of his poetry from these years was to be remembered, except for the pieces that were incorporated into later work. He had confined himself to the rectory magazines and periodical publications without great effect. But he had broken the bounds of Christ Church and, with his camera, caught a lion or two. At thirty, the young mathematician had become a man of the world.

Of the years between his graduation and his thirtieth birthday, two relics are by far the most resonant. One was an inspired pastiche of Anglo-Saxon verse, as he called it, which did not sound Anglo-Saxon in the least. In 1855, in the rectory magazine *Misch-Masch*, there appeared a single opening stanza with explanatory notes. It was an omen of that future fame which was to carry his name around the world as the most popular English writer since Shakespeare.

> 'Twas brillig, and the slithy toves
>   Did gyre and gimble in the wabe;
> All mimsy were the borogroves,
>   And the mome raths outgrabe . . .

There was no more, no Jabberwock as yet. His glossary of terms was, in truth, redundant. Meaning lay in sound and suggestion, not in definitions. It was inimitable and inexplicable.

The second relic of these years was more private. It was a photograph of a knowing little barefoot beggar-girl, dark-eyed and dark-haired, in a ragged dress slipping off one shoulder. Her sidelong glance suggested that she could think the photographer's thoughts for him. The model was Alice Liddell, daughter of the Dean of Christ Church. Tennyson, on receiving a copy, pronounced it 'the most beautiful photograph he had ever seen.' It was certainly the most portentous that Charles Dodgson ever took.

7

Alice in the Golden Afternoon

THE 1860S WITNESSED Dodgson's supreme literary achievement and the most famous book ever to come out of Oxford.
Yet *Alice in Wonderland* was only one version of his Oxford life in
this new and more exhilarating decade. He was still involved in the
religious debate whose disputes lingered from the 1850s, yet his self-
published satires related increasingly to university politics. In 1864,
he opposed the new Examination Statute which allowed candidates
in Science and Mathematics to give up Latin and Greek after Moderations. The statute was passed in Congregation on 2 February and
later in Convocation by 281 to 243. Dodgson's innate cultural conservatism was affronted by this devaluation of traditional Oxford
disciplines. He wrote an open letter to the Vice-Chancellor on 2
March, which was reprinted in the *Morning Post* two days later,
resigning as Public Examiner in Mathematics. He had already
composed a satire in rhyming couplets on those 'who might, could,
would, or should have voted' in Congregation.

> A is for [Acland], who'd physic the masses,
> B is for [Brodie], who swears by the gases; . . .
> I am the Author, a rhymer erratic –
> J is for [Jowett], who lectures in Attic:
> K is for [Kitchin], than attic much warmer,
> L is for [Liddell], relentless reformer . . .[1]

Next year he wrote *Dynamics of a Particle*, in three parts, the last
being a reprint of his joke at Jowett's expense in *The New Method of
Evaluation*. The first chapter of the new booklet was a parody on the

Definitions, Postulates, and Axioms of Euclid, as they might apply to modern politics.

> Plain Superficiality is the character of a speech, in which any two points being taken, the speaker is found to lie wholly with regard to those two points.[2]

The second chapter includes a Euclidean satire on the forthcoming parliamentary election for the University of Oxford, in which Gathorne-Hardy was to defeat Gladstone. There is also a glancing blow at Jowett as a contributor to *Essays and Reviews*.

> This last indicates the 360th degree, and denotes that the particle in question (which is 1/7th part of the function $\overline{E + R}$ 'Essays and Reviews,') has effected a complete revolution, and that the result $= 0$.[3]

Despite its abstruse nature, the satire was reprinted twice in its year of publication.

Of more general interest were Dodgson's pamphlets of 1867 and 1868, *The Deserted Parks* and *The Offer of the Clarendon Trustees*. The first, a parody of Oliver Goldsmith's poem *The Deserted Village*, followed a resolution to use part of the University Parks as college cricket grounds. Though the decision was reversed and only the university team continued to play its matches in the parks, Dodgson's poem depicts how things will be when the change is made.

> Amidst thy bowers the tyrant's hand is seen,
> And rude pavilions sadden all thy green;
> One selfish pastime grasps the whole domain,
> And half a faction swallows up the plain;
> Adown thy glades, all sacrificed to cricket,
> The hollow-sounding bat now guards the wicket;
> Sunk are thy mounds in shapeless level all,
> Lest aught impede the swiftly rolling ball;
> And trembling, shrinking from the fatal blow,
> Far, far away thy hapless children go . . .
> Iced cobbler, Badminton, and shandy-gaff,
> Rouse the loud jest and idiotic laugh;
> Inspired by them, to tipsy greatness grown,
> Men boast a florid vigour not their own;
> At every draught more wild and wild they grow;
> While pitying friends observe 'I told you so!'[4]

Among exiles from the present Eden, Dodgson sees his old adversary, Benjamin Jowett, his salary at last augmented.

> A man he was to undergraduates dear,
> And passing rich with forty pounds a year.
> And so, I ween, he would have been till now,
> Had not his friends ('twere long to tell you how)
> Prevailed on him, Jack-Horner-like, to try
> Some method to evaluate his pie,
> And win from those dark depths, with skilful thumb,
> Five times a hundredweight of luscious plum . . .[5]

By the late 1860s, in his middle thirties, Dodgson exuded contentment with Oxford as it was. He had, to all appearance, achieved that equilibrium where creative work was possible, after the self-doubt and disillusionment of the 1850s. Even in his satire, he writes as if he loved the riverside pasture, the parks and the cast-iron and railway Gothic of Benjamin Woodward's nearby University museum. Indeed, the matter of providing facilities for study or research at the museum was then under consideration. *The Offer of the Clarendon Trustees* in 1868 was Dodgson's letter on the topic to the Senior Censor of Christ Church. He suggested a very large room for calculating Greatest Common Measures; a piece of ground for keeping Roots, especially Square Roots, which were more liable to damage; a room with a cellar for reducing Fractions to their Lowest Terms; and another room with a magic lantern for displaying Circulating Decimals. Finally, he suggested a narrow strip of ground, needed for 'investigating the properties of Asymptotes, and testing practically whether parallel lines meet or not: for this purpose it should reach, to use the expressive language of Euclid, "ever so far."' Not for the last time, Dodgson punctured the pompous claims of the more fanciful types of academic research with lightness and grace.[6]

*

The two illustrious figures of Oxford life with whom Dodgson remained most preoccupied were still Jowett and Liddell. Despite his translation from Westminster to Christ Church, Liddell gives the impression of one who was nature's housemaster. At Westminster, no boy could look him in the face and tell a lie, Frank Markham recalled. He was efficient, active, careful, and suspicious. He lacked small talk and showed no wish to acquire it. At Christ Church, undergraduates recalled their Collections at the end of each term, presided over by Liddell with his eyeglass and withering air.

> The green baize covered table; the row of Tutors who knew each victim's failings, and had often told him of them; the Dean seated at the north end of the table, with the terminal report before him; – and then the examination badly done; the fatal record of lectures unattended, or other and graver misdeeds; at last the plain unvarnished words of rebuke which fell from the Dean's lips: this was no agreeable experience, and left no happy memory behind.[7]

Dodgson called him a relentless reformer, but the reforming days died in the 1860s and had not been particularly remarkable in their results. Liddell's greater activity was now architectural, having at first demolished parts of the Deanery interior and reconstructed them in his own manner. Hence the so-called 'Lexicon staircase' with its carved wood and lions to represent the Liddell family crest, a structure built upon his share in the proceeds of the *Greek–English Lexicon* compiled by Liddell and Robert Scott, Master of Balliol. A bath was installed but, ever the prudent housemaster, he ensured that only cold water was supplied to it. He was the practical, modern man who, when Dr Acland brought a German professor to see him, was announced as being 'down the drain' in Christ Church Meadow, ensuring that the college sewage was flowing as it should.

Outbreaks of cholera at Oxford still claimed their victims. As late as January 1875, the Queen's youngest son Prince Leopold, a Christ Church undergraduate, fell seriously ill with typhoid contracted through defective drainage at his Oxford accommodation in Wykeham House. Only to so sensitive a conservative as Dodgson did Liddell seem a dangerous reformer by the middle 1860s. Rather, he gave his energies to university committees, the running of the new museum and the university press, as well as such public enterprises as the drainage of the Thames valley.

Social life at the Deanery was spoken of by such Christ Church men as Max Müller with open admiration.

> The Deanery of Christ Church was not only made architecturally into a new house, but under Dr Liddell, with his charming wife and daughters,

became a social centre not easily rivalled anywhere else. There one met not only royalty, the young Prince of Wales, but many eminent writers, artists, and political men from London, Gladstone, Disraeli, Richmond, Ruskin, and many others.[8]

There were receptions and musical evenings to which some Students of the College were invited. The social ambitions of the Liddells were not in question. It was even hoped in the 1870s that Alice Liddell might be married to Prince Leopold. On hearing this rumour, unkind friends nicknamed the ambitious Mrs Liddell 'The Kingfisher'. Of Liddell as co-author of the famous *Lexicon*, however, Müller noted his 'consummate sobriety', a term which attached more readily to him than social gaiety. At college meetings, according to Müller, the Dean raised the tone of discussion, even while he doodled ivy-clad walls and woodland scenes on his pink blotting paper. Yet, as Tuckwell and others insisted, behind the stern and brusque manner, he was at heart a shy man. This made him ill-matched with Dodgson. W. B. Richmond, who painted the Liddell sisters in 1864, remarked that Liddell was impatient of shyness in others because under his aloof manner lay shyness of his own.[9]

Mrs Liddell, née Lorina Reeve, was spoken of as a catch in the marriage market, with a 'Spanish' beauty. She could be charming when public duty demanded. She could also be small-minded and foolish, as Liddell himself indicated, describing how they had demolished the intellectually fashionable Little Holland House set in London. Mrs Liddell nicknamed the salon the Agapemoné, after a house in Somerset where the clergyman Henry Prince, claiming to be the prophet Elijah, practised free love with a colony of women rumoured eagerly in the neighbourhood to number 2,000. There was a scandal over his assurance to a Miss Paterson, as they copulated on the billiard table, that she would not become pregnant – which she did – and over a case in 1860 when two followers prosecuted him for obtaining money under false pretences.

Having coined this witticism, Mrs Liddell was indiscreet as well as waspish. It came to the ears of Mrs Prinsep of Little Holland House. With stories of the billiard table and false pretences circulating, Mrs Prinsep failed to see the joke. According to Liddell she 'was very angry and gave all the gentlemen notice to quit.' The Liddells moved on, scattering this wreckage in their wake. Later in life they were commemorated in the Balliol rhymes, some of which circulated in manuscript after the 1881 broadsheet, *The Masque of B–ll—l.* A letter of 1881 from Cecil Spring-Rice to Dodgson's friend G. W. Kitchin includes a portrait of the Liddells.[10]

> I'm the Dean of Christ Church; – Sir
> There's my wife, look well at her.
> She's the Broad and I'm the High:
> We're the University.

Liddell was said to pronounce 'university' as 'universi-tie', as though in a more aristocratic form, hence the rhyme with 'high'. A variant description of the Dean and his wife also followed the publication of the Balliol rhymes.

> I am the Dean and this is Mrs Liddell:
> She plays the first, and I the second fiddle.

In the early 1860s, Dodgson was on better terms with the Liddells than he was soon to be. Both Alice and William Blake Richmond, who painted the Liddell sisters, remembered him staying in 1864 at the family's summer home, Penmorfa at Llandudno. Richmond was in error. Dodgson was in the Isle of Wight at that time. Even Alice's memory seems to have been at fault in her old age. Yet Dodgson stayed near the governess Miss Prickett and the children at Charlton Kings near Cheltenham in April 1863, escorting them to Oxford a few days later.

Even in the days of her 'Spanish' beauty, there is not much to suggest that Dodgson liked Mrs Liddell or she him. 'Unfortunately,' wrote Alice, 'my mother tore up all the letters that Mr Dodgson wrote to me when I was a small girl.' It is not clear whether Mrs Liddell did this in a single fit of expurgation, or whether they were routinely torn up soon after being read. Dodgson, commenting on the *tableaux vivants* which formed the entertainment at the evening party for the Prince of Wales, told his family that they were too good to have been devised by Mrs Liddell, from whose taste in such matters he had suffered on previous occasions.

He was not a particularly welcome guest at the Deanery as time went by. When Alice broke her thigh and was in bed for six weeks, she noted that he never came to see her. Perhaps Mrs Liddell drew the line at allowing Dodgson to pass his time in her daughter's bedroom.

Alice, the second Liddell daughter, had entered Dodgson's life as far back as 1856, when she was not quite four years old. He, the novice photographer, and his friend Southey had tried to take pictures of Alice, Lorina, and Edith in the Deanery garden on 25 April, only to find that the girls were too impatient to keep still. In his diary, it was one of those auspicious days the Romans had marked with the 'white stone' of chalk, and one which the poet Catullus hoped might be marked by his mistress with an even whiter stone.[11]

Thereafter, Alice Liddell became his photographic model, posing as 'The Beggar-Child' in 1859, the knowing pseudo-waif in a torn gown who had so pleased Tennyson. It was certainly a curiosity. Alice Liddell looks a little too clean and well-fed to be a beggar-maid, despite the tattered dress slipping off the shoulders, bare feet, bare knee drawn up, as she regards the camera with soulful stare. The winsome female beggar was a poignant image in Victorian England, admired in paintings like Burne-Jones's *King Cophetua and the Beggar-Maid*. More important, visitors like Dostoevsky were shocked to find among the ranks of Haymarket prostitutes, girls as young and younger than Alice Liddell, in dresses so torn as to show bare flesh and bruises. That they usually solicited clients for older women rather than for themselves was small comfort. By the criteria of the London streets that were among the best-known to Dodgson, Alice as beggar-maid was a hygienic and appealing pastiche of a less agreeable reality. Seen thus in the Haymarket, she might not have lacked admirers.

To suggest that anything other than the joy of photography and a delight in children motivated him consciously in choosing such subjects would be unjust. He was, by his highest standards, scrupulous in his dealings with his young models. Alice Liddell, in old age, recalled the excitement of being photographed and of the dark room where the black art worked its magic. First, however, he entranced his restless young visitors with 'fantastical tales, drawing on a large sheet of paper all the time.' The tale was 'slowly enunciated in his quiet voice with its curious stutter,' the children either side of him on the sofa. Then there was the novelty of dressing up and being photographed in costumes from his collection, many of them stage cast-offs.

But much more exciting than being photographed was being allowed to go into the dark room, and watch him develop the large glass plates. What could be more thrilling than to see the negative gradually take shape, as he gently rocked it to and fro in the acid bath? Besides, the dark room was so mysterious, and we felt that any adventure might happen there! There were all the joys of preparation, anticipation, and realisation, besides the feeling that we were assisting at some secret rite usually reserved for grown-ups![12]

Alice remembered summer days with Dodgson and her sisters on the river and the winter dusk in his room. Before five o'clock tea became a Victorian institution, Dodgson made use of the beverage to keep little girls content. When the weather or the season was unsuited to outdoor expeditions, he would say, 'Now then, it's a rainy day, let's have some tea,' which he made by walking up and down, waving the tea-pot about, and continuing the flow of story or conversation.[13]

Yet Alice's memoir is markedly reserved as regards the love or affection that might have lingered thirty years after his death. Love or infatuation on his side, if they existed, perished when she reached adolescence – the transition as he called it. Nor was Alice a favourite at home, at least she was not a favourite of the governess, Miss Prickett, known as 'Pricks'. Miss Prickett was not, Alice's son recalled, 'the highly educated governess of the present day, but she brought up the Liddell children successfully according to the ideas of those days.' After that, she married, dying in considerable prosperity as proprietress of Oxford's Mitre Hotel. Dodgson became alarmed at one point when his regular visits to the Deanery were rumoured to indicate a courtship of Miss Prickett, who stood a good many rungs below him on the social ladder.[14]

The Deanery was part of Cardinal Wolsey's design for the College, looking on to the Great Quadrangle at one side and on to its own garden on the other, though the garden was itself overlooked on the north by the library. On Dodgson's visits to the children, there was croquet on the lawn, or card games of Pope Joan, Beggar My Neighbour and Whist for afternoons indoors.

The other childish attraction at the Deanery was a pair of cats, Villikins and Dinah. 'Villikins and his Dinah' was a popular song of the Coal Hole and the 'chaunting cribs' of London's fledgling music halls. Even Dodgson with his moral dislike of such entertainments can hardly have been unaware of the verses, in which the star-crossed cockney lovers, Villikins and Dinah, are parted by Dinah's father, whose daughter then takes 'pisen'.

Now all you young ladies don't fall in love, nor
Like wilful Miss Dinah don't wax your guv'nor,

And all you proud par-ients, when your daughters claps eyes on,
Nice young men like Villikins, remember the pisen . . .

There was a feline irony in the song for the Deanery cats, since it was the unfortunate Villikins who accidentally ate poison and died. Dinah, who belonged to the eldest sister Lorina but was looked after by Alice, lived to wear immortal fame as the Red Queen in *Through the Looking-Glass.*

The children's life at the Deanery was strictly regulated. They were not to make a noise in the College or to run about. Their upbringing was spartan and, indeed, Liddell was known at Westminster for his willingness to lay about him. On the marriage of the Prince of Wales to Princess Alexandra in 1863, the sisters planted three trees on the bank of the Cherwell while Dodgson watched, naming them Alexandra, Albert and Victoria. He and his brother Edwin took Alice by either hand that evening and led the excited eleven-year-old into the Oxford streets to see the fireworks and illuminations. Dodgson had still been unlucky with the Prince of Wales in his attempts to persuade his royal victim to sit for a photograph.

In letters of fire the High Street now wished the royal couple, 'May they be Happy!' Alice was so taken by this display that Dodgson drew it for her. However, under the lettering he added two hands holding 'very formidable birches' for bride and groom with the words 'Certainly not.' Whether this was an uneasy private joke about the Deanery regime, or an initiation into the thriving humour of punishment, it seemed a curious gloss on the notion of marriage for a girl of her age. She thought the joke 'not very good,' but wished she still had the drawing. He marked this day with a white stone.[15]

*

The summer river was an escape to paradise. Alice recalled that outings with Dodgson and an adult companion took place four or five times during eight weeks of summer term. Usually they were afternoon trips, arriving back at Christ Church during the evening, but sometimes they lasted all day. Dodgson appeared in white flannel trousers and straw boater, the only occasion when he abandoned clerical dress. Though five o'clock tea might not yet be in fashion, he brought a basket of cakes and a kettle to be boiled under a haycock for the half-day outings. If they set out in the morning from the Folly Bridge boating station, the basket was larger, containing chicken, salad and all that was necessary for lunch. The three sisters, Lorina, Alice and Edith, were sometimes chaperoned by Miss Prickett, sometimes by one of Dodgson's brothers, even on occasion by his sisters, and sometimes by his friend Robinson Duckworth of Trinity, who was favoured for his excellent singing voice.

On longer expeditions, the party would row downstream from Folly Bridge, which carried St Aldate's across the river just below Christ Church, aiming for Nuneham and the park where Vernon Harcourt had provided huts for picnickers. Cutlery was borrowed from the cottagers and, after lunch, there were stories or rambles in the woods before rowing back to Oxford in the long summer evening. The children sat in the stern of the little boat, Alice acting as cox on their most famous voyage, while Dodgson rowed bow and Duckworth rowed stroke at the centre of the boat. Through the sunset and the dusk, they sang on the homeward journey, 'Star of the evening, beautiful star,' or 'Twinkle, twinkle, little star,' soon to be more famous as parodies. Dodgson recalled how, throughout these journeys, his 'jaded Muse was goaded into action' by the children, and how tales were told, but never written down, until the famous 4 July 1862: 'they lived and died, like summer midges, each in its own golden afternoon.'[16]

Afternoon trips lay upstream from Salter's boat-yard at Folly Bridge, past Gerard Manley Hopkins' 'base and brickish skirt' of working-class Oxford, the river winding out through Binsey to the green spaces of Port Meadow with its haycocks at harvest time. The ruined nunnery by the bridge of Godstow was the ultimate destination. Mooring the little boat, they made for the shade of a haycock to boil the kettle and make tea. Dodgson told his stories and then the children called for more. He closed his eyes and pretended to have fallen asleep, was roused like the Dormouse, and began again. In those summer fields of the 1860s, there was no village within half a mile and only a single farmhouse. Three miles off, the towers and spires of Oxford rose above the trees beyond the wide water-meadows. If there was heaven on earth for these children, it was here. Nine years earlier, Matthew Arnold had pictured the same pastoral idyll of Godstow at early harvest in *The Scholar-Gipsy*.

And above Godstow Bridge, when hay-time's here
  In June, and many a scythe in sunshine flames,

Men who through those wide fields of breezy grass
Where black-wing'd swallows haunt the glittering Thames,
 To bathe in the abandon'd lasher pass,
  Have often pass'd thee near
Sitting upon the river bank o'ergrown . . .

On 17 June 1862, the three sisters, with Dodgson and Duckworth, were joined by Dodgson's sisters, Fanny and Elizabeth, who were visiting Oxford with Aunt Lucy. The party set off before lunch to row downstream to Nuneham for a picnic lunch. Alice and her sisters looked with apprehension at the Misses Dodgson. 'They seemed to us rather stout, and one might have expected that, with such a load in it, the boat would have been swamped . . . we were awed by the "old ladies," for though they can only have been in their twenties, they appeared dreadfully old to us.'[17]

The two sisters also had the effect of subduing Dodgson and Duckworth. There were no stories and no songs. After lunch, the seven picnickers walked in the park and then began the upstream journey home. Within a mile or so of starting on the return to Oxford, the party faced a less idyllic evening. The English summer weather did its worst, the clouds gathered and heavy rain began. Within a short time, Dodgson decided that they must moor the boat and find their way back to Oxford by land. He took the children to a nearby house in Sandford to dry their clothes, Duckworth and his sisters following. Then he and Dodgson walked to Iffley to hire a fly for the women and children. They had tea in Dodgson's rooms at half-past eight and the children were then returned to the Deanery.

The experience provided a private joke in *Alice in Wonderland*, when Alice, the Duck, the Dodo, the Lory and the Eaglet scramble from the pool of tears and stand on the bank with the other birds and animals in the third chapter, 'all dripping wet, cross, and uncomfortable.' The Dodo announces, 'I know of a house near here, where we could get the young lady and the rest of the party dried.' In the story, the Duck was Duckworth, the Dodo was Dodgson (his stutter led to him occasionally pronouncing his name Do-Do-Dodgson), the Lory was Lorina and the Eaglet was the youngest sister Edith.

From the day of the rain storm until Commemoration on 2 July Dodgson was fully occupied with examinations and social engagements. As the honorary degrees were awarded in the Sheldonian Theatre, he saw for the first time Lord Palmerston, who was one of the recipients. On the following day he went to lunch at the Deanery, planning to take the children down the river afterwards. When lunch was over, however, the summer rain came on. With memories of the last trip, Dodgson and the Liddell sisters postponed their expedition. The clouds lifted sufficiently for a game of croquet on the Deanery lawn, preceded by the children singing the negro minstrel song, 'Sally Come Up', which Dodgson was later to parody in the Mock Turtle's 'Salmon Come Up'. The following day was decided upon for an afternoon's expedition, if the weather was fine.

The weather on Friday 4 July 1862 was not particularly good. Yet the memories of those who went in the little boat to Godstow were of blazing sun and perfect summer. Perhaps, in the six hours of absence from Christ Church, the weather cleared sufficiently to give that impression. Or perhaps they sailed into another dimension of eternal summer, commemorated by Dodgson in his concluding verses to the famous story.

> A boat, beneath a sunny sky
> Lingering onward dreamily
> In an evening of July –
>
> Children three that nestle near,
> Eager eye and willing ear,
> Pleased a simple tale to hear –

During the morning of 4 July, Dodgson was occupied by a visit from friends who came to his rooms to look at his album of photographs. They stayed to lunch. Having seen them off to the museum, he and Duckworth went across the Great Quadrangle to the Deanery. His diary has a brief but momentous entry: 'I made an expedition *up* the river to Godstow with the three Liddells; we had tea on the bank there, and did not reach Christ Church till half-past eight.' They then went to his rooms and were back at the Deanery by nine. This was the day, Dodgson added, 'On which occasion I told them the fairy-tale of 'Alice's Adventures Underground,' which I undertook to write out for Alice.[18]

Alice depicted to her son the three little girls, in white with shady hats, clinging to the hands of Dodgson and Duckworth in their flannels and boaters, the basket with the tea things in Dodgson's free hand, as they made their way down to Folly Bridge. 'Ina', as Lorina was known, was the tallest with brown hair and clear-cut features,

Alice wore her black hair cut in its familiar fringe, Edith was conspicuous by her bright auburn hair. Alice recalled 'that blazing summer afternoon with the heat haze shimmering over the meadows where the party landed to shelter for awhile in the shadow cast by the haycocks near Godstow.' The heat was such that the party deserted the boat for 'the only bit of shade to be found, which was under a new-made hayrick.' As the kettle boiled, there came from the three children the familiar refrain of 'Tell us a story.' Dodgson began, as he said many years later, by sending his heroine straight down a rabbit hole, 'without the least idea what was to happen afterwards.' After a while he stopped and said, 'And that's all till next time.' 'Ah, but it is next time!' the children cried with a simple logicality. The story continued in the boat on the way home.

Dodgson, as usual, rowed bow, facing the children in the stern, Alice again acting as cox. Duckworth rowed stroke, between Dodgson and the girls, so that he recalled the famous tale being spoken over his shoulder. However, this was so different to the others, so composed and polished, that Duckworth turned round and asked, 'Dodgson, is this an extempore romance of yours?' 'Yes,' said Dodgson, 'I'm inventing as we go along.' Seldom had literary inspiration of such genius been so public.[19]

Quarter of a century later, Dodgson remembered that return journey, the figure of Alice Liddell and the heroine of his tale merging in one.

Full many a year has slipped away, since that 'golden afternoon' that gave thee birth, but I can call it up almost as clearly as if it were yesterday – the cloudless blue above, the watery mirror below, the boat drifting idly on its way, the tinkle of the drops that fell from the oars, as they waved so sleepily to and fro, and (the one bright gleam of life in all the slumberous scene) the three eager faces, hungry for news of fairy-land, and who would not be said 'nay' to: from whose lips 'Tell us a story, please,' had all the stern immutability of fate.

The party reached Christ Church again at quarter past eight and the children were returned to the Deanery as usual by nine o'clock. As they parted from the sisters, Duckworth heard Alice say to his companion, 'Oh, Mr Dodgson, I wish you would write out Alice's adventures for me.' Dodgson said that he would try. He later told Duckworth that he had sat up most of that night, writing down in a manuscript book what Duckworth called, 'his recollections of the drolleries with which he had enlivened the afternoon.'[20]

However little sleep he got, he was up in time to catch the train to London at two minutes past nine. At Oxford station, he met the Liddells, presumably the Dean and his wife without the children, who were going up on the same train. It seems that he had little conversation with them since, by the time the train pulled into Paddington, he had composed the headings for the sections into which his story was to be divided.

*

His days on the river with the Liddell sisters continued, though he noted on 6 August that he thought it was the last time Lorina would be allowed to come. He gives no specific reason for thinking this. Lorina was now thirteen and legally 'marriageable,' having passed the age of consent at twelve. It may be that Mrs Liddell felt the time had come for her to put away childish things in favour of concentrating on the marriage market. It was the first shadow but not the last to fall on the happiness of that summer.

In October, Dodgson thought he had been out of favour with Mrs Liddell ever since a disagreement over Lord Newry. Viscount Newry was a Christ Church undergraduate, a protégé of the Liddells, who was denied permission to hold a private ball in the College. It seems an unlikely cause for falling out since Mrs Liddell, even if she favoured Newry, must have realized that a private ball would be inconsistent with college regulations.

The world of croquet and river picnics had also been shadowed by tragedy. Victorian mortality took its toll on the Liddells again when, in May 1863, for the second time in their marriage an infant son died. Liddell was called from chapel urgently to baptize the baby, who died the next day. He had lived just long enough to have the Prince of Wales as a godfather.

On 25 June 1863, Dodgson was a member of another boating party. It included the Dean and his wife, their three daughters, Liddell's father, the baby girl Rhoda, with Harcourt and Lord Newry. It seemed that Dodgson was there merely to take an oar. After reaching Nuneham, the others returned home in a carriage, leaving him to bring the children back alone. *Mirabile dictu!* as he said on such occasions.

The marvel was short-lived. Perhaps Viscount Newry at nineteen was a possible match in the medium term for Lorina at thirteen. The thought surely crossed Mrs Liddell's mind, and possibly Dodgson's as well. He was still allowed to take the three sisters on the river during that summer of 1863 but the chaperone was now the conscientious Miss Prickett, who did little to inspire another literary masterpiece. In May 1864, Dodgson as usual asked Mrs Liddell for permission to take Alice, Edith, and the younger sister Rhoda for a boat-trip. He was refused. In future none of them would be allowed to come, even with Miss Prickett in attendance.

Dodgson's parting from Alice Liddell was his most public experience of his 'shipwrecked' child-friendships. In March 1863 he tried to embody her in a poem which was to appear at the beginning of *Through the Looking-Glass.*

> Child of the pure unclouded brow
> And dreaming eyes of wonder!
> Though time be fleet, and I and thou
> Are half a life asunder
> Thy loving smile will surely hail
> The love-gift of a fairy-tale.

Neither Alice nor her mother seemed to want his gift. The later photographs, paintings and reminiscences of Alice Liddell do not suggest a particularly appealing personality but a rather dull member of a rather dull class. To her, Dodgson was dead and done with, as he recognized in his own lines.

> I have not seen thy sunny face,
> Nor heard thy silver laughter:
> No thought of me shall find a place
> In thy young life's hereafter.

That seemed true, by the time the poem appeared in 1871. The Liddells were patrons of culture, as rulers of such little worlds as theirs are apt to be. They nodded to it but they did not bow. In that respect, Dodgson's judgement of Liddell as self-made architect and designer was correct.

The poem he addressed to her might seem wasted on Alice Liddell or her parents, yet it contained lines which were among the most resonant in all Victorian poetry. In them, he compounded death with

1. Archdeacon Dodgson as a young man

Daresbury Parsonage

The only sister who would write to her brother, though the table had got "laid today dinner"! The other sisters are de-picted "sternly resolved" to set off to "Halnaby & the battle", tho' it is yet "early early morning". —— Rembrandt.

3. A caricature of his sisters, drawn by Charles Lutwidge Dodgson in his youth

4. Croft Rectory with members of the Dodgson family in the garden

5. Christ Church Hall, from Rudolph Ackermann,
A History of the University of Oxford, 1814

7. Henry George Liddell, Dean of Christ Church, 1855–91, from a crayon drawing of 1858 by George Richmond, RA

6. Charles Lutwidge Dodgson in 1855

8. Benjamin Jowett as Master of Balliol, from a photograph by Hay Cameron, 1893

9. Alfred Lord
Tennyson, Poet
Laureate, from a
photograph by
Dodgson, 1857

10. Hallam
Tennyson,
from a
photograph
by Dodgson,
1857

11. Alice Liddell as 'The Beggar-Child', from a photograph by Dodgson, 'which Tennyson said was the most beautiful photograph he had ever seen.'

than she expected: before she had drunk half the bottle, she found her head pressing against the ceiling, and she stooped to save her neck from being broken, and hastily put down the bottle, saying to herself "that's quite enough— I hope I sha'n't grow any more— I wish I hadn't drunk so much!"

Alas! it was too late: she went on growing and growing, and very soon had to kneel down: in another minute there was not room even for this, and she tried the effect of lying down, with one elbow against the door, and the other arm curled round her head. Still she went on growing, and as a last resource she put one arm out of the window, and one foot up the chimney, and said to herself "now I can do no more — what will become of me?"

12. *Alice's Adventures Underground*, illustrated by its author, 1864

13. 'The ugliest boy I ever saw. I wish I could get an opportunity of photographing him,' from a sketch by Dodgson, 1860

14. 'What I look like when I'm lecturing,' from a sketch by Dodgson

15. Dante Gabriel Rossetti, Christina Rossetti, their mother, and William Michael Rossetti (*left to right*), from a photograph by Dodgson, October 1863

16. Ellen Terry, from a photograph by Dodgson, 1865

17. Kate Terry as 'Andromeda', from a photograph by Dodgson, July 1865

18. *Top left:* Lorina (*left*) and Alice Liddell in oriental costume, from a photograph by Dodgson

19. *Top right:* Evelyn Dubourg (*left*) and Kate O'Reilly in servants' costumes, from a photograph by Dodgson

20. 'Xie' Kitchin as a Chinaman, from a photograph by Dodgson, 1873

21. The Jabberwock,
from *Through the Looking-Glass*, 1871,
illustration by John Tenniel

22. *The Hunting of the Snark*, 1876,
illustration by Henry Holiday.
The figure of the barrister was thought
to resemble Edward Vaughan Kenealy,
counsel for the Tichborne claimant

23. Gertrude Thomson
(undated photograph)

24. Irene Vanbrugh, née Barnes. From a
sketch by Dodgson, 1887

25. 'The fourth is its fondness for bathing-machines, which it constantly carries about,
and believes that they add to the beauty of scenes. . .' The Grand Parade, Eastbourne

26. Dodgson's study on Staircase 7 at Christ Church, 1868–98

27. Dodgson in later years
(undated photograph)

28. 'Tea at the Hotel Cecil', from 'Saki', *The Westminster Alice*,
illustration by Sir F. Carruthers Gould, 1902

29. Dodgson as a problem to be solved, from Harry Furniss,
The Confessions of a Caricaturist, 1901

child's play, while his little nursery sisters are one with the reluctant virgin-bride who fears the prospect of being deflowered. No one knows whether Alice's rejected suitor ever understood what he himself had written.

> Come harken, then, ere voice of dread,
>   With bitter tidings laden,
> Shall summon to unwelcome bed
>   A melancholy maiden!
> We are but elder children, dear,
> Who fret to find our bedtime near.

He drew away from the Liddells and mocked the Dean's architectural taste. His comments on Mrs Liddell in his diary suggest an armed truce. There were rumours in both families that he had asked for Alice Liddell's hand, had been refused, and that Alice resented this. To have asked in 1863, when she was eleven, would have been possible. It was Minnie Sidgwick's age when the future Archbishop Benson confided in her parents. It was not, however, likely. Thereafter, the hostility of Mrs Liddell would guarantee a rebuff, as he must have known, even if he contemplated such an approach. On 5 December 1863, at amateur theatricals in the College when Mrs Liddell and the children were present, he kept his distance. A fortnight later, he was invited to the Deanery and calculated that he had scarcely seen them for six months. He cannot have been surprised when Mrs Liddell told him next summer that he would not be allowed to take her daughters on the river. Alice became a subject for elegy rather than a marriage hymn.

> Long has paled that sunny sky;
> Echoes fade and memories die:
> Autumn frosts have slain July.
> Still she haunts me, phantomwise,
> Alice moving under skies
> Never seen by waking eyes.

He wrote of her by 1872 as if she were dead. Even in May 1865 he thought she had not changed for the better in the awkward stage of 'transition.'

His meetings with the Liddell girls were now accidental. They were at a bazaar in St John's for the visit of the Prince and Princess of

Wales in June 1863, selling white kittens. Alice was too shy to offer one. Dodgson asked the Prince whether the Princess would like a white kitten. The Princess turned and said she had one already. Next year he met them with Miss Prickett at a Horticultural Fête in New College gardens. In April 1865 he admired, with reservations, Richmond's painting of them which he saw at the British Institution. More than eighteen months later, he was invited to dinner at the Deanery, after a tutors' meeting on 5 December 1866. The evening was enjoyable. He spoke to Mrs Liddell, who showed him some new photographs of her daughters. They were not, of course, his. Five months later, in May 1867, he had a long conversation with Mrs Liddell in the Deanery garden, something that had not happened for years.

Alice waited longer than most young women of her generation before finding a husband. She was twenty-eight when she married Reginald Hargreaves, son of a wealthy family and an undistinguished Christ Church undergraduate somewhat her junior, in 1880. Thereafter, Dodgson wrote to her as 'My dear Mrs Hargreaves.' On 1 March 1885, when he asked permission to reproduce his Alice manuscript in facsimile, he thought his letter would be like a voice from the dead. They were mutually polite, considerate, and nominally friends. Whatever love there had been was immortal in remembrance only and Dodgson had surely written its epitaph.

> In a Wonderland they lie,
> Dreaming as the days go by,
> Dreaming as the summers die:
> Ever drifting down the stream –
> Lingering in the golden gleam –
> Life, what is it but a dream?

Dodgson began writing his 'fairy-tale' in earnest on 13 November 1862, four months after he had told the story on their river outing. He had spoken to the sisters in the quadrangle that day, which he now called a rarity. The manuscript was ready in three months and the fair copy with his own illustrations was finished and sent to Alice Liddell as *Alice's Adventures Underground* on 26 November 1864, two years later. It evidently circulated earlier than this without illustrations, since Dodgson had agreed with Alexander Macmillan by the autumn of 1864 that it should be published. The published version was longer than the tale written down for Alice Liddell and was to have the title, *Alice's Adventures in Wonderland.*

Dodgson lent the manuscript to the MacDonalds in May 1863. Mrs MacDonald wrote enthusiastically and suggested that it should be published. While the manuscript was not yet illustrated, Henry Kingsley paid a visit to Dean Liddell and read it. He at once urged Mrs Liddell to persuade Dodgson to publish it. Duckworth recalled Dodgson's response.

> On hearing this, Dodgson wrote and asked me if I would come and read *Alice's Adventures,* and give him my candid opinion whether it was worthy of publication or not, as he himself felt very doubtful, and could not afford to lose money over it. I assured him that, if only he could induce John Tenniel to illustrate it, the book would be perfectly certain of success, and at my instance he sent the MS. to Tenniel, who soon replied in terms of warm admiration, and said that he should feel it a pleasure to provide the illustrations for so delightful a story. Every time that a batch of Tenniel's drawings arrived, Dodgson sent me word inviting me to dine, and to feast after dinner on the pictures which the world now knows so well.[21]

Who would publish it? Dodgson first met Alexander Macmillan in Oxford on 19 October 1863, though the purpose of the meeting had nothing to do with Alice. The two men met through Thomas Combe, Director of the Clarendon Press and Printer to the University, when Dodgson wanted Macmillan to print a number of Blake's *Songs of Innocence* for him. Alexander and his elder brother Daniel had set up a bookselling and publishing business at Cambridge in 1843–4. By the time that Dodgson met Alexander, Daniel was dead, the firm had moved to London, and its first successes included Charles Kingsley's *Westward Ho!* and *The Water Babies* and Thomas Hughes' *Tom Brown's Schooldays*. It had also founded *Macmillan's Magazine* in 1859 to serialize work before publication in volume form. With the demise of the publisher Edward Moxon in 1858 and the extension of the mid-Victorian reading public, there was room for a new and innovative firm. Alexander Macmillan became established as one of the foremost publishers of the age, with a list of authors that included Tennyson, Matthew Arnold, Arthur Hugh Clough, George Meredith, Thomas Hardy and Charlotte M. Yonge. He was also a pioneer in printing cheap editions of classic literature in the *Golden Treasury* series for the growing middle-class market.

The agreement to publish Dodgson's manuscript was not one which involved Macmillan buying the book and taking the risks in the modern sense. *Alice in Wonderland* was to be published on commission, a common practice in the Victorian period. Dodgson would pay the costs of production, which were about a third of the published price. He would decide the form of the book and even the length of the print-run, on Macmillan's advice. Macmillan would sell the book to the booksellers and receive a commission on the proceeds. To that extent, he would get a share of the profits, if any. The major part of the risk was the author's and for that reason Dodgson the man of letters was for the rest of his life no less Dodgson the man of business. It was small wonder that he had told Duckworth he could not afford a loss. A single printing might cost him £500, a sum that most people of the time would take ten years and more to earn.

In this case, he faced a further expense. It was important that a children's book should be illustrated. He wanted this done by the *Punch* political caricaturist John Tenniel. Having opened discussions with Macmillan, Dodgson wrote in 1863 to his friend Tom Taylor, also a friend of Tenniel's, inquiring if Tenniel might be prepared to draw for a children's book. Tenniel agreed to do the illustrations and work began in the middle of 1864. Dodgson had hoped that the book might appear that year. However, there was a delay when Tenniel's mother died in the autumn and by November there was no hope of the book appearing before Christmas. At least the title was now chosen. Dodgson had decided against *Alice's Adventures Underground*, in case it should be mistaken for a child's introduction to coal-mining. He wanted something supernatural in the title, perhaps including elves, goblins and their kind, but finally chose *Alice's Adventures in Wonderland*.

On 21 December 1864, he called on Macmillan while in London and discussed the revised schedule of the book. It seemed that binding would begin in March and publication might be on 1 April. He marked 21 December with a white stone, but that was because he had at last met Ellen Terry. He was less fortunate with the production of the book. It was almost the end of May 1865 before he was sent a dummy of the volume with a specimen binding. A month later, on 27 June, Macmillan received the first finished copies. But then Tenniel intervened. He was dissatisfied with the printing of the illustrations. Tenniel told the engraver Dalziel in the autumn of 1865 that he had protested so strongly that Dodgson had withdrawn the edition. Richard Clay who now replaced the Clarendon Press as printer was to do most of Dodgson's future work.[22]

When the first impression of *Alice in Wonderland* was withdrawn,

Dodgson was dismayed by the cost this would incur. He was even more dismayed on learning from Macmillan that when the book was reprinted it would cost £100 more than the £500 for the first impression, whose printing had been done at Oxford. The first two printings, 4,000 copies in all, would leave him £200 out of pocket, even if all the copies were sold. Only on the next 2,000 would he be in profit. He considered the possibility of holding back the faulty printing for future issue. Forty-eight bound copies had been given away. Fortunately the remainder were still in sheets, which were now sold to Appleton of New York in April 1866 and, with new title pages, became the first American edition. Dodgson agreed this with Macmillan's partner George Craik, husband of the novelist Dinah Mulock whom Dodgson had admired since reading *The Head of the Family* in 1855. Copies of the rejected printing of *Alice in Wonderland* were to become, ironically, rarer and more valuable than those of the edition which supplanted it in London.

By the end of November, five hundred copies of the reprinting had been sold in England, a promising start. It did not prevent Dodgson from complaining in March 1866 that the sales were smaller than he had hoped, that Macmillan was failing to advertise the book effectively, and that he was being overcharged for complimentary copies sent out. He kept a vigilant eye on the quality of each impression. When the third printing appeared at the end of 1866, he informed Macmillan that the margins were too narrow and instructed him to have this remedied in any copies not yet cut. All the same, he noted on 3 September that a new impression of 3,000 copies would get him out of debt and probably into profit. He also gained by experience. Within a year or two he was proficient in the mysteries of printing, paper, type and binding, as well as the marketing of his books.

By April 1867, French and German translations had been proposed. Macmillan produced them both in 1869, and an Italian edition in 1872. On 24 August 1868, Dodgson calculated that 13,000 copies had been printed and that his profit was a substantial sum of £395. In the following January, Macmillan told him that 3,000 copies had been sold in the months before Christmas. Though the book was pirated in New York by *Merryman's Magazine*, there seemed no doubt that the overseas earnings would be substantial. By August 1866, less than a year after the publication of *Alice in Wonderland*, Dodgson told Macmillan that he was thinking of a sequel. By the spring of 1868 he was trying hard to persuade the now reluctant Tenniel to illustrate it.

Private letters and public reviews of the first book were uniformly encouraging. Henry Kingsley received his copy while still in bed and refused to get up until he had finished it. Dante Gabriel Rossetti thought the comic verses wonderful. Among early reviews, *The Reader* on 18 November 1865 announced, 'From Messrs. Macmillan and Co. comes a glorious artistic treasure, a book to put on one's shelf as an antidote to a fit of the blues; *Alice's Adventures in Wonderland* by Lewis Carroll, with forty-two illustrations by John Tenniel, sure to be run after as one of the most popular of its class.' By Christmas, the praise had been taken up by the *Illustrated London News*, the *Illustrated Times* and the *Pall Mall Gazette*, the last of which commented, 'This delightful little book is a children's feast and triumph of nonsense.' The *London Review* on 23 December was one of the first to see that it was not merely a book for the young. The reviewer thought it 'a delightful book for children,' while for adults, it was 'a piece of downright hearty drollery . . . crammed full of curious invention.' The *Spectator* on the same day added, 'big folks who take it home to their little folks will find themselves reading more than they intended, and laughing more than they had any right to expect.'

Not all the reviews were favourable, since reviewers were divided between those who had a sense of the ridiculous and those who did not. When *The Times* on Boxing Day described it as a book of drawings by John Tenniel, 'the letterpress of which is by Lewis Carroll,' it perhaps slighted Dodgson but accurately foresaw that for a great majority of readers the Tenniel illustrations were to be an integral part of the text. Yet the *Athenaeum* of 16 December, which complained that 'any real child might be more puzzled than enchanted by this stiff, overwrought story,' was soon to be proved wrong by the sales.

*

Dodgson protested that his masterpiece was made of 'bits and scraps.' This was true even to the extent that *Through the Looking-Glass* relied sometimes on the same jokes as its predecessor – cutting no cake and drinking no wine – as well as on revisions of such youthful pieces as 'Jabberwocky' and 'The Aged Aged Man'. The immediate source for *Alice in Wonderland* was, of course, the shorter version which he had written out for Alice Liddell as *Alice's Adventures Underground*, the illustrated manuscript finished in September 1864 and sent to Alice in November. There are minor variations and significant additions in the published version of *Alice in Wonderland*. The earlier story is far more dominated by Alice. There is no Pig and Pepper, no Duchess, no Cheshire Cat, no Mad Tea Party. The trial of the Knave of Hearts is a device of a single page for bringing the story to an end, when Alice dismisses the court and its officials as a pack of cards.

The first version also has Dodgson's illustrations. Alice looks rather older than Tenniel's heroine and supports Anne Clark's suggestion that with her long centrally-parted hair she appears 'a type dear to the Pre-Raphaelite brethren.' Moreover, Dodgson's own drawing of the Caterpillar has a facial resemblance to Benjamin Jowett, which Tenniel's does not. Shane Leslie in 1933 argued that the entire book is a satire on the Oxford Movement, with Jowett as the severely rational Caterpillar and Cardinal Wiseman as the Cheshire Cat. Though this may seem far-fetched, Dodgson's drawing of the Caterpillar is accompanied by its fastidious use of words and Socratic style of conversation, matching Jowett's tutorial manner. With questionable social graces, the Caterpillar might have spoken for the Jowett of legend, when a member of a tiresome group of visitors to Balliol said apologetically, 'Master, what must you think of us?', and the quiet voice replied, '*We* don't think of you at all.'[23]

As for the Cheshire Cat, whether or not it surfaced as a memory of Dodgson's early childhood, its immediate inspiration seems to have been in the bound volumes of *Notes and Queries* which stood on the shelves of his Christ Church rooms. The phrase 'grinning like a Cheshire Cat' had prompted two letters from correspondents. The first, written from Bath and published on 16 November 1850, remarked that 'Some years since Cheshire Cheeses were sold in this town moulded into the shape of a cat, bristles being inserted to represent the whiskers.' The second letter, published on 24 April 1852, offered a fuller explanation.

I remember to have heard many years ago, that it owes its origin to the unhappy attempts of a sign painter of that county to represent a lion rampant, which was the crest of an influential family, on the sign-boards of many of the inns. The resemblance of these *lions* to *cats* caused them to be called by the more ignoble name. A similar use is to be found in the village of Charlton, between Pewsey and Devizes, Wiltshire. A public-house by the roadside is commonly known by the name of *The Cat at Charlton*. The sign of the house was originally a lion or tiger, or some such animal, the crest of, I believe, Sir Edward Poore.

There was much in Dodgson's life and in the lives of his young audience on the famous river trip that was to be parodied or subverted in the book. The driest thing the Mouse has ever heard is an extract from Havilland Chepmell's *Short Course of History*, just published in its second edition in 1862 and in use at the Deanery for the children's lessons. It was a somewhat pedestrian schoolbook history which dealt principally with Greece, Rome and the Middle Ages, stopping short at the reign of George II. The dullness of Havilland Chepmell's history is allowed to speak for itself but the songs of Dodgson's story are energetic parodies of popular or moralistic verses familiar to the children from their Deanery performances. In years to come, Dodgson would surely have been more sensitive to the material he was debunking. Even in the 1860s, it is perhaps surprising that in his version of Southey's lines, '"You are old, Father William," the young man said,' he should have parodied such verses as,

'I am cheerful young man,' Father William replied,
  'Let the cause thy attention engage;
'In the days of my youth I remember'd my God!
  'And He hath not forgotten my age!'

Dodgson insisted that there was no moral intention or teaching in his story. He certainly seemed free of moral or theological second thoughts to an extent that he seldom showed again.

To explain the existence, let alone the nature, of *Alice in Wonderland* and *Through the Looking-Glass* is tempting but perilous. Most literary critics of whatever persuasion who peer into the narratives see little more than their own faces peering out again. In more practical terms, Dodgson's own experience and interests account for some of the books' characteristics.

Later generations, not merely psychoanalysts, were taken aback at much that was macabre, cruel, and what was later called sadistic, in his entertainment for children. Yet he was in tune with his times and with a long span of corrupted romanticism which saw cruel events as a rich source of humour, from Sade at one end to Saki and Evelyn Waugh at the other.

Dodgson had grown up in that age of post-romanticism which Victor Hugo described as the art of the grotesque. Horror and moral absurdity squinted uneasily from the young Robert Browning's 'Madhouse Cells' in 1836. Children were entertained by 'The Execution.

A Sporting Anecdote,' in *The Ingoldsby Legends*, where the joke depends on a man being hanged while the voyeurs sleep through his death agonies and miss all the fun. Thomas Hood entertained the little ones with the humour of 'the nice fresh corpse.' Hood's poem 'Miss Kilmansegg and her Precious Leg' ran for two years in the *New Monthly Review* of 1841–3 and now stood upon Dodgson's bookshelves. Its Carrolingian legal conundrum was echoed in the Trial of the Knave of Hearts.

This boisterous literary mood was scarcely modified in the 1860s. Swinburne's *Poems and Ballads* of 1866 brandished the sexually and morally aberrant with a schoolboy brilliance of technique. At the mid-point between *Alice in Wonderland* and *Through the Looking-Glass* stood one of the greatest English poems to be driven by sexual violence and a knowing enthusiasm for it on the part of half its characters. Robert Browning's *The Ring and the Book*, appeared in four volumes in 1868–9 to accusations of its author's interest in 'morbid anatomy.' At the beginning of the story, the heroine and victim, Pompilia, is the same age as Alice Liddell when Dodgson first presented the illustrated manuscript of his tale to her.

Nor were children in the early nineteenth century, who became the poets of mid-century, spared such educational treats as Nathaniel Wanley's *Wonders of the Little World* with its curious Puritan learning in the arts of murder, execution, torture, monstrous births and abortions, or Richard Baker's *Chronicle of the Kings of England* with its keen eye for bloodshed and mutilation, not least in the pursuit of justice. Alice, in the gentler world of 1860s childhood, encountered no more than promises of beheading.

The first version of her story was rather oddly entitled *Alice's Adventures Underground*. Despite Dodgson's apprehension over the association with coal-mining, there was a more obvious interpretation which he was not inclined to made. Most people who are underground are dead. The story takes the form of a dream and among the most famous dreams of literature were those that offered the means by which Odysseus and Aeneas made their respective visits to the shades of the underworld. Long before and after Dodgson's time, Homer and Virgil were the foundation of an education in classics at school, let alone at Oxford. Among the most familiar texts were accounts of the underworld in Book XI of the *Odyssey* and Book VI of the *Aeneid*, particularly the latter.

That Dodgson intended a parallel or was conscious of being

influenced by his reading is beyond proof. He certainly used figures from Virgil's account in *Euclid and his Modern Rivals* (1879), when two of the judges from the courts of Hades in the *Aeneid*, Minos and Rhadamanthus, act as mathematical examiners in a dream of contemporary Oxford. Whether or not the pool of tears in the second chapter of *Alice in Wonderland* is an image of the Styx, its victims marooned on the bank have a curious resemblance to those in the *Aeneid*. Virgil compares them to a flock of birds. Dodgson calls them 'This queer-looking party' of birds with 'draggled feathers' and animals. Yet the only figures in the narrative or shown in Tenniel's drawings apart from birds are the Mouse and the Crab. Specific mention is made of the Duck, the Dodo, the Lory, the Eaglet, a Magpie and a Canary.

In 1887, Dodgson described the Queen of Hearts and the Red Queen as Furies – the former 'a blind and aimless Fury,' the latter a Fury with a passion that was 'cold but calm . . . the concentrated essence of all governesses!' The Furies belong by tradition to the underworld. They await Aeneas on its threshold with spectres and monsters, the Centaurs and the Hydra, Briareus the giant with his hundred hands, the Gorgon, Geryon with his three bodies and Chimaera armed with flame. These form a menagerie of hideous shapes and sizes, of spectral properties, to which the more amiable and domestic figures of the Cheshire Cat or the Mock Turtle are a reassuring contrast.[24]

The Cheshire Cat might claim the Chimaera as an ancestor. Like the Chimaera, which consisted of a lion's head, a goat's body and the tail of a dragon, the Cheshire Cat comes in sections. The Chimaera breathes insubstantial flame and the Cheshire Cat boasts an insubstantial grin which, like flame, may linger independently of the creature. In common English usage, 'chimaera' had long described an image or idea that would vanish by the light of reason, not unlike the Cheshire Cat. According to Dodgson's copy of *Notes and Queries*, the grin of the Cheshire Cat was the result of a badly painted lion, whose features the Chimaera shares.

There is a Gryphon in Virgil, though not in the sixth book of the *Aeneid*. When *The Oxford Companion to Classical Literature* was published in 1937, it directed the reader in search of an image of the monster to 'Tenniel's illustrations of the Gryphon in "Alice in Wonderland."'

The Queen of Hearts would have been peculiarly at home in Virgil's underworld. Minos and Rhadamanthus preside over the courts of the dead, but hand over the guilty to Tisiphone, Queen of the Furies, for punishment. Virgil describes the procedure of the court of Rhadamanthus. 'Castigatque auditque dolos,' he chastises them and then listens to the account of their crimes. Dodgson's contemporary, John Conington, the first Professor of Latin at Oxford and editor of Virgil in three volumes, published between 1858 and 1870, remarked that this legal procedure of Rhadamanthus in line 567 was ὕστερον πρότερον, that is to say, putting the second thing first. Or, as the Queen of Hearts insisted, 'Sentence first – verdict afterwards.' Dodgson's Wonderland and Virgil's underworld have strikingly similar judicial systems.[25]

It may not be irrelevant that the year in which Conington published his edition of Book VI of the *Aeneid* with his comment on the justice of the underworld was the year in which Dodgson was writing out his own story for Alice Liddell, including this judicial dictum of the Queen of Hearts. Dodgson knew Conington and included him next year in his *Examination Statute*, 'C is for Conington, constant to Horace.' In 1861 he had also supported Conington against Jowett as a scholar. Another Oxford classicist Arthur Sidgwick, a younger friend of Dodgson's, remarked that Virgil's was 'a famous line from its inversion of the natural order of justice.' In 1894, T. E. Page illustrated it by quoting the instance of Keate, as Headmaster of Eton, 'who flogged the candidates for Confirmation first and *then* allowed them to explain that they were not the victims whom he had been expecting.' In *Through the Looking-Glass*, where time runs backwards for the White Queen, she explains that the King's Messenger is being punished in prison, though his trial is not until next Wednesday and only after that will the crime be committed. Both Dodgson and Virgil, the one with humour and the other as an act of national piety, describe what a new century of totalitarianism would recognize as the courts of tyranny.[26]

As in Wonderland so in the underworld, the Queen of the Furies presides over the punishments, in ways more colourful than a mere command of 'Off with his head.' One of her torments is to prepare a banquet for the sufferers but then to snatch away the delicacies before they can eat. They, too, might find Wonderland familiar. Alice gets nothing at the Mad Tea Party nor any cake from the Lion and the Unicorn. It is not etiquette to cut the leg of mutton and the pudding talks back defiantly. The cover seems glued on to the dish in which the fish has been served. Psychoanalysts were later to see in this frugality grave evidence of the author's oral sadism. Whether or not he was an oral sadist, he had certainly read Virgil.

Alice, like Aeneas, emerges unscathed from the dream, he by the gate of horn and she to the Oxford river bank. The horrors and predictions which Virgil's hero encountered were implacable and unalterable. But Alice triumphs. However cruel their humour or authoritarian their manner, the figures of tyranny are, at last, 'nothing but a pack of cards,' and the Red Queen as Fury 'really *was* a kitten after all.' Since Aristotle and the Old Testament, dreams had been seen as a reworking of the past, anticipation of the future, or in some way symbolic. In 1864, the year before publication of *Alice in Wonderland*, I. H. Fichte in *Psychologie: Die Lehre vom Bewussten Geiste des Menschen* had also acknowledged that dreams might be self-healing. Alice had confronted her demons, as Aristotle might have called them, and put them to flight. Even the condemned are safe. Beheadings may be ordered, but the Gryphon tells her that none have taken place.

Logic and law ran deep in Dodgson's interests, the one nourished by his profession, the other by his family. A good deal of the subject-matter of the stories relates to logic rather than law. Though the courts of Wonderland were an exercise in comic topicality, the Trial of the Knave of Hearts juggles logic as well as judicial procedure.

'Take off your hat,' the King said to the Hatter.
'It isn't mine,' said the Hatter.
'*Stolen!*' the King exclaimed, turning to the jury, who instantly made a memorandum of the fact.
'I keep them to sell,' the Hatter added as an explanation, 'I've none of my own. I'm a hatter.'

The inquest verdict on Miss Kilmansegg and her ownership of the golden leg is echoed. However, there is no time in this case to explore the true meaning of ownership as the King exhorts the witness, 'Give your evidence, and don't be nervous, or I'll have you executed on the spot.' The Hatter does his best, which is not good enough. He is on his way out when the Queen says to one of the officers, '– and just take his head off outside.'

Dodgson's letters and diaries show a familiarity with such moral and legal absurdities of Victorian life as the Court of Chancery and breach of promise suits. He teased his correspondents with references to Blackstone's *Commentaries on the Laws of England* and *Coke upon*

Littleton. His correspondence with his cousin James Hume Dodgson in 1891 suggests that he was well able to hold his own in matters relating to the law of property. He grew well informed on issues of copyright. He watched the trials at Oxford Assizes in July 1863, while writing the fuller version of *Alice in Wonderland,* and followed further cases in March 1865.[27]

The Court of Chancery would have been even more suited to Wonderland than to *Bleak House.* Until the Chancery Amendment Act of 1858, 'Lord Cairns' Act' as it was called, Chancery was accustomed to tell some of those who won their cases after years of litigation that it could now do no more for them. They might be entitled to damages, but that was not Chancery's business. They must go elsewhere to seek them and start all over again.

No one with an interest in current events, particularly with lawyers in the family, could have been unaware of living through the most profound changes in the English legal system since the seventeenth century. The anomalies and absurdities of the old system were current news. In the ten years before Dodgson first told his story on the river, there had been Common Law Procedure Acts in 1852, 1854 and 1860, which abolished the medieval categories of civil actions and substituted contract and tort. The new laws also enabled some litigants to obtain remedies in law and equity from a single court. In 1861, Sir Henry Maine in *Ancient Law* thought a developed law of contract was the true mark of modern civilization.

In other areas, within those ten years, the divorce court was set up after the Matrimonial Causes Act of 1857 and modern divorce procedure first implemented. Much of the criminal law was codified by the Offences Against the Person Act and accompanying legislation in 1861. Despite the enthusiasm for cutting off heads in the courts of Wonderland, the 160 capital crimes which existed in English law in 1800 had now been reduced effectively to murder and treason with provision for such military crimes as mutiny. In 1853 Lord Cranworth had tried to catch the tide of reform by advocating a scheme for the codification of the entire law of England. The suggestion failed but twenty years later the court system itself was to be abolished by the Judicature Acts and a fresh start made in the administration of justice for the first time in eight centuries.

While Dodgson was writing *Alice in Wonderland* a legal reform of a different kind was in progress by which the haphazard system of private law reports was replaced by a modern comprehensive system in 1865. Yet there was never a more famous law report than Dodg-son's own in that year. By the time *Alice in Wonderland* was published, the trial of the Knave of Hearts had expanded from a single page to fill almost two of the book's twelve chapters. In doing so, it presented a burlesque version of the system whose reform was a major topic of news and discussion in English society at mid-century. English judicial behaviour had often been less than decorous in the earlier years of the century. It was public knowledge in 1830, for example, that Lord Chancellor Brougham had such 'a touch of love' for Lady Fitzroy Somerset that he confessed he could no longer attend to the arguments of counsel or the business of the court in which he sat, thereby throwing the administration of equity into chaos. As holder of the highest legal office in the land, he played games of hunt-the-thimble with the Great Seal of the realm and called his lord chancellor-ship 'a mere plaything, and there is nothing to do.' Baron Parke, first of King's Bench and then of the Exchequer Chamber, appeared so 'extraordinarily ridiculous' as he tried a case of bestiality that the entire proceedings took place amid roars of laughter. Art, in Dodgson's courtroom, followed life.[28]

Elsewhere, life imitated art. In the year of Dodgson's death, for example, *Through the Looking-Glass* was quoted in a House of Lords judgment in *Eastman Photographic Materials Company v. Comptroller General of Patents, Designs, and Trademarks* (1898). The issue was what constitutes an invented word and the decision was that a trademark which consists of or contains an invented word is capable of registration. In the course of his judgment, Lord Macnaghten referred to Dodgson's work, 'a book of striking humour and fancy, which was in everybody's hands when it was first published.' Dodgson had written of 'two meanings packed up into one word.' They might be invented words, Macnaghten added, but 'a meaning is wrapped up in them if you can only find it out.'[29]

No less significant an area in which Dodgson's interest continued and developed was that of madness. The collision of pure rationality and immoveable insanity combined two of his preoccupations. As the Cheshire Cat remarks, 'We're all mad here.' The nature of insanity, the law relating to it, and provision for the mentally ill had been public issues during the 1850s. Now Dodgson followed the further developments in criminal psychiatry, as it was later to be termed, and showed himself to be a careful reader of such texts as Henry Maudsley's *Responsibility in Mental Disease*, a supporter of Dr

Conolly's insistence that forensic medicine is the 'only friend' of the accused who is mentally afflicted. The alienist must stand his ground in the face of a sceptical judiciary. 'Not the voice of the people calling for executions, nor the severities of the bench frowning down psychological truth, should shake his purpose as an inquirer and a witness.'[30]

Dodgson followed this even to the extent of offering unsolicited advice to Lord Denman on a murder case in which a defence of partial insanity might have been possible. If he let loose psychopathic royalty and the mentally alienated bourgeoisie in the pages of Wonderland it was perhaps because he kept company with 'Kleptomania, pyromania, suicidal monomania, homicidal monomania, perverted desires and deranged impulses,' as Maudsley described them, in the pages of the new science.[31]

Against madness he balanced stark rationality. Philosophy provided him with jokes which children could see and some adults might understand. The 'null' class was a favourite.

'I see nobody on the road,' said Alice.
'I only wish I had such eyes,' the King remarked in a fretful tone. 'To be able to see Nobody! And at that distance too! Why, it's as much as *I* can do to see real people, by this light!'

Vision and reality were a preoccupation of Wonderland no less than they were of George MacDonald, whose family encouraged Dodgson to publish the story. MacDonald was fond of quoting Novalis, 'Our life is no dream, but it ought to become one, and perhaps will.' MacDonald himself also employs the uncertainty of dream and waking in his *Lilith*. He noted in his essay 'The Imagination', that 'Indeed, a man is rather *being thought* than *thinking*, when a new thought arises in his mind.'[32]

'He's dreaming now,' said Tweedledee: 'and what do you think he's dreaming about?'
Alice said: 'Nobody can guess that.'
'Why, about *you*!' Tweedledee exclaimed, clapping his hands triumphantly. 'And if he left off dreaming about you, where do you suppose you'd be?'
'Where I am now, of course,' said Alice.
'Not you!' Tweedledee retorted contemptuously. 'You'd be nowhere. Why, you're only a sort of thing in his dream!'

'If that there King was to wake,' added Tweedledum, 'you'd go out –
bang! – just like a candle!'

As Bertrand Russell added, 'A very instructive discussion from a
philosophical point of view. But if it were not put humorously, we
should find it too painful.' The exchange recalls Bishop Berkeley's
theory of vision, that things are known to exist only because they are
perceived. 'There is therefore some other Mind wherein they exist,
during the intervals between the times of my perceiving them.' When
they are not perceived by human sense, they continue to exist in the
mind of God, a guarantee of their continuity and a simultaneous
proof of the necessity of God's existence.[33]

Roger Holmes in 1959 detected Cartesian Dualism in the White
Knight's comment, 'What does it matter where my body happens to
be? My mind goes on working all the same.' Other philosophers
approached problems in ways similar to Dodgson. William James
asked whether a man who walks round a tree on which there is a
squirrel that never turns its back to him can be said to have walked
round the squirrel. It was a matter of definition, as is the question
of whether the Cheshire Cat, when existing only as a head, can be
beheaded.[34]

> The executioner's argument was, that you couldn't cut off a head unless
> there was a body to cut it off from: that he had never had to do such
> a thing before, and he wasn't going to begin at *his* time of life.
>
> The King's argument was that anything that had a head could be
> beheaded, and that you weren't to talk nonsense.
>
> The Queen's argument was that, if something wasn't done about it in
> less than no time, she'd have everybody executed all round. (It was this
> last remark that had made the whole party look so grave and anxious.)

Even the Caterpillar's 'Who are you?' is not polite interest but a
philosophical question of identity and Alice takes it as such by saying
that she does not know. Already, in the first chapter, the reader learns
that 'this curious child was very fond of pretending to be two people.'
The question of identity raised in the first chapter of *Alice in Wonderland*
is echoed in the last chapter of *Through the Looking-Glass*: 'Which
Dreamed It?' In whose head has the reader been all this time? Was
the Red King part of Alice's dream, or was she part of his? Only
Dinah the Deanery cat might know the answer, but Dinah is too
busy washing a paw to attend to the question.

Dodgson's treatment of time and space was to prompt comparisons with Einstein and Eddington. The Red Queen runs to stay still and the White Queen lives in a world where time runs backwards. As with Keate's unfortunate Confirmation class, punishment comes first and evidence follows. Most memorably, it is eternally six o'clock at the Mad Tea Party. This, at least, has an explanation that is simpler than quantum physics. Victorian England, Charles Dodgson most notably, had discovered a world where time stands still, places never change, people grow no older and even the dead may live. It was the world of the photograph, the moment of time caught for ever, a commonplace by the 1860s that would have seemed like a miracle to preceding centuries.

By their games with true and false philosophical ideas, the two Alice stories have a claim to be the cleverest fiction ever written in English. It was a strength to Dodgson in this case but a potential weakness in the appeal of his later work. The English do not on the whole like cleverness, either in their rulers or their writers. 'Too clever by half . . .', 'Too clever for his own good . . .', 'I suppose you think that's clever . . .', 'Don't try to be clever . . .' These phrases speak for themselves. 'Be good sweet maid,' wrote Charles Kingsley in 1858, 'and let who will be clever.' Dodgson in his stories of Alice was triumphantly clever. Of course, he was being clever for the benefit of children, which put him in a more tolerable position. Adults who might have gaped at his philosophical conundrums otherwise had no need to feel under threat.

So the dreams end and their little heroine wakes. Dodgson quickly provides natural explanations for the stimuli of Wonderland by making Alice's elder sister share the account of it with eyes closed but mind conscious.

So she sat on, with closed eyes, and half believed herself in Wonderland, though she knew she had but to open them again, and all would change to dull reality – the grass would be only rustling in the wind, and the pool rippling to the waving of the reeds – the rattling tea-cups would change to tinkling sheep-bells, and the Queen's shrill cries to the voice of the shepherd boy – and the sneeze of the baby, the shriek of the Gryphon, and all the other queer noises, would change (she knew) to the confused clamour of the busy farm-yard – while the lowing of the cattle in the distance would take the place of the Mock Turtle's heavy sobs.

Whether it was also possible to account for the figures of Wonderland by matching them to real people was a question that was to exercise readers and critics. Was 'Queen Alice' a representation of Victoria Triumphans? Was the Red King a spectre of Archdeacon Dodgson? Was the Mouse with its schoolbook history another Miss Prickett? Was the Red Queen or the Queen of Hearts a caricature of Mrs Liddell? The Dodo, the Duck, the Lory, and the Eaglet are, of course, Dodgson, Duckworth and the two other Liddell sisters. If any other resemblance rings true it is that of the White Knight to Dodgson. Both are Alice's escorts and protectors. Both have an inventive knack and a certain impracticality. Both are amiable and ungainly. More generally, it is difficult not to link the revival of the extinct Dodo, the fabulous Gryphon and Unicorn, the Mock Turtle with his sorrow, even the doomed Bread-and-Butter Fly, with the Darwinian debate of 1859–60 – the publication of *The Origin of Species* in the former year, the famous meeting of the British Association at Oxford in the latter – and the pre-historic exhibits at the University Museum.

In politics, 'The Lion and The Unicorn' in Tenniel's illustration might represent Gladstone and Disraeli – or Tenniel's Mad Hatter might represent Gladstone alone – because the illustrator evidently used his *Punch* cartoons of Gladstone as a basis. Could Alice at her coronation be taken for Queen Victoria? It would hardly have been possible in the 1860s. In Dodgson's childhood, the little princess who became a queen at eighteen faced the late-Regency brashness of her elders in politics. Charles Greville, dismissing her as 'a short, vulgar-looking child,' spoke in the accents of Wonderland. When Dodgson's contemporaries read of the King of Hearts in his story, the last King of England was still William IV who had died in 1837. 'Silly Billy' was not a bad match for the unregal King of Hearts. Quirky, irascible, kindly, unpredictable, William never cured himself of such homely midshipman's habits as wiping his nose on his forefinger or spitting out of the window of the royal coach on state occasions. His sanity was questioned. Greville allowed that he had fits of good nature but deplored his 'burlesque character' and at last described him as 'only a mountebank, but he bids fair to be a maniac.'[35]

William's dumpy consort, Queen Adelaide, with her corkscrew ringlets, would scarcely have done for the Queen of Hearts. Victoria's mother, the Duchess of Kent, might. If not a Fury, she seemed to the court of King William, and indeed to her daughter's court, like a belligerent and humiliating nuisance. Though no queen herself, she was attached to the idea of acting as regent for the young Victoria. If there was anything in this parallel at all, then it was surely Lord Melbourne who became Victoria's White Knight. However slight individual identification may be, there is much in the monarchy of Wonderland to suggest the legends of England's pre-Victorian House of Brunswick.

Alice in Wonderland has a speed and vitality which *Through the Looking-Glass* lacks. It takes most of a chapter for Alice to pass through the looking-glass. Within four sentences, in the earlier story, she is bored by her book, has seen and heard the White Rabbit, and set off down the rabbit-hole. There are memorable moments beyond the looking-glass, the encounters with Humpty Dumpty or Tweedledum and Tweedledee, the poetry of 'Jabberwocky' or 'The Aged Aged Man', but the style has less a feeling of flawless accomplishment, where not a word is out of place and the reader feels it to be as nearly perfect as such a book could be. To that extent, the *Academy* of 22 January 1898, in its praise of his work at the time of Dodgson's death, was right to distinguish the two books by saying of the latter, 'we now and then hear the pump at work.'

Through the Looking-Glass appeared at the end of 1871. Dodgson had begun it in 1868, sent the first chapter to Macmillan in 1869 and finished the book in 1870. When it was in preparation, two difficulties occurred. The text contained the chapter of 'The Wasp in a Wig'. Tenniel wrote to Dodgson firmly about the difficulty of illustrating this participant, concluding that 'a *wasp* in a *wig* is altogether beyond the appliances of art.' The ordeal of illustrating the book was considerable, even without the Wasp. Tenniel later wrote that 'with *Through the Looking-Glass* the faculty of making drawings for book illustrations departed from me, and notwithstanding all sorts of tempting inducements, I have done nothing in that direction since.' The Wasp in the Wig was omitted and the chapters were thereby reduced from thirteen to twelve.

Dodgson's other doubt concerned the frontispiece. He had intended to use Tenniel's illustration of the Jabberwock but wondered if it might not be too frightening for small children. He sent a circular letter to thirty mothers of small children, who were to try the effect of it upon their offspring. The verdict was distinctly against the Jabberwock, which was relegated to the main text of the book and replaced as a frontispiece by the White Knight.

On 1 November 1871, specimen pages were printed by Clay's for

Dodgson's approval. A first edition of nine thousand copies was run off, ready in December 1871 but dated 1872. Alexander Macmillan realized that the demand was larger still and hastily ordered a second impression of six thousand. On 17 December, Dodgson intervened and ordered that the illustrated pages of this reprinting must not be pressed but stacked and left to dry naturally, so that the quality would not be impaired. If that meant the book would not be ready until the end of January, it was a small price to pay for perfection.

Not everyone agreed with Henry Kingsley that *Through the Looking-Glass* surpassed *Alice in Wonderland*, yet its success was immediate. Eight thousand copies were sold even before Dodgson received his presentation volumes. Kingsley added, 'I lunch with Macmillan habitually, and he was in a terrible pickle about not having printed enough copies the other day.' The second impression was exhausted, sales reaching fifteen thousand in a few weeks. By October 1872 the sale was what Dodgson called tremendous, having reached twenty-five thousand. Though it slackened thereafter, when the second edition (correcting the single misprint) appeared in 1878 it was announced as the Forty-Fifth Thousand.

The true value of *Alice in Wonderland* was never better estimated than by Walter De La Mare in 1932. 'On the afternoon of 4 July 1862, in the Long Vacation, a minute expedition set out from Oxford up the river to Godstow. It returned laden with a treasure compared with which that of the *Golden Hind* was but dross.'[36]

*

The 'Mathematical Lecturer of Christ Church' entered upon his reward. With the demolition of the Chaplains' Quadrangle and his removal on 30 October 1868 to the set of rooms which Lord Bute had occupied, in the north-west corner of the Great Quadrangle, Dodgson entered a phase of his life which was most memorable to the little girls who knew him.

As might be gathered from his books, he is a genuine lover of children, and his beautiful suite of rooms in the northwest corner of Wolsey's great quadrangle, looking over St Aldate's, were at one time a veritable children's paradise. Never did rooms contain so many cupboards, and never did cupboards contain such endless stores of fascinating things.

Musical boxes, mechanical performing bears, picture-books innumerable, toys of every description, came forth in bewildering abundance before the child's astonished eyes; no wonder, then, that in the childish years a day spent with 'Lewis Carroll' was like a glimpse into a veritable El Dorado of innocent delights!

Ethel Arnold published her recollections in *Harper's Magazine* in July 1890, while Dodgson was still alive. For her, as for others, the enchanted world was more mysterious for that other magic of the camera.

For many years he was a considerable amateur photographer, and amused himself by taking his little friends in all sorts of odd and fanciful costumes, till his albums became filled with Japanese boys and girls, beggar-maids in picturesque tatters, or Joans of Arc in glittering armor. The smell of the collodion he used to pour on to the negative, his small 'subjects' watching him open-mouthed the while, lingers in the memory still, and the sight of the box in the dark room which used to be pulled out for them to stand upon, in order that they might watch more comfortably the mysterious process of 'developing,' served not long ago to remind one at least of his quondam child friends, humorously if a little painfully, of the flight of time.[37]

His rooms were remembered for the fireplace with its red William De Morgan tiles and the paintings of child-friends above it, which faced the large St Aldate's window. Before the fire was the capacious red sofa matching the brocade curtains. To either side were the large tables and the tall reading-desks at which he stood when he worked. With its green wallpaper and turkey carpets this was the scene that welcomed his visitors. His smaller book-lined dining room was the venue of *tête-à-tête* dinners brought from the kitchens by college servants. Afterwards, Dodgson would turn the handle of the orguinette and fill the room with such popular melodies as 'Santa Lucia'.

As Alice Liddell grew to womanhood, their names were still linked in Oxford wit and Oxford gossip. Indeed, his supposed infatuation with all the Liddell sisters was gossip beyond Christ Church for some years after there could have been any substance to it. In 1874 an undergraduate satire on the Liddells was published, which depicted the Dean and his wife marrying off their daughters for money. It was called *Cakeless*, an echo perhaps of the tea parties of Dodgson's fiction. Its undergraduate author, John Howe Jenkins of Christ Church, was sent down for his effrontery. He had written a second attack on the Liddells, *The Adventures of Apollo and Diana*, which was suppressed. Publication of *Cakeless* followed the marriage of the eldest Liddell daughter, Charlotte Lorina, to William Baillie Skene, who is discovered in the satire to be less rich than the Liddells had hoped.

The attack is in the form of a verse drama with the Liddell parents as Apollo – a 'walking Lexicon' – and Diana. The three girls still unmarried, Alice, Edith and Rhoda, appear as Ecilia, Rosa and Psyche. A marriage is proposed between Ecilia and Yeruba, an unsubtle reversal of Aubrey Harcourt, son of the High Sheriff of Oxford and grandson of the Earl of Sheffield. Rivulus, the future Earl of Warwick, is ensnared by Rosa, while Psyche has 'trapped a Prince,' an echo of the rumour that one of the Liddell daughters was destined for Prince Leopold. As it happened, Aubrey Harcourt became engaged to Edith, rather than Alice, though Edith died of peritonitis soon afterwards.

In the satire, whose verse is pastiche Shakespeare, including *Othello*, *Macbeth* and *The Tempest*, a triple wedding is prepared, though the promised wedding cake fails to arrive. Dodgson, as 'Kraftsohn' is one of those present, biting his nails, as he seems to do throughout.

KRAFTSOHN   (*interrupting*)
I do protest against this match, so let me speak.

APOLLO   (*irate*)
Strip, strip him, scouts! This is the knave we seek.

KRAFTSOHN   By circles, segments, and by radii,
Than yield to these I'd liefer far to die.

ROMANUS   (*moving his hand*)
Arm, arm, ye brave! and rush upon the foe,
Who never did to early temple go,
Nor taste in lordly hall the luscious steak,
Nor would his frugal luncheon e'er forsake.

(*Scouts advance, throwing their 'perquisites' at the head of Kraftsohn, who takes refuge in the cloisters*)

ROMANUS   Take him through trench and tunnel to the chest,
Nor ever leave the cursed fiend at rest.
Leave him in Wonderland with some hard-hitting foe,
And through the looking-glass let him survey the blow;
Confine him in the belfry, not in Peck,
And make him sign at pleasure your blank cheque.
(*Scouts obey and lock Kraftsohn in the Belfry*)

References to Wonderland, the looking-glass, and the titles of Dodgson's printed satires, *The New Belfry* and *The Blank Cheque*, left no doubt as to his identity in the poem. The frugal lunch and absences from Hall match his reputation as a man who increasingly withdrew from college life. That he never went to early chapel, matches Liddon's later complaints of Dodgson lying in bed until half-past nine. Perhaps he also had a reputation for biting his nails.

At the end of the last scene Kraftsohn is thrown into Mercury, the original Christ Church reservoir, now a fountain at the centre of the Great Quadrangle.

> Full fathoms five e'en now he lies,
> Of his bones are segments made.
> Those circles are that were his eyes.
> Nothing of him that doth fade
> But doth suffer a sea-change
> Into something queer and strange.
> Goldfish hourly ring his knell.
>   Ding dong.
> Hark! now I hear them, ding, dong, bell.[38]

Such, in Oxford satire, was the fate of the man who had courted the daughters of Dean Liddell.

As for his teaching, in December 1864 Dodgson was giving five lectures a day. In the following October he went to see Liddell and pointed out that he was now responsible for seventy undergraduates and that it was too much. He suggested that he should be given an assistant, even offering to pay some of the cost himself. In 1868, Samuel Bosanquet, who had come next to Dodgson in the First Class list of December 1854, became Reader in Mathematics. In 1867, Bartholomew Price had agreed to take eight more of Dodgson's remaining pupils for a fee of £50 a term. At last he had regained some of his freedom.

In December 1867, however, he was appointed Pro-Proctor of the University on Bayne's nomination and went his rounds with the Junior Proctor to supervize the behaviour of undergraduates. He seems an unlikely figure to have been patrolling in cap and gown with two 'bulldogs' in attendance, entering those haunts of moral danger from which junior members of the University were banned. All the same, he did so. Lord Kilbracken, a Balliol undergraduate of the 1860s, recalled having gone with a friend after Hall to play billiards in a public billiard-room. During the game, Dodgson entered in his clerical academic dress and demanded the prodigal's name and college. He then asked Kilbracken to call upon him next day at his Christ Church rooms. The offender received 'a short lecture' on such places of ill-repute as public billiard-rooms and was fined ten shillings.[39]

The image of Christ Church in the 1860s was somewhat more tarnished than myths of gilded youth might suggest, at least in the memory of some who were undergraduates at the time. W. T. Thistleton-Dyer recalled the College in 1863.

> There was a dull apathy amongst the men, and a good deal of sullen discontent which broke out occasionally in coarse rowdyism. They did [little] in the Schools, the Westminsters who should have led the House were chiefly remarkable for getting into debt and getting ploughed. The appearance on the river was ignominious. The Etonians would not play cricket. 'Peck' was a barbarous community dominated by the Duke of Hamilton and mainly occupied with hunting.[40]

His contemporary, A. B. Simeon, found that for all its wealth and reputation, Christ Church under Liddell seemed in decline. Small wonder that fathers who cared about their sons' education were more likely to send them to Balliol or New College.

> At that time Christ Church was not a leading College, and there was a great deal too much card-playing, drinking, and rowdyness. There were a lot of young noblemen and rich men ... But it was some help to be living in the Old Library instead of in Peckwater where all the rowdy men lived. There were wine parties almost every night, and we had to give at least two a term ... Ch. Ch. in those days was cut up into sets, and you were bound to join one unless you lived an unsociable life.[41]

The worst instances of indiscipline in the 1860s would have been quite beyond Dodgson's control. He was appointed Pro-Proctor in the wake of the so-called 'bread riot' of 1867. The usual Oxford rowdyness between town and gown, which accompanied Guy Fawkes celebrations on 5 November, had continued longer than usual. The riots in the town were not to be quelled by proctorial authority but by a company of the Guards, sent to Oxford by the Home Secretary, Gathorne-Hardy, to keep order in the city.

Rowdyism was never far below the surface of Oxford life. It caused such outbursts as that in the Sheldonian Theatre at Encaenia in June

1870. Dodgson's friend Liddon, a popular figure in the University, received his honorary Doctorate of Civil Law to great applause. He was followed by Robert Lowe, a senior member of Gladstone's cabinet as Chancellor of the Exchequer. Lowe's appearance was greeted by groans and hisses from the assembled junior members who now saw the enemy in the flesh, their disapproval temporarily drowning the proceedings.

Yet Christ Church, which had been in the front line of resistance to reform in the 1850s, was not immune to it a decade later. Indeed, on 5 December 1866 at a tutors' meeting in the Deanery, Dodgson managed to push through a reform of his own. For years he had tried to get agreement that the Collections faced every term by undergraduates should consist of one annual examination only and that the other two occasions should be formalities. This time he won the vote.

He had a sharp disagreement with Liddell, whom he accused of unconstitutional conduct, in January 1864. A notice had appeared in *The Times* announcing that six Junior Studentships would be awarded to Christ Church undergraduates and that one of these would be 'adjudged to the candidate who shows the greatest proficiency in Mathematics.' Dodgson wrote to Liddell at once, telling him that he had no right to publish such a notice. The ordinance governing the election specifically empowered the electors to decide which candidate they thought most fit. Perhaps it might not be the man who had the greatest proficiency in mathematics. Back from the Deanery came a note in which Liddell accused Dodgson of having made a 'hypercritical and unnecessary' objection. All the same, Liddell said, he would follow the rules on future occasions.

Next morning Dodgson wrote again. It was not enough to obey the rules on future occasions. They must be observed in the present instance. Either that, or Dodgson would refuse to act as assessor for the candidates in Mathematics. Liddell wrote back saying that he had no intention of altering the present notice. Dodgson replied that he would refuse to act as assessor. With this exchange a hostile silence settled on the Great Quadrangle.

Fundamental reforms of the Christ Church constitution were needed and this time they had Dodgson's support. He noted in his diary on 11 February 1865 that he had been to a meeting of Senior and resident Students called by T. J. Prout to discuss what measures should be taken to alter the government of the College. On 15 February, Liddell suggested that three of the Students should meet three of the Canons to discuss the matter. The effect on Dodgson was to inspire an opaque satire on the dispute, *American Telegrams*, which lampooned the developments at Christ Church, while purporting to be news of the Civil War.

The reforms of the 1850s had done little for the position of the Students. Christ Church was still governed by the Dean and Canons of the cathedral, which stood in the College. In the middle of the 1860s, its senior members felt their position to be intolerable. On 7 December 1864, a letter had appeared in *The Times* from 'Ex-Censor', condemning the exclusion of the Students who were senior members of the College from the government of Christ Church. Behind this signature was Dodgson's colleague, T. J. Prout, a Third Class man in Classics, Perpetual Curate of St Margaret's, Binsey, who still held his Studentship when he died at Christ Church in 1909, having lived there for almost seventy years. By February 1865, Prout was campaigning openly for change. A petition to parliament was suggested but Dodgson's friend Liddon would not support further parliamentary interference in the affairs of the College.

On the evening of Saturday 11 February, Prout called a meeting in his room of Students who were in residence. No minutes were kept. Eighteen of those invited were there, including Dodgson and Bayne.

> Mr (afterwards Dr.) Bigg proposed that the position of the students should be raised, and that proposal was carried by thirteen votes to four. Mr Prout, supported by Mr Dodgson, then carried *nem. con.* a proposal 'that the carrying out of the above proposition involves the admission of the Students into the Corporation of The House, with a due share of the administration of the revenues and in the government of the same, and also the possession of such rights and privileges as commonly attach to the Fellows of other Colleges.[42]

It was only three days before the Dean and Canons set up a committee of the Dean, Sub-Dean, Treasurer and Dr Pusey to listen to the complaint which Prout and Dodgson had formulated. On 18 February, led by Prout and Dodgson, the Students repeated their demand for a share in the government of the College and the rights of fellows. It was unacceptable that the College should be governed by the Canons, some of whom held their Canonries merely because they were professors in the University and who belonged to other colleges.

Dodgson and Bigg also chose these negotiations to introduce a demand that the college servants 'should receive fixed salaries, and not be paid by monopolies,' which were a cause of the so-called 'bread and butter row' of 1865. Not only did the row preoccupy the College, it filled the columns of the national press.

Sir William Hardman read these press reports and thought of his own days as a Cambridge undergraduate under the system. College servants supplied the meals to members in Hall and charged them directly, rather than receiving a salary. They were, in that respect, contractors rather than servants. Dodgson had long since tried to get the system changed to one where salaries were paid but Hardman seemed to think the present arrangement worked well in principle.

> In the dearth of news *The Times* and *Pall Mall Gazette* have given up their columns to the discussion by undergraduates of both Universities of the excessive charges for bread and butter, and the evil arrangements of Hall. Christ Church has been the chief Oxford complainant, and Trinity and Downing have taken up the cudgels on our side. *Tempora mutantur*, and I don't think in our day we should have done anything of the kind. Eightpence is certainly a long price to pay for a loaf of bread which can be bought for fourpence; 2s. 3d. for dinner in Hall is not out of the way.[43]

Dodgson wanted the issue to be examined by a joint committee of Canons and Students. But Christ Church acted quickly to stifle the unwelcome publicity by electing a Steward and introducing fixed salaries at last.

So far as the Students' demands for a share in college government were concerned, Liddell, sensing a reform that might carry all before it, announced that he wished 'as far as possible to be considered neutral' in the argument between the Canons and the Students. It was agreed that there should be arbitration on the demands which Prout and Dodgson had formulated. The two sides settled on five eminent referees, including Archbishop Longley; Sir Roundell Palmer as Attorney-General in Lord John Russell's government; Sir John Coleridge, Justice of the Queen's Bench; William Page Wood, Vice-Chancellor in the Court of Chancery; and Edward Twistleton, barrister and commissioner. Though Dodgson did not give evidence to the referees, he made his views known to Archbishop Longley, his father's friend and patron. The recommendations of the referees, as amended in discussion, became the Christ Church, Oxford, Act of 1867. This instituted a governing body of Dean, Canons and Students, while reserving to the Dean and Chapter the right to decide matters relating to the cathedral and its diocesan buildings.

Though college politics absorbed much of his time in 1865–7, Dodgson found scope for university controversies as well. He continued to say of himself, 'First an Englishman, then a Conservative,' and some of his gibes were overtly political. In November 1866, the Stowell Professor of Law and Professor of Modern History, Goldwin Smith, who was a Liberal, published a letter to the Senior Censor of Christ Church deploring the results of the recent elections to the University's Hebdomadal Council. The elections had given the Conservatives a majority of two. Goldwin Smith was dismayed, and demanded that in future the election should be restricted to fellows of colleges, that the Hebdomadal Council itself should be abolished, and that the legislative function of resident Masters of Arts and others in Convocation should be removed.

Dodgson's ironic verse satire *The Elections to the Hebdomadal Council* appeared early in November and accused Goldwin Smith of not being sufficiently radical in his demands. It was not enough to demolish most of the University's government and disenfranchise non-academic electors in the city.

> My scheme is this: remove the votes of all
> The residents that are not Liberal –
> Leave the young Tutors uncontrolled and free,
> And Oxford then shall see – what it shall see . . .
>
> Disfranchise each Conservative, and cancel
> The votes of Michell, Liddon, Ward, and Mansel!
> Then, then shall Oxford be herself again,
> Neglect the heart, and cultivate the brain –
> Then this shall be the burden of our song.
> 'All change is good – whatever is, is wrong –'
> Then Intellect's proud flag shall be unfurled,
> And Brain, and Brain alone, shall rule the world![44]

For a Conservative of Dodgson's type, however, far more profound changes than those of the 1867 Christ Church Act were at hand. With the exception of theological degrees and professorships, the University Tests Act of 1871 enabled a man to take degrees at Oxford and hold office without subscribing any article or formulary of faith.

No person was required to hold a religious faith or to attend any form of worship.

Further legislation in 1877 diverted the private income of individual colleges to more public university purposes. Christ Church was the most fruitful source of revenue. It owned more land throughout the kingdom than any other Oxford college. More strikingly, as the richest of the colleges, its income was £57,000 a year, compared with £39,000 for its most affluent rival, Magdalen. In return for this, Christ Church had just 145 undergraduates.

No less significant for college life at Christ Church and in the University, the requirement of celibacy among fellows was abolished, except for certain specific categories of clerical and residential fellowships. It seemed that Dodgson in his forties might marry if he chose and still remain a Lecturer in Mathematics.

The old order took time to die. Dodgson's generation lingered on in hall and common room, into the early years of a new century. They lived and died in colleges which had elected them when they were scarcely more than boys. The new order made its way softly but persistently. In the face of it, some of the older men withdrew to lives of their own or lives elsewhere, assailed by the twin demons of rowdyism and reform. It was later said of Dodgson that at Oxford he became a recluse, in rooms which looked out on the quiet traffic of St Aldate's and whose backs were turned to the hunting and drinking sets of Peckwater. Yet before that, he became a man about town.

8

Man about Town

IF DICKENS WAS correct in believing that the dandy of the Regency
had become the High Churchman of mid-century, Charles Dodgson in the decade of *Alice in Wonderland* might have seemed a convenient example of the change. Yet, with his bandbox neatness, he
was a less unusual figure as the extreme poverty of the 1840s and
the intellectual earnestness of the 1850s dissolved in the greater affluence and raffishness of 1860s London.

With the coming of the railway by the 1840s, London was a day's
excursion from Oxford. Twenty years later, England's capital had
never seemed so lively and so self-consciously modern. Dodgson's
obsession with invention and ingenuity was entirely in sympathy with
the new developments. There was adventure in the first travel by
underground with the opening of the Metropolitan Railway in 1863.
'I am spirited to Bayswater before I know we have started,' wrote Sir
William Hardman. 'The only difficulty is not to pass your station, for
the stations are all precisely alike.' Dodgson travelled for the first
time by this wonder of urban transport on 15 July 1864, on a family
visit to Kensington. The year of *Alice in Wonderland* in 1865 was also
that of the cable to New York, the first carpet-sweeper and mechanical
dish-washer. Before *The Hunting of the Snark* came electric light, a mains
drainage system, the typewriter, the bicycle, colour photography, even
the 'abecedarium' or 'logical machine' of W. S. Jevons. In other
respects, of course, London was still much as Dickens had described
it in *Bleak House*. The fogs of 1868 were so bad that on one occasion
Dodgson overslept at the United Hotel, waking at eleven o'clock in
the morning when day had still not broken.

Dodgson's West End was celebrated by novelists like R. S. Surtees in *Mr Sponge's Sporting Tour* (1853) and by journalists like Henry Mayhew in *London Labour and the London Poor* (1851–62), as a scene of pleasures, innocent or profane. The theatre grew more glamorous and glittering with the advent of Dodgson's idols, performers and managers like Henry Irving, Squire Bancroft and Ellen Terry. Astley's amphitheatre in Westminster Bridge Road combined drama with spectacle, stage with circus ring, in one auditorium. The Polytechnic became the nearest approach to cinema with its 'dissolving views,' which he described to his sister Mary in 1860. Art galleries and exhibitions were more numerous. An Act of Parliament in 1866 encouraged public exhibitions in England and, in 1875, the Public Entertainments Act removed restrictions on matinée performances, to which Dodgson preferred to take his little girls. 'The day-return ticket from the outer suburbs, the tea-shop, and the visit to the Grosvenor Gallery, count for something in the greater liveliness of Late Victorian England,' wrote G. M. Young.[1]

By no means all pleasure was so innocent. At the heart of Dodgson's London, the web of streets which led from Portland Place, down Oxford Street to Piccadilly and down the Haymarket to Pall Mall, was the sentry-go of hundreds of what Henry Mayhew called 'circulating harlotry'. From the slums of Westminster, another vein of prostitution ran upwards to Whitehall, Trafalgar Square and Cockspur Street, joining its rival at Waterloo Place. The number of girls and women who made some or all of their livings in this way was unnerving. Mayhew and Dr Henry Philpotts, the Bishop of Exeter, estimated the number at 80,000 full-time and casual prostitutes when the capital's population was some 2,800,000. They were at their most evident in the heart of the West End and among the kiosks, temples, platforms and crystal lights of the Cremorne pleasure gardens at Chelsea. Behind Regent Street or in the Haymarket were the well-known rendezvous, the dance-floor, gallery and alcoves of the Argyll Rooms or Kate Hamilton's Night House, Barron's Supper Rooms and the cafés of the Haymarket. In the houses of the little streets beyond, the blinds were drawn down, the lights were dim and the notices in the windows promised that 'beds are to be had within.'[2]

Nearby, at the United Hotel in Charles Street, Dodgson made his London headquarters for most of his life. A walk down the main thoroughfares after dark could have left him in no doubt of a moral anarchy that lay about him.

The 'social evil' was also reflected in art and entertainment, as in

Formosa; or, The Railroad to Ruin, a Drury Lane production of 1861 by one of Dodgson's favourite dramatists, Dion Boucicault, whose daughter he wanted to photograph and who became the father-in-law of another child-friend, Irene Vanbrugh. In the same year at the Royal Academy, whose annual summer exhibitions Dodgson visited, 'Skittles', alias Catherine Walters, a virago of the streets whose conquests included the future Duke of Devonshire, appeared as Kate in Sir Edwin Landseer's painting *The Taming of the Shrew*.

Whatever distaste Dodgson may have felt for the scenes that surrounded him, it was tempered by the rush of artistic and intellectual excitement of London in the 1860s. Twenty years hence he wrote of a young actress in danger of seduction and perhaps genteel prostitution, 'she had better have died, a thousand times better,' and he felt it impossible to mix with those of whose sexual morals he could not approve. Happily this seemed to be a later development in his character.[3]

In the worlds of art and literature, an impatient younger generation of Victorians, born in the 1830s, shouldered its way through the ranks of those, like Tennyson or Dickens, who had established themselves at the time of Victoria's accession. Dickens, Thackeray and the Brontës had given way to George Meredith and Wilkie Collins, as well as to the more relaxed popular fiction of Anthony Trollope, or the romance of 'Ouida', whose 'late Victorian' romantic fiction *Under Two Flags* actually appeared in 1867. As London seemed more brightly lit, more affluent, and more gaudy, so the decade of *Alice in Wonderland* was that of a literary bohemia which grew, for example, out of the more conscientious Pre-Raphaelitism established in 1848.

Pre-Raphaelitism, once largely identified with the Rossetti family, was soon to become the common property of young men like Burne-Jones and William Morris (whom Swinburne announced fiercely as a greater poet than Tennyson), and to some extent of Swinburne himself. Yet of all those who gathered in Chelsea at Tudor House, Cheyne Walk, Swinburne was the proclaimed rebel, the disciple of the Marquis de Sade, the young poet whose *Poems and Ballads* had been withdrawn by Moxon in 1866 under threat of a prosecution for obscene libel, one who appeared to the new generation of men like Edmund Gosse as 'not merely a poet, but a flag, and not merely a flag, but the Red Flag incarnate.' The drawing-rooms and deaneries of England shuddered at the scenes of lesbianism or sado-masochism that the young poet thrust upon them. Robert Buchanan denounced the rottenness of the new writing as 'The Fleshly School of Modern Poetry,' in the *Contemporary Review* for October 1871. Charles Dodgson, however, was content to be friend and court photographer to the new Tudors.

There was a limit to his tolerance. He was unlikely to have smiled when Hardman regaled the household with a joke about a school bible examination, where a dim-witted lad misheard Samson's killing of a Philistine with the jawbone of an ass as 'jobbed him in the arse.' Dodgson's limit was the story of a boy who, on hearing of Lot's wife, inquired, 'Where does salt come from that's not made from ladies?' Nor would he have been amused by Hardman seeing a name-sign above a tailor's shop in St Paul's Churchyard, 'Mann, Rogers and Greaves', and taking it as a translation of 'omne animal post coitum triste est.' Dodgson noted, in awe, the visit of the Sultan of Turkey to Buckingham Palace, while Hardman reported slyly that the royal guest had saved Victoria the embarrassment of housing a team of concubines under her roof by bringing 'a boy or two,' which caused her no misgivings.[4]

Dodgson's 'treats' at the theatre took place on almost every night that he was free during his London visits and followed an established pattern. Shakespeare was varied by farces and dramas at the Olympic, the Adelphi and the Strand, sometimes the dramas of Boucicault or the farces of his friend Tom Taylor, whose great success had come with the character of Lord Dundreary and 'Dundreary whiskers' in *Our American Cousin*. Dodgson's reception of these undemanding plays was appreciative and tolerant. His first general criticism of the morality of the London stage appeared in 1865, when he increasingly deplored comedy that appeared coarse or plays that were rubbish or entertainment that he found low or vulgar. These shortcomings were still the exception, however, and he enjoyed productions of dramas like Robertson's *Caste* or operas like *The Magic Flute*. He liked opera in its proper place but objected in 1873 to the performance of Bach's *St Matthew Passion* in Christ Church cathedral. In this he echoed those of Bach's contemporaries who attacked the composer for having treated sacred texts in the musical style of the opera house.[5]

Dodgson's severest criticism was reserved for productions that might inadvertently be seen by children. After a visit to the Haymarket in 1871, where he saw a comedy called *An English Gentleman*, he resolved not to take any children to a London theatre again without first discovering whether the play was suitable. In this case, he had offered to take Lord Salisbury's children, though the invitation was not accepted. At the Olympic, where he had customarily enjoyed the plays, he found that *Without Love* was clever but unpleasant.

He was particularly upset when anything 'coarse' crept into a panto-mime or the harlequinade which followed it. He disliked what Sir William Hardman praised in 1862 as 'legitimate Pantomime,' without transformation scenes and extravaganzas. Hardman was delighted by Harlequin Lord Dundreary, derived from Tom Taylor's stage hero, a pantomime 'in which nobody uttered a word, but simply grimaced, gesticulated, and hit each other cracks on the head and kicks on the bottom.' When Dodgson took three little girls to the Princess's Theatre pantomime in 1873, they left before the harlequinade which he knew to be 'coarse', a word that he was to use constantly in the years that followed. The next year there were two productions to which he was advised not to take children and ten years later he recorded that *Whittington and his Cat* at the Avenue Theatre had been sullied by a piece of indecent fun in the harlequinade.[6]

By contrast with Dodgson, the amiable curate of Clyro, Francis Kilvert, called *Whittington and his Cat*, 'the best pantomime of the season' in 1870. 'There were some laughable passages in the harlequin-ade afterwards as when the policeman, upon whom most of the jokes turn, posts a Grenadier Guardsman in a sentry box unseen by the clown, and when the clown is engaged with the policeman the soldier takes the clown very much in the rear.' Kilvert and Dodgson shared an intense affection for young girls, though Kilvert's sexual enthusi-asms were directed towards mature women. Yet Kilvert's diary describes without censure scenes that were worlds away from Dodg-son. Clergymen's daughters held young lambs while they were cas-trated, 'seeming to enjoy the spectacle,' a scene almost from another century as well as from another class to the Christ Church Deanery. Nor would Dodgson have comprehended how Kilvert could join in the 'roars of laughter at an improper story,' told after dinner by a female guest in 1870 'about a child's misconception of the meaning of "committing adultery."'[7]

Dodgson's own attempt to write a drama, *Morning Clouds*, in 1866 was not encouraged by those to whom he showed the text. Yet his interest in the backstage world never faded. In 1867 he was particularly charmed by the child actresses and actors whom he met behind the scenes at a children's theatre in the Haymarket. Those who would not visit a theatre under any circumstances were depriving themselves of many innocent pleasures. He tried in vain to persuade his friend Liddon to abandon his decision never, as a clergyman, to see a play.

Dodgson always insisted that he was not trying to impose a puritanical taste on the theatre but merely to ensure that nothing was performed which a 'true lady' would rather not see. When his protests were ignored, however, he was implacable. Virginia Bateman provided Dodgson and the Dubourgs with the royal box at the Lyceum in 1874 for Irving's performance of *Hamlet*, followed by a farce in which she herself appeared. The farce contained the word 'damn', used once, which might be thought milder than the use of language in certain passages of *Hamlet*. However, Dodgson wrote her a letter of protest to which she did not reply. From then on, he regarded himself as a stranger to Mrs Bateman and her husband.

He was an enthusiast for the circus and for girl-acrobats, notably the young Lulu whom he admired in 1871, and for stage magic. He was astonished by the skill of the tricks of Maskelyne and Cooke and their stage seance, though he guessed how one of the tricks was performed.

Nothing, however, would reconcile him to music hall. It had grown in the 1850s from sing-songs and amateur performances in the larger taverns, the Canterbury Arms in Westminster Bridge Road or the 'London Pavilion', once the Black Horse in Piccadilly. There were also the 'penny gaffs', shops that were gutted and turned into makeshift working-class theatres. Draymen or costers earned coppers by singing to the packed and sweltering penny audiences, young girls danced more revealingly than on the legitimate stage. 'Show their legs and all, prime!' as one street boy assured Mayhew. There was community singing from the 'Flash Songsters' published during the 1850s with heavy innuendo on 'My long-tailed jock' and such phrases. There were also bawdy parodies of sentimental or popular ballads. It could hardly be expected that a man of Dodgson's type would regard them as anything but a social evil to be stamped out. They posed a further danger of a working-class culture, unregulated by the Lord Chamberlain or a respectable theatrical management. To Dodgson, it was entertainment for the 'roughs'.[8]

The effect on the audiences of such exhibitions could not be in doubt. Dodgson's view was that the stage might be either a moral influence or an immoral example. He insisted he was not priggish.

Yet there were good reasons to object, for example, to the stock figures of clergy in stage comedy. 'The pale young curate,' was not in reality the figure of fun that he appeared on the stage but 'pale and worn with the day's work, perhaps sick with the pestilent atmosphere of a noisome garret where, at the risk of his life, he has been comforting a dying man.' Dodgson asked his readers if they would as easily 'Laugh also at that pale young doctor, whom you have summoned in such hot haste to your own dying child: ay, and laugh also at that pale young soldier, as he sinks on the trampled battlefield, and reddens the dust with his life-blood for the honour of Old England!'[9]

He still maintained that he was not a prig, allowing that even the use of profanity might be justified by the requirements of realism. In *The Golden Ladder*, a British naval captain defended the hero against a French pursuer with the defiant words, 'Then, damn it, come on board and take him!' This was quite different, in Dodgson's view, to the gratuitous profanity of the chorus singing, 'He said "Damn me!" He said "Damn me!" in *HMS Pinafore*. 'How Mr Gilbert could have stooped to write, or Sir Arthur Sullivan could have prostituted his noble art to set to music such vile trash, it passes my skill to understand.'[10]

A Student of Christ Church, even a mathematical lecturer, was master of his own time. Dodgson found that in term and vacation alike he was free to spend a few days in town if he felt like it. When there was a day free from teaching, he would invariably stay the night in London and go to the theatre. Sometimes, he returned to Oxford from Paddington by the first train in the morning, arriving in good time for his day's work. In the early 1860s, he was still patronizing the Old Hummums Hotel in Covent Garden, convenient for the opera. In 1865 he moved briefly to the Trafalgar Hotel in Spring Gardens, just behind Whitehall. In January 1868 he transferred his custom permanently to the United Hotel in Charles Street.

The United was within walking distance of such other attractions as Parliament and the courts at Westminster. In 1867 and 1868 Dodgson was a guest at the House of Commons by courtesy of Christ Church men who were now members, including Ward Hunt, the Chancellor of the Exchequer. He listened to debates on the Reform Bill and on the proposal to disestablish the Church in Ireland. He was also Lord Salisbury's guest at the House of Lords in 1872. Prior to the building of the new law courts in the Strand, the courts were housed in Westminster Hall, which was the most easily accessible of all the public arenas from Dodgson's *pied à terre*.

*

In April 1857, Dodgson noted in his diary that he had been lent a book on 'Pre-Raphaelitism'. That summer, Dante Gabriel Rossetti, Val Prinsep, William Morris, Edward Burne-Jones and their companions descended upon Benjamin Woodward's new debating chamber at the Oxford Union. They were to embellish the ceiling bays with scenes from Malory's *Morte d'Arthur*, in exchange for their keep. Among the group was Arthur Hughes, whom Dodgson came to know well in the 1860s and 1870s and whose daughters were among his child-friends.

As his visits to London grew more frequent and prolonged, Dodgson made the acquaintance of a considerable number of artists and sculptors. He was affluent enough to be their patron but he was primarily a fellow worker as photographer and man-of-letters. It was with the sculptor Alexander Munro, whose work he had been photographing, that he first visited Dante Gabriel Rossetti at Tudor House in Cheyne Walk, Chelsea on 30 September 1863. By then, the queen of Pre-Raphaelite stunners, the red-haired Lizzie Siddal, had been wooed from behind her shop counter, become Lizzie Rossetti and died from an overdose of chloral in February 1862.

When the future novelist and biographer Arsène Houssaye was sent to England in 1836 by the *Revue de Paris*, he reported that London differed from Paris in having 'no artistic friendships, no groups, no schools.' Pre-Raphaelitism in 1848 had changed that view of art. Dante Gabriel Rossetti, and what might pass for a bohemian commune, now occupied a large house and extensive gardens in Cheyne Walk. The old house looked out over the Thames foreshore, the bustle of Cremorne gardens a little way to the west.[11]

Whatever Dodgson's reservations over the domestic arrangements, they had some similarity to the fantasies of his most famous story which he was now revising for publication. The sixteenth-century brick house with its panelled rooms and secluded gardens housed a shifting population of artists, Rossetti, his brother William Michael, George Meredith, Algernon Charles Swinburne, William Morris, and visitors who included Frederick Leighton, James McNeill Whistler and Frederick Sandys. There was also Rossetti's menagerie. A wombat slept contentedly on the dining-table. An armadillo and a kangaroo lived in the gardens. Ford Madox Brown, a painter-guest, believed that the wombat was Dodgson's inspiration for the Dormouse in A Mad Tea-Party.

Henry Treffery Dunn, a young artist in Rossetti's household, recalled that, '"Lewis Carroll," the author of *Alice in Wonderland*, was another frequent guest at Cheyne Walk in the early days of Rossetti's occupancy of the house there.' The other guest whom Dunn vividly recalled and whom Dodgson met now, even if he had not done so in Darlington, was the notorious Charles Augustus Howell. He had fled abroad in 1857, returning to England in 1864.

The two favourite gossips at Rossetti's dinner parties were Howell and the painter Frederick Sandys. Howell always had 'some monstrous story to tell about anybody who happened to be enjoying notoriety at the time, with whom he would claim to have a perfect intimacy.' Rossetti planned the seating of his guests. 'We'll have Howell here; so-and-so is slow and he shall sit next to him; he'll be sure to be amused and wake up when that droll fellow begins pouring out his Niagara of lies. And here . . . Sandys shall have his place, just opposite, so that whatever Howell relates, Fred shall have a chance of capping his romances with some more racy.'

Such genial acceptance of Howell came at a high price. Correspondence of the day refers to 'that cur Mr Howell,' 'so infamous a libel,' 'this disgusting farce,' and so forth. Howell pleaded with William Michael Rossetti that 'accusations of slipperiness in money affairs are cruel untruths.' At the time of Dodgson's appearance as a dinner guest, Howell was contemplating how best to hold Swinburne to ransom over his sado-masochistic escapades in a brothel at Circus Road, Regents Park. He had letters enough from the young man for that purpose. Dante Gabriel, in grief at Lizzie's death, had buried his poems in her coffin. In 1869 it was Howell who arranged the exhumation. When Rossetti 'begged Howell to hold his tongue' about the business, Howell worked his favourite trick of pawning the sensitive letters with a confederate for a high price and requiring a large sum to redeem them. Perhaps, at the dinner table, Howell's speculative gaze rested on Dodgson the unworldly don. In 1864, however, a platonic enthusiasm for little girls was scarcely the stuff of which blackmail might be fashioned.[12]

That Dodgson ceased to attend Rossetti's dinner parties was not necessarily a sign of disapproval. Rossetti and his cohabitants went their own way as the idyll of bohemia was tarnished by domestic reality at Tudor House. The wombat ate the cigars. Meredith proved wittier than the others and made fun of Rossetti in front of his guests. Rossetti threw a cup of tea in his face. Swinburne's shrill enthusiasm for the Marquis de Sade and the sexual relations of Byron with his own sister got on Rossetti's nerves, as did Swinburne's nervous energy, 'dancing all over the studio like a wildcat.' William Michael Rossetti found his brother's boisterous late hours an impediment to work. He also objected that he had never heard Dodgson say anything 'funny or quaint.' When Dodgson tried to be clever William Michael found him tiresome and too whimsical. Swinburne wrote his Victorian Greek Tragedy *Atalanta in Calydon*. Dodgson followed it with 'Atalanta in Camden-Town', in *Punch* on 27 July 1867, the story of an unhappy suitor with whom Atalanta grows bored after he has spent all his money.

> I had been to the play
> With my pearl of a Peri –
> But for all I could say,
> She declared she was weary,
> That 'the place was so crowded and hot, and she couldn't
> abide that Dundreary.'

The disintegration of the Chelsea ménage continued. Meredith was revolted by Rossetti's gargantuan breakfasts. Swinburne knocked William Morris into a cupboard and smashed Rossetti's expensive china. With a newcomer, Simeon Solomon, Swinburne romped naked about the house, sliding down the banisters and waking the echoes. Rossetti found a new mistress, Fanny Cornforth, who was known to others as 'The Bitch', out of loyalty to poor dead Lizzie. Meredith, driven to fury by the constant shrillness and din which accompanied Swinburne's presence everywhere, swore that he would certainly have kicked the poet downstairs 'had he not foreseen what a clatter his horrid little bottom would have made as it bounced from step to step.'[13]

On 6 October 1863 Dodgson made his most famous visit to Cheyne Walk, taking his camera. While he was unpacking it, Rossetti's sister Christina arrived and Rossetti introduced them. Dodgson was already an admirer of her poetry, notably *Goblin Market*, which he had read the year before. Though Christina was rather shy, he persuaded her to sit for two portraits. Dodgson also photographed Dante Gabriel, a portly figure who looked more like a bank manager than a bohemian. He stayed to dinner and was back the next day, photographing individual members of the Rossetti family and groups. As well as the two sisters, Christina and Maria Francesca, and the two brothers, their mother was visiting Tudor House. One of the group photographs, taken in the garden, shows the two brothers and Mrs Rossetti and Christina by a flight of steps leading up to the garden door. The intimacy and informality of this family group make it one of the most appealing of all Victorian photographs. Dodgson also tried to take the five members of the family together. At that moment the October rain began to fall. He took the photograph but, as Maria Francesca remarked, 'we appear as if splashed by ink.'[14]

During the rest of that week, Dodgson photographed Rossetti's drawings and Madame Beyer, the painter's model for *Joan of Arc*. The friendship between the two men developed and, on a later visit to Cheyne Walk, Dodgson was introduced to Swinburne. The eccentric occupants of the old house and the no-less-unusual menagerie which Rossetti kept among the trees and shrubs of the gardens seemed to Dodgson like the stuff of fiction.

Of all those who frequented Cheyne Walk, Dodgson felt closest to the shy and devout Christina, who lived with her mother. He presented *Alice in Wonderland* to Christina in 1865. Characteristically, she liked the White Rabbit and the puppy but 'of the hatter's acquaintance I am not ambitious, and the March hare may fairly remain an open question.' Dante Gabriel read his sister's copy of the book and was delighted by Dodgson's verse parodies. He thought these parodies, mocking the solemnity of schoolbook poetry, among the funniest things he had read.[15]

Dante Gabriel's declining health in the 1870s, his use of chloral and delusions of persecution, marked a separation from many friends, including Dodgson. In 1876 he concluded that *The Hunting of the Snark* was a personal attack upon him. Despite this estrangement, Dodgson's temperamental sympathy with Christina and her instinctive respect for the role of the clergy sustained a link between them which endured until her death in 1894. In November 1882, Dodgson called on her and gave her his negative of Dante Gabriel who had died that year on Easter Sunday. He visited Christina and her mother from time to time when he was in London. The year before her death he inscribed for her a copy of *Sylvie and Bruno Concluded*, a moral tale with which she may have felt more at ease than with *Alice in Wonderland*.

Dodgson's admiration of Rossetti as an artist was undimmed by his friend's interpretation of *The Hunting of the Snark*. In 1883 he saw Rossetti's painting *Found* at Burlington House.

A picture of a man finding, in the streets of London, a girl he had loved years before in the days of her innocence. She is huddled up against the wall, dressed in gaudy colours, and trying to turn away her agonized face, while he, holding her wrists, is looking down with an expression of pain and pity, condemnation and love, which is one of the most marvellous things I have ever seen done in painting.[16]

Among other acquaintances in the Pre-Raphaelite circle during 1865 was the family of John Everett Millais. Dodgson visited the artist's studio and photographed the three daughters, as well as Mrs Millais, the young Effie Gray who had ended an earlier unconsummated marriage to John Ruskin. Dodgson did not seem deterred by moral scruple or personal embarrassment, as he was later, when the young Ellen Terry left George Frederick Watts for a lover.

Though Dodgson was acquainted with Millais and Holman Hunt, his closest friend among the Pre-Raphaelites was Arthur Hughes, an exact contemporary, who first exhibited at the Royal Academy in 1856 and was illustrator of Christina Rossetti and George MacDonald. Among Hughes's paintings, Dodgson admired the three-panelled *Lady of Shalott* and purchased *The Lady with the Lilacs*, which hung in his Christ Church rooms for the rest of his life. The Hughes daughters, Agnes and Amy, were by now his child-friends. They and their parents were also among his subjects for photography.

While at Hastings, consulting Dr Hunt over his speech impediment in 1859, Dodgson had been introduced to George MacDonald and his family. Though the MacDonalds made their home in Italy from 1877, Dodgson became their intimate friend during their years in London. George MacDonald's early poetry had been admired by Tennyson and Lady Byron. When Dodgson met him he had just published a 'faerie prose romance' of 1858, *Phantastes*, a book including a large white rabbit not dissimilar to its successor in *Alice in Wonderland*. MacDonald was also a clergyman, author of three series of *Unspoken Sermons*, published between 1867 and 1889. Like Dodgson, he was a devotee of F. D. Maurice's preaching. MacDonald's wife Louisa combined theatre with philanthropy. Dodgson was entranced by the performances given by the family, in their garden, to audiences of the poor.

He met two of the eleven children, Greville and Mary, in London in 1860, where the parents and children became his photographic models. While they remained in England, the house at Elm Lodge, Hampstead, was presided over by George MacDonald in the roles of ex-Calvinist mystic, children's friend, and disciplinarian. Within the family, he was less like the gentle mystic. 'When appeal to an undeveloped moral sense failed,' wrote Greville Macdonald, 'corporal punishment, sometimes severe, was inevitable.'[17]

Dodgson stayed with the MacDonalds at Elm Lodge in July 1863, though his first night was unintentionally spent elsewhere. Like the caricature of 'Stage-Door Johnny', he returned from the theatre at 1.30 a.m. and could get no one to answer the door after half an hour of knocking and singing. Like the resourceful man about town that he was, he walked back to Euston and at about 3 a.m. found a bed in Windsor's Coffee House. The MacDonald children remembered him with unequivocal affection, as Greville MacDonald recalled.

> Our annual treat was Uncle Dodgson taking us to the Polytechnic for the entrancing 'dissolving views' of fairy tales, or to go down in the diving-bell, or watch the mechanical athlete *Leotard*. There was also the Coliseum in Albany Street, with its storms by land and sea on a wonderful stage, and its great panorama of London. And there was Cremer's toy-shop in Regent Street – not to mention bath-buns and ginger-beer – all associated in my memory with the adorable writer of *Alice*.[18]

Cremer's was more than a toy-shop. It was better known as W. H. Cremer's Saloon of Magic at 210 Regent Street, specializing in 'Illusions, Magic, Optics', with a platform like a small stage at one end where tricks were demonstrated by a resident magician.

When the MacDonald family returned to England from Italy in 1879 to put on their production of *Pilgrim's Progress*, which Dodgson rather oddly did not consider unsuitable for the stage, he and George MacDonald met Mark Twain at dinner on 26 July. Like some of Rossetti's guests, Mark Twain found Dodgson unexpectedly reserved and not at all the clever man of reputation.

> We met a great many other interesting people, among them Lewis Carroll, author of the immortal *Alice* – but he was only interesting to look at, for he was the stillest and shyest full-grown man I have ever met except

'Uncle Remus.' Doctor MacDonald and several other lively talkers were present, and the talk went briskly on for a couple of hours, but Carroll sat still all the while except that now and then he answered a question. His answers were brief. I do not remember that he elaborated any of them.[19]

*

Writing to Gertrude Thomson in January 1879, Dodgson suggested that she might like to be introduced to artists of his acquaintance. Apart from Ruskin, they included Leighton, Millais, Holman Hunt, Woolner, Hughes, Paton, Joseph and George Sant. He also included Henry Holiday, who described himself and Dodgson as 'friends on the spot' when they first met and who was the illustrator of *The Hunting of the Snark*. Dodgson, with his camera, was a guest of the Holidays in July 1870, photographing at the artist's home the children of Lord Salisbury, two of the Terry sisters, and the daughters of Arthur Hughes. Among his other subjects on that occasion was Theo Heaphy, the youngest child of the painter Thomas Heaphy. By the time of Dodgson's letter to Gertrude Thomson, Thomas Heaphy was dead and Dodgson had become a kindly mentor to Theo in her own career as an artist. The list which he offered to Miss Thomson made up a fair proportion of the Victorian artistic establishment. He arranged for Ruskin to look at her drawings in 1883, as the Slade Professor of Art at Oxford who was about to lecture on Fairyland.

His relationship with Gertrude Thomson was to develop into one of the most important of his later life. Miss Thomson described how they first met by arrangement near the Schliemann Exhibition at the South Kensington Museum in the early summer of 1879.

Just as the big clock had clanged out twelve, I heard the high vivacious voices and laughter of children sounding down the corridor.

At that moment a gentleman entered, two little girls clinging to his hands, and as I caught sight of the tall, slim figure, with the clean-shaven, delicate, refined face, I said to myself, '*That's* Lewis Carroll.' He stood for a moment, head erect, glancing swiftly over the room, then bending down, whispered something to one of the children; she, after a moment's pause, pointed straight at me.

Dropping their hands he came forward, and with that winning smile of his that utterly banished the oppressive sense of the Oxford don, said simply, 'I am Mr Dodgson; I was to meet you, I think?' To which I as frankly smiled and said, 'How did you know me so soon?'

'My little friend found you. I told her I had come to meet a young lady who knew fairies, and she fixed on you at once. But, *I* knew you before she spoke.'[20]

The Schliemann Exhibition of the gold of Troy was a likely venue. Dodgson was a regular visitor to the Royal Academy, to the exhibitions of British artists, and to the Grosvenor Gallery. With his little girls in tow, he visited galleries as the admirer of an art in which he had little talent of his own. As a photographer, however, he had established a sufficient reputation in the 1860s to be regarded with respect by his peers. In 1864 his photographs were shown to the Queen, who commanded that he be told that she admired them very much.

Dodgson's opinions on photography appeared in a review of the Photographic Exhibition, in the *Illustrated Times* on 28 January 1860. 'The merits and demerits of photographs are, generally speaking, so entirely chemical as to leave little subject for art criticism ... The artist himself is mainly responsible in views for choice of point of view and time of day, and (occasionally) the arrangement of foreground accessories ... and in portraits, for choice of light, altitude, and grouping.' The great problem of portraits is the position of the hands. He advises the photographer to resist the temptation to arrange the hands himself. 'He generally produces the effect of the proverbial bashful young man in society who finds for the first time that his hands are an encumbrance, and cannot remember what he is in the habit of doing with them in private life.' He also deplores photographs that are mathematically correct in their arrangement.

> A common fault in point of choice of view is getting the principal object exactly into the centre, or, at all events, so near to it that the calculating faculty is at once aroused instead of the imaginative, and the spectator longs for a foot-rule to ascertain whether the picture is exactly bisected or not.

In April 1862 and July 1864, he spent holidays at Freshwater on the Isle of Wight, partly in the hope of meeting Julia Margaret Cameron and Tennyson. On the first occasion he saw very little of Tennyson and not much of Mrs Cameron, though he did meet Benjamin Jowett who was staying with the Tennysons. His three-week holiday in 1864 was more productive in enabling him to meet Mrs Cameron so that they might look at one another's photographs. Though she assured him that she was longing to see his work, the encounter was not entirely amicable. Dodgson thought that all Mrs Cameron's photographs were taken out of focus with the result that some looked picturesque and others hideous. For her part, Mrs Cameron seemed to regard her photographs as great art and made no comment on Dodgson's beyond saying that she would have liked the chance to take some of his subjects. Dodgson reported that he had merely said the same about hers. It was less a meeting of minds than a collision of egos.

Other workers in the field of art were more congenial. Sophie Anderson and her husband had a beautiful model of twelve, Elizabeth Turnbull. Dodgson bought Mrs Anderson's oil painting of the girl's head in profile against a background of lilacs. He discovered that the couple also employed her as a servant so that she would be constantly available to model. Two weeks after seeing her, in July 1865, Dodgson photographed her at Millais' house in the same pose as the picture. In return, Dodgson urged the Andersons to submit some of their paintings for the Royal Academy summer exhibition and promised to use his influence with the 'hanging committee'. He talked and wrote like a man of importance in the world of mid-Victorian art. To fulfil his promise, he approached the painter George Richmond, to whom he had been introduced and who was on the Royal Academy committee. He urged the claims of Mrs Anderson's painting *The Bath*, for which Elizabeth Turnbull had posed, but without getting it selected. The picture showed the girl with shoulder bared preparing for the bath, a subject which might have appealed less to Dodgson in the 1890s when he warned Gertrude Thomson that all partly clothed figures suggested impropriety.

A triumphant day as a photographer came to him on 14 July 1865 when at last he photographed Ellen Terry, who was by then eighteen years old and married in the previous year to the painter George Frederick Watts, thirty years her elder. He also photographed the other Terry sisters and their parents. His pursuit of the sisters had lasted almost two years. On 29 September 1863, he wrote in his diary that all his intended subjects had been available in London except the Terrys. The following year, he went to their house at 92 Stanhope Street with a letter of introduction from Tom Taylor. Mrs Terry was at home and agreed that he might take photographs in October. That autumn he persisted with his visits but there were no photographs. He called on 28 October and told stories to the younger children, returned on 20 December and was entertained by Kate Terry, then finally met Ellen – now Mrs Watts – on the following day. Ellen no longer lived at Stanhope Street but with her husband, at Little Holland House. Dodgson was invited to lunch in April and at last, in July 1865, arrived at Stanhope Street with his camera.

Ellen Terry's beauty was an enigma, as the novelist Charles Reade thought.

> Her eyes are pale, her nose rather long, her mouth nothing in particular. Complexion a delicate brickdust, her hair rather like tow. Yet somehow she is *beautiful*. Her expression *kills* any pretty face you see beside her. Her figure is lean and bony; her hand masculine in size and form. Yet she is a pattern of fawn-like grace. Whether in movement or repose, grace pervades the hussy.

But the enigma of her beauty was as nothing, in Reade's view, to the tiresome personality of the young actress.

> Soft and yielding on the surface, egotistical below ... always wanting something 'dreadful bad' today, which she does not want tomorrow, especially if you are weak enough to give it her, or get it her. Hysterical, sentimental, hard as a nail in money matters, but velvet on the surface. A creature born to please and to deceive.[21]

Such was Dodgson's angel of the London stage, a model whose pose is suffused with petulant indifference to his camera. Kate Terry, more obliging, consented to be trussed up and photographed in the Stanhope Street drawing-room under the pretext of being Andromeda. Ellen gave the distant appearance of one who does the photographer a favour by consenting to have her picture taken at all. That alone made the photo a triumph. From Ellen Terry, Dodgson endured signs of indifference that would have ended other friendships. She ignored the contents of correspondence, as well as a gift of *Alice in Wonderland*. When he called to see her she had not, apparently, bothered to get up. He forgave her everything and sympathized with her complaints of being tired. As surely as his fellow novelist and Oxford don, Charles Reade, he was bound by enchantment.

There was a memorable afternoon on 11 May 1867, when Dodgson went to an amateur benefit performance of Morton and Sullivan's

Box and Cox and Tom Taylor's *A Sheep in Wolf's Clothing* at the Adelphi. He sat with the Terrys in the stage box while the plays were performed by a cast including George Du Maurier and the luminaries of *Punch*: Tom Taylor, John Tenniel, Mark Lemon, and Hardman's friend Shirley Brooks. By 1868, he was taking the youngest Terry girls, Polly and Flo, to the Drury Lane pantomime. Yet the afternoon at the Adelphi was a parting. He was not to meet Ellen Terry again for twelve years.

In 1866 Dodgson heard that she had left Watts and was living in lodgings. At first he felt sorry for her and hoped she would continue her stage career. Like Effie Ruskin, she was almost the child victim of an unconsummated marriage. Theologically, such unions might be no marriage at all. Ellen was barely seventeen when she married a man who was not far off fifty. The break with her came when Dodgson discovered that she had eloped with the architect Edward William Godwin, by whom she was to have two children. Theology could find no excuse for that. Not only was it unseemly for Dodgson to continue the friendship, it might be imprudent. He continued to admire her from a distance on the stage and wrote about her acting in superlatives but their next meeting was not until 18 June 1879, by which time she had remarried, her husband being the actor Charles Clavering Wardell. Friendship in the intervening years had been impossible for Dodgson, who recorded that he had deliberately broken it off and then as deliberately renewed it.

During the years of estrangement, the elder sister, now Kate Terry Lewis, showed a constant affection for him. In 1867 she married a prosperous silk merchant, Arthur Lewis, and went to live among the gardens and trees of Kensington at Moray Lodge, Campden Hill. Dodgson was a frequent visitor on such occasions as the garden-party of 11 June 1869, with Millais, Tom Taylor, and Boucicault, where 350 guests were entertained by a band and an impressive variety of food and drink.

By 1879, Ellen Terry was no longer an egotistical girl in her teens but a woman of thirty-two who responded to Dodgson's kindness by getting him tickets for the theatre, receiving his awestruck little girls backstage, and helping him in the matter of his cousin Minna Quin who had ambitions to be an actress and to whom she gave an audition. In the last summer of his life, Dodgson took his guest at Eastbourne, Dolly Rivington, to Winchelsea where the famous actress was staying. His last memory of Ellen was of her next to Dolly

Rivington as the two swung in a pair of hammocks in the sunlit garden on that August afternoon.

A Sunday morning in London in the 1860s usually saw him attending F. D. Maurice's services at Vere Street Chapel. He once offered to assist at Communion when there was no one else available and so made the acquaintance of the famous heretic. Maurice took Jowett's side against Pusey in the attempted prosecution for heresy before the Vice-Chancellor at Oxford in 1863 and Dodgson corresponded with Maurice on the issue. Though Dodgson may have felt less sympathy with Maurice's attachment to Christian Socialism, his own later religious development was as critical of biblical fundamentalism as Maurice's. Another of Dodgson's friends, Frederic Harrison, who had also been brought up as a High Churchman, recalled their experience of hearing Maurice preach.

> Maurice, Coleridge, Carlyle and F. Newman, in different ways and often without intending it, would fill me with horror and shame at many passages of Scripture and many dogmas of the Church which I felt to be repugnant to morality and even to human nature. I never can forget poor dear old Maurice stammering through the story of Dinah, when that horrible chapter of Genesis came to be read in its turn.

For Harrison, Maurice's sermons 'demolished what remains of orthodoxy I had.' The effect on Dodgson was less dramatic but Maurice seems to have been a powerful influence in his later rejection of such doctrines as eternal punishment.[22]

The world of the law embraced both Dodgson's family and those he knew socially. He was wedded to a picturesque past of English law rather than to the reformist present. He still threatened young Alice Crampton playfully in 1877 with the Court of Chancery, four years after it was abolished by the Judicature Acts. In these matters, he was well informed by friends and family, including men like Russell Gurney QC, Recorder of London and Privy Councillor, and Henry Charles Hull, Conveyancing Counsel to the Court in the new Chancery Division. Hull's daughters Agnes and Jessie were among the first conquests at Eastbourne in 1877.

As he told George Denman, he had read a good deal on the subject of insanity and criminal responsibility. Medical books made up a significant proportion of Dodgson's library, some from England and others from Philadelphia. Since the M'Naghten Rules of 1843 had laid down the definition of insanity for the purposes of the criminal law, it had been a topic of unresolved debate, not least in the matter of partial insanity. It was in April 1876 that Dodgson raised with Denman a case over which his friend had presided. Rose Ann Rue, a seventeen-year-old servant, had been sentenced to penal servitude for life at Taunton Assizes for killing a child. Dodgson was familiar with Henry Maudsley's *Responsibility in Mental Disease*, which had appeared in 1874. He drew Denman's attention to Maudsley's discussion of partial insanity, in case that had not been considered. Lunacy and the law, thanks to Uncle Skeffington, remained associated in Dodgson's mind. Indeed, anyone who had read the unedifying saga of Mad Windham and Miss Willoughby in the daily press might be thought to have a grounding in the subject.[23]

George Denman admired *Phantasmagoria*, whose verses, he told Dodgson, he had read repeatedly and 'enjoyed many a hearty laugh, and something like a cry or two.' The Denman daughters, Edith and Grace, had been Dodgson's models in the 1860s and he remained on affectionate terms with them. Whether the suggestion was correct that he was in love with Edith Denman in the late 1870s, when she was in her early twenties, is something only Dodgson knew. The difference in their ages might have seemed perilously close to that between Ellen Terry and G. F. Watts, though many such marriages had been a success. Dodgson held the traditional Christian view that marriage, other than for love of the other party beyond anything but the love of God, was a form of blasphemy. In 1885 he also told Tommy Bowles that while it might not be a lady's first duty to look beautiful, a wife's duty was to make the home pleasant and beautiful. Since she was an element in the home, her role was, 'still to be neat, still to be dressed.'[24]

A trial which preoccupied Dodgson in the early 1870s and was thought to be connected with *The Hunting of the Snark* was the Tichborne Case. Following the collapse of his civil action as claimant in 1871–2, Arthur Orton was indicted as an impostor in 1873 for having claimed falsely to be the missing baronet Sir Roger Tichborne, heir to the Tichborne estates. Dodgson's interest was sufficient for him to have got news of Orton's conviction by telegram at Christ Church on 28 February 1874. It seemed that the barrister in *The Hunting of the Snark* was a caricature, at least in Holiday's illustration, of Orton's counsel, Edward Vaughan Kenealy. Dodgson, with his facility for anagrams, told the future Dean of Christ Church, Francis Paget, that

'Edward Vaughan Kenealy' was an anagram for 'Ah! We dread an ugly knave!' He had worked it out in bed, another device for keeping evil thoughts and desires at bay while he lay sleepless.[25]

*

It was small wonder that gaps began to appear in his diary or that in June 1874 he could only manage a summary of a few pages to record what had happened in the previous three months. His days in London were crowded. A morning and afternoon of photography would be followed by an evening at the theatre before he returned to his camera next day. Lunches with child-friends or their families, treats and trips, dinner and amateur theatricals with the MacDonalds or the gossip and tall tales of Rossetti and his circle, the stories in and out of court, followed one another in his recollections. For Dodgson, as the man about town, even travel was an adjunct rather than an interruption of his pleasures.

Isa Bowman recalled him as a meticulous traveller, one who used to 'map out exactly every minute of the time we were to take.' Arrangements for the journey were made down to the last detail, including his usual plans for avoiding unnecessary cab fares when luggage could be wheeled. He always carried two purses, each divided into a number of compartments, so that the exact amount of money required for train fares, cabs, porters, newspapers and refreshments might be easily and separately accommodated. Others might find this obsessive but strict accounting even for trivial sums was the most natural thing in the world to Archdeacon Dodgson's family.[26] His fear of being cheated by cabmen led him to inquire in advance the correct fare in unfamiliar towns. As he remarked in 1872, travellers were likely to be 'done' by cabmen in towns that were unfamiliar to them.

The object of his meticulous preparations, however, was never in doubt.

> Three little maidens weary of the rail,
> Three pairs of little ears listening to a tale,
> Three little hands held out in readiness,
> For three little puzzles very hard to guess.
> Three pairs of little eyes, open wonder-wide,

At three little scissors laying side by side.
Three little mouths that thanked an unknown Friend,
For one little book, he undertook to send.
Though whether they'll remember a friend, or book, or day –
In three little weeks is very hard to say.[27]

Such was the self-portrait of Dodgson the railway traveller of
1869 in 'To Three Puzzled Little Girls from the Author', the inscription in a copy of *Alice in Wonderland* addressed to the 'Misses Drury',
Minnie, Ella and Emmie. The encounter, on a train to Sandhurst
where Dodgson found himself sharing a carriage with the children
and their nurse, typified many others. The nurse was telling a story
to the children. Self-conscious in a stranger's presence, she stopped.
To the delight of the little girls he finished the story. Then he took
off his grey and black cotton gloves and produced from his bag three
puzzles for them. Then came the three pairs of scissors for cutting
out patterns. Finally, as the train slowed down, he promised to send
them the book he had written, *Alice in Wonderland*.

By the time the book had arrived, and Mrs Drury had thanked
him, and Dodgson had called, photographed and entertained the girls,
they were his friends for life. However odd the rest of the world
might think it, the family remembered only kindness, visits to theatres,
pantomimes and galleries.

Even when the encounter in a railway carriage did not lead to
an exchange of names, he was known to write to those whom he
thought might be the parents of the children and ask for photographs of the girls, since he was a collector of such items and
an amateur photographer. It was a matter in which he felt no self-
consciousness.[28]

He travelled meticulously, provided with everything that he might
need. As if in anticipation of *Through the Looking-Glass*, the travelling
bag of the 1860s with its intriguing contents also held his 'in statu
quo' chess set, designed so that the pieces remained in place despite
the vibration of the train, enabling him to challenge any adult companion to a game.

A good many of his letters written to children in these years were
calculatedly odd and perhaps some appeared odd without calculation.
As an excuse for not coming to see the Drury sisters he forwarded
a letter written by himself to himself commanding him to attend a
Buckingham Palace garden party and signed 'Victoria R.' At other

times, as his mind turned to the story of *Sylvie and Bruno*, he signed letters to children as their 'affectionate little fairy friend, Sylvie.' There was also a most interesting distinction between letters in which he was Lewis Carroll and those in which he was C. L. Dodgson. Writing in 1870 to Mary Marshal, another little girl whom he had met on a train, he was C. L. Dodgson writing on behalf of Mr Lewis Carroll. Writing to Magdalen Millard in 1875, there were two other people in the room with him who had both asked to be allowed to sign the letter, which they did, as 'Lewis Carroll' and 'C. L. Dodgson'. For other correspondents, like Gertrude Chataway who was to be his 'child-friend' for the rest of her life, 'even when your hair is grey,' the magic circle opened and he signed himself as her loving friend, 'Lewis Carroll.' In 1874, he feared that Edith Jebb at sixteen had ceased to be a child and sent her father his love to daughters who were not too old. Yet a few, like Gertrude Chataway, were immune to this affliction of growing up.[29]

*

On 24 June 1867, Dodgson went to the Taylorian teacher of French at Oxford for his fourth French lesson, hoping to visit Paris for the International Exhibition. On 11 July his passport arrived from London. By that time, however, he had heard that his friend Henry Parry Liddon was free to accompany him. Their principal destination was not Paris but Moscow. Liddon had suggested Russia to him and found that Dodgson was very much taken with the idea. Next day, Dodgson left Christ Church for Dover, where the two men met.

As he remarked, it was an ambitious journey for one who had never left England and who, indeed, was never to do so again. The appeal of the Orthodox and Catholic churches, which Liddon visited and Dodgson for the most part avoided, may have prompted Liddon's suggestion that they should travel east. Dodgson was a High Churchman by belief but Liddon was of the type known as Ritualist and soon to be described as Anglo-Catholic. Cuddesdon theological college near Oxford, of which Liddon had been Vice-Principal, was still regarded as a Tractarian seminary, dangerously sympathetic to Rome. Perhaps the drama and theatricality of Ritualism made up for his vow never to enter a theatre.

The two friends travelled to Calais, Brussels, Cologne and Berlin, where they spent several days. Both kept journals of the expedition. There was time to visit Cologne cathedral, where Liddon noticed that Dodgson was overcome by the beauty of its interior.

> I found him leaning against the rails of the Choir, and sobbing like a child. When the Verger came to show us over the chapels, he got out of the way. He said he could not bear the harsh voice of the man in the presence of so much beauty.

Recollecting the experience in tranquillity, Dodgson described Cologne cathedral as 'the most beautiful of all churches I have ever seen, or can imagine. If one could imagine the spirit of devotion embodied in any material form, it would be in such a building.'[30]

They took an overnight train from Cologne to Berlin with seats that pulled out to make two beds. Dodgson found it comfortable. 'I am sorry to say Liddon did not sleep.' From the Hotel de Russie they visited the museums and churches near the Unter den Linden. The approach to the royal palace reminded Dodgson of the streets of Whitby. They rode on the top of an omnibus to the palace and grounds of Charlottenburg, and on Saturday morning went to the Jewish Synagogue, which Dodgson found 'perfectly novel to me, & most interesting.' The afternoon was spent in the gardens and palaces of Potsdam, the 'gem' of Sans Souci and the New Palace which had been built in the style of an English manor house for Victoria's eldest daughter on her marriage to the Crown Prince, Friedrich Wilhelm. 'The amount of art lavished on the whole region of Potsdam is marvellous,' Dodgson wrote.[31]

They left Berlin for St Petersburg by way of Danzig and Königsberg. Most English travellers in the heat of European summer and at the mercy of the local water supply were overtaken at some point by diarrhoea or enteritis. Few were conscientious enough to keep an account of their afflictions. Liddon was struck down on arrival at Königsberg, the symptoms so alarming that Dodgson called a doctor during the night. An application of blotting-paper soaked in mustard and the consumption of morphine powder and camomile tea put the patient right by next day. Since Liddon refused to enter a theatre, Dodgson went alone. He thought the acting quite good, the singing better, though he understood little of the plot.

At St Petersburg, where they arrived on 27 July, it was Dodgson's turn to be briefly incapacitated. He was enthusiastic over the architecture of the imperial capital, the wide streets and handsome buildings, the galleries of the Hermitage, and the gardens of the Peterhof, which they visited by taking a steamer down the Gulf of Finland. The gorgeousness of the Orthodox ceremonial, however, made him long for the 'plain, simple' service of the Church of England. The interior of the Cathedral Church was 'magnificent rather than beautiful' and he watched without enthusiasm a woman handing a soldier money for the offertory box by St Peter's picture before praying for her sick child. 'One could almost read in her worn, anxious face, that she believed what she was doing would in some way propitiate St Peter to help her child.'[32]

They travelled to Moscow on 2 August. Dodgson was impressed by the 'conjuring trick' performed by the guard who revolved the backs of their seats and turned them into beds. Moscow had a distorted beauty, like the city of a dream.

We gave 5 or 6 hours to a stroll through this wonderful city, a city of white & green roofs, of conical towers that rise one out of another like a fore-shortened telescope; of bulging gilded domes, in which you see as in a looking-glass, distorted pictures of the city; of churches which look, outside, like bunches of variegated cactus (some branches crowned with green prickly buds, others with blue, & others with red & white), & which, inside, are hung all round with Eikons and lamps, & lined with illuminated pictures up to the very roof; & finally of pavement that goes up & down like a ploughed field, & droshky-drivers who insist on being paid 30 per cent extra today, 'because it is the Empress' birthday.'[33]

They met members of the English community, attended a Russian wedding, visited the Petrovski monastery and St Basil's cathedral. On 7 August, they took the train to Nijni Novgorod, with its Tartar mosque and markets. Dodgson went alone to 'a burlesque of Aladdin and his lamp.' The journey was not without its difficulties. The train broke down and they had to walk a mile through heavy rain to reach the town.

Liddon showed a certain irritability with his companion. They were almost stranded at Verviers 'owing to Dodgson's delay about the tickets.' 'Spent the greatest part of the morning [in Berlin] in going about to shop for photographs for Dodgson ... After church a long argument with Dodgson ... Dodgson did not get up until 9.30 ... A great argument with Dodgson on the character of Russian religion – he thought it too external ... Our whole morning was lost. Dodgson did not get up until 9.30 . . . I had a warm argument with Dodgson about Prayers for the Departed . . .' Dodgson insisted on sketching a Russian cottage, 'but in this was lost ¾ of an hour . . .' Visiting shops in search of photographs and toys, which Dodgson did habitually, was evidently not Liddon's idea of time well spent.[34]

They returned to St Petersburg and from there travelled to Warsaw on 28 August. At Breslau they found the playground of a girls' school, 'a very tempting field for a photographic camera,' Dodgson wrote wistfully. Though he had brought his telescope, his camera had been left in England. He thought the girls appealing. 'After the Russian children, whose type of face is ugly as a rule, and plain as an exception, it is quite a relief to get back among the Germans with their large eyes and delicate features.'[35]

At Dresden there was another disagreement. Dodgson went with Liddon to the Catholic church but announced that it was 'like a Concert-room' and left. There were three Protestant churches but he suspected that at least two were Dissenting and so went to none of their services on Sunday.

The two men reached Ems, crossed the Rhine and travelled on to Paris. Dodgson went alone to the Théâtre Vaudeville and an open-air concert in the Champs Elysées. He liked Paris with its sense of elegance and design and was not surprised that its inhabitants should think London 'triste.' On 14 September he was back in England. He found the tour instructive and occasionally amusing. Though overwhelmed by the beauty of Cologne cathedral, his comments on the journey in general were appreciative but commonplace. It seemed to have made no great impression on him and he showed no wish to go abroad again. A consequence of experiencing what he regarded as the excessive ceremonial of Orthodox ritual, and Liddon's more favourable response to it, was his conclusion that he was not truly a High Churchman in the fashionable sense. He also told Liddon that he objected to the use of the term 'Catholic' when applied to the Church of England because it 'connected us with Rome.' Liddon, on the other hand, showed little objection to either the Orthodox religion or to Roman Catholicism in those places where the Church of England was not to be found.

*

There was one event in the 1860s which affected him more than any other. At Christ Church on 21 June 1868, Dodgson had just finished marking papers for Moderations, sitting up until 4 a.m. to complete the task. He was making plans for the publication of *Phantasmagoria*. He was also completing arrangements to move into rooms vacated by Lord Bute in the north-west corner of the Great Quadrangle, overlooking St Aldate's. He hoped to have alterations made there and to find space for a photographic studio. Before this he had been renting a studio in a tradesman's yard for £6 a year.

On 22 June, while occupied with these matters, he received a message that his father had died the previous evening. 'The greatest blow that has ever fallen on my life,' he told Edith Rix shortly before his own death, the worse for being so abrupt and unexpected. Archdeacon Dodgson's death, like that of his wife, came with little warning. He was sixty-eight and had been mildly indisposed, though not sufficiently to prevent him performing his duties. His daughters were caring for him and had not thought the symptoms alarming enough to alert their brother. Dodgson left Christ Church at once for Croft, abruptly and unwillingly succeeding as the head of his family.[36]

Croft Rectory, the scene of so much family happiness and jollity in the past twenty-five years, was suddenly a house of mourning, as he described it to his child-friend Edith Rix many years later.

> In those solemn days, when we used to steal, one by one, into the darkened room, to take yet another look at the dear calm face, and to pray for strength, the one feature in the room that I remember was a framed text, illuminated by one of my sisters, 'Then are they glad because they are at rest; and so He bringeth them into the haven where they would be!' That text will always have, for me, a sadness and a sweetness of its own.

The rector's last years had been marked by his pamphlet war with Dr Goode, Dean of Ripon, on the Catholic versus Evangelical claims of the Church of England. Yet he had earned tributes during his lifetime from the Churchwardens of Daresbury, where he had revitalized the little church and taken the gospel to the bargees and navvies. He was remembered more than sixty years later, in the *Northern Echo* of 5 January 1932, as a philanthropist who had been the moving spirit behind Croft National School. These survivors saw him, as his sermons suggest that he saw himself, as enlightened and progressive, not least by holding firm to religious observances which promoted the interests of the new working class.

Grief was tempered by the need to make arrangements for his family. The rectory must be vacated. A new incumbent was waiting, though protesting there was 'no hurry.' In this, Dodgson's qualities as businessman and lawyer *manqué* served him well. He had seven unmarried sisters, the eldest forty, the youngest twenty-five. There was also Aunt Lucy who kept house for Archdeacon Dodgson as a widower. Dodgson spent seven weeks at Croft, clearing the house, and arranging the sale of his father's effects. Worst of all, the undertakers had been given a free hand. Their bill was so enormous that Dodgson had difficulty in proving the will in Doctors' Commons. Despite all this, by 1 November, the family had a new home.[37]

Dodgson had taken a lease on 'The Chestnuts' at Guildford, a detached house built in 1860 in the Georgian style. He went to Guildford on 14 August and met Walter Anderson, the husband of Sophie Anderson, the painter of Elizabeth Turnbull, also in search of a house. The two men looked at property, finding none to compare with this. It stood near Guildford Castle, close to the High Road. It was on four storeys and had eight bedrooms, none too many for Christmas or family gatherings. On occasion, Dodgson was obliged to lodge elsewhere, with friends or at hotels like the White Lion and the White Hart.

Guildford had much to be said for it. To act at Christ Church as head of the family, dealing with the financial affairs of his siblings at Croft, would have been impractical. Guildford could be reached easily by train from Oxford via Reading. It was convenient for London and the south coast. 'The Chestnuts' was to be the scene of parties, charades and amateur theatricals for family and friends. Little girls like Isabel and Maud Standen came there to be photographed.

The home life of the family, preserved after his mother's death by the arrival of Aunt Lucy, seemed safe for another generation. Its older members died, full of years. Dodgson was present at Guildford to comfort Aunt Lucy's last hours in 1880. Aunt Margaret had died in 1869, Aunt Henrietta in 1872, and Aunt Caroline, Hassard Dodgson's wife, three years later. When his cousin and godson, Charlie Wilcox, then twenty-two, was dying of tuberculosis in 1874, Dodgson helped to nurse him at Guildford for several weeks, taking his turn to sit up with the young man at night. He also stayed with the Wilcoxes at Sandown, when Charlie was well enough to travel, but was back at Oxford when the young man died in November.

Dodgson presided over leases on properties in which his sisters' funds were invested, the problem of unsatisfactory tenants, the investments in shipping. He acquired nephews and nieces from the marriages of his sister Mary and from that of his brother Wilfred to Alice Donkin. By 1870, when his sister Mary's first son was born, Stuart Dodgson Collingwood, he already had five godchildren and told Mary that though he was prepared to act as godchild in this instance, his consent was now to be regarded as an exception.

Of the elder generation, Uncle Hassard became Master in the Court of Common Pleas in 1872, when nearly seventy, and Dodgson went to visit him in his new quarters on 10 January. Indeed, Hassard survived until 1884, dying at eighty-one.

In 1865 Uncle Skeffington moved to 101 Onslow Square. His nephew visited him frequently and introduced him to the painter George Sant, whose pictures Skeffington purchased. In January 1869, Dodgson was in London, staying with Skeffington while working with Hassard and Wilfred on the executors' accounts of his father's estate. That evening Hassard came to dinner in Onslow Square, accompanied by Dodgson's brothers, Wilfred and Edwin. After dinner Skeffington put on an exhibition of an early form of electric lighting, using 'Geissler's Tubes'.

Skeffington's last years were a chapter of accidents. In August 1871 he was injured by a blow to the head when someone threw a stone at the train in which he was travelling. Dodgson escorted him to Scotland in September, presumably to recuperate, but Skeffington was still an invalid in January. By June he seemed better, Dodgson dined with him at the Clarendon Hotel and in Onslow Square. Almost a year later, in May 1873, Dodgson received a message that Skeffington had been injured at Salisbury. He left Oxford at once and reached the White Hart in Salisbury to be told that his uncle had been struck again, this time by a lunatic. Sir James Paget and a surgeon were on hand and it seemed that Skeffington was improving. Dodgson returned to Christ Church, only to receive a telegram next day, warning him that his uncle was worse. He and Paget set out for Salisbury at once, as did Aunt Lucy and Fanny, but arrived a few minutes after Skeffington died.

With the deaths of his uncles, the remaining lawyers in the family were James Hume Dodgson, Hassard's son who was now a partner in a firm of solicitors, and Charles Pollock, Baron of the Court of

Exchequer, who had married Dodgson's cousin Amy, another of Hassard's children. Charles Pollock also became a founder of the *Law Quarterly Review*. Dodgson was a visitor to Oxford Assizes and, in February 1877, accompanied Charles Pollock and his brother judge to the Taylorian and All Souls, as guests of the Vice-Chancellor at dinner.

In Dodgson's friendships, as well as in his family, the law was as important as in his most famous writings. His Oxford friend Reginald Southey, with whom he learnt photography in the 1850s, was, like Uncle Skeffington, a Commissioner-in-Lunacy as well as a physician. His friend and adviser James Wilkes was also a Commissioner. He remained on close terms with Lord Denman, the High Court judge whose father was Lord Chief Justice. He was a friend of Russell Gurney, the Recorder of London; and a fellow lodger during East-bourne holidays was Samuel Waddy, Recorder of Sheffield and counsel for the Salvation Army leader William Branwell Booth, who was acquitted at the trial of W. T. Stead and others, following the white slavery scandals of 1885. Christ Church lawyers of Dodgson's acquaintance included George Ward Hunt, Bencher of the Inner Temple, who became Chancellor of the Exchequer in Gladstone's cabinet in 1868, and Roundell Palmer, who was to be the reforming Lord Chancellor Selborne. Among his other friends, to whom he sent puzzles for solution, was Sir Hardinge Giffard, the first counsel for Governor Eyre of Jamaica in the attempted prosecution for murder, second counsel for the Tichborne claimant and, as Lord Chancellor Halsbury, the future author of *Halsbury's Laws of England*.

These associations ran parallel in Dodgson's middle years with the biggest upheaval in the English legal system since the seventeenth century and, in some respects, since the reign of Edward I. Small wonder that *Alice in Wonderland* had the trial of the mouse by Old Fury, and that of the Knave of Hearts, that *Through the Looking-Glass* had the case of the King's Messenger, or that a section of *The Hunting of the Snark* was taken up by 'The Barrister's Dream.' Scattered throughout his works were passing references, no less famous for that.

> 'In my youth,' said his father, 'I took to the law,
>   And argued each case with my wife;
> And the muscular strength, which it gave to my jaw,
>   Has lasted the rest of my life.'

To Dodgson, even logic was the ideal of platonic forensic argument, where a case might be proved as absolutely as in mathematics but without the sordid realities of murder, rape, assault or theft in the proceedings. These he had watched in court and studied at second-hand in the volumes of William Acton on prostitution and Henry Mayhew on the criminal underworld. Conversely, his contemporary, the logician and inventor of the 'reasoning machine or logical abacus, adapted to show the working of Boole's logic in a half mechanical manner,' W. S. Jevons, cited in *The Principles of Science* the role of the barrister as that of the reasoner who adapts logic to reality.[38]

Uncle Skeffington had also encouraged his nephew to share his enthusiasm for gadgets, inventions and scientific curiosities. Finally, in his last years, he had provided the means for one of Dodgson's happiest and most fruitful encounters. It occurred on 17 August 1868, less than a month after Archdeacon Dodgson's death. Dodgson was staying at Uncle Skeffington's house in Onslow Square with his sister Fanny and Aunt Lucy. A little girl was playing in one of the nearby back gardens while Dodgson paced up and down Skeffington's strip of lawn, hands clasped behind him. Hearing the child called 'Alice', he asked her if that was her name, adding that he was very fond of Alices.

Alice Raikes was, unknown to him at this point, another cousin. 'Would you like to see something that is rather puzzling?' he asked. He led the little girl to a room full of furniture with a tall mirror across one corner. He gave her an orange and asked her which hand she was holding it in. Alice Raikes told him that it was the right hand. He then asked her to look in the mirror and tell him again on which side the orange was. The left hand, she said, feeling 'perplexed'. Dodgson asked her to explain the contradiction and the child said, 'If I was on the *other* side of the glass, wouldn't the orange still be in my right hand?' Dodgson laughed and said, 'Well done, little Alice. The best answer I've had yet.'[39]

Three years later, his fictional Alice passed through the looking-glass to the world beyond. Alice Raikes herself passed into the ranks of child-friends.

*

As his middle years passed, Dodgson's self-searching commitment to God's service in his New Year's Eve diary became briefer and less conscience stricken. By 1869 he simply hoped that he might do more than he had yet done. The precise nature of his allegiance to the Church of England and its doctrines was more apt to be modified than his loyalty to the Conservative party. He had a parliamentary vote in Oxford, as a member of the University, and another in Guildford as leaseholder and ratepayer. He made the effort to travel to Guildford in order to cast this second vote for the successful Conservative candidate, as the constituency abandoned its Liberal preference. As an amateur in politics, Dodgson the insomniac lay awake puzzling out anagrams for Disraeli and Gladstone. It was the limit of his practical assistance.[40]

Charity, in the sense of giving money, was something with which Dodgson was seldom at ease. There were undeserving poor and dishonest beggars whose only disability was their idleness. He was not callous or mean but he was careful. On 24 January 1867, in the *Pall Mall Gazette*, he argued for a National Philanthropic Institution. Those who wished to give money to charity would send it to this body for 'the objects designated.' The organization would then hand over the donation to an appropriate charity 'without deduction.' In return, the Institution would report on the charities to their benefactors.

In many respects, however, Dodgson was not the typical Conservative of the 1870s. He grew to dislike most forms of sport which involved the killing of animals. Though he had never tried, like Robert Browning, to live as a vegetarian, he advocated the painless killing of animals for human food. He wrote of his success in catching and setting free a sparrow trapped in his room and the bird's uncanny trust in him. Edith Litton, a child-friend, attributed her own love of animals to his example. In fantasy he was cruel, feeding a white cat ink to turn it black. In reality he found it quite natural to write a letter of commiseration to a friend whose dog had just died. 'I am very sorry to hear of your sad loss. Well, you have certainly given to *one* of God's creatures a *very* happy life through a good many years – a pleasant thing to remember.' When mice invaded his Christ Church rooms, he devised a trap that caught them alive. The compartment could then be plunged in water and the mice drowned instantly, rather than having 'an agonized struggle on the surface.' By 1893 he was working on a pamphlet, 'The Morality of Sport', analysing the arguments for and against fox-hunting, a sport for which he never expressed approval.[41]

In his middle years, Dodgson's routine became well-established. After work in the morning, or perhaps a little photography in the summer, there would be a walk in the afternoon with a child-friend or a colleague, dinner in Hall, followed by Common Room, perhaps conversation with a guest in his rooms, then more work and bed. He did not sleep well, perhaps because puzzling over mathematics and anagrams, aided by the use of an ingenious invention of his own for taking notes in the dark, and all the mental acrobatics and pillow problems designed to keep evil thoughts and desires at bay, actually warded off sleep. His nephew's account strongly suggests this.

> Like most men who systematically overtax their brains, he was a poor sleeper. He would sometimes go through a whole book of Euclid in bed; he was so familiar with the bookwork that he could actually see the figures before him in the dark, and did not confuse the letters, which is perhaps even more remarkable.[42]

As though in search of further prescriptions to ensure insomnia, he corresponded with the poet C. S. Calverley in November 1872 as to the possibility of reducing well-known poems to acrostics, 'and making a collection of them to hoax the public.' Calverley replied that he had already thought of this but had been deterred by the complexity of the task. Therefore, he had told two girls that Gray had already written his famous *Elegy* in the form of acrostics and offered 'a small pecuniary reward' to whichever girl could discover them in half an hour, thus saving himself the labour.[43]

In general, Dodgson refused to accept invitations for lunch, except from Prince Leopold or his former child-friend Lady Wolmer and her kind, nor did he accept invitations for Sundays. Eventually he declined all invitations, or so he said. When the summer came, he found it impossible to work in Christ Church and began a routine of seaside holidays, settling on Eastbourne in 1877 and spending weeks or months there every year for the rest of his life.

He still consulted specialists about his family's collective speech impediment. James Hunt the speech therapist died in 1869 and Dodgson thereafter sought the advice of Hunt's brother-in-law, Henry Rivers. It was Rivers whom he told in 1874 that six of his seven sisters also stammered to varying degrees. Two years later he was much improved, able to get through family prayers without a single hitch. He also did a good deal for himself, continuing his practice of reading aloud a scene of Shakespeare every day.

In 1871, as he approached his fortieth birthday, Dodgson's correspondents noticed a vivid change in his style. It was not in the language but in the colour of the ink. He had always written in black ink. Now his letters and manuscripts blossomed into purple. Just short of forty, it seemed he was embarking on a new intellectual and artistic freedom, a purple period as significant as any painter's. It was to last for twenty years until, in 1891, the black ink returned as a portent of what lay ahead.

9

The Man of Letters

To the world at large, the ten years from 1869 to 1879 showed Dodgson at his most productive. *Phantasmagoria, Through the Looking-Glass, The Hunting of the Snark, Euclid and his Modern Rivals*, were accompanied by the collection of his Oxford pamphlets under the title of *Notes by an Oxford Chiel*. All but the last of these were published by Macmillan. He was also at work on his sprawling and moralistic fairy-tale *Sylvie and Bruno*, the first fragment of which appeared in *Aunt Judy's Magazine* in 1867. Moreover, as Warren Weaver calculated, he produced some two hundred little pamphlets during his life, many of them in this period. About sixty of the total were concerned with mathematics or logic, thirty with puzzles, fifty with quarrels or contentions at Christ Church, fifty more on miscellaneous topics. These were also the years of his most intense social activity, a dedication to the photographing of young girls, who wore less and less as the years passed, and his discovery of the summer pleasures of Eastbourne.

So far as his major publications were concerned, relations with Macmillan were amicable but exacting in some of his personal demands on the firm. In 1870, he hoped that Alexander Macmillan might solve the problem of the youngest Dodgson brother, Edwin, by taking him on as a clerk and then making him a partner. He also expected the firm to run errands for him and he would write or telegraph from Oxford commanding the purchase of tickets from the box-office of such theatres as the Adelphi or the Globe, almost always in the stalls, never behind the conductor of the orchestra, whose waving arms impeded his view. On one occasion, for which he drew a sketch-map of the theatre, the seats were to be in the upper circle

so that his little girls should have a good view of the Adelphi pantomime. The boy who went for the tickets was to be given a shilling,
unless he was Macmillan's son, in which case he was to get nothing.

In April 1889, Dodgson asked Macmillan to note certain seats
which were not suitable for him and also to leave the tickets for him
to collect at an address in the Strand. By 1893, he insisted that he
must be in the front row of the stalls, on the right-hand side, because
of the deafness in his right ear. For good measure, Macmillan was
also to send Dodgson's watches for repair and make sure they were
fetched by a reliable person.

For all that, Dodgson proved himself adept in acquiring a knowledge of the production and marketing of his books. Indeed, on one
occasion he undertook to see through the press a children's book by
W. W. Follett Synge, a friend first met at Guildford and then at
Eastbourne. His correspondence with Macmillan showed him to have
a good sense of the problems of copyright as applied to foreign
editions and to dramatizations, as well as the danger offered by imita-
tions of his work. In the production of a book he watched keenly
for the width of the margins and the quality of the blocks in each
printing, as well as being alert to problems in translation. He was
acutely conscious of such matters as the importance of the Christmas
market, his diaries for November and December 1893 being filled
with forebodings that the withdrawal of a shoddy reprint of *Through
the Looking-Glass* would mean that a new impression, as well as the
first printing of *Sylvie and Bruno Concluded*, would miss the most lucra-
tive season for sales. Twenty-six Decembers before, he was already
pressing Macmillan for Christmas sales figures and the possibility of
getting *Alice in Wonderland* into such 'Xmas Books' articles as that of
the *Saturday Review*.

Dodgson had first wanted *The Hunting of the Snark* to catch the
Christmas market in 1875 but the poem itself was not even complete
in October and it would take the block-maker three months to cut
the blocks for the illustrations. In January 1876, Dodgson was still
writing and still absorbed in the positioning of illustrations in the
book, pressing his suggested innovation of having the title of so slim
a volume lengthways down the spine. Since it was to be an Easter,
rather than a Christmas book, he thought 1 April would be a suitable
publication date.

Such dealings with Macmillan were no more free of demands or
complaints than his collaboration with the artists who illustrated his

books. Charles Morgan, in his history of the House of Macmillan, aptly described Dodgson's vigilance, noticing errors in the production of his books 'as an old lady feels draughts. Uneven inking, cropped margins, irregular levels of opposite pages – he missed nothing.' Apart from a perfectionism in the production of his books, he protested that his letters were not being answered; he complained of delays in payment, and of the division of the profits on *Alice in Wonderland* and *Through the Looking-Glass*; he declined to have his warehoused books and wood-blocks insured by Macmillan, believing he could get better rates from a general insurance company. In April 1871 he told Macmillan bluntly that overseas sales were resulting in a loss to himself but a profit to the publisher. While not wishing to write for money alone, he could not afford to make a loss on the books. There was no loss, however, and by 24 June 1890 he admitted that his sales had become a respectable source of revenue. Even so, he argued that he should now get better terms because the financial demands made upon him by his family were enormous. Macmillan refused and stuck to the agreement.

Seven years earlier, in 1883, Dodgson had refused to comply with the system of discounts to booksellers, insisting that the agreement for publication allowed his books to be supplied to the trade only at a fixed price. In this he appeared to anticipate the Net Book Agreement of 1900. He, as author, had taken the financial risk of publication. Why, then, should the bookseller get 37 per cent of the sale price, the publisher 11 per cent and the author who paid all the costs of the book less than 20 per cent, the remainder being the cost of production? Dodgson, the entrepreneur who might lose everything, was getting half the return of the bookseller as parasite.

On 4 August 1883, a letter in the *Bookseller* on 'Authors as Dictators' and signed by 'A Firm of London Booksellers' maintained that it would be impossible to abolish discounts for certain authors and not for others. If Dodgson insisted on refusing a discount, then 'rather than buy on the terms Mr Lewis Carroll offers, the trade will do well wholly to refuse to take copies of his books, new or old, so long as he adheres to the terms he has just announced to the trade for their delectation and delight.' The magazine's editorial, however, was favourable to the abolition of the discount system and on 5 September the original 'Firm of London Booksellers' insisted it did not intend a total boycott, rather they would not stock Mr Carroll's books but would order them for any customer who asked.

The last act of the drama is somewhat obscure. Dodgson's nephew and biographer, Stuart Dodgson Collingwood, recorded that Dodgson wrote a pamphlet in reply on *The Profits of Authorship* and that Macmillan published it in 1884. No copy of it is known to exist but Collingwood quotes a passage, which may be from a manuscript that was never printed. In it Dodgson deals not with the injustice to the author but the effect of the discount on the publisher, who gets less than half the bookseller's share.

> The publisher contributes about as much as the bookseller in time and bodily labour, but in mental toil and trouble a good deal more. I speak with some personal knowledge of the matter, having myself, for some twenty years, inflicted on that most patient and painstaking firm, Messrs. Macmillan and Co., about as much wear and worry as ever publishers have lived through. The day when they undertake a book for me is a *dies nefastus* for them. From that day till the book is out – an interval of some two or three years on an average – there is no pause in 'the pelting of the pitiless storm' of directions and questions on every conceivable detail. To say that every question gets a courteous and thoughtful reply – that they are still outside a lunatic asylum – and that they still regard me with some degree of charity – is to speak volumes in praise of their good temper and of their health, bodily and mental. I think the publisher's claim on the profits is on the whole stronger than the bookseller's.[1]

Whatever the merits of Dodgson's case against discounts and however influential his efforts as a best-selling author in bringing closer a Net Book Agreement, the passage is at least an affectionate and perhaps apologetic tribute to Alexander Macmillan from one of his more difficult authors.

*

No other book of Dodgson's ever rivalled the two adventures of Alice, either in quality or popularity. Yet a good many readers, like Dante Gabriel Rossetti, had found the greatest charm of those two stories in their verse parodies. In March 1876 there appeared Dodgson's finest poem, *The Hunting of the Snark*, illustrated by his friend Henry Holiday. It represented a last flaring brilliance before Carrolingian genius dwindled to a mere sparkle of Dodgsonian cleverness.

He had gone to Guildford on 17 July 1874 to help with the nursing of his godson Charlie Wilcox. He took his turn to sit up with the young man and on the next day left the sick room to walk over the downs. A single detached line of verse came into his mind, a gift from heaven or the subconscious mind. 'For the Snark *was* a Boojum, you see.' Thirteen years later, he wrote simply, 'I knew not what it meant then, I know not what it means now; but I wrote it down: and some time afterwards, the rest of the stanza occurred to me, that being its last line: and so by degrees, at odd moments during the next year or two, the rest of the poem pieced itself together, that being its last stanza.' 'The Ancient Mariner', another famous voyage of the doomed, began with the ill-omened encounter with an albatross. Dodgson ended with the Baker's fateful discovery of the Snark-as-Boojum in the last stanza.[2]

> In the midst of the word he was trying to say,
>   In the midst of his laughter and glee,
> He had softly and silently vanished away –
>   For the Snark *was* a Boojum, you see.

It was a book of eighty-four pages, 141 four-line stanzas. The Snark, so far as Dodgson imagined it, was a cross-breeding of the snail and the shark. The poem described a voyage by members of Victorian professions and trades to capture this elusive creature. Under the command of the Bellman, the complement consists of a Boots, a maker of Bonnets and Hoods, a Barrister, a Broker, a Banker, a Billiard-Marker, a Beaver as the only non-human member, a brave but absent-minded Baker who can only bake bridecake, and a Butcher who knows only how to kill beavers. The Baker recalls his uncle's last words of warning. Only if the Snark is, tautologously, a Snark, can he be sure of avoiding danger.

> But oh, beamish nephew, beware of the day,
>   If your Snark be a Boojum! For then
> You will softly and silently vanish away,
>   And never be met with again.

The voyage, the landing and the hunt end with the impetuous Baker last seen alone on a crag. There follows his plunge into a chasm and a cry, 'It's a Snark!' followed by, 'It's a Boo——'

Then, silence. Some fancied they heard in the air
   A weary and wandering sigh,
That sounded like '——jum!' but the others declare,
   It was only a breeze that went by.

They hunted till darkness came on, but they found
   Not a button, or feather, or mark,
By which they could tell that they stood on the ground
   Where the Baker had met with the Snark.

Not even in his stories of Alice had Dodgson contrived so rich a distillation of the macabre, while juggling non sequitur and paradox. Two halves of a statement move towards one another, apparently destined to meet in mutual sense, as two and two meet to make four. At the last moment it is evident they are on separate tracks, passing and fading into opposite distances. Yet the tone of the narrative is so confidently rational that nonsense seems at any moment about to resolve itself into plain meaning. The verse follows a vertiginous cliff-edge of reason, never quite firmly on the cliff-top, never quite falling into the abyss. The reader clutches for support at a hope of realism in a swoop of intellectual vertigo. There is sequence without apparent sense. The lolloping rhythm allows not a pause, but canters along, driving its victims onwards with the plausible logic of the asylum. Statements, advice, exhortations, beginning in the most rational manner, never transgressing rules of syntax or grammar, breathing a voice of authority and reason, end in a black hole of the mind's stellar space. So, the Butcher instructs the Beaver on cooking the Jubjub bird:

You boil it in sawdust: you salt it in glue:
   You condense it with locusts and tape:
Still keeping one principal object in view –
   To preserve its symmetrical shape.

The humour of the macabre which flavours the poem owes much to Thomas Hood as the doomed voyage is reminiscent of Coleridge. The first line identifies the protagonist as the Bellman, the one non-Victorian trade among the hunters. The most famous bellman in English literature was perhaps in Dodgson's mind because his friends the MacDonalds were preparing their production of *Macbeth* while he was writing his poem.

> It was the owl that shriek'd, the fatal bellman,
> Which gives the stern'st good-night.

The bellman's tasks, two centuries before Dodgson's poem, included calling the names of the dead in the streets, or being 'the bellman which goeth before a corpse.' In John Webster's *Duchess of Malfi*, the nature of the stern good-night is made sinisterly plain.

> I am the common Bellman,
> That usually is sent to condemn'd persons
> The night before they suffer.[3]

Such was the guide whom Dodgson had hoped to have ready to greet little girls on Christmas morning 1875.

Like a latter-day William Buckland, eating his way through the animal kingdom, the Bellman instructs his companions how to recognize the Snark not by its appearance but by its taste, 'Which is meagre and hollow, but crisp,' or by its habit of 'getting up late,' which Liddon had complained of in Dodgson's case, and then by its fondness for bathing-machines, the haunt of Dodgson and his little girls at Sandown and Eastbourne.

There is a casual intermingling of blood and death with Victorian entrepreneurial skills and sentimental comradeship. When the Butcher confesses he only knows how to kill beavers, the Baker advises the Beaver to procure a second-hand dagger-proof coat and to insure its life with 'some Office of note.' The Baker offers to hire or sell to the Beaver,

> Two excellent Policies, one Against Fire
> And one Against Damage from Hail.

> Yet still, ever after that sorrowful day,
>   Whenever the Butcher was by,
> The Beaver kept looking the opposite way,
>   And appeared unaccountably shy.

In a Carrolingian volte-face, during the Butcher's instructions on how to cook the Jubjub bird, the Beaver begins to cast 'affectionate looks' upon him and the two representatives of their species, killer and victim, walk reconciled, hand-in-hand.

The poem presents the commercial and legal world of mid-Victorian England as if in a distorting mirror. It was thought that

'Fit the Sixth: The Barrister's Dream' was a representation of the Tichborne case, though this rested principally on one of Holiday's drawings resembling Dr Kenealy, counsel for the Tichborne plaintiff. The Tichborne case was certainly a hunt for the true identity of the claimant and it dragged its way through a daunting variety of legal procedures in Chancery, Common Pleas and Queen's Bench, but there the similarity seemed to end. Dodgson saw a different parallel between his work and the complexity of the trial, writing to Mrs Horatia Gatty in February 1872 of the proposal that her son might set 'Jabberwocky' to music. 'I hope your brother has largely abridged the poem, as I should think that the whole, if sung to a slow air, would remind one more of the Tichborne trial than of any other form of entertainment now popular.'[4]

The Barrister's Dream is more elaborate than the trial of the Mouse by Cunning Old Fury or the trial of the Knave of Hearts in *Alice in Wonderland*. The Snark appears as defence counsel in the case of a pig which has been prosecuted for deserting its sty.

> The Witnesses proved, without error or flaw,
>   That the sty was deserted when found:
> And the Judge kept explaining the state of the law
>   In a soft undercurrent of sound.

At the end of the defence case, in which the Snark claims to have proved an alibi, the judge confesses that he has never summed up evidence before. He is plainly at a loss and so the Snark sums up instead. The jury, however, decline to find a verdict because they cannot spell the word and ask the Snark to act for them. How can you find a word, in a dictionary or elsewhere, that you cannot begin to spell? The Snark thereupon finds its client guilty and pronounces sentence of transportation for life, 'And *then* to be fined forty pound.' The cheers of the jury are checked, however, by the arrival of the gaoler. He informs them, 'with tears,' that the pig was dead for years before the case began.

If Dodgson was influenced by current events in the law, it seems less likely to have been the Tichborne case than the consequences of the two Judicature Acts of 1873–5, what the poem calls 'the state of the law,' which the judge has continuously to explain. 'The Barrister's Dream' was written after the main poem and two years after the Tichborne case. In 1873–5, however, reform went even further than in the 1850s by abolishing all the existing courts of law, which had evolved from the Norman period, and setting up those which were to determine the structure of the system until the present. Not only was this a matter of supreme importance to the Dodgson uncles and cousins, Charles Dodgson's own path had crossed those of men who were most closely involved. Roundell Palmer, who as Lord Selborne was Gladstone's Lord Chancellor and prime architect of the reforms, was a Christ Church man who had been one of the referees in the discussions leading up to the Christ Church, Oxford, Act of 1867, for which Dodgson bore some responsibility. Dodgson's parliamentary friend Ward Hunt, another Christ Church man, was a member of the Royal Commission whose deliberations preceded the first Judicature Act.

The abolition of the Court of Chancery and the modernization of justice were welcome. Yet where a major provision of the 1873 Judicature Act could not take effect until its successor was on the statute book there was ample scope for uncertainty and contradiction. By abolishing the appellate jurisdiction of the House of Lords, for example, the Act of 1873 proposed to abolish by far the most important function of the highest court in the land. But in February 1874 the Gladstone government, which had secured the first Judicature Act, was defeated in a general election and the second government of Disraeli was formed. Such measures as the abolition of the House of Lords' powers as an appeal court were dropped from the Judicature Act of 1875 that had been intended to implement them. When Dodgson wrote 'The Barrister's Dream', the Lords' powers had been reprieved yet still faced reform, which came eventually in the Appellate Jurisdiction Act of 1876, without yet knowing what the reform would be.

More fundamentally, the distinction between administration of law in the Courts of Exchequer, Common Pleas or King's Bench, and administration of more flexible rules of equity in the Court of Chancery was also done away with. From now on, law and equity would be administered simultaneously in all the courts, though where there was a conflict equity was to prevail. Small wonder that in Dodgson's trial neither judge, nor jury, nor witnesses feel able to discharge their duties confidently.

No less important to a later reading of the poem was a perception that 'The Barrister's Dream' reflected the realities of totalitarian justice with a precision that Dodgson can scarcely have anticipated. Victims of Soviet show trials, notably the purge trials of 1937–8, or the courts of Nazi Germany, or the United States Senate investigations of alleged Communists by Joseph McCarthy were apt to describe the experience as 'dream, nightmare, fairy-tale, or *Alice in Wonderland*,' in Elizabeth Sewell's summary. The commonest literary parallels were Franz Kafka and Lewis Carroll. Soviet defence counsel rivalled the Snark in ensuring the conviction of their clients by co-operation with the authorities.

In Senator McCarthy, the Snark would have recognized a singularly apt pupil. He was, as J. A. Wechsler described him in *The Age of Suspicion*, 'very much the judge now, handing down the decision in favour of the prosecutor (who happened to be himself).' 'The Barrister's Dream' is strictly speaking extraneous to the main action of the poem, yet it was prophetic of a future in which nightmare was to be translated into history.[5]

For the rest, psychoanalytic interpreters were able to nod significantly over such lines as 'Then the bowsprit got mixed with the rudder sometimes,' not least because in the preface Dodgson felt he had to explain the mishap as a 'painful possibility.' When the bowsprit was unshipped for painting and the time came to replace it, 'no one on board could remember which end of the ship it belonged to . . . so it generally ended in its being fastened on, anyhow, across the rudder.'

A plainer reflection of the poem's author is the Baker's inability to complete a word in the last stanza or the description of the Banker's horror on being attacked by the Bandersnatch, a reaction that might be a subconscious self-portrait of Dodgson struggling with his speech impediment.

> To the horror of all who were present that day
> He uprose in full evening dress
> And with senseless grimaces endeavoured to say
> What his tongue could no longer express.

It was just as Margaret Mayhew remembered him when words would not come.

If Dodgson's poem appeared inspired, compelling and incomparable in its deranged narrative, on publication in 1876, some sixty years later, it was also to be the stamp on his credentials as a pioneer of surrealism. Its most significant resting place was not in collections of his own work but in Henri Parisot's translation with the illustrations of Max Ernst. More generally, it showed a sinister intellectual brilliance in bending a reader's mind from contact with reality, as surely as the interrogators of a totalitarian age. In less scrupulous hands, such power was more effective than the rubber truncheon or the cattle prod.

The poem was issued in an edition of 10,000 copies. It was reprinted in December 1876 but then incorporated in Dodgson's collection *Rhyme? and Reason?* in 1883. Among its readers was John Henry Newman who admired the dedication to Gertrude Chataway with her bucket and spade almost more than the poem. He thanked Helen Church for 'the amusing specimen of imaginative nonsense' but added, 'The little book is not all of it nonsense, though amusing nonsense . . . the "Inscription to a dear child," the style of which, in words and manner, is so entirely of the School of Keble, that I think it could not have been written, had *The Christian Year* never made its appearance.'[6]

Dodgson gave his poem and its interpreters a sardonic epitaph, writing to Mary Barber at Eastbourne in the year before his death.

I meant that the Snark was a *Boojum* . . . To the best of my recollection, I had no other meaning in my mind, when I wrote it: but people have since tried to find the meanings in it. The one I like best (which I think is partly my own) is that it may be taken as an Allegory for the Pursuit of Happiness. The characteristic 'ambition' works well into this theory – and also its fondness for bathing-machines, as indicating that the pursuer of happiness, when he has exhausted all other devices, betakes himself, as a last and desperate resource, to some such wretched watering-place as Eastbourne, and hopes to find, in the tedious and depressing society of the daughters of mistresses of boarding-schools, the happiness he has failed to find elsewhere.[7]

When the poem appeared, however, his twenty-one sunlit summers at Eastbourne lay in the future. That the Snark was a creature of his subconscious mind, from which it floated to the surface as he walked across the Surrey downs on a July day in 1874, was seldom doubted by his successors. Was the poem a voyage of self-discovery, Lewis Carroll hunting the Reverend C. L. Dodgson, an echo of the two voices and two people whom Alice herself contained? The abstemious, slightly-built clerical don, who tipped the scales at 10 st 3½ lbs, fully dressed, when he weighed himself on Eastbourne pier six years later at the age of fifty, might be 'meagre and hollow but crisp.' The occasional fault of getting up late and a fondness for bathing machines seemed applicable. The Snark's final quality was ambition. Dodgson was ambitious, as a perfectionist and as one who seeks his own moral completeness, yet like all interpretations, this too would softly and silently vanish away under his own sceptical observation.

*

In the rest of his life, Dodgson wrote nothing to rival the two stories of Alice or the celebration of the Snark. Had he died in his mid-forties, posterity would have lost much of C. L. Dodgson and little of Lewis Carroll. In 1869 he had published his collection *Phantasmagoria*. Apart from the title poem, there was little of importance that had not appeared already. The title poem concerns a thoroughly modern ghost, a ghost with a cold, a believer in the rights of ghosts. There are rules of conduct for ghosts and a Ghost Inspector Kobald to enforce them. Yet the thoroughly modern spirit, with its literary agent and its knowledge of current events, sounds more like the creation of W. S. Gilbert than of Lewis Carroll. The subject is too slight and the poem too long to sustain the idea. When it was reprinted in *Rhyme? and Reason?* it was further 'padded' by extra verses to fill up blank space.

Rhyme? and Reason? appeared in 1883, a collection which reprinted *The Hunting of the Snark* and part of *Phantasmagoria* with nothing new apart from two riddles and two very short poems. His other major work of the 1870s was *Euclid and his Modern Rivals*, which appeared in 1879 with a second edition in 1885. Loyal to the certainties of Euclid, he showed their superiority to modern textbooks of geometry. At Eastbourne in 1877, he decided that his book should take the form of a dialogue, in which Euclid would demonstrate his pre-eminence when confronted by a succession of modern rivals. Dialogue form would make the book more popular and enable 'chaff' to be used. He began to write it in November that year and sent it to the press in February 1879, as the work of C. L. Dodgson, MA, Senior Student and Mathematical Lecturer of Christ Church, Oxford. The reign of Lewis Carroll was almost over.

The book describes Minos the Examiner in his college study at midnight with two gigantic piles of candidates' scripts before him. His colleague Rhadamanthus visits him, complaining about some of the answers. After Rhadamanthus leaves, Minos falls asleep and is visited by Euclid's ghost, who wants his great Manual to be left alone and unrevised. He asks Minos to judge between him and his modern critics, though allowing the moderns to be represented by the ghost of a German professor, Herr Niemand, a champion who can defend any proposition, 'true or untrue.'

By this device the textbooks of the moderns are examined in turn, principally W. D. Cooley's *Elements of Geometry Simplified and Explained* (1860) and J. M. Wilson's *Elementary Geometry* (1878). Though the points made about them are seriously intended, the books are dealt with in a less than rigorous style. Dodgson, for example, allows Minos to remark that the modern device of superimposing triangles 'reminds one a little too vividly of the man who walked down his own throat.' *Euclid and his Modern Rivals* was clever, readable, but of limited appeal. The points it dealt with belonged to elementary textbooks rather than to the adventurous frontier of mathematics. At the same time, it was too much a critique of school and university textbooks to have a wider appeal.

A Tangled Tale was a further attempt at popular mathematics, this time in the form of a series of short stories. Dodgson calls each story a 'knot,' embodying a mathematical problem. The book appeared in volume form in 1885, the stories having been contributed in the previous five years to the *Monthly Packet*, edited by Dodgson's friend and photographic subject Charlotte M. Yonge. Some of the stories drew on the stuff of his experience, railway journeys and seaside lodgings at Little Mendip, where sensible travellers demand to know 'Does the window open? . . . Does the chimney *smoke*?' In more fanciful episodes the travellers arrive in the realm of a despotic radiant empress where the mathematical calculations revolve about how much she will have them caned and how many rods will be needed.

Apart from this puzzle of corporal punishment, in which Dodgson like Sade is obsessed by mathematical sets of blows, Phyllis Greenacre in *Swift and Carroll* saw in *A Tangled Tale* his 'recurrent preoccupation with cords and knots.' This led him to send Macmillan a diagram to be posted up, showing how he wished parcels to be tied when they were sent to him. Alice, of course, ties the baby in a knot and the mouse's tail is knotted. Kate Terry tied up as Andromeda was a potent image to him. Victorian contemporaries were less uneasy at such symbols in an age of heroes who were free at a single bound. Yet it seems unlikely, had he written for the young a century later, that such indulgences would have escaped the frown of a politically sensitive editor.[8]

In the same spirit as *A Tangled Tale*, *Pillow Problems* in 1893 offered mathematical problems to be pondered in the dark by those who found sleep elusive and sexual images persistent. This book was also the second part of *Curiosa Mathematica*, whose first part had appeared in 1888 as *Curiosa Mathematica: A New Theory of Parallels*. Like all his work on mathematics, it bore the name of the Reverend C. L. Dodgson.

The Game of Logic (1886) and *Symbolic Logic* (1896), the second part of which was in proof at his death, confirmed the narrowing of his scope. The problems themselves were more interesting than their answers, presenting sets of premises from which conclusions were to be drawn.

1. Babies are illogical;
2. Nobody is despised who can manage a crocodile;
3. Illogical persons are despised.

The conclusion to which is that babies cannot manage crocodiles.

1. All members of the House of Commons have perfect self-command;
2. No M.P., who wears a coronet, should ride in a donkey-race;
3. All members of the House of Lords wear coronets.

The answer to which is that no MP should ride in a donkey-race unless he has perfect self-command.

As he progressed, Dodgson's problems in symbolic logic became longer and more complex, the number of premises to be reconciled putting him far beyond the reach of most of his readers.

1. The only animals in this house are cats;
2. Every animal is suitable for a pet, that loves to gaze at the moon;
3. When I detest an animal, I avoid it;
4. No animals are carnivorous, unless they prowl at night;
5. No cat fails to kill mice;
6. No animals ever take to me, except what are in this house;
7. Kangaroos are not suitable for pets;
8. None but carnivora kill mice;
9. I detest animals that do not take to me;
10. Animals, that prowl at night, always love to gaze at the moon.

Therefore, the conclusion is, I always avoid a kangaroo. It was scarcely surprising that young girls, singly or in classes at Oxford High School, tried, struggled, and gave up. Yet it was easy to see the attraction of such problems for one who, like Dodgson, had a taste for law and the processes of law. The mastery of logic was again shown to be the highest forensic skill, the construction of a perfect and unanswerable case. In logic a man might exercise the same skill without contaminating his mind by the disquieting details of criminal evidence.

That mind was perpetually and fussily busy with such mental devices as the Memoria Technica, as he memorized dates or the logarithms of all primes under a hundred by giving the consonants of words a numerical equivalent and incorporating the words in easily remembered rhyming couplets. He varied popular games, introducing three dice at backgammon to adjust the odds of winning, and invented the card game Court Circular. For the summer garden, he devised Croquet Castles, the balls being soldiers or sentinels while the hoops and flags were castles to be invaded. For rainy days he added Arithmetical Croquet, which was played by naming sets of numbers.

There were also puzzles that might have amused children but over whose solution even eminent mathematicians could not agree. A rope ran over a pulley. At one side a weight was attached to it. On the other side was a monkey of exactly the same weight. What would happen if the monkey began to climb the rope? Some Oxford mathematicians thought the weight would rise, others that nothing would happen. With such Dodgsonian contrivances, which the recipient could neither answer certainly nor put from his mind, he drove his colleagues to distraction, as Claude Blagden recalled. Worse still, he cheated or at least tricked them. What number is closer to 10 than 9 or 11? Having worn them out with this, he would explain that the answer was 0, because nothing is closer to 10 than 9 or 11.

He turned such ingenuity upon his political opponents. In a letter to the Conservative paper the *St James's Gazette* on 23 March 1882 he announced that Mr Gladstone had evidently discovered the Perpetuum Mobile, a clock that wound itself up whenever it ran down. The proof was in allowing a House of Commons vote that a closure motion could be passed by a bare majority. The provision was itself passed by a bare majority. The architect of this iniquity was Gladstone, 'on whose great mind it has dawned, for the first time in the world's history, that a body of men can *confer on themselves* rights over another body of men which they do not already possess. Mr Pyke introduced Mr Pluck, entitling Mr Pluck to introduce Mr Pyke.

Pseudonymously, Dodgson fell victim to the popular belief that such ingenuity as his lay next to madness. Variant stories reached him, sometimes directly, in railway trains or theatres, of the tragedy of Lewis Carroll who was now known to have gone utterly and irreclaimably mad. He feigned innocence and retained his sanity. Whether he might drive others to distraction was a different question.

*

In 1881, at the age of forty-nine, Dodgson acknowledged that he was financially secure and could afford to retire. He relinquished the Mathematical Lectureship soon afterwards, remaining a Senior Student of Christ Church for the rest of his life. As a businessman who had put money into his own publications, he might gain or lose and, therefore, must be prudent. He had told Gertrude Thomson in 1879 that, much as he admired her drawings, he could not afford to buy them. On the other hand, he was prepared to take photographs of them, which would provide him with copies cheaply and allow her to have duplicates.

Having escaped from his lectureship in mathematics, he turned to logic, teaching it to such private pupils as Edith Rix and to almost any class in a girls' school whose headmistress would allow him to do so. In a wider circle, his sisters and his Wilcox cousins were visitors to Oxford. He also visited conscientiously Loui Taylor, the niece of his sister Mary. Loui was in Cowley Hospital in 1885, afflicted by paralysis. He ordered devices which would make it possible for her to read by having the book held above her or to one side. When she was moved to a hospital in London, he wrote to her suggesting that by an effort of will she might walk again. Loui broke off the correspondence because she felt he regarded her as a malingerer, and she never wished to see him again. Dodgson wrote to his sister Elizabeth that he wished he could offer money to help in caring for Loui, but in the wake of a financial setback caused by faulty printing of an edition of *Through the Looking-Glass* he could do nothing.

His charity was enlightened but prudent. In 1877 on his first holiday in the town, he met Thomas Dymes, a master at Eastbourne College. The Dymes daughters, Margaret and Ruth, were among his child-friends that season and the friendship had thrived. Their relationship with Dodgson was still close in 1883, when Dymes lost his job. He was soon in debt, having by then eight children and a wife to support with no income. He could not pay his rent and the landlord had taken some of the family's furniture for sale.

The two girls whom Dodgson had first met six years previously were now fourteen and thirteen. Dodgson sent a printed circular to 180 friends, explaining the facts and asking if they could provide employment for Dymes or other members of his family. He wrote to Frederic Harrison, one of those who had helped Dymes financially, revealing that he himself had settled Dymes' debt with his landlord and made him a further long-term loan. In exchange, Dymes had given Dodgson a bill of sale on his furniture, to secure the loan. Dodgson had not the least intention of making a claim on Dymes' furniture. It was a tactic to prevent anyone else being able to do so. Having gone so far, Dodgson did not think that any friends of Dymes should be expected to help the family any further. This certainly did not diminish his attachment to the Dymeses, whose daughters were among his child-friends at Eastbourne the following year. Yet there came a point when even the most unfortunate, like Loui Taylor, must help themselves.

From time to time, Victorian mortality claimed a child-friend as its victim. In June 1876, he heard that Gertrude Chataway's sister Alice, a companion on the beach at Sandown the previous summer, had died suddenly in Dresden of scarlet fever. Three days before this news, on 26 June, death had come closer still. Alice Liddell's sister Edith, the youngest of the three on the famous river-trip, had died with little warning in Christ Church Deanery. She was twenty-two and had become engaged the week before to Aubrey Harcourt.

During the festivities of Commemoration Week, the procession of boats on the river, the Commemoration Ball in the Corn Exchange and Encaenia in the Sheldonian Theatre, Edith was not to be seen. She was suffering from measles. On 25 June, she experienced acute stomach pains. Dr Acland was summoned, and in turn called in Sir James Paget. It was evident that Edith had appendicitis, as surely a death sentence for her as it was to be for the diarist Francis Kilvert three years later. The appendix burst and peritonitis followed. By the following day she was dead. The mental anguish of the family, what Dean Liddell called, the 'actual watching' of his daughter's last hours was something that 'cannot soon be overcome.'[9]

In January 1885 Dodgson heard of the death of Edith Draper, formerly Edith Denman, who had married the Reverend William Draper, Vicar of Alfreton. Dodgson had stayed with the Drapers the previous summer and it seems that Edith's death had also come suddenly. She was twenty-nine and it was only a few years earlier that there had been speculation as to whether Dodgson was, in the adult sense, in love with her.

His faith was philosophic. He believed, as he wrote to Ethel Barclay in July 1879, that those who were lost to him became his 'friends in the other world.'

> Many people believe that 'our friends in the other world can and do influence us in some way, and perhaps even 'guide' us and give us light to show us our duty. My own feeling is, it *may* be so. That the angels do so *is* revealed, and we may feel sure of *that*: and there is a beautiful fancy (for I don't think one can call it more) that 'a mother who has died leaving a child behind her in this world, is allowed to be a sort of guardian angel to that child.'[10]

Stoicism in the face of death, however, did not diminish reverence for life. When *Alice in Wonderland* was staged, he ordered the removal of an additional verse which the adaptor had added and which treated the drowning of unwanted kittens 'from the humorous point of view.' It was to be removed, his nephew recalled, 'lest the children in the audience might learn to think lightly of death in the case of the lower animals.'[11]

*

His moral equilibrium in social matters was not quite always as steady as his assertion of principles might suggest. Sunday was to be observed. In 1893 he informed Gertrude Thomson that no drawings or sketches commissioned by him were to be undertaken on a Sunday. Yet Sunday, years before, had not seemed an inappropriate day for him to visit Edmund Yates on the business of the *Comic Times* nor did it now seem the wrong day to write correspondence on matters of business to Alexander Macmillan, or to discuss technical details of book production, or, indeed, to sign a commercial agreement with the firm.

In matters of religion as well, his interests and responses were sometimes unpredictable. He deplored the vulgarity of the Salvation Army and the street preacher, yet attended the performances of Joseph Leycester Lyne, 'Father Ignatius', the self-appointed abbot and leader of the Benedictine Order, revived within the Church of England. The Abbot of Llanthony was as eager for the priesthood, refused him on all sides, as Dodgson was steadfast in avoiding it. Ignatius, who claimed to have raised the dead and with his followers had seen visions of the Virgin Mary on their Welsh hillside at Capel-y-ffin, was a consummate stage performer, promising haunted houses and infidelity in Oxford, but giving his audience 'Jesus only,' as his motto was. Perhaps it says something for the radiant sincerity of Ignatius that Dodgson tolerated the showmanship by which the Abbot of Llanthony conveyed his message.

Dodgson's toleration still did not extend to the music hall. The Reverend Stuart Headlam, a future Fabian Socialist, tried to interest him in the Church and Stage Guild of 1879. But Dodgson recognized him as the man who had lately given a lecture praising music halls and had carried on a 'defiant' correspondence with the Bishop of London. Headlam was banned from officiating in the diocese. Dodgson replied that he had no sympathy either with his enthusiasm for music halls nor for his attitude to the bishop.

Towards the end of his life, however, he relented a little. Isa Bowman wrote that one of his objections was that music halls were not 'properly managed,' a reference perhaps to the prostitutes who frequented the promenade bars. The vulgarity of the songs also caused him to 'speak harshly' about such 'variety theatres.'[12]

Elsewhere, his ears were alert and his nose was keen for the least sound or scent of the unwholesome. In 1880, he disapproved of Wilkie Collins' novel *Fallen Leaves* for depicting a heroine who spent the night under the same roof as Amelius, even with the best intentions. In the same year, he told Tom Taylor that *Oliver Twist* was 'one of the most detestably realistic plays I ever saw.' The murder of Nancy was 'brutal,' as indeed it had been in the novel.[13]

Isa Bowman recalled that when a young actress among his friends took the part of a morally flawed character, she was apt to feel his displeasure. Isa experienced this during the run of *The Wicked Squire*. Polly Terry had been demeaned in Dodgson's view by being cast in Taylor's play *Lady Clancarty* in 1874 in a role that made her seem too pert.

Though he failed to persuade Sir Arthur Sullivan in 1877 to set the songs of *Alice* to music for a projected stage version, he was relieved to find that the famous Savoy operas were not offensive, with the exception of the use of 'Damn me!' in *HMS Pinafore*. It was a special relief, on going to vet *Patience* at the Savoy Theatre before taking a child in December 1881, that Gilbert's humour had now become unobjectionable. Four years later, he was quite won over by *The Mikado*, which he thought funny and charming.

His moral sensitivity was, if anything, more pronounced as he reached his middle forties. Such a development was common enough in a man's maturity. In Dodgson's case, it might seem a little curious that it occurred in the two or three years when his own importunate enthusiasm for hours with naked little girls romping in his rooms and before his camera suggested a man who had abandoned discretion and was burning his boats down to the last beam and log of which a raft might have been made.

IO

Dreaming as the Summers Die

MUCH OF DODGSON'S adult life was preoccupied by the 'treats', 'outings', and the diversions of childhood. Theatres, pantomimes, charades, puppets, conjuring, excursions, games, puzzles, magic lanterns, mechanical toys, 'ghosts' on the ceiling and paper 'pistols' were the complement to Euclid and personal theology. In the light of this, it was scarcely surprising that he should have indulged himself increasingly in the greatest treat of its kind that the mid-Victorian bourgeoisie had devised. Summer holidays at Whitby had been familiar to him from childhood. By the 1870s, however, the new and grander seaside was more than a few weeks' respite to him. It became, as he termed it in 1882, his 'headquarters' and in the 1890s his second home, to the extent that he spent two or three months of the year there. By the 1890s, as autumn came, he seemed less and less inclined to leave his seaside lodgings for Christ Church.

More poignantly than Oxford or London, the seaside was the story in little of the last twenty-five years of his life. The weeks of leisure, the beaches with their groups of little girls alone or in family parties, the sketching and photography, the undemanding entertainments, the relaxation of inhibitions, all offered so many pleasures that the threats to his moral self-esteem and the undercurrent of social malaise appeared more plainly. He was not, as he might have been at Christ Church, denied opportunity, though protected within its walls. By the seaside, there was opportunity for adventure but also the danger of scandal. In consequence, he was reduced to pleading in his early fifties that he was an aged, aged man, who could not possibly be a threat to young girls.

In 1860, in *College Rhymes*, he had published 'A Sea Dirge', a comic lament for the vicissitudes of those more homely resorts of the 1850s like Whitby.

> I had a vision of nursery-maids;
>   Tens of thousands passed by me –
> All leading children with wooden spades,
>   And this was by the Sea . . .
>
> There is an insect that people avoid
>   (Whence is derived the verb 'to flee'),
> Where have you been by it most annoyed?
>   In lodgings by the Sea.
>
> If you like your coffee with sand for dregs,
>   A decided hint of salt in your tea,
> And a fishy taste in the very eggs –
>   By all means choose the Sea.

The development of the railway system throughout the 1850s had brought most major centres of population within a few hours' journey of the coast, even if it was only the London, Brighton and South Coast Railway's 'Brighton and Back for Three-and-Six'. The families of urban workers, who thirty years before might never have seen the sea in their lives, discovered the more accessible resorts. The professional class took its summer holidays at Ilfracombe or Tenby, Newquay or Sandown, beyond the reach of the 'trippers'. Dodgson describes the more select seaside towns of mid-century in the second chapter of his most famous tale. 'Alice had been to the seaside once in her life, and had come to the general conclusion that, wherever you go to on the English coast, you find a number of bathing machines in the sea, some children digging in the sand with wooden spades, then a row of lodging houses, and behind them a railway station.'

By 1873, in the years of his fame, Dodgson had settled on Sandown as a summer choice, after a preliminary month with his Aunt Lucy Lutwidge at Hastings. The little resorts of the Isle of Wight had a gentility far beyond the crowded Margate sands of William Powell Frith's famous painting or even the older charms of Whitby. 'Culver Cliff stretching far out into the bright blue sea,' wrote Francis Kilvert in 1874, 'Sandown Bay and town and forts and Cliffs on our left, below us and on our right the village of Shanklin and the bright sandy bay busy with bathers and bare-legged children paddling in the water or digging in the sand among the boats and machines.' For four years, from 1873 to 1876, Dodgson spent his summers at Sandown, first at the King's Head and then in Culverton House, one of the boarding houses, which 'stretched along the front, each with its balcony on the upper floor and standing in a little garden with steps leading down on to the shore.'

He was by no means always alone. As he remarked, his relatives trooped in from all directions, his brother Wilfred and sister-in-law Alice, the Hassard Dodgsons and a host of cousins. His Christ Church friend Edward Sampson also spent part of the holiday with him. Yet his happiest moments were with a succession of little girls, 'child-friends old and new,' who passed before his camera and his sketch-book. Gertrude Chataway, almost nine and daughter of the Reverend James Chataway in the next-door lodging house, was his conquest of 1875 at Sandown.

> We had all been taken there for a change of air, and next door there was an old gentleman – to me at any rate he seemed old – who interested me immensely. He would come on to his balcony, which joined ours, sniffing the sea-air with his head thrown back, and would walk right down the steps on to the beach with his chin in air, drinking in the fresh breezes as if he could never have enough. I do not know why this excited such keen curiosity on my part, but I remember well that whenever I heard his footstep I flew out to see him coming, and when one day he spoke to me my joy was complete.

'Little girl,' Dodgson asked, 'why do you come so fast on to your balcony whenever I come out?' 'To see you sniff,' she said. 'It is lovely to see you sniff like this' – she threw up her head and drew in the air.

Dodgson was delighted with Gertrude and she with him. She recalled how she sat for hours on the wooden steps leading down to the beach, listening to his stories, which he tailored to her own remarks so that the tales seemed what she called, 'a personal possession.' It was a season of ease allowed to few contemporaries, a month, two months and eventually three months of summer spent in this way.

The proper amount of costume suitable for sea-bathing was something which Dodgson considered in Gertrude's case. Decent covering in such resorts was still a matter of debate, treated in earnest or humorously according to taste. The recommendations for bathers and swimmers ranged from nudity to something like a sailor's uniform. Dodgson was pleased with Gertrude 'because my mother let me run in and out of the sea in little bathing pants and a fisherman's jersey,' much less than a full costume. She was one of the girls who appeared in his Sandown sketch-book, dressed in jersey and shorts. The picture, dated 7 October 1875, was drawn when she was nine years old. Her costume gave the girl a juvenile androgynous look, as Dodgson remarked in dedicating *The Hunting of the Snark* to her, 'In memory of golden summer hours and whispers of a summer sea.'[1]

> Girt with a boyish garb for boyish task,
>   Eager she wields her spade: yet loves as well
> Rest on a friendly knee, intent to ask
>   The tale he loves to tell.

Memories of Sandown lingered at Christ Church throughout the following winter as Gertrude was brought over to be photographed. 'You must beg hard to be brought over to Oxford again,' Dodgson wrote on 2 January 1876. He seemed to have no interest in photographing her in any other form of dress than the jersey and bathing pants. He even enquired after the measurements of her pants and jersey, so that he could acquire some for use in Christ Church photographs. More dangerously, on 28 June 1876, he enquired of Mrs Chataway what was the very least covering in which she would permit her daughter to pose, offering to do a nude study of the girl that would be entirely suitable for hanging in the drawing-room. More boldly, on 21 October, he suggested that Gertrude and another girl he had met at Sandown, Lily Gray, daughter of the Clinical Lecturer in Medicine at Oxford, should pose naked for him together, one perhaps sitting on the other's knee. He had already taken nude photographs of Lily Gray alone and found her quite unselfconscious about it. However, it seemed that his new enthusiasm had made him too impetuous. By the next month the topic of correspondence was whether or not some existing negatives of Gertrude should be erased.[2]

Whatever the outcome of these requests to parents, Dodgson kept faith with his principle of never inducing one of his models to do more than she wished to herself. In consequence, Gertrude Chataway's friendship for him persisted, ending only at his death, by which time she was in her thirties. It did not truly mature. Despite their closeness, he insisted that she would always be a child to him.

Whitby, Sandown and then Eastbourne seemed to offer all the material and emotional comforts of Dodgson's life in one town. Yet the more general opinion of the seaside in the 1860s and 70s was tinged with a ribaldry that had much to do with the problems of sea-bathing and decorum. Despite the advent of the bathing-machine with its cabin for changing and its steps down to the water, the argument over seaside costume continued. A more outspoken diarist than Dodgson, Francis Kilvert, was also at Sandown in 1874, where he deplored 'the detestable custom of bathing in drawers' rather than naked. The rough sea tore them down to his ankles and he stumbled in the shallows as he found his feet 'fettered'. He rose from the shingle 'streaming with blood' and minus the drawers, to find a group of ladies 'looking on' with unconcealed interest. At Seaton, in August 1871, it was the girls, 'naked from the waist downwards' as they held their skirts up to wade in the sea, who had caught Kilvert's attention in an age before drawers were common.[3]

Onlookers like Sir William Hardman and his friend, the novelist George Meredith in 1870, treated the moral dilemma with scant respect. Meredith wrote to Hardman describing the scene at Eastbourne that year. Naked men came 'scampering' out of the bathing machines into the water while, in the distance, 'I have beheld antique virgins spy-glass in hand towards the roguish spot.' On the same topic, the magazine *Paul Pry*, founded by Robert Martin in 1856 and a precipitator of the Obscene Publications Act of 1857, scented a reek of cant as plainly as Charles Greville had done from the loftier perspective of the Privy Council. The magazine denounced the hypocrisy of 'Young prim Miss,' whose nerves were shocked at the least indelicacy in town. By the sea, without conscience or scruple, she borrowed 'Charles's telescope, or Alfred's opera-glass' to complete her education in male anatomy. She would not learn much, chuckled Sir William Hardman, citing the detumescent effect of cold water on the male genitals.[4]

Dodgson's ambivalence typified what was comedy to others. He liked little girls before his camera in bathing drawers or, indeed, without them. Yet, for example, he disapproved of the fashion of tight dressing to the extent that when he had boots made for his young friends they were of a deformed utilitarian ugliness. Tight dressing was deplored by respectable seaside newspapers like the *Eastbourne Gazette* for its 'draperies out-lining, with the faithfulness of sculpture, all the beauties and defects which for propriety's sake should be discreetly veiled.' The sexual sensibilities of the prudes had already been tinder dry when *Paul Pry* denounced the cant of seaside decency in presenting the paper's own engravings of bathing belles. It did not forget the likes of Charles Dodgson.

> Shame where is thy flush? Left behind in London to be worn again on a fitting occasion ... At a time like the present, when humbug reigns triumphant and miscreants in white chokers croak for the safety of Christian England, we make no apology for showing a little of the disgusting depravity of respectability, and its seaside bathing monstrosities.[5]

*

After four summers at Sandown, it was Eastbourne that was to be Dodgson's 'second home' for the rest of his life. If ever he was happy, it seems to have been here, carrying his safety-pins, so that a girl who wished to wade into the sea might pin her skirts up clear of the water.

> There he loved to sit and look at the children playing on the sands. Sometimes he tried to sketch them, and he usually ended by enticing one of them to come and talk to him, but, with a true artist's sense of discrimination, he had his likes and dislikes and made his choice deliberately ... Of course he remained incognito, but would reveal himself at last as 'Lewis Carroll' by sending one of his books with an inscription 'from the author' to greet his new acquaintance on her return home.[6]

The choice of Eastbourne seemed a perfect match for Dodgson's sense of decorum and his own estimate of his social rank. Eastbourne was not part of that 'rim of pasteboard-like bathing towns,' with which, as the *Saturday Review* complained in 1856, the coast of England was being disfigured. A new town of elegance and culture was under construction in the 1870s along a stretch of Sussex coast east of Beachy Head, beyond the old town of Eastbourne, on land owned by the Dukes of Devonshire. It had developed remarkably in the seven years since Meredith's visit.

The new resort looked out towards France, and seemed to have more in common with Boulogne or Trouville than with Brighton or Margate. By 1881, the *Daily News* thought that Eastbourne 'evidently emulates Continental towns.' By the following year it had overtaken Trouville, 'the premier French seaside resort,' in the view of the local press. Yet Eastbourne never lost sight of Anglo-Saxon morality. It warned off the tight dressers and made bathing, other than from a bathing-machine, a criminal offence. Equally, it had nothing to say if a child took off her clothes and posed before the camera on a more secluded stretch of beach with the chalk cliffs as a backdrop.

When Dodgson spent his first of twenty-one summers at Eastbourne in 1877, the core of the new town was complete. How quickly and recently much of the development had occurred was shown by the population figures which increased from 1,600 in 1861 to over 10,000 in 1871. Under the shelter of the downs, the residential area of the Meads had been planned as 'the Belgravia of Eastbourne,' in red brick and cream gables, just two hours by rail from London. The shopping streets of the town itself, principally the tree-lined Terminus Road which ran from the railway station to the sea front, already offered bookshops and circulating libraries, confectioners and homoeopathic chemists, a photographer and artist, banks and billiard rooms. For the summer visitor there were shops which sold swimming corsets and vests, skating-rink boots for Devonshire Park, and opera glasses whose only probable use was on the sea front.

To the east towards Pevensey, fringed by the broad shingle bank of the Crumbles, the land was flat. To the west, the parades by the sea had been formed in part by cutting away the low sandstone cliffs to provide promenades at three levels, known as 'The World', 'The Flesh', and 'The Devil'. A pier had been built, for pleasure rather than commerce, and Devonshire Park with Captain Holman as its secretary was to be the venue for middle-class sports and entertainment, from lawn tennis and county cricket to orchestral concerts. The design of its Winter Garden imitated the Crystal Palace and, from 1884, the nearby Devonshire Park Theatre with its square Italian towers brought West End plays to summer visitors.

There was no doubt as to the sort of visitors Eastbourne hoped to attract. Dodgson's first two summers coincided with those of the Queen's daughter and son-in-law, Princess Louise and the Marquis of Lorne, who were visiting Her Majesty's grandchildren, the children of the Crown Prince and Princess of Prussia. There followed the Grand Duke and Duchess of Baden, Prince Ludwic and Princess Victoria, the Grand Duke and Duchess of Hesse and others whose names might better have suited a Devonshire Park musical extravaganza.

The national press listed the numbers of the 'Upper 10,000' who spent their summers there, the *Eastbourne Gazette* and the *Eastbourne*

Chronicle each having a weekly 'Fashionable Visitors' List'. In a lowly portion of the *Eastbourne Chronicle*'s list of 28 July 1877 appeared the name of the Reverend C. L. Dodgson. He was staying on the sea front at Grosvenor House, 44 Grand Parade, where he had arrived on 10 July. The Grand Parade ran westwards from the pier and looked out across the promenades to the green waves of the Channel breaking on a shingle beach. The other guests at Grosvenor House were the family of Samuel Waddy, a Member of Parliament and Recorder of Sheffield. The daughter Louise was at the head of Dodgson's conquests for the summer.

When he left Eastbourne at the end of his first September, Dodgson recorded a list of the child-friends he had acquired during his stay. There were more than in any previous year of his life. The easy-going routine of the seaside, where children played alone or were rather distantly supervised, filled the beach with candidates for his selection. Neither nursemaids nor parents were likely to be alarmed by the gentle figure of the clergyman, simply but formally dressed in what *Paul Pry* called his white choker and clerical black. Sometimes the hunter disturbed the prey, however. In August 1883, his eye fell upon a twelve-year-old girl who was sketching a boat. He was disappointed that he frightened her away by his admiring observation. Such disappointments were few. At the end of September 1877, like a sultan calling the role of his harem, he ticked off twenty-six girls, surname first, Christian name second. To these he added nine more whom he had got to know but who were not yet friends. Though he habitually used the neutral term 'friends', there were, of course, no boys among them. In adding them up, he was more Casanova than Romeo.[7]

In common with a true Victorian philanderer like 'Walter' of *My Secret Life*, Dodgson's accounts of his conquests were more interesting to himself than to any reader. Yet within four days of his arrival, he was writing to his cousin Menella Wilcox of his first encounters. Some were fleeting, and perhaps flirting, in the extreme.

There was a little girl running up and down the parade yesterday, and she always ended her run exactly where I was sitting; she just looked up in my face, and then off she went again. So when she had been about six times, I smiled at her, and she smiled at me and ran away again; and the next time I held out my hand, and she shook hands directly; and I said, 'Will you give me that piece of seaweed?' and she said 'No!' and ran away again. And the next time I said, 'Will you cut off a little bit of the seaweed for me?' And she said, 'But I haven't got a pair of scissors!' So I lent her that folding pair of scissors, and she cut off a little bit very carefully, and gave it to me and ran away again. But in a moment she came back and said, 'I'm frightened that my Mother won't like you to keep it!' so I gave it back again, and I told her to ask her mother to get a needle and thread, and sew the two bits of seaweed together again; and she laughed, and said she would keep the two bits in her pocket. Wasn't she a queer little vegetable?[8]

In what even susceptible contemporaries might have seen as banality, Dodgson found charm. However facetiously, he regarded children as grown women and, sometimes, grown women as little girls. There were little girls who ran away, and little girls who betrayed one male admirer with another. To one of the latter he wrote a letter laden with comic self-pity, a reproach of the kind which he imagined a disappointed suitor might compose in earnest.

I kept my promise yesterday afternoon, and came down to the sea, to go with you along the rocks: but I saw you going with another gentleman, so I thought I wasn't wanted just yet: so I walked about a bit, and when I got back I couldn't see you anywhere, though I went a good way on the rocks to look. There *was* a child in pink that looked you [*sic*]: but when I got up to her it was the wrong child: however that wasn't *her* fault, poor thing. She couldn't help being a stranger. So I helped her with her sandcastles, and then I went home. I didn't cry *all* the way.[9]

Then there were girls who were difficult but might be persuaded. Such was the case of five-year-old Edith Blakemore, known familiarly as Dolly, whom Dodgson met with her parents on the pier. He met them again, asked the child her name and address and walked home with them. Next day he left a little box as a present for her but when he met her again with her parents on the pier she could not face him and fled. Describing her as if she was an adult, he thought her behaviour coquettish, though he believed the parents teased Dolly about his interest in her and added to her shyness. He feared, however, she might grow up an hysterical type. He wrote to Mrs Blakemore offering to give her up, while not forgetting a suggestive allusion to a Russian custom of a young man like himself courting a difficult young lady like Dolly.

His patience and tact were rewarded, as was his talent for story-telling. By the end of the summer, her parents acting as go-betweens,

Dolly was won over. Dodgson went to read to her a story that was later to be Chapter XV of *Sylvie and Bruno Concluded*. It was the story of the three little Foxes shut in a hamper with bread and apples which they had been forbidden to eat. When the hamper was opened at intervals, first the bread and apples were missing, then the Foxes, one by one. 'Eldest little Fox . . . I'm *afraid* you've been eating your little sister . . .' Finally there is just a mouth in the hamper. 'Eldest little Fox, have you been *eating yourself*, you wicked little Fox?' Bruno opens the mouth and extracts the rest of the eldest Fox, its two siblings, the apples and the bread.

Translated into Victorian family morality, the episode might have been more resonant to psychoanalysts than the oral sadism they professed to find in *Alice in Wonderland*. Whether the punishment of the Foxes reflected Dodgson's experience or observation, whether it was a fancy of the Eastbourne summer, was not revealed. 'First you'll go up to the nursery, and wash your faces, and put on clean pinafores. Then you'll hear the bell ring for supper. Then you'll come down: and *you won't have any supper*: but you'll have a good *whipping!* Then in the morning you'll hear the bell ring for breakfast. *But you won't have any breakfast!* You'll have a good *whipping!* Then you'll have your lessons . . .' The episode ends happily. 'And ever after that, they *were* such good little Foxes! . . . and they never ate each other any more – and *they never ate themselves!*' Their reward was buns, cake, jam and sugar plums. The virtues of decency and cleanliness were seldom so curiously embodied as in this baby-talk tale told by Sylvie and Bruno to Dodgson as 'Mister Sir'.

Dolly Blakemore, at five years old, was favoured with this moral instruction. Perhaps the voices of the story were echoes in Dodgson's mind from the governess or nursery regimes of Christ Church Deanery, or Croft, or a dozen other Victorian family homes of his acquaintance. Yet the dinner bell, clean pinafores, spoons in hands, followed by the table and white cloth with nothing but a large whip upon it might just as easily have graced Minski's banquet in Sade's *Juliette*.

The Blakemores were regular visitors to Eastbourne and Dodgson met them again in the next few years, Dolly gracing his sketch-book in 1880, by which time he had abandoned photography. She thereafter became 'Edith' to him and was a friend for the rest of his life. When she was nineteen, she visited him in Oxford, though she did not become his companion in Eastbourne that year, as he had suggested. When she was twenty-three he wrote to her, asking if she remembered how he had first addressed her on Eastbourne pier with the effrontery that was characteristic of the easy-going social morality of visitors at the seaside in the 1870s. As a comment on the opportunities which the resort afforded him, he wrote without exaggeration.

If there was ambivalence in his dealings with such children it was perhaps that, while he behaved as a Victorian suitor might to the girl of his choice, he disliked any indication that the children were precocious. When, for example, he approached Edith Nash on the beach, with her sister and cousin, he first took them to better sand for building castles, where he might also make their acquaintance. Then, like the most respectable of admirers, he took them back to the house in Lushington Road, where they were staying with their parents, and sent in his card. The family made him welcome. After that, he was allowed to 'borrow' one or more of the girls as he wished.

Edith Nash at nine years old was acceptable because, despite the facetious parody of courtship, she behaved like a child. Yet Dodgson was dismayed by an American child at Eastbourne in 1880 who talked like a girl of fifteen or sixteen and refused to be kissed as she left. He concluded that there were no true children in America. No doubt she was precocious by the standards of the day, but perhaps she was also intuitively aware of something which the girl sketching a boat, whom he had frightened away on Eastbourne beach, had also felt. Responses of this kind were rare but upsetting, not least because, presumably, they confronted him with questions about the nature of his own feelings.

*

Three weeks after his arrival at Grosvenor House on the Grand Parade, Dodgson moved to 7 Lushington Road, a large and almost semi-detached house with a small balcony and a canopy over its ground-floor bay. It was a little distance behind the sea front and, rather more grandly, it sometimes called itself Glenmore Villa. The house was mid-Victorian in yellow brick and stone facings, uniform in design with its neighbours. Here, as the guest of Mrs Dyer, he was to lodge for the next nineteen summers. When her lease expired and she found other premises in the last two years of his life, Dodgson followed her. The Grand Parade was not, after all, for him. The very address spoke of extravagance. Chambers' *Handbook for Eastbourne* of

1876 had conceded that the prices for lodgings were 'exorbitant'; such a house on the Grand Parade was likely to cost between twenty and thirty pounds a week in the summer season. The local press defended the high prices, insisting that the season was short and the town must make money while it could.

Glenmore Villa was not a summer residence for the Upper 10,000. Mrs Dyer's husband was a postman and between them they provided summer lodgings from June until October, though there was little demand after September. Dodgson occupied a bedroom and the sitting room with the balcony on the first floor, looking out over a tree-lined road with wide pavements, a view which might have been almost anywhere in the new suburban England of Victoria's later years.

His dealings with Mrs Dyer suggest that, like many of the town's visitors, it was Eastbourne's reputation for cleanliness that particularly attracted him. Other resorts were less fortunate as the summer crowds gathered and sanitation failed. Newquay, for example, had suffered a serious outbreak of typhoid in 1872. Dodgson still had a marked fear of infection but he had reason to feel safer at Eastbourne than almost anywhere else. The latest Registrar-General's figures showed that while annual mortality for the kingdom as a whole was 21.3 per 1,000 of the population, in Eastbourne it was a mere 13.9. The Duke of Devonshire had supervised a new water supply system and there was a comprehensive system of sewerage with an outfall at Langney Point, which passed the problem further down the coast.

All this was a matter of great importance to the new arrival. Irene Vanbrugh, who had been one of his child-friends, recalled the impression of 'extreme cleanliness' about him. Even literature and drama was apt to be criticized as wholesome or otherwise. Hardly had he moved from the Grand Parade to Lushington Road than he joined a dispute in the local newspapers over vaccination.

The controversy was caused by a prosecution before Eastbourne magistrates of Philip Luck, who refused to have his child vaccinated against smallpox. He was supported by the Anti-Compulsory Vaccination League, on whose behalf William Hume-Rothery wrote to the *Eastbourne Chronicle* on 31 July. Vaccination involved 'forcing corrupt matter directly into the blood,' wrote Hume-Rothery. He quoted figures to show that in various recent epidemics of smallpox, in London, Berlin and Bavaria, some eighty to ninety per cent of those who caught the disease had been vaccinated. Vaccination was therefore no protection. It spread the disease and very probably caused it in the first place.

Dodgson had a strong belief in homoeopathic medicine. When a patch of hard red skin appeared under his arm, for example, he used calendula externally and graphites internally. When he needed a homoeopathic physician, he consulted Dr James Compton-Burnett, whose daughter Ivy Compton-Burnett was to be a major influence in the fiction of the mid-twentieth century. Jenner's theory of vaccination was, in principle, homoeopathic. Rather than 'like cures like', however, it also suggested that 'like prevents like'.

Dodgson wrote a letter which was published in the *Eastbourne Chronicle* on 18 August, signing himself, 'Charles L. Dodgson, Mathematical Lecturer of Christ Church, Oxford.' He cited the statistics which Hume-Rothery had given and added, 'Now it cannot be too widely known, or too often repeated, that this argument is a fallacy, and that these statistics by themselves prove nothing; we need to know as well what per centage of the population have been vaccinated and then to compare the two per centages together.' Only by taking the two groups, vaccinated and unvaccinated, would it be possible to see what effect vaccination had. 'I heartily wish that these simple facts could be brought to the notice of all members of that well-meaning, but most mischievous association, the "Anti-Vaccination League."'

On 25 August, there was a long and angry reply from Hume-Rothery. He denounced Dodgson as being 'in error' over the treatment of statistics. Those Hume-Rothery had quoted were sufficient to show that vaccination was not protection against smallpox. In any event, his own argument was against the principle of introducing contaminated matter into the blood and incurring such added dangers as 'syphilitic inoculation.' He also quoted figures to show that deaths from smallpox were forty times higher in the 'most vaccinated' departments of France than in the 'least vaccinated.'

Dodgson came back on 8 September to accuse Hume-Rothery of being 'a little uncourteous to him' and repeating that the anti-vaccination campaigners habitually quoted the figures for smallpox among those who had been vaccinated, while giving no figures for the disease among the unvaccinated. The present figures alone 'prove nothing.'

On 15 September, Hume-Rothery was a good deal more 'uncourteous'. He deplored the 'comical' performance of 'our Christ Church mathematical lecturer.' If those who had been vaccinated contracted smallpox, vaccination was self-evidently worthless and that was an end of the matter. The unfortunate Mr Luck had been prosecuted at Eastbourne 'because he has a healthy child and will not allow that child to be diseased. I trust that all lovers of true liberty will help Mr Luck in his battle against State-medical despotism.'

Dodgson closed the contest on 22 September. The fact that those who were vaccinated sometimes caught smallpox proved nothing. Might vaccination not protect them by making the attack milder and the chance of survival greater? As to Hume-Rothery, if he meant what he had written, 'I can only say that we do not take quite the same view either as to what is honourable in controversy, or as to what is courteous in language.'

The bad-tempered exchange ended. Yet Dodgson's fear of infection was unappeased. When Mrs Dyer's children caught scarlet fever in 1878, he cut short his stay and went back to Oxford. In August 1886, for the second time, he suffered a feverish attack at Lushington Road and was convinced it was caused by bad drainage. The following year, he warned Mrs Dyer that he was sending a man at his own expense from Oxford to Eastbourne to examine her drains and make a report to him. Anything that was amiss must be put right before he could consent to stay in the house again. He sought sanitary improvements at Christ Church but could not enforce them. In Lushington Road he was in a position to lay down the law.

In April 1888, he sent Mrs Dyer a ferrometre designed to purify the sewage from water closets by the use of iron sulphate. She was ordered to install it and make use of the supply of accompanying chemicals. Despite all this, he did not escape further maladies while staying in the house. There was a boil on his left wrist which lasted a month, migraine which involved seeing 'fortifications' but with no headache, and attacks of synovitis or 'housemaid's knee' in alternate knees, which required bandaging. These ordeals, however, were bearable compared with the threat and filth of unseen infection from drains and sewage.

His other phobia at Eastbourne was more carefully cultivated, a fear of lion hunters and of being generally known in his new home as Lewis Carroll. He need not have worried. The press dropped him from its distinguished visitors list for long periods to make room for lesser beings, evidently having no idea who he was. At other times he appeared misprinted as 'Rev. G. L. Dodgson,' and as 'Rev. C. L.

Dobgson.' Unless he gave the secret away himself, it was safe. He moved in a small world, since Glenmore Villa was not large enough to hold more than two or three sets of visitors. Sometimes the rest of the house was occupied by his Christ Church friend Edward Sampson and sometimes by his friends the Bennies and their children, whom he had first met at Whitby in 1868.

Later still, it was to be his own child-friends, or those who had been child-friends a few years earlier, who came to Lushington Road as his summer guests, despite the frown of 'Mrs Grundy', as he never tired of pointing out. At last, when the adolescent Isa Bowman was his companion, Dodgson at fifty-seven wrote to Winifred Holiday on 28 February 1889, 'I'm a *very* old fogey, now, you know; so I defy "Mrs Grundy" fearlessly!' On 1 April that year, he told Mary Brown,

> I go down every summer to Eastbourne, & I still make friends with children on the beach – & sometimes even (being an old man who can venture on things that 'Mrs Grundy' would never permit to a younger man) have some little friend to stay with me as a guest. That will give you some idea what an 'aged aged man' I have become.[10]

From 1877, there was little doubt that Eastbourne was to be a permanent summer residence. It was hard to imagine that sixty miles away from this carnival of middle-class leisure on the Sussex coast, the scenes of slum life which were described in publications like *The Bitter Cry of Outcast London* (1883) remained the daily reality of millions. In cities away from the sunlit beach where Dodgson flirted with his Alices and Barbaras and Dollys and Ediths, adolescent girls changed hands for a few shillings each at the brothels of Mary Jeffries or Anna Rosemberg. It was better not to taint the minds of young men with consciousness of such scenes. It was certainly better that they should not be revealed in the public press. Dodgson was to urge the prosecution of those who did so.

Within four years of his first summer, Eastbourne was, in the words of the *Daily Chronicle*, 'a frontage of superb mansions and hotels, flanked at the back by streets of valuable house property and splendid shops; the shingly beach, dotted with white bathing-machines; its long-shoremen, nautical in dress and phrase, ready to be the medium of a boating excursion; the pier projecting far into the sea with the reflection of its coloured lights twinkling at night in the dark water.' For Dodgson it was also the Devonshire Park Theatre and the new Theatre Royal and Opera House in Seaside Road, visits by circuses of 'Lord' George Sanger and his competitors, circus children, the fireworks and fêtes of Devonshire Park.[11]

There were also daily orchestral concerts in the park, and the skating rink, whose couples were commemorated by an anonymous Eastbourne poet, 'The Observing Eye' in verses 'At the Rink.'

> But they will glide through life together soon,
> Ah! happy pair! together stand or fall . . .[12]

Devonshire Park was one of the 'treats' for Dodgson and his girls. Its lawns were 'well mapped out with the chalky outlines of the tennis court, and either from snug seats hidden in the surrounding greenery, or from conspicuous benches in the open field, you may daily watch the animated game of man and maiden with racket and tennis ball.' The South of England Tennis Tournament was held here from 1881, four years after the first All-England Tournament at Wimbledon. As he watched this new diversion of the affluent, Dodgson was struck by a logical anomaly. A system by which those beaten in successive rounds are eliminated gives the best player the first prize. Yet the three next places are decided by chance rather than skill. 'As a mathematical fact, the chance that the 2nd best player will get the prize he deserves is only 16/31sts; while the chance that the best 4 shall get their proper prizes is so small, that the odds are 12 to 1 against its happening!'

In August 1883, as the tournaments were in progress at Devonshire Park, he issued a pamphlet whose title speaks for itself. *Lawn Tennis Tournaments. The True Method of Assigning Prizes with a Proof of the Fallacy of the Present Method.* By Charles L. Dodgson, M. A. Student and Late Mathematical Lecturer of Ch. Ch. Oxford. His method replaced sets by the playing of games until one competitor was clear of the other. Those who had beaten a player or an intervening player who had beaten that player became the first player's superiors. 'So soon as any name has 3 "superiors" entered against it, it is struck off the list.' The system was logical and equitable. It was also complex enough with its filling in of mathematical tables to have reduced players, scorers and onlookers to a state either of frenzy or stupor.[13]

While the Eastbourne theatres provided him with the plays of Arthur Wing Pinero and the operettas of Gilbert and Sullivan, the churches of the town offered a variety of ceremonial. He had visited Holy Trinity and St Saviour's, the latter criticized soon after its completion in 1872 as being too Continental and redolent of Catholicism. It was, more accurately, a red-brick pro-cathedral of the Tractarian movement. Holy Communion – 'Mass', as the parish was soon calling it – was celebrated twice every Sunday instead of once a month elsewhere. Later, Dodgson visited Ocklynge Mission Room, on the hill that climbed from Eastbourne towards Lewes and London, even preaching there in later years.

His permanent association, however, was with Christ Church, Eastbourne, a Victorian Gothic church of Sussex flint at the eastern end of Seaside Road. It was here that he attended morning and evening service on almost every Sunday, taking with him any child-friend who happened to be his guest at Lushington Road. He took part in the life of the parish, informing the vicar that 'Christ Church was the only church he really cared for in the place.' It had an infants' school in one corner of its grounds and Dodgson preached at children's services, as well as giving talks and telling stories to the schoolchildren. One sermon of 1897 included his allegorical story 'Victor and Arnion', whose purpose was 'to illustrate the temptations to which children are exposed and to teach them how they might be avoided and conquered.'[14]

Like its Oxford namesake, Christ Church was not merely pietistic and certainly not self-denying. It was infected by the spirit of summer as surely as the fashionable areas to its west. It had its Lawn Tennis Club with mixed doubles and refreshments on the vicarage lawn. It held bazaars at Devonshire Park, patronized by the Grand Duke and Duchess of Baden, Princess Victoria, Prince Ludwic and Lady Fanny Howard. There were choir outings which took the members to Pevensey for dinner and a cricket match against another local team. The social life of the parish was far removed from the earnestness of religious debates over *Tract XC* or *Essays and Reviews*. A safe, undogmatic decency suited parishioner and visitor alike.[15]

As autumn came and, by the beginning of October, the Oxford term was imminent, Dodgson left Lushington Road and returned to the ancient formal life of Christ Church. He did so with increasing reluctance. On each occasion, however, he took away with him a list of child-friends acquired that summer and the memory of a season in paradise.

Away, fond thoughts, and vex my soul no more!
  Work claims my wakeful nights, my busy days –
Albeit bright memories of that sunlit shore
  Yet haunt my dreaming gaze![16]

*

Whether or not there was a serpent in this summer Eden, there was certainly a tree of knowledge. The 1870s was the last decade of innocence before the more sophisticated Victorians bit deep into the fruit. Childhood sexuality was soon to become a focus of criminal reform, raising the age of consent from thirteen to sixteen, while adult sexuality was a matter for the new science of psychopathology. Eastbourne's garden of high life by the summer sea faced a closer threat. The 1880s were years in which towns of its kind strove unavailingly to maintain the illusion of being select or 'separate', less affected by crime, death and the presence of a deprived class than the rest of the nation. It was soon evident that they were not exempt from such things and that, indeed, they never had been.

To some extent Dodgson's letters and diaries during his summers at Eastbourne reflect merely the advance of age during a period of more than twenty years. Yet his very pretence of being an 'aged aged man' at a time when he thought his health was vigorous and his capacity for work undiminished was presented by him as a protection from those who might question his moral right to familiarity with girls of all ages.

There were other changes in his conduct. His facility for attracting little girls on the beach or the pier seemed to have left him. The Casanova-like lists of summer conquests dwindled and died. From 1885 onwards he spoke instead of his loneliness at Lushington Road, writing to his cousin Menella Wilcox on 20 July 1886, 'I'm down here all alone, but happy as a king – at least, as happy as *some* kings – at any rate I should think I'm about as happy as King Charles the First when he was in prison.'[17]

He made a point of referring to the amount of work he now took with him to fill the time at Eastbourne, as well as a stack of unanswered letters. 'I get about 2000 letters off, every year,' he told Mary Brown, 'but it isn't enough.' In October 1887, he wrote to Anne Thackeray that he had spent four months at Eastbourne working some six hours a day. In February 1888 he predicted another four months of hermit existence in the summer. So it seemed. On 15 August he assured Edith Rix that he had been on his own for three weeks and begged her to come and stay at Lushington Road, despite Mrs Grundy. He had had no child-friend that year and his one attempt to acquire a girl of twelve from a neighbouring house had foundered when she proved to be one of six sisters, the eldest of whom was far too ancient at twenty-five. Even by the end of the season of 1887, ten years after his first visit, he concluded that Eastbourne was for work rather than for holiday. The greatest work to be completed was *Sylvie and Bruno*.[18]

Throughout these years he also complained gently that death would overtake his plans. There was so much to be done. He proposed a 'Child's Bible' purged of coarseness and terror, and a 'Girls' Shakespeare.' The latter was intended for girls between ten and twenty. Small children did not need it and grown women might read Shakespeare unexpurgated. Between these ages, Dodgson felt that the sensitive years required a more heavily censored Shakespeare than even Thomas Bowdler had produced in 1818. Reading Bowdler's version, he was so astonished at the objectionable material left in it that he wondered why Bowdler had bothered to undertake the task at all. 'I have a dream of Bowdlerising Bowdler,' he wrote to Marianne Richards, the mother of a child-friend, 'i.e. of editing a Shakespeare which shall be absolutely fit for *girls*. For this I need advice from *mothers*, as to which plays they would like to be included – Could you put down for me the names of those you think might be made good reading for girls (from ten to twenty years old, let us say).'[19]

Writing of his plans for the Bible and Shakespeare in 1894, he added, 'I fear neither of these ever will be done – at least by me. Life is very short! I'm 62, &, though I'm in good working order now (I can easily work 10 hours a day) I can't in reason expect many more years of it.' Perhaps he measured his prospects by the lifespan of his father, who had died at sixty-eight, though the Archdeacon's brother Hassard Dodgson had lived to eighty-one. If time were short, however, it might appear odd that a man whose genius produced the two Alice books and *The Hunting of the Snark* should contemplate the expurgation of the Bible and Shakespeare, which a conscientious hack could as easily have done. Before the end of his fifties, however, he seemed to have lost something which in a more usual constitution might have been termed libido.[20]

By 1890 he wrote of solitary walks at Eastbourne, many of which were up to Beachy Head, sometimes over the high downland to Polegate, out to Pevensey, even the one-way walk of eighteen miles to Hastings, which he commonly took in the last summer of his life without feeling tired by it. Solitude was to his taste now, he wrote, and he was losing touch with friends. He no longer seemed the slim, debonair figure, who lured and beguiled little girls on the beach by his puzzles and story-telling.

In his fifties his manner and movements, as well as his appearance, had a certain oddity. Isa Bowman remembered his eyes as a deep blue and his hair as silver-grey, worn somewhat longer than was then the fashion. He was clean-shaven and this emphasized what seemed to be a strangely 'womanish' quality in his look. He had a suggestion of youth in his face, which was remarkably unlined, though this was belied by his white hair. This was also the period in which he had begun to suffer from prolonged attacks of synovitis, which gave an odd jerkiness to his walk. He still wore no overcoat in winter but grey and black cotton gloves all the year round. It was possible to be misled by his gentle look. As Isa Bowman pointed out, though he was a man of firm belief and of strong character, there was little to show it in his face. His speech impediment was usually taken for the droll hesitation of the raconteur but occasionally, under pressure, he found it impossible to speak the words he had intended.[21]

His tastes had not changed. To the end of his life he asked, even importuned, existing child-friends – some of them well past the awkward age – to stay with him in Eastbourne. His sketch-book enthusiasm for 'little nudities' was undimmed. What had changed, more obviously in this seaside town than on his own ground at Christ Church, was the world and his perception of it.

Eastbourne had never been anything like the select resort its promoters claimed. Terminus Road with its shops and new department stores, complete with ladies' lounges and gentlemen's smoking-rooms, divided two communities. To the west were the hotels of the Grand Parade, the diversions of Devonshire Park and the spacious 'Belgravia' of the Meads. To the east, towards the Crumbles and Pevensey, was a degree of poverty and crime which belied the resort's title of 'Empress of the South'. Even Dodgson did not remain unaware of this world, though only on one occasion was he provoked into action.

Petty theft and the arrests of those who were found drunk and disorderly were the routine of the local courts. Domestic violence and the neglect of children were commonplace. Dodgson was a reader of the Eastbourne press, indeed a contributor to it. The existence of that other world, ten minutes walk from Lushington Road, was distressingly and increasingly plain. After a few years it was also more menacing.

The tales of mean streets beyond Terminus Road that greeted him in the weekly papers were surprising only to those who imagined that Eastbourne had no mean streets. Ellen Breach, a servant girl of Cavendish Place, claimed that she woke to find J. W. Hopkins, the family grocer who employed her, kneeling on her chest wearing nothing but his shirt, having 'attempted familiarities' with her. Henry Fox of Seaside inadvertently stabbed his wife Sarah to death with a knife during some naked marital romping late at night and was prosecuted for manslaughter. Alexander Sparks of Lower Cavendish Place was charged with the manslaughter of his wife by ill-treatment and depriving her of sufficient food to sustain life.[22]

The most striking aspect of such reports was the number of cases in which children had been subjected to cruelty or neglect. Children were certainly not worse treated in the 1880s than previously, yet their ordeals became more newsworthy. While the daughters of a professional middle class listened to Dodgson's fairy-tales on the sands, ten-year-old Sarah Martin waited fifteen minutes' walk distant, tied to a bedpost in Marine Drove on a diet of bread and water, for her step-father to flog her yet again with cord and strap for allegedly stealing a coin and some fruit. The child's mother was said to have treated her even worse. There was crime on the very spot where Dodgson entertained his little friends. Henry George, a boy described as unemployed and destitute, made his way on foot to Eastbourne. Tired, hungry and penniless, he crawled into a boat drawn up on the beach to find a night's shelter. For this trespass, the Eastbourne magistrates sentenced him to a month in prison with hard labour. A week later a destitute woman was arrested and brought before the magistrates. Her crime was singing in the street, which she had done to get food for her children. Was she the woman whom Dodgson heard singing in Lushington Road while writing to Isabel Standen on 4 August 1885? He shut the window to keep out the voice, which gave him no pleasure, being harsh from too much use in the open air.[23]

By 1896 the National Society for the Prevention of Cruelty to Children was busy in working-class Eastbourne. Earlier, the fate of children in the 1880s was most forcibly brought to public notice by letters like 'The Cry of the Children', which appeared in the *Eastbourne Gazette* on 15 July 1885. J. T. Markley pointed out that 'this model town is not above suspicion' in the matter of cruelty to children, citing the case of 'the alleged semi-starvation of two children' a fortnight earlier. Elsewhere, a girl of five had been locked in a cupboard as a punishment by her schoolmistress, and forgotten when the teachers left the building. Small children were routinely being beaten, or starved, or both. 'No wonder,' wrote Markley, 'that "Societies for the Protection of Children" are being formed all over England.'[24]

A far greater impetus had been given to the issue in the same month by W. T. Stead's revelations in the *Pall Mall Gazette* that girls in their teens were being bought and despatched to brothels abroad, as well as imprisoned in brothels at home, through the agency of those, like Mary Jeffries, who were agents of a white slave trade. Dodgson was furious at this sensationalism, specifically at what he regarded as the lewdness of Stead's narrative. Yet public attention shifted from cruelty in the more limited sense to the fate of children at the hands of what psychopathology in the 1880s had begun to call paedophiles. By August 1885 the Criminal Law Amendment Act raised the age of consent to sixteen.

In the autumn of 1885, Stead was urging his readers to be on the lookout for sexual predators who might insult or molest women or children and, if necessary, to take the law and a horsewhip into their own hands. How might such vigilantes react to the sight of a man in his fifties approaching, perhaps accosting, a little girl on the beach and then leading her away to 'better sand'? He might not have given a good account of himself. Isa Bowman noticed that even in Christ Church meadows his composure failed him if he met an adult acquaintance while out with a child-friend.[25]

Eastbourne was still, to appearances, the resort of a professional class where such hooliganism as Stead threatened was out of character. How long would it remain so? Not long, it seemed. By Dodgson's penultimate summer of 1896, there was a near riot on the promenade as 'Some trippers of a very objectionable type caused a disturbance on the sea front.' Thirty or forty of them were rounded up and a number were fined at the magistrates court.

Where the minor royalty of Europe had strolled at ease twenty years before, the trippers of the 1890s swarmed over the promenades. The council instituted a 'parade police' to keep order and preserve decorum. On 3 September 1887, *Modern Society* reported on the decline of Eastbourne. Even its mayor and councillors now welcomed the 'invaders', in this case an outing of the Licensed Victuallers Association. The view of Eastbourne residents was that 'the upper middle class used to frequent the place more than they do now. Can it be that the excursions have anything to do with the change?'[26]

Isa Bowman, a frequent guest of Dodgson in her teens, at both Eastbourne and Oxford, described him as 'of strong conservative tendencies. He viewed with wonder and a little pain the absolute levelling tendencies of the last few years of his life.' His outrage at the social decay of Eastbourne was reserved for a far more improbable target than the trippers or even the victims listed in 'The Cry of the Children.' His displeasure was levelled at the Salvation Army, which he abominated for the manner in which it had vulgarized Christianity. 'We shudder to hear yelled along our streets the vile blasphemies which the Salvation Army has made so common,' he wrote in the *St James's Gazette* on 6 December 1890.[27]

Nor was he placated when the Salvation Army thought Eastbourne in need of its philanthropic and missionary attentions. In 1891, almost no distance from Lushington Road, it marched with its bands playing on Sunday afternoons and provoked pitched battles with the bystanders. Believing that his acquaintance Thomas Gibson Bowles of *Vanity Fair* had been elected to Parliament, Dodgson wrote to him in August 1892, urging him to persuade the legislature to outlaw the Salvation Army's marches. The playing of the band had now been made an offence under a by-law. Yet he assured Bowles that the marches brought together nothing but 'a mob of all the worst and noisiest of the roughs.'[28]

July 1891 was the month which had seen street fights between the procession and the onlookers, almost within earshot of Lushington Road. The Salvation Army charged the *Eastbourne Standard* with inciting a breach of the peace by suggesting that the townspeople would make short work of it, if police protection were withdrawn. This case was dismissed on 29 June. It was followed by street fighting on 12 July, when local men encouraged by Thomas Gibb, known to the police as 'a Brighton rough,' tried to wrench the instruments from the bandsmen. The Salvation Army gave as good as it got.[29]

By now Dodgson's Eastbourne of the late 1870s, the summers of innocence and pleasure, had long gone as the town's Fin-de-Siècle Orchestra entertained a wider public at Devonshire Park. The beach where he had charmed little girls was now given over to trippers, among them perhaps the vigilantes of whom Stead dreamed.

It was not simply the threat of being pursued down the sea front at his first attempt to enchant a little girl, which may have deterred him. Dodgson was conscious of his rank in society and self-confessedly cautious about associating with a girl who was markedly inferior to him. The notable exception to this was in the case of child actresses. He noticed that Eastbourne's girl children of the 1890s belonged to a less covetable class than their predecessors.

To the artist Edith Shute he complained in July 1890 that he knew neither adult nor child in Eastbourne that year. The children on the beach were not his type, they were vulgar-looking. Their families belonged to the ranks of small shopkeepers, with whom he declined to associate. He must look elsewhere. A few days later he was in Mrs Shute's London studio making sketches from the model of Maud Howard, a fourteen-year-old with a plain face but pretty figure. Despite her advanced age, she was soon admitted to the ranks of his child-friends.

Even among those who knew him, Dodgson was no longer quite the harmless oddity he had once appeared. In October 1893, Mrs Marianne Richards of Eastbourne forbad her daughter Marion from dining or walking with him again. In the following summer, Mrs Miller wrote to tell him that there was talk of his activities, and that she would prefer him not to invite one of her daughters to dine unless chaperoned by the other. Roger Lancelyn Green was told that Mrs Catharine Moore at Oxford thought him 'a bit odd' and put a stop to his plans. In 1894, Mary Newby's teacher read a letter that Dodgson wrote after meeting the fifteen year old on a train. The teacher, like Mrs Moore, dismissed him 'with some suspicion.'[30]

Yet Eastbourne remained his summer home and when, in 1896, Mrs Dyer's lease expired and she moved to Bedford Well Road, he accompanied her. The larger red brick house with its cream gable was further inland, beyond the railway station, looking out over flat land towards the Pevensey levels. Now his pleasures were shared only when one of his former child-friends consented to stay with him under Mrs Dyer's chaperonage or when he went up to London by train for a day of nude sketching in the studios of Gertrude Thomson or Edith Shute.

His enthusiasm for naked girl-children sustained him until the end of his life. In his last summer of 1897 he wrote a wistful letter on

10 August to Gertrude Thomson, who was on holiday at the seaside, where she reported that the little girls played naked on the sands. Dodgson wondered whether the boarding-houses would have room for him, or whether the temperature might drop and the girls put some clothes on. It would be difficult for him to approach one of the naked girls but Miss Thomson might do it on his behalf. At the least, could she not use her camera to take pictures of individuals and groups? He was even prepared to reward the little models with copies of his books.

As undesirable little girls and their parents of the shopkeeper class filled the Eastbourne beaches, he turned to existing friends for company. From 1885, a sequence of child-friends passed a few days or even weeks at Lushington Road and Bedford Well Road, where his landlady was chaperone and the servant acted as maid. Dodgson's self-proclaimed agedness guaranteed the safety of his young visitors in the bedroom across the landing from his own. Among others, the ten-year-old actress Phoebe Carlo stayed with him in 1885. Marie Van der Gucht followed in 1886; Edith Vanbrugh, Irene Vanbrugh and Isa Bowman, child actresses, in 1887; Isa Bowman again in 1888 and 1889; Edith Lucy, Katie Lucy and Isa Bowman in 1890; Ethel Hatch and Isa Bowman in 1891; Polly Mallalieu, Maggie Bowman and Angela Vanbrugh in 1892; Gertrude Chataway in 1893; Beatrice Hatch in 1894; Marie Van der Gucht in 1895; his niece Edith Dodgson in 1896; and Dolly Rivington in 1897. The Hatch sisters and Gertrude Chataway were in their twenties. Of the others, almost all were in their teens and quite a number, like the Bowman and Vanbrugh girls, were actresses. As a rule he made light of what the world might think. Like a pop-eyed comedian who warns his audience of the censorious manager in the wings, Dodgson teased his visitors and those who refused his invitations to stay at Eastbourne with the threat of Mrs Grundy.

Despite this defiance of convention, as he saw it, his behaviour with a succession of pubescent and adolescent girls at Eastbourne seemed irreproachable. Isa Bowman, who was one of those taught to call him 'Uncle', left the fullest account of the routine at Lushington Road. The visitor had her bedroom across the landing from Dodgson's rooms. If, in the morning, the newspaper still protruded under his door, she was forbidden to enter. When it was withdrawn, she might come in. After breakfast, they would read a chapter of the Bible together. Then he would take her swimming at the Devonshire

Park Baths, though he did not swim himself. Sometimes he took her bathing in the sea, which occasioned a reprimand when Isa complained that the salt had left her hair stiff as a poker and Dodgson told her not to exaggerate.

A curiosity of Isa Bowman's stay was his insistence that each visit to the baths should be followed by one to the dentist. Dodgson himself went regularly to the dentist in Eastbourne and what sounds like a daily visit by the girl was probably a course of treatment during the few days or weeks of her stay.

At lunch, he would have nothing but sherry and a biscuit, while Isa ate her mutton and rice pudding. Then he gave her a lesson in backgammon, followed by a walk. The usual walk was up the open downland from Eastbourne to Beachy Head with tea in one of the coastguard cottages. Though he was reluctant to force a Sunday routine on his young visitors, in practice he took them to Christ Church. He still maintained that nothing should be required of a child which would make her dread the boredom and restriction of uncompromising Sabbath observance.

His regime at Lushington Road appeared as a benevolent despotism to the girls who visited him. At longer range he would direct letters of curious archness on their naughtiness and punishment. 'Oh, you naughty, naughty, bad wicked little girl! You forgot to put a stamp on your letter, and your poor old uncle had to pay *TWOPENCE*! . . . I shall punish you severely for this when once I get you here. So *tremble*! Do you hear? Be good enough to tremble!' or 'Oh, you naughty, naughty little culprit! If only I could fly to Fulham with a handy little stick . . .' Even in the pleasantries of correspondence, the benevolent despot reminded his subjects that they were his to command.[31]

Four days after this letter, he faced naughtiness of another kind. His sister Mary Collingwood wrote to warn him that his habit of having girls to share Lushington Road – especially teenage actresses – was causing scandal. He replied sharply and unrepentantly on 21 September 1893, yet the further problem in this case was that girls like Isa Bowman were in their teens and of an age to give their consent to sexual relations.

The great curiosity of this was that Dodgson might seem Mrs Grundy's natural supporter. Isa Bowman found that although among children he lost his reserve, among adults he was 'almost old-maidishly prim.' His public utterances confirmed this. During the controversy over child prostitution in the summer of 1885, for example, he announced in the *St James's Gazette* of 22 July that 'there is but one step from prudishness to pruriency.' Better to be a prude. Like his conduct at Eastbourne with adolescent guests, this public warning suggested that Mrs Grundy had little to reproach him with. He assured Mary Collingwood that he was guided in his dealings with girl-children by the light of religion and by avoidance of anything which would not be sanctioned by the girls' parents. Yet while Mrs Grundy remained the imagined foe, there soon appeared another form of Grundyism, unilluminated by the light of faith but seeking to subordinate natural love to a perverse intellectual discipline.[32]

11

Mrs Grundy and the Baron

Enid Shawyer, née Stevens, who at twelve years old became
Dodgson's child-friend in 1891, thought 'The Victorian mind
saw possible evil' in that friendship. Hence her parents' refusal to
allow her to stay with her admirer at Eastbourne. After a year he was
addressing her as 'My darling,' and 'My darling Child,' from 'Your
very loving C. L. D.' With habitual hunger for affection, he rebuked
her in correspondence for omitting to describe herself to him as 'your
loving' Enid. Nothing less would do.[1]

The earlier Victorian mind, even in the 1870s, had not as readily
seen such a degree of possible evil in a man's friendship with a little
girl. Enid Shawyer was born in 1882 and had been too young to
remember anything but the new age of apprehension. Relationships
of the sort that existed between Dodgson and his child-friends were
more publicly questioned in the 1880s. Mrs Grundy abandoned her
evangelical mask for those of the social reformer and the psychopathologist.

That female children between the ages of twelve and sixteen might
be the objects of desire was recognized and tolerated by the English
law until the final quarter of the nineteenth century. When the age
of consent was raised to thirteen in 1875, there were some misgivings.
For example, Lord Chief Justice Coleridge felt that it was inconsistent
to make the alteration when the age at which a marriage might be
contracted had for so long been twelve. However, when the age of
consent was further raised to sixteen by the Criminal Law Amendment
Act of 1885, the argument in favour of this was based almost wholly
on the need to curb adolescent prostitution.

Even where a man broke the law before 1875, the courts were

more lenient than at any time subsequently. Sir William Hardman dealt with such cases as Chairman of Surrey Quarter Sessions. In 1866, for example, 'I gave one dirty old cats'-meat man twelve months penal servitude for carnally knowing a girl between ten and twelve years of age; he himself was sixty-five.'[2]

The age of sixteen was a factor in the attitude of society and the courts, even before 1875. It was not the case that girls between the ages of twelve and sixteen had anything like adult status before the new law protected them. Section 55 of the Offences Against the Person Act 1861 already made it a criminal offence for anyone to take a girl under the age of sixteen out of her father's possession against his will. Beyond that, marriage would normally require the sanction of her parents until she was twenty-one. In *R. v. Prince* (1875) the defendant was convicted because the offence was regarded as one of strict liability and it was therefore no defence to show that the girl looked or acted as though she were older than sixteen. In *R. v. Hibbert* (1869), however, a man who met a girl of fourteen in the street and had intercourse with her was acquitted because it was not proved that he knew her to be in the custody of her father.

Life and literature reflected these attitudes. In 1852, while Dodgson was an undergraduate, E. W. Benson, a future Archbishop of Canterbury, confided to his diary his love for Minnie Sidgwick. He was then twenty-three and she was eleven. The following year, while 'she sat as usual on my knee, a little fair-haired girl of twelve with her earnest look,' he suggested marriage. Minnie, like her mother whose permission Benson had already asked, was delighted. She accepted at once, saying that of the three great gifts in Tennyson's poem *The Princess*, 'Love, Children, Happiness,' two were now hers. They were married when Minnie was seventeen.[3]

In very different circumstances, Lieutenant Harry Smith had seen a Spanish girl of fourteen running from the sack of Badajoz in 1812, ears bleeding from the ripping away of her ear-rings by the looters. Struck by her beauty, Smith went to her rescue and married her that year. As General Sir Harry Smith VC, he was now to be one of Victoria's most illustrious soldiers and Governor of the Cape, where the town of Ladysmith was named after his young bride of the Peninsular War.

Among lifelong bachelors, Swinburne was credited with an unrewarded passion for Jane Faulkener, the adopted daughter of Burne-Jones's friend John Simon. By his own account, Swinburne made his one proposal of marriage in 1862, the year of Dodgson's famous river-trip with the Liddell sisters. Swinburne's first biographer Edmund Gosse added that the proposal was made to Jane Faulkener, then ten or eleven years old, and that she spoilt the occasion by bursting into nervous laughter. Swinburne withdrew and embodied his reproach in 'The Triumph of Time'. That Jane Faulkener was so young at the time did not make the story of Swinburne's proposal impossible.

In the Dodgson family, the author of *Alice in Wonderland* was not unique. He caused less trouble by child-friendships than his younger brother Wilfred did by announcing that he intended to marry Alice Donkin. She was the niece of William Donkin, Savilian Professor of Astronomy at Oxford. In 1865, when Wilfred announced his intentions, he was twenty-seven and she was just fourteen. Charles Dodgson discussed the matter with his brother in October and advised him to keep his distance from the girl for a couple of years. Wilfred married Alice Donkin but not until 1871, when she was twenty.

In mid-century, adolescent girls as brides or common-law wives were not everywhere but nor were they a rarity. In a harsher world than Christ Church, the facts of early Victorian life had made it unrealistic that the young should remain celibate. The average age of death was forty, but in the earlier part of the Queen's reign, expectation of life in some of the manufacturing districts was seventeen. The next generation should be produced as early as possible. At the other extreme of society, Victoria and Albert permitted Princess Beatrice to fall in love and become engaged at thirteen in what Charles Greville described caustically from the vantage of his Privy Council clerkship as a 'nursery Courtship.'[4]

Public attitudes to men as husbands or lovers of much younger women were nonetheless unpredictable. So it happened that Lord Dudley was jeered in the street as an old man who had taken a very young bride. 'Walter,' the diarist of *My Secret Life*, relates his affair towards the end of the 1840s with Kitty, a young prostitute in the Strand who was fifteen at the time of their first meeting. As a cab took them to rooms in Bow Street, the driver showed his disgust by charging five times the proper fare and shouting after Walter, 'Yer haught to be glad to be let orf with ten bob. Think yerself lucky a peeler don't drop on you for taking a young girl like that, – yah! you're a swell, ain't yer? – yah! – yah! – poop!' The last exclamations were presumably directed to the horse rather than to Walter.[5]

The same division of opinion existed in literature. While Mrs Wetherell's *Queechy* might show the wholesome attraction of a religiously inspired romance between a man of experience and a young girl, one of the greatest pieces of Victorian literature, Browning's 'Roman Murder Case', *The Ring and the Book*, published in 1868–9, offered a contrasting story of intimidation and violence. Based upon the records of a Roman trial in 1698, the poem is the drama of Pompilia, bought from her parents at twelve years old as the bride of Guido Franceschini, a decayed nobleman of fifty, after he had watched her playing with her toys. In the poem, as in reality, Pompilia was murdered by him after five years of cruelty and persecution. Browning triumphs in his sustained characterization of psychopath and saint. Yet at the end of the 1860s the poem also served to remind its readers that the child-victim playing with her toys was of the age of consent in mid-Victorian England.

*

In his child-friendships, Dodgson passed through several stages of development, the first of which related to his friendship with the Liddells and his particular attraction to Alice.

Then, from about 1865 until 1880, the Liddells and Alice were replaced by a score of otherwise uninteresting little girls, to whom and to whose parents he became photographer, admirer and court jester. He made and secured demands on families usually flattered by his interest in their daughters and who seldom saw harm in his requests.

The true test came when he asked if he might photograph the girls naked. Some mothers agreed and some did not. Occasionally there was an argument and the threat of scandal, as Margaret Mayhew, the youngest daughter of the Chaplain of Wadham, recalled.

> My mother raised no objection to my youngest sister, aged about six or seven, being photographed in the nude, or in very scanty clothing – I cannot now remember which – but when permission was asked to photograph her elder sister, who was probably then about eleven, in a similar state, my mother's strict sense of Victorian propriety was shocked, and she refused the request. Mr Dodgson was offended, and the friendship ceased forthwith.[6]

Many years later, the friendship was resumed but in the spring and early summer of 1879 Dodgson's correspondence with the Mayhew parents, principally with Mrs Mayhew, confirms the course of events. He had permission to photograph the Mayhew daughters in their bathing drawers, presumably including twelve-year-old Ethel and, as a wild hope, thirteen-year-old Ruth. It was not enough for him. He insisted to Mr Mayhew that there could be no reasonable objection to Ethel at twelve being photographed nude from the back, though bathing drawers might be decorous for frontal views. Nor could there be objection to the God-given beauty of nude girls at twelve or thirteen before his camera.

His appeals grew more imploring and importunate throughout that spring, Dodgson pleading the rarity of opportunity which he had for such nude studies, citing himself as a victim of Mrs Grundy. Then came the explosion which any rational being might have foreseen. Dodgson's letters on the subject show little rationality and even less discretion. He accused the Mayhews of not trusting him and he declined to discuss the matter face to face. The final insult seems to have been Mrs Mayhew's insistence that she must be present to chaperone her elder daughters, one of whom was of the current age of consent. Dodgson washed his hands of them and declined even to print certain negatives for the family because their associations were too painful for him to contemplate.

The Henderson girls, Annie and Frances, were seven and eight years old in 1879, their father, like Mayhew, a Fellow of Wadham. Throughout Trinity Term, Dodgson had been photographing them naked in his Christ Church studio, sometimes with the assistance of his new friend, the artist Gertrude Thomson. Next summer, when they were eight and nine, he resumed his activities. On 29 May 1880 they spent two hours as naked Zulus in his studio on the college roof.

There was no evidence that Mrs Mayhew had gossiped about the contretemps of 1879, yet a dispassionate observer might wonder how long Dodgson's activities could continue without gossip or scandal. It was not nude photography that would spark such consequences but rather the manner of his importunate correspondence and appallingly coy euphemisms for nudity. There were, of course, models who let it be known that they intended to be fully clad and that neither bathing drawers nor acrobats' costume would suit them. One such was Xie Kitchin, of whom Dodgson took splendid photographs that were far ahead of the winsome nude studies. Among his favourite subjects was Xie Kitchin as a captive princess, or King Cophetua's beggar-maid bride – famous elsewhere in the Burne-Jones painting – or in Greek or Chinese costume.

Mrs Alice Kitchin, wife of Dodgson's mathematical colleague G. W. Kitchin, was persuaded in 1880 to act as go-between in acquiring stockings, bathing-pants and other female attire which Dodgson was too bashful to obtain for himself. It was also to Mrs Kitchin, in 1880, that he revealed a new trouble. On 5 February, he had kissed Henrietta Owens, known as 'Atty. He had thought she was under fourteen, the age at which he considered it proper to ask permission. But 'Atty was seventeen. Neither she nor her mother was amused, least of all by Dodgson's facetious letter of apology. Relationships were strained between Dodgson and the family, whose father Sidney Owens was Reader in Law at Christ Church. Dodgson, as if oblivious to this, then asked their permission to photograph 'Atty. The next time he saw Sidney Owens, he reported, the Reader in Law looked black as thunder. The Owens family now began to spread gossip about him, as he thought. They condemned him for taking photographs of other people's daughters. 'Ladies tell me "people" condemn these photographs in strong language: and when I inquire more particularly, I find that "people" means "Mrs Sidney Owens."'[7]

Ten days before this letter to Mrs Kitchin, on 15 July 1880, Dodgson used his camera for the last time. He may have intended to resume his hobby when the fuss died down but he never did. The following year he discovered that Mrs Henderson had on her drawing-room table one of his nude studies of her daughters. He approved of this display, which he hoped would entice the mothers of good-looking daughters to let their children be photographed naked. Clothes were not mentioned as an option, except for the ugly. As for the gossip which was still circulating, he professed to care nothing for it but thought it prudent to be told what it was.

Perhaps he would have continued photography if others had procured models for him. To the end of his life he encouraged female friends who were artists – Gertrude Thomson and Edith Shute – to obtain young girls as nude models for him to sketch and for them to photograph on his behalf. If Mrs Henderson's photographs had lured mothers and their girls to him, his photography might have been resumed. It seems that Oxford gossip made them think twice. There is no evidence that he ever again asked such favours for himself.

Such embarrassments might have induced him to abandon photography. He suggested that the true reason, which his obsessive creation of work for himself would support, was that he no longer had the time for the laborious wet-plate process. Photography was progressing from the wet collodion to the dry collodion plate, but he thought this new technique less satisfactory.

Perhaps his extreme reaction to gossip had a further cause. He cannot have been unaware of the less agreeable uses of the camera, even before the 1870s. He was a regular visitor to the farces at the Olympic Theatre in Wych Street, one of the shabby little by-ways north of the Strand. Three shops in Wych Street and six more in its neighbour, Holywell Street, were regarded as the source of the mid-Victorian trade in pornography. The prints and photographs displayed in their windows, let alone the less inhibited material found by the 'Vice Society' and the police in the back rooms, were a constant cause of complaint in the 1860s, despite the Obscene Publications Act of 1857.

Erotic postcard photography, some of very young girls in pictures attributed to J. T. Withe from 1844 onwards, was available while Dodgson was still a boy at Rugby. When he first visited the Olympic, most sexual vices had become the property of the camera and were a photographic stock-in-trade of men like William Dugdale in the streets off the Strand. Auguste Belloc provided lesbian subjects by 1850–2. A posed photograph of 1853 by Jacques Moulin showed a mother raising a birch over the naked body of her daughter, a child of Alice Liddell's age at the time of the famous river-trip, the father looking on.[8]

Dodgson can no more have been unaware of such images than he could ignore the prostitutes parading in hundreds on the pavements of the Haymarket or Waterloo Place, a stone's throw from the Union Hotel which was his regular London accommodation. It surely made him the more prudent in dealing with young models and their mothers. The disagreeable incidents of 1879 and 1880, fear of Oxford gossip and abhorrence of what existed in the lower depths of the art, combined with pressure of work and the technical changes for the worse – as he saw it – may all have played a part. There is no evidence that he made a conscious decision to abandon his camera, rather that he may have intended to use it again but became less inclined to do so as the years passed.

*

After the indiscreet appeals and the gossip, which put a stop to photography, the 1880s marked a third stage in Dodgson's development during which he became a good deal more cautious. This caution was to a great extent the consequence of the new attitude in society towards its children and an awakening to certain unpleasant truths of sexual conduct in English life. That awakening might have occurred at almost any time in the previous twenty years but events determined that it should be dramatically evident at this time. Much was to be heard of child prostitution and the reasons for it. More was to be heard about the sexuality of children themselves. An age of innocence, both in the life of the child and in the development of mid-Victorian England, now seemed to have been an illusion.

Thereafter, in his fifties and sixties, Dodgson cast himself as the 'aged aged man'. Well in advance, he dwelt much on his hastily acquired old age and the approach of death. In 1893 he wrote to Edith Miller, thankful to God for the absence of temptation but ever watchful for its return. He consoled himself with child-friends now grown up, or at least in their teens, and by sketching nude models hired for him by Gertrude Thomson and Edith Shute.

His philosophy of sexuality was plain in his reference to 'relations of *sex*, without which purity and impurity would be unmeaning words.' He was vigilant for purity. He dreaded evil against children, as he repeatedly insisted. If a girl was reluctant to pose naked, he warned Gertrude Thomson that 'it would be a crime in the sight of God to persuade her to consent.' Female beauty was a dangerous gift, particularly when possessed by a child actress or a daughter of the poor. The fate of one whom he had known as a child and who, he hinted, fell prey to promiscuity or even prostitution was such that he thought it would have been a thousand times better for her to be dead. Dodgson disapproved of hyperbole in such matters and there seems no reason to doubt that he meant just what he said.

The control of sexual feeling, preferably its suppression, was important enough to be a main reason for compiling his book of mathematical problems for bedtime, *Pillow Problems*, in 1893. He might have found strange bedfellows in such matters. Indeed, he might even have claimed a pupil in the patient cited next year in the first English translation of Krafft-Ebing's *Psychopathia Sexualis*, a man who tried to combat masturbation by a mental 'inhibitor' based on calculations relating to the number 13. A few pages later, Krafft-Ebing describes a similar case of a student of theology and science, 'retiring, preoccupied with self, and given to much reading.' In a comment that might almost have applied to *Pillow Problems*, Krafft-Ebing adds, 'Now and then the patient suffers with onomatomania. He is compelled to think of the most useless problems and give up to an interminable distressing and worrying thought.'[9]

Sexual desire could not be sublimated, transmuted or dealt with otherwise than by banishment. Among Dodgson's early reading on the subject were sermons of Edward Monro, published in 1850. They seem to have been the nearest thing to youthful sexual instruction that he ever received and he quotes them in the *St James's Gazette* as a model of conduct in suppressing the images of desire.

> The mere dwelling on its forbidden pollutions, even to combat them, forms evil habits, and withers holiness. We are often led to bring the objects of sinful desires before us, and that with the best intentions, when we pray against it, when we examine ourselves on it, when we are regretting the past, when we unfold our grief to another, when we compare ourselves with ourselves. But on all these occasions as far as possible shun the image; do not let the coloured lights fall into a shape or outline, nor suffer, if you can help it, your vision to centre them in a focus; if they are dimmed, leave them so, and do not restore the view; repress even the slightest image, lest it should strengthen and invigorate evil desire; you are too weak to bear it.[10]

These 'wise words,' as Dodgson calls them, came complete with the curiously apt photographic metaphor of image and focus. When he was fortunate enough to 'centre in a focus' the nakedness of Lily Gray, or Ethel Hatch and Beatrice Hatch, or Annie and Frances Henderson, or Ella Monier-Williams, he saw only the purity of 'fairies'. Those who saw evil in such images by the 1880s misunderstood. Children offered him a refuge because even in these circumstances he was safe from having sexual demands made upon him or from feeling that he need entertain such thoughts himself. They were, as he put it, a 'tonic' to his mind.[11]

Though he had women as friends, he usually kept a prudent but not unkindly distance in the relationship. To Gertrude Thomson he was a 'beloved friend,' yet he wrote to her most of the time like a business client, sometimes abruptly and with no sign that she might be beloved by him. He sent cheques or bills to be receipted. At his warmest, he was 'Very sincerely yours,' and always C. L. Dodgson, in fourteen years of friendship. Krafft-Ebing's platonic admirer of

little girls had shown a similar coolness towards young women. This
was not quite Dodgson's case, of course. With some young women
who had once been his child-friends he seemed entirely at ease. Yet
when he wrote to the mothers of his photographic models or to
those whose daughters he hoped would stay with him in Eastbourne,
he could never quite disguise a lack of interest in these women or in
anything other than his own pursuits.

The differentiation of girl-children from women was as important
to him as, for contrary purposes, it would have been to most men.
It haunted his subconscious mind causing him perplexity in the dream
of 1879, when he dreamt simultaneously of Polly Terry as the child
he had known and the actress of twenty-six that she now was. It
might be easy to suppose a fear of mature young women in one who
had witnessed, among his friends, the marital disaster of G. F. Watts
with Ellen Terry or, indeed, Ruskin with Effie Gray.

A presumed cause of those two domestic tragedies was the discovery that feminine physical maturity was far from the pure beauty
of a statue, a painting, or a child as model. At times, Dodgson showed
a taste for the androgynous. He was not interested in boys, yet, as
he told Henry Savile Clarke in 1888, girls could be made to look
charming when dressed as boys. Boys must never be dressed as girls.
What of womankind? Among his own female creations, the young
woman of the 'false, false lips' in his early poem 'Stolen Waters' and
the suggestion in *A Tangled Tale* that the letters 'E. W.' stand both
for 'Early Womanhood' and 'Envenomed Wickedness' have a certain
emotional resonance. Despite his literary reservations, however, there
is at least a hint that in middle age, and under the right circumstances,
he had not quite given up all thought of taking a wife. He can
scarcely have avoided hearing talk about the Ruskins. It would be
understandable, in any event, that he might inform himself on the
physical nature and demands of marriage.

Female children had the self-evident attraction of being more easily
controlled or curbed than women. After Thomas Day's *Sandford and
Merton* it also seemed that they might be educated to a required pattern
prior to marriage. In more prosaic terms, there is an imagery of cords
and knots in Dodgson's work, as Phyllis Greenacre noted in 1955.
Indeed, the 'fair' women readers of Charlotte M. Yonge's the *Monthly
Packet* were to be tied by each 'Knot' of Dodgson's *Tangled Tale* from
1880 until 1885. More explicit is the photograph taken on 15 July
1865 of Kate Terry, then twenty-three years old, as Andromeda, held

captive by cords from the drawing-room ceiling with her wrists rather lavishly trussed together. The setting is not remotely antique but a Victorian sexual melodrama. Dodgson recorded taking the photograph with the facetious regret that Kate Terry had to remain 'draped!' Even clothed she would perfectly illustrate a Victorian erotic novel like *The Yellow Room: or, Alice Darvell's Subjection*. Elsewhere he makes recurrent references to naughtiness and punishment, facetious and not remarkable at the time, except as reflecting the authority of the giver of treats over his child recipients and of the photographer over his models.[12]

Allied to this authoritarianism was a humorous cruelty in his writing and an evident willingness to dispense with girls who failed to meet his standards. He dismissed all those he saw at Margate as being merely of the commercial class and made increasing objections of the same sort at Eastbourne. He was, after all, a gentleman not a trader or a shopkeeper. Little girls who failed to appreciate his cleverness also got short shrift. However intense Dodgson's interest in her, Ruth Gamlen's father warned his daughter, 'a day will come when he will drop you like a hot potato.' So he did, when she proved to be inept at a board game he had invented. As a parting present, he sent her a copy of *Symbolic Logic*. Another failure was the daughter of the Master of University College, Margaret Bradley, whom he met on a railway journey but who failed to answer the 'arithmetical puzzles' which he shot at her from the far corner of the compartment. 'He doubtless concluded me to be a stupid girl, for he took no further notice of me.'[13]

To other girls he wrote of knocking heads off cats, feeding them on rat-tail jelly and buttered mice, how they might use forks and carving-knives on each other. Like a playful vampire, he wrote to Gertrude Chataway about 'drinking her health,' at a time when child mortality touched most families. ' "Boo! hoo! Here's Mr Dodgson has drunk my health, and I haven't got any left!" And how it will puzzle Dr Maund, when he is sent for to see you! "My dear Madam, I'm very sorry to say your little girl has got *no health at all*! I never saw such a thing in my life!" '[14]

Even those to whom he was attached had to be teased a little with such cruel humour. Edith Litton remembered letters from him on her habit of sucking her thumb, which combined homily with ingenious terror.

I received a long letter with funny little pictures of a small family of birds who would suck their thumbs (claws). They looked so comical in a row, on a branch, with their claws in their beaks, and the father- and mother-birds below with a pot of bitter aloes, a birch-rod, and long muslin bags to tie up the claws in. The next picture showed the little birds weeping, with their claws in bags, the father and mother enjoying a good repast, and the naughty little birds 'had none'! And so on all the way through this most interesting pictorial letter, till the little birds had no claws left. All sucked away! . . . Mary Pearson always read this letter to me whenever I sucked my thumb more than usual, and protested my thumbs were disappearing as the birds' claws did, and I was terribly frightened; for Mr Dodgson used to say Mary was quite right, and I should be spoken of as 'the little girl without thumbs.'[15]

That Dodgson was loved by some of his child-friends as he loved them was not in doubt, though the nature of that love was not always reciprocal. Sometimes affection and authority were in opposition within him, in which case authority prevailed. In 1889 he arrived fresh from what he called his month's 'honeymoon' in Eastbourne with Isa Bowman who was by then fifteen. They called on Mary Manners to whom Dodgson explained that he had forgotten to bring a collapsible tumbler which he used for drinking on railway journeys.

'Oh, Goosie,' broke in Isa, 'you've been talking about that tumbler for days, and now you have forgotten it.'
He pulled himself up, and looked at her steadily with an air of grave reproof.
Much abashed, she hastily substituted a very subdued 'Uncle' for the objectionable 'Goosie,' and the matter dropped.

Ultimately, he was the master, a benevolent despot. Yet Isa Bowman's slip also hinted at an intimacy which was not intended to be glimpsed by others.
That he was not a conscious sexual predator is self-evident. He strove to be true to what he saw as the laws of God. That he was ignorant of the sexual underworld of his age is disproved by his personal library, even had it not been made improbable by his observation of life.[16]

*

So far as Dodgson showed evidence of sexual development, it was in the rumours of intended marriage cherished by younger members of the Dodgson and Liddell families. Whether he was ever deeply enough attached to any woman to consider marriage is a matter of conjecture.

In 1898 his nephew, Stuart Dodgson Collingwood, thought 'the shadow of some disappointment' in love lay upon his uncle's life. In 1932, however, Collingwood disclaimed any other source than family gossip, which evidently suggested that Dodgson had been in love with Ellen Terry. However, by the time that Dodgson met her, the seventeen-year-old actress was already married to George Frederick Watts.

There was also Alice Liddell, whom both the Dodgson and Liddell families thought he had hoped to marry. Liddell family stories had Dodgson proposing and being rejected by Alice's parents. It seems unlikely. The Liddells discouraged his affection from the time Alice was ten. He showed no sign that he liked her any the more as she grew up. Meeting her in May 1865, when she was thirteen, he found her spoilt by adolescence. At no point, before or after, did he sound like a suitor. In the autumn of 1866, he discussed with Uncle Skeffington the matter of someone referred to as 'A. L.' They also talked about his brother Wilfred's wish to marry fourteen-year-old Alice Donkin. Wishful thinkers might conclude that the conversation also dwelt on Alice Liddell as a child bride. There is nothing apart from initials to suggest it. The initials might refer to her. They might as easily refer to someone like Arthur Lewis, whose rumoured engagement to Dodgson's friend Kate Terry was in danger of being confused with rumours of Ellen Terry's separation from Watts.

In the 1860s marriage would, of course, have cost him his place at Christ Church, where celibacy was still required. However, this was not an issue by 1879, when he expressed interest in books by a Dr Meigs of Philadelphia, which the American artist A. B. Frost was to get on his behalf. Frost discovered there was more than one doctor in Philadelphia of that name. Indeed, there were at least three and Frost was evidently not sure which one Dodgson had in mind. John Forsyth Meigs busied himself principally with catalogues and lectures. James Arthur Meigs had written a book on children's diseases but that was published by H. K. Lewis in London and Dodgson had no need whatever to write to America for it. The most famous of the three was Charles Delucena Meigs. He was a gynaecologist, author of such books as *Woman, Her Diseases and Remedies*, translator of Marc Columbat d'Isère's *Treatise on the Diseases and Special Hygiene of Females* and inventor of a pessary ring. As others were to note, Dodgson's bookshelves at the time of his death still contained such titles by other authors as *The Physical Life of Women*.

Short of prurient curiosity, it might seem odd that a clerical bachelor in his late forties should have taken such a subject so seriously, unless there was the most simple explanation of all. Free to marry following a change in college statutes and a self-sufficient income, though far too late to marry Alice Liddell whose wedding to Reginald Hargreaves took place in 1880, Dodgson perhaps contemplated taking a wife. Some of his contemporaries sought to acquire a preparatory knowledge of sex by experience of prostitutes or reading of pornography. Far more often they resorted to the little volume known politely as *Aristotle's Masterpiece*, which despite its racy reputation was an encouragement to marital fidelity, a popular treatise on midwifery, and a warning of the horrors of syphilis. Charles Meigs and his kind were a step up from this.

If Dodgson pondered marriage, there seem to have been two possible partners at the end of the 1870s. One was Edith Denman, born in 1855, whom he had photographed when she was a child. She was certainly his social equal, always a factor in Dodgson's calculations. Her father was a High Court judge and her grandfather had been Lord Chief Justice. Edith Denman had artistic gifts and shared Dodgson's enthusiasm for figure drawing. A marriage between a man in his late forties and a young woman in her mid-twenties was by no means unthinkable. As it happened, Edith Denman married the Reverend William Draper in 1883 and died the following year. At the time of the engagement, Dodgson wrote to Frost telling him not to worry about Dr Meigs.

A less likely bride was Gertrude Thomson who had assisted in his photography of naked girl children at Christ Church in 1879. She was a friend for the rest of Dodgson's life, eighteen years his junior and almost thirty at the time of their meeting. His letters to her, however, were cool and businesslike, although he was personally kind to her, as in letting her use his Eastbourne rooms when he was not there. She does not seem to have been invited when he was in residence. His attitude towards her was one of courteous dependence for assistance and facilities rather than one of love. Gertrude Thomson, on the other hand, seemed to worship the man she wrote of openly after his death as 'my beloved friend.'[17]

*

There was a colder truth about the sexual appeal of young girls to contemporary mankind than anything in the benevolent desires of men like Benson, Smith or Swinburne. It lay about Dodgson from his infancy and during the greater part of his life. Almost within sight of Daresbury, in the first ten years of his childhood, was another world. Many of its inhabitants had come from the villages and towns in the surrounding countryside. Most had been born into that class of the poor and destitute to which Charles Dodgson senior did his best to minister. While the infant Dodgsons played in their parsonage garden or learnt the games of the nursery, little girls like Jane Doyle and Ellen Reece confronted stranger terrors than anything in Alice Liddell's middle-class Wonderland.

To Edwin Chadwick's missioners, Jane Doyle described how she and 'a deal of little girls' who had run away from their parents in the neighbourhood, lived in the cellar of the George's Head in Garden Street, Liverpool, with a bawd who called herself 'Old Granny'. Their ages were between twelve and fourteen. Jane Doyle was found by her mother, taken home, beaten and locked in her room without her clothes. She managed to run away again and this time worked the streets for Mrs Gaffery, under the tutelage of the eldest girl, Mary Ann Hammond, who was fifteen. Mary Ann showed them the town and put Jane Doyle and Jane Shaw to work in the Playhouse Square.

They were first picked up by a well-dressed man of about fifty. He gave ten shillings for them because they were both virgins. Jane Doyle was found by her mother again, beaten with a rope and kept without clothes on bread and water for a fortnight. But she ran away once more and at the age of nineteen was sentenced to ten years transportation for theft. Her story was one among thousands on the geographical and moral horizon of the Dodgson children.[18]

Such prostitution in the new industrial cities, which paralleled Dodgson's childhood in Darlington as well as Lancashire, became a thriving trade. From 1868, it was his custom to stay at the United Hotel in Charles Street on his visits to London, within a few minutes' walk of an area of theatres and entertainment whose pavements were notorious in that decade and subsequently. Dostoevsky, exiled in London, recalled his horror at the scene, writing in *Vremya* in April 1863.

In the Haymarket I saw mothers who had brought their young daughters, girls who were still in their teens, to be sold to men. Little girls of about twelve seize you by the hand and ask you to go with them. Once I remember seeing among the crowd of people in the street a little girl who could not have been more than six years old. Her clothes were in tatters. She was dirty, barefoot and beaten black and blue. Her body, which could be seen through the holes in her clothes, was all bruised. She was walking along aimlessly, hardly knowing where she was, and without apparently being in any hurry to get anywhere. Goodness knows why she was roaming about in the crowd: perhaps she was hungry. No one paid any attention to her. But what struck me most about her was that she looked so wretched and unhappy. Such hopeless despair was written all over her face that to see that little creature already experiencing so much damnation and despair was to the highest degree unnatural and terribly painful. She kept shaking her dishevelled head from side to side, as though debating some highly important question with herself, waving her little hands about and gesticulating wildly, and then, suddenly, clapping them together and pressing them to her bosom. I went back and gave her sixpence. She seized the small silver coin, gave me a look of startled surprise, and suddenly began running in the opposite direction as fast as her little legs would carry her, as though terrified that I should take the money away from her.[19]

Here was the reality parodied by girls like Alice Liddell, masquerading before Dodgson's camera, winsome little 'beggar-maids in picturesque tatters,' as Ethel Arnold recalled them, admired for their teasing sweetness. Was there, in his subconscious mind, an attempt to find in this subject a more 'wholesome' representation of the importunate little creatures who solicited as a rule for their elders in the London streets with which he was most familiar?[20]

The Haymarket did not change much before the 1880s. Giving evidence to the House of Lords Select Committee on the Law relating to the Protection of Young Girls in 1881, C. E. Howard Vincent, Director of Criminal Investigations at Scotland Yard, reported that a recent calculation had found five hundred prostitutes at 12.30 a.m. in the few hundred yards 'between Piccadilly Circus and the bottom of Waterloo Place.'[21]

On this evidence, the ground had been marked out for one of the great social and political controversies of the entire Victorian period. It was scarcely one that Dodgson could ignore. So far, it appeared that he had either excluded from deliberate consideration what was called euphemistically 'The Great Social Evil' or that he had kept his thoughts on it to himself.

It was possible, of course, to believe that prostitution on this scale was so deeply rooted in social circumstances and economic necessity that the cure was beyond any available remedy. There was also a school of thought, which included Dodgson's great Oxford contemporary Benjamin Jowett, that felt the cure was a moral impossibility. If men and women chose to live in such a manner, the attempt to prevent them was probably in vain. Jowett wrote to Florence Nightingale on 17 October 1869 about Josephine Butler, who had taken up the cause of prostitutes and those suspected of being prostitutes, who were subjected to forcible medical examination under the Contagious Diseases Acts. 'She is thought to do good, but is very excitable and emotional,' wrote Jowett, 'of an over-sympathetic temperament, which leads her to take an interest about a class of sinners whom she had better have left to themselves.'[22]

There may have been something of that in Dodgson's judgement. The women of the Haymarket were sinners, in this view, they knew they were sinners, and proposed to continue being sinners. By analogy with his comments on Sallie Sinclair, Dodgson would have thought them better off dead. It cannot have helped matters that one of the London prostitute's more frequent salutations at this time was, 'Hello, Charlie!' To hear the 'Charlie' of his mother's childhood endearments tossed at him in this manner must have been profoundly repellent.

The campaigner of the 1880s with whom Dodgson found himself in conflict was W. T. Stead, son of a Congregational minister and ironically a man far better known in Darlington than the Dodgsons. Born with journalism in his heart, by 1871, at the age of twenty-two, he was editor of the *Northern Echo*, making Darlington's morning paper a force in national politics. The Darlington which he saw was far removed from Dodgson's world of rectory magazines, the paddocks, model railway and marionettes of Croft.

With his campaigns for a relief column to rescue General Gordon at Khartoum in 1884 and his warnings on the weakness of the Royal Navy by contrast with its European rivals, Stead had made his name in London as editor of the *Pall Mall Gazette*. Like many campaigners, he saw the raising of the age of consent as a first essential step in suppressing child prostitution. After the revelations of the House of Lords Select Committee in 1881, their lordships had passed a Criminal Law Amendment Bill which, among other provisions, raised the age of consent to sixteen. Stead demanded the passage of the Bill into law.

The Bill was sent to the Commons and was dropped. Lord Dalhousie introduced it again in the Lords in 1884 but it was sacrificed in the Commons in the debate on the new Reform Bill. It was introduced again in 1885, though it was felt prudent to make the age of consent fifteen. It came before the Commons on 22 May, the night of the adjournment for the Whitsun recess. Only twenty members were in the chamber when the second reading was moved. Conservative members were hostile and it was talked out, 'much to his own satisfaction' as Stead reported, by Cavendish Bentinck. Bentinck, a son of the Duke of Portland, was suspected of acting on behalf of Mary Jeffries, owner of eight London brothels whose clients included the King of the Belgians and 'patrons of the highest social order,' as she termed them. By 5 May, Mrs Jeffries was on trial at London Sessions for her activities. Bentinck was greeted from the opposite benches of the Commons by cries of 'Pity the poor fornicator!'

On 4 July, in the *Pall Mall Gazette*, Stead announced that his next two issues were not intended for 'all those who are squeamish, and all those who are prudish, and all those who prefer to live in a fool's paradise of imaginary innocence or purity.' The full truth of juvenile prostitution was to be revealed in two parts of 'The Maiden Tribute of Modern Babylon'. Public opinion, informed by the investigation of the *Pall Mall Gazette*'s 'Secret Commission', would demand the passage of the Criminal Law Amendment Bill in its original form with the age of consent at sixteen.

Stead had the support of Archbishop Benson of Canterbury, Frederick Temple as Bishop of London, Cardinal Manning, Archbishop of Westminster, the Congregational Union, the Salvation Army and many others. 'The Maiden Tribute of Modern Babylon' mingled sermon and striptease in a classic of sensational journalism. The articles were reprinted as a pamphlet and the sub-headings appeared on the news-vendors' placards in the London streets. 'The Violation of Virgins . . . The Confessions of a Brothel-Keeper . . . The London Slave Market . . . Why the Cries of the Victims Are Not Heard . . . Strapping Girls Down . . . A Child of 13 Bought for £5 . . . I Order Five Virgins . . . The Police and the Foreign Slave-Trade . . .'

Dodgson deplored the way in which the scandal had been forced on the public, 'the whirl and din of this popular Maelstrom.' Like many Conservative MPs and the Conservative press, he was appalled by what he read in Stead's articles. He was not so much appalled by the revelations themselves, rather by the fact that Stead had not been prosecuted for displaying his placards in the London streets and publishing his magazine. Whether or not Dodgson noticed the prostitutes of the Haymarket on his visits to the United Hotel, he was evidently well aware of the fate of children. After one of the 'little nudities' had attended Gertrude Thomson's studio for him, 'a very charming child whom I had engaged specially for him,' he discovered that she had travelled from north London alone. The girl said she was 'used to it.' Dodgson was uneasy, as he explained to Miss Thomson.

> I don't quite like the idea of that small and pretty child going all that way alone on my account. If she got lost or stolen I should feel an awful responsibility in having caused her to run the risk. I fear such beauty, among the very poor, is a very dangerous possession.[23]

The awakening from innocence had come earlier to Dodgson than to many others. His friend George Bradley had been Headmaster of Marlborough and then Master of University College, Oxford. Bradley's daughter Margaret was one of Dodgson's photographic models. In 1871, she was travelling by third-class rail, an adolescent passenger alone. Dodgson saw her at Reading, and left his first-class carriage to join her for the rest of the journey, when he realized she was unaccompanied. 'This horrified him; not quite so unreasonably as we thought, for there were traps set for young girls on journeys, of which my innocent mother was as ignorant as myself.'[24]

In thought, Dodgson was no stranger to the reality of enforced prostitution of young girls. Its images were to be banished by the precepts of Edward Monro's sermons, not brought into lurid focus by the press. Like the rest of Stead's critics, he had no wish that the issue should be discussed in the terms that the *Pall Mall Gazette* had chosen. Unfortunately, some of Stead's other critics were differently motivated. Cavendish Bentinck, in the House of Commons, demanded to know why Stead was not being prosecuted for obscene libel. The Home Secretary was said to be consulting the law officers of the Crown. It was also said, however, that Stead had the names of Mrs Jeffries' illustrious clients. If he were prosecuted, he would have them subpoena'd and cross-examined as hostile witnesses, Cavendish Bentinck included.

Among the Conservative press, Dodgson's regular newspaper the *St James's Gazette* published a series of reports and letters on the case before he made his own intervention. It described how the City solicitor had prosecuted twenty-three newsboys who had sold issues of the *Pall Mall Gazette*, which contained Stead's revelations. The Lord Mayor, sympathetic to Stead's 'high and honourable views,' dismissed the charges, saying that if the government refused to undertake a prosecution, 'I simply decline to go on with the case.'[25]

The *St James's Gazette* published letter after letter comparing the *Pall Mall Gazette* with Holywell Street, the centre of the pornography trade. It quoted the *Leeds Mercury* on Stead's 'prurient word-painting in the style of Zola.' Henry Vizetelly was soon to go to prison for publishing Zola in English. Zola, to the paper's readers, was known by Vizetelly's 1884 edition of *Nana*, with its frontispiece of the young courtesan riding her kneeling lover like a savage equestrienne, or La Mouquette in *Germinal*, who, 'when only ten years old . . . had already made acquaintance with all the dark corners of the ruins, not as a green and timid chit like Lydie, but as a fully developed hoyden, a fit partner for the bearded youths . . . Ah! youth, how it indulged and enjoyed itself.'[26]

The paper's attack on Stead was interrupted by a change of government on 25 June. Gladstone was defeated on a Finance Bill amendment and Lord Salisbury formed a minority Conservative administration. Salisbury was a reluctant Prime Minister but he held office for ten of the remaining thirteen years of Dodgson's life, a friend in Downing Street as well as at Hatfield.

On 22 July there appeared an article in the *St James's Gazette* signed 'Lewis Carroll.' It was entitled 'Whoso Shall Offend One of These Little Ones . . .' However, the title did not refer to the 'little ones' in brothels or on the streets but to those – not so little – who might read the distasteful details of Stead's articles. The issue, he insisted, was not whether the evils existed or whether public opinion should be roused, but whether Stead's exposure of such evils was not 'doing more harm than good.'

I plead for our young men and boys, whose imaginations are being excited by highly-coloured pictures of vice, and whose natural thirst for knowledge is being used for unholy purposes . . . I plead for our woman-kind who are being enticed to attend meetings where the speakers, inverting the sober language of the apostle, 'It is a shame even to speak of these things which are done of them in secret,' proclaim that it is a shame not to speak of them . . . Above all, I plead for our pure maidens, whose souls are being saddened, if not defiled, by the nauseous literature that is thus thrust upon them ... For all these I plead, with whosoever has the power to interfere, to stay, before it is too late, the flood of abomination with which we are threatened.

The article justified Dodgson's fear of such subjects in general by his single revealing comment, 'There is but one step from prudishness to pruriency.' If he believed this – and his whole life was consistent with such a belief – a man of decency and self-respect, let alone respect for others, had a moral duty to be a prude. Had he always thought so or was it a defence against the new culture at the century's end? Did he believe himself to be a prude as he spent some of his happiest hours with the little Henderson girls, naked as Zulus, on the roof high above the collegiate walls of Oxford or with the models whom Gertrude Thomson and Mrs Shute later obtained for him to sketch? Probably he did. To be a prude in the circumstances of the 1880s would show him to be wise as well as virtuous.

Despite his alarm at the 'flood of abomination with which we are threatened,' it should be said that anyone who expected to find 'highly-coloured pictures of vice' in Stead's articles was likely to be disappointed. A good deal of the material was distressing but, if the headlines induced readers to confront it, Stead felt that he had done his job as a crusader. Indeed, after five years of frustration, the Criminal Law Amendment Bill passed through the Commons and received the royal assent in August 1885. In the 1860s, Hardman had thought twelve months long enough for the old cats'-meat man who had intercourse with a girl under twelve years of age. From now on, intercourse with a girl under sixteen was punishable by two years or, where she was under thirteen, by penal servitude for life. Public policy, if not public opinion, had undergone an incalculable change in its view of childhood and sexuality.

As for the flood of abomination, Dodgson had already written to Salisbury on 7 July, after the first part of 'The Maiden Tribute', demanding a prosecution for obscene libel. The new Prime Minister acknowledged the letter personally but did nothing. Dodgson wrote again on 31 August, urging that even if it were too late to prosecute the *Pall Mall Gazette*, there were later publications to be dealt with. The offending articles had been reprinted as a pamphlet and Stead was to issue 'specials' of his newspaper. Dodgson referred in his letter to the possibility of a private prosecution being brought by a society.

Indeed, the National Vigilance Association was founded in March 1886, an offshoot of the 'Maiden Tribute' scandal. It was led by John Kensit, also leader of the Protestant Truth Association, and soon numbered Rabelais, Balzac, Zola, Maupassant and Sir Richard Burton among its victims. In its Annual Report for 1888, it warned publishers 'to have regard to the change of manners' which had taken place in late-Victorian society.[27]

Stead lacked such regard. He was not prosecuted for obscenity, however, but for buying and taking from her family Eliza Armstrong. It was a stunt, intended to show how a pubescent girl might be purchased and shipped overseas. Stead and his fellow defendants were convicted in October. He was sentenced to three months' imprisonment, the judge taking the chance to add that the 'Maiden Tribute' articles – for which Stead was not on trial – had 'deluged' the country with filth. Their publication, 'has been – and I don't hesitate to say, ever will be – a disgrace to journalism.' Mary Jeffries, the doyenne of the white slave scandal, had escaped with a fine. On three days she was seen handing out baskets of rotten fruit in the street for the crowd to throw at the defendants in the October trial.[28]

Stead issued his *Pall Mall Gazette* 'special' on the Criminal Law Amendment Act of 1885. In these pages he advocated vigilante groups to watch and follow men who solicited women or young girls, with a view to their 'chastisement by young fellows chivalrous enough to take the chance – which, after all, would be very remote – of going to gaol for horsewhipping a scoundrel who habitually made improper proposals to virtuous girls.' It was not likely that Dodgson's activities would put him in danger of such treatment from those he habitually termed 'roughs.' Yet public indignation was roused and a man who appeared to be accosting a young girl was the object of a new popular suspicion. Mrs Grundy, the middle-class matron, now appeared at the head of a mob.[29]

The events of 1885 caused a shift in opinion which was not to be reversed. Yet a further sentence in Dodgson's *St James's Gazette* article of 22 July had ominous resonance. He spoke of knowledge 'being used for unholy purposes by the seducing whisper "read this, and your eyes shall be opened, and ye shall be as gods, knowing good *and evil.*"' The age was in the mood to read and, as in the matter of tasting forbidden fruit, an early reward was a new sexual self-consciousness. Activities that had been quaint or odd, matters of folklore or amusement, now became suspect. The 'Maiden Tribute' scandal had perhaps defiled the innocence of girl children in their view of grown men. For men of Dodgson's temperament, however, there was worse to come.

*

If the Garden of Eden meant anything in terms of mid-Victorian sexual awareness, it was an innocence – rather than an ignorance – of psychopathology. By the 1880s a new vocabulary of sexual behaviour was enlightening – or blighting – the world in which men like Dodgson, Benson or Francis Kilvert, the Curate of Clyro, had found emotional fulfilment. Grundyism acquired through the political debate of 1885 a new secular power beyond anything it had known before. 'What will Mrs Grundy say?' She now said, 'Sadist, masochist, homosexual, lesbian, fetishist, and paedophile.'

Until the penultimate decade of the nineteenth century, such terms would have meant nothing to educated Victorians. Some years earlier, for example, Henry James had been to a luncheon party with the Tennysons at Aldworth. A female guest had mentioned the name of her kinswoman, Laure de Sade. Tennyson burst into a prolonged and passionate denunciation of 'the scandalous, the long-ignored, the at last all but unnameable' Marquis of the same family name. No one, apart from James, had the least idea what the Poet Laureate was talking about. Before the 1880s were over, however, names like Sade and Sacher-Masoch had been purloined by psychopathology as labels for the most deplorable sexual deviations, at a time when the unfortunate author of *Venus in Furs* (1870) was still alive. The island of Lesbos was similarly colonized, though as late as 1915 Ronald Firbank in his novel *The Artificial Princess* could make use of the ambiguity of the term for comic effect. Paedophilia was not in use as a word among the Victorians but had someone contrived it before this, it would have been taken as meaning 'love of children' without any suggestion of sinister overtones.[30]

Of course, curious forms of behaviour had always existed and drawn comment. Sarah Ponsonby had 'eloped' with Eleanor Butler in 1778, and they had lived together as the so-called 'Ladies of Llangollen' for fifty years. It had not prevented them from being a social attraction to the Duke of Wellington and others. In the seventeenth and eighteenth centuries women were occasionally brought before the courts for having masqueraded as men in order to marry other women. Krafft-Ebing himself cited three such cases, Henry Fielding chronicled another and the diarist Anthony á Wood a fifth. It was a crime regarded generally with some amusement and was usually assumed to be a means whereby the 'husband' was simply a female fraud who hoped to benefit financially from the property of the 'wife' before deserting her.

In another area, at least as far back as 1597, English satire in Sir John Davies' *Epigrammes* had a victim whose sexual potency required the stimulus of whipping by 'his whore.' There were workhouse masters and mistresses who appeared as Wackford Squeers in reality, famous disciplinarian headmasters said to recognize their pupils more easily by their bottoms than by their faces. There were others like Vaughan of Harrow whose conduct, as a 'pederast' rather than a 'homosexual', led to his enforced resignation. A man might treasure a lock of hair or a garment from a woman he loved without seeming deviant. Other men loved little girls gently and benevolently, like Francis Kilvert who wrote of one occasion in 1870. 'Shall I confess that I travelled ten miles today over the hills for a kiss, to kiss that child's sweet face. Ten miles for a kiss.' The confession is not one a clergyman would be well advised to make a century and a quarter later.[31]

Such manifestations of behaviour, perhaps curious, sometimes foolish, but not regarded as sexually sinister except where they broke the law, were now to find a place in the black museum of the Baron von Krafft-Ebing's *Psychopathia Sexualis*. The very people who might have found evangelical prudery ridiculous were perhaps the most likely to be impressed by this curator and his exhibits. Once again, Mrs Grundy could have found no more powerful, if unlikely, partner.

What now of the Reverend C. L. Dodgson writing to Gertrude Chataway about the dimensions of her bathing pants or offering to buy from Mrs Kitchin the bathing dress that Xie had used last year on the pretext that it would photograph better than a new one? What of his confessed shyness about such garments and his urging of Mrs Kitchin to buy female accessories on his behalf? What of the little girls who spent hours naked with him in his studio? Much worse, what of the fact – for fact it now seemed – that they might have had sexual feelings about the experience even if he did not? What of the jokes about marital birching with Alice Liddell, the story for Edith Blakemore of the little foxes in nursery pinafores just like hers, finding instead of breakfast or dinner a large whip waiting on the table ready for use upon them? What of the letters signed by this middle-aged clerical don as 'Your fairy friend Sylvie'? Reinforced by German scholarship, Mrs Grundy became formidable indeed. For the rest of his life Dodgson made a game of defying her and yet acknowledged her power by name in letter after letter.

Her new ally, Krafft-Ebing, was only eight years younger than Dodgson, born at Mannheim in 1840. He held professorships in medicine successively at the universities of Strasbourg, Graz and Vienna. His first major publication, a textbook of forensic psychopathology, *Lehrbuch der Gerichtlichen Psychopathologie*, appeared in 1875, two years after *Through the Looking-Glass* and the year before *The Hunting of the Snark*. The more famous *Psychopathia Sexualis* was published in 1886, the year following the scandals of 'Modern Babylon'. It had gone through no less than nine editions by 1894. Krafft-Ebing gave an inscribed copy of the ninth edition to a promising young colleague, Sigmund Freud.

Whether Dodgson ever read or heard discussion of the great psychopathologist is conjecture. Even Christ Church was certainly not isolated from the advance of thought and Alice Liddell in old age was to recall seeing Verlaine, Mallarmé and a Communard as the college guests of Dodgson's 'bohemian' friend and colleague Frederick York Powell. Dodgson's Common Room colleague, Max Müller, had earned his footnote in the *Psychopathia Sexualis* as a linguist. Ignorance, if not innocence, would have been hard to preserve.[32]

Dodgson's own reading of medical books or journals and their publishers' catalogues would very probably have alerted him to Krafft-Ebing's existence. His letter of 5 April 1881 to the American illustrator A. B. Frost indicates that he was obtaining medical books from a publisher in Philadelphia, which was also the source of English translations of Krafft-Ebing. Indeed, Krafft-Ebing's work was circulating beyond medical circles in England well within Dodgson's lifetime. In 1918, in the Pemberton Billing libel case, Lord Alfred Douglas was asked whether Oscar Wilde was studying the *Psychopathia Sexualis* while writing *Salomé* in 1893, 'Yes, he was. He showed me the book in his room. He was continually reading it and talking about it.' Wilde was, of course, fluent in German. However, Douglas told Bernard Shaw that he himself had read the book 'long before Havelock Ellis,' presumably from the English translation of 1894, issued by F. A. Davis, the medical publishers in Philadelphia.[33]

Ideas are apt to travel faster than books and to circulate far more widely. Karl Marx's hypotheses in *Das Kapital* were discussed while the book waited twenty years for its translation from German. Whether from the circulation of ideas or text, the new psychopathology can have brought Dodgson little comfort. Krafft-Ebing was its first great systematizer but a glance at his sources shows how far back the investigation had gone before 1886.

So far as an interest in little girls was concerned, Krafft-Ebing categorized paedophilia in the juridical section of his work, 'Pathological Sexuality in its Legal Aspects.' Discussion of the aberration expanded throughout successive editions of the *Psychopathia Sexualis*, until the twelfth edition, the last to be published in the author's lifetime. Conforming to German and Austrian legal definitions, Krafft-Ebing took fourteen as the age of consent. From that standpoint, as surely as any alarmist of the late twentieth century, he saw by 1886 that 'Criminal Statistics prove the sad fact that sexual crimes are progressively increasing in our modern civilisation.' And just as surely, 'This is particularly the case with immoral acts with children under the age of fourteen.' He cites an eightfold increase in crimes against children in France during the half-century to 1875 and a similar increase in England for the quarter century to 1857. 'Today, rape on children is remarkably frequent.' Of the 22,017 cases of rape tried in France between 1851 and 1875, 17,657 were rapes of children. As surely as Stead and his campaigners, Krafft-Ebing ascribes this to the increasing 'mildness of the laws' which punish such offences.[34]

Women seemed as criminally inclined towards children as men, perhaps because their employment or position in the family gave them constant access. What Krafft-Ebing calls 'a large percentage of cases' was represented by 'lewd servant girls, governesses and nursemaids, not to speak of female relatives, who abuse the little boys entrusted to their care, for sexual purposes and often even infect them with the gonorrheal poison.'[35]

Apart from the mentally deficient, Krafft-Ebing classifies those who prey on little girls as 'young men who lack courage or have no faith in their virility' or '*roués* who have, to some extent, lost their power.' The precise word which Dodgson himself used to describe the failure of child-friendships at puberty – 'my child-friendships get shipwrecked at the critical point, "where the stream and the river meet"' – is used by Krafft-Ebing: 'The only presumption is that these individuals have suffered shipwreck in the sphere of morality and potency.'[36]

Finally, Krafft-Ebing draws a portrait of the innocent or 'platonic' lover of little girls, as if attempting to hold the mirror up to the author of *Alice in Wonderland*.

> In addition to the aforesaid categories of moral renegades, and those afflicted by psychico-moral weakness ... there are cases in which the sexually needy subject is drawn to children not in consequence of degenerated morality or psychical or physical impotence, but rather by a morbid disposition, a *psycho-sexual perversion*, which may at present be named *paedophilia erotica*. In my own experience I have come across four cases only. They all refer to men. The first case is of more value than the others for it appears in the form of platonic love; but it manifests its sexual character in the fact that this (paranoic) lover of children is only stimulated by little girls. He is quite callous towards the grown-up woman and, as it appears, a hair-fetichist [*sic*].[37]

Like Henry Maudsley, in *Responsibility in Mental Disease*, which Dodgson had cited to Lord Denman in 1876, Krafft-Ebing criticized the courts for insufficient attention to the mental state of defendants. In the case of paedophilia, however, the defendants should be treated as criminals, not as patients. 'Irresponsibility should, as a rule, not be claimed in these cases, for experience teaches that paedophilic impulses can be mastered, unless a weakening or total loss of will power has been superinduced by pathological conditions, such as neurasthenia gravis or dementia paralitica.'[38]

At some point, the theories of the alienist had to give way to the pragmatic realities of criminal justice. On the day before the Criminal Law Amendment Act received the royal assent it was legal to have carnal knowledge of a consenting girl of thirteen. The following day, it was a felony. Yet it would have been strange to insist that conduct regarded as medically normal on one day should have been treated as a pathological perversion two days later. 'Such acts, which especially deserve legal punishment, seem only exceptionally to have psychopathic significance,' Krafft-Ebing concluded.[39]

Yet the creed of Krafft-Ebing was uncompromising. For the platonic lover of little girls, who held to the gospel of purity, the laws of conscience and of God, there was little comfort. 'Sexuality is the most powerful factor in individual and social existence ... Thus all ethics and, perhaps, a good part of aesthetics and religion depend upon the existence of sexual feeling ... Notwithstanding all the ethics which love requires in order to develop into its true and pure form, its strongest root is still sensuality. Platonic love is an impossibility, a self-deception, a false designation for related feelings.'[40]

What of the little girls themselves, as sexual creatures? From Cesare Lombroso and Démétrius Alexandre Zambaco, Krafft-Ebing drew cases of sexual awakening in girls as young as three. In the section on General Pathology there followed such examples as case sixteen, in which a woman in childhood had a compulsion to expose herself to men. The happy afternoons at Christ Church with an eager child-model, indifferent as to dress, or with the Henderson girls running about naked for hours, might now be seen in a different light. Were the children merely obliging benevolent Mr Dodgson or, perhaps, deriving some sexual pleasure of their own from the experience? And when he dressed them in rags, or as boy acrobats, or in bathing-pants or bathing-dresses which he had procured for them through Mrs Kitchin, was he not behaving very much as some of Krafft-Ebing's patients had felt the need to behave with grown women? Once the notion of childhood sexuality was admitted to the Victorian garden of earthly delights, was he not in danger of awakening in certain of these girls excitements that had better have lain dormant?[41]

'Read this, and your eyes shall be opened, and ye shall be as gods, knowing good *and evil.*' The warning had a sadder note in the light of the new learning than with respect to anything in Stead's journalism. It was not a case of a single book nor of such schools as Zola's naturalism. A novelist like Henry James could now put aside the terms 'painful', 'unpleasant' and 'disgusting', to publish *What Maisie Knew*, whose child heroine confronts an underworld more sinister than Alice's, and gently adapts herself to its vicious morals. The next year, in *The Awkward Age*, James claimed acquaintance with a society whose tone was 'as far as possible removed from that of the nursery and the schoolroom,' to house what Mrs Brookenham called, 'my innocent and helpless, yet somehow at the same time, as a consequence of my cynicism, dreadfully damaged and depraved daughter.'[42]

The great English historian G. M. Young once suggested that the thirty-six years before 1900 actually produced far greater changes than the thirty-six years after, despite the proclaimed 'modernism' of the later period. During the 1880s particularly, the ground of moral certainty rocked beneath the feet of such men as Dodgson. Yet, curiously, the century was dying in a shroud of earnestness that made the energy and inconsequence of the 1860s, when even Dodgson wrote without moral purpose, seem a sunlit memory. The protection of children through the National Society for the Prevention of Cruelty to Children grew from the scandal of 1885. Eastbourne town hall, like halls across the country, welcomed Mrs Fawcett and her sisterhood with their lectures on Women's Rights. Oscar Wilde went to Reading Gaol, but voices – including Krafft-Ebing's – demanded legalization of homosexuality, a practice which gained the doubtful attraction of a persecuted faith. There were wrongs to be righted and grievances to be remedied in a culture which seemed to have been innocent or ignorant of them in the past.

In the last summer of his life Dodgson invited Hettie Rowell to dinner at Christ Church. She was eighteen, one of his pupils in logic. He had not known her as a little girl. As they walked back from Christ Church, she told him what a happy evening it had been. Dodgson explained that there was no such thing as present happiness. To say 'I *am* happy now,' was untrue, only, 'I *was* happy then.' Thirty-five years, almost to the day, had passed since the afternoon on the river which had given birth to *Alice in Wonderland*. Of course he was older and the sunlit decades of energy and enthusiasm glimmered on a remote horizon. Yet his letters and diaries give every impression that he was so much happier in the 1860s and 1870s than ever before or since. Was it the new world of worthy causes and censorious instincts, that sadder and alien landscape, which now gave such a ring of melancholy to the 'aged, aged man'?[43]

12

Christ Church Hall

'EXCEPT TO LITTLE girls, he was not an alluring personage,' wrote William Tuckwell, a former Fellow of New College, in 1900, describing Dodgson at Oxford. Tuckwell seems only to have known by sight 'the homely figure and the grave, repellent face,' yet he and New College had heard of the difficulties that the creator of 'Alice' was said to have caused to his Christ Church colleagues. 'Austere, shy, precise, absorbed in mathematical reverie, watchfully tenacious of his dignity, stiffly conservative in political, theological, social theory, his life mapped out in squares like Alice's landscape, he struck discords in the frank harmonious *camaraderie* of College life.'[1]

Opinion among the senior members of Christ Church was divided between those who thought Dodgson behaved with the petulance of an overgrown child and others who saw in him a kindly nature, a gift of humour that moved laughter without ridicule, and a disposition to do good in his role as a clergyman and Christian gentleman. In his own habits, there was no question that he had become a recluse or that his happiest hours were spent in the company of 'little misses', as Tuckwell called them, rather than in adult conversation. Words like 'remote' and 'inconspicuous' attached to descriptions of him after 1880. By 1882, even Dodgson wrote uneasily of himself as 'a selfish recluse.'

He had resigned his Mathematical Lectureship in November 1881, and had already agreed a reduction in his stipend from £300 to £200. As he said, 'I have been many years able to retire.' He was content to remain merely a Student of Christ Church who might tutor or lecture if he wished. At the age of forty-nine, he was free to live as he chose. With his friend Vere Bayne, he was one of the last of those who held the old life fellowships. He was as secure, in that respect, as Dr Martin Routh who had been a senior member of Magdalen for almost eighty years, and still held office in his eighteenth-century wig when Dodgson first came into residence at Christ Church.[2]

Dodgson's new leisure was not to be equated with idleness. He was 'a great worker but not a very great reader', as his colleague Frederick York Powell described him. Confirming this, T. B. Strong remarked that Dodgson 'read very little of the other logicians or of mathematicians who had dealt with the same subjects as himself.' He was, as Powell described him, 'a born inventor' and, Strong added, in logic or mathematics he would 'evolve the whole out of his own mind.' Even those who found him antipathetic did not dispute the tenacity with which he returned to his rooms after dinner and stood at his desk until four or five in the morning, fashioning his moral tales and mathematical problems.[3]

When, a few days after Dodgson's death in 1898, the new Dean of Christ Church, Francis Paget, referred in a sermon to 'that real and touching child-likeness that marked him in all fields of thought,' it was a partial view of him as mathematician and colleague. If he was a child, there were those at Christ Church who saw in him that more fractious 'grown-up child' whom Tuckwell had described. A self-indulgent childishness was apparent to Michael Sadler, Steward from 1886 of the Christ Church Common Room, a post similar to that of Junior Bursar in other colleges.[4]

Sadler was a recent President of the Oxford Union, a new type of married don, whose personal mission was to widen access to higher education. His sense of political obligation was divided by two generations from Dodgson's whom he described as 'the most prolific malcontent . . . ever on the *qui vive* for negligence on the part of the College servants or minor inconveniences affecting his own comfortable life.' Almost fifty letters of complaint have survived in which Dodgson takes to task the unfortunate Steward. Sadler, however, who as Master of University College fifty years later was a reluctant and abrasive host to Joachim von Ribbentrop, Hitler's appointment as German Ambassador in London, was not easily overawed.[5]

Sadler arrived at Christ Church to be greeted first by a complaint from Dodgson that he had been overcharged for his dinner on the previous Tuesday. Close on this came a protest that he had been sent nine-tenths of a pint of milk, which he had carefully measured, instead of half a pint. Further letters followed. His scout had almost started a fire in his rooms. The drains were defective on the staircase next to the Common Room. Dodgson was distressed by the amount of his crockery being broken by the clumsiness of his scout. When Sadler received his MA degree a year after his appointment, Dodgson's letter of congratulation also contained complaints about the college cooking, in which he found fault with the beefsteak, both the mashed and the boiled potatoes, the onions, the apple dumplings and the cauliflower. He insisted that he did not regard himself as 'fastidious' and hoped that Sadler would not be upset by his complaints.

As time went by, the protests and urgings became more varied. In the course of a letter complaining that Sadler had not sent him a receipt, he also demanded that ferrometres should be installed in the college lavatories to purify the sewage. He complained that the 3 p.m. post had gone before Tom finished striking the hour but then insisted that the college messengers were not clearing the boxes quickly enough. He reprimanded Sadler for allowing puddles to form in the Great Quadrangle when it rained. With his usual compulsion for detail, Dodgson added that the puddles were oval and that they measured between three and four feet long and two inches deep. Why had Sadler not sent servants to sweep them dry? Perhaps, he suggested caustically, the servants had not yet had their wits sharpened by Sadler's reformist enthusiasm for University Extension Lectures.

Dodgson was also sensitive about other matters, which did not in the first place depend upon the Steward. Dinner should not be served at 7 p.m. on Sundays because it interfered with services held for the college servants, at which Dodgson himself preached. He was dismayed on a weekday morning to find no undergraduates at chapel, now that attendance was no longer compulsory. Grace before dinner was being treated with such scant reverence that it had become a mockery. Whether inside Common Room or outside it, there seemed much of which to complain. Christ Church was in decline. The same conclusion was noted by Claude Blagden, forty-two years younger than Dodgson, who thought that by 1890 Liddell had lost his grip of college government.

Sadler was soon sick to death of Dodgson: 'The gas supply is inadequate to a new asbestos grate which Mr Dodgson wishes to instal. He requires an electric bell-push in each of his two bedrooms. Please tell the kitchen to send him *no more smoked ham*. If ginger-beer can be supplied in bottles with glass-ball stoppers instead of corked, Mr Dodgson, who is accustomed to stack them head-downwards to prevent effervescence, would not, out of a dozen, find five completely empty and two half empty. And so on; and so on.' What made it worse, as Sadler knew perfectly well, was that the ginger-beer was destined for the refreshment of the 'little misses' who infested Dodgson's rooms.[6]

Such hostile views of Dodgson in his later years were by no means universal. Frederick York Powell, the Christ Church historian, friend of Mallarmé, Verlaine and the Communards, was politically far removed from him yet personally sympathetic. Mrs Shute, a Christ Church widow, called Powell a 'bohemian'. He was described by Strong as representing 'modernising views in the extreme form' and was in the habit of bringing 'strange foreigners' to High Table. Dodgson called them 'Powell's assassins.' They were frequently political refugees. Powell himself was not unaware of Dodgson's limitations but thought him at his best in the Common Room, where he excelled as an after-dinner speaker. 'The whimsical thought, the gentle satire, the delicate allusions to the various characteristic ways of his hearers, the pleasant kindness that somehow showed through the veil of fun, made his few post-prandial orations memorable.' Powell praised Dodgson for qualities which appear nowhere in his dealings with Sadler: the quiet humour of his voice, the slight hesitation before a clever remark, his natural patience and kindness. With his friend Henry Parry Liddon he 'long made the House Common-room a resort where the weary brain-worker found harmless mirth and keen but kindly wit.'[7]

John Simon, a young graduate during the last years of Dodgson's life, recalled him enlivening dinner by 'quizzing' his neighbours with mathematical problems of the kind that appeared in *Pillow Problems*. By contrast with this, H. A. L. Fisher knew Dodgson only as a man who said very little at dinner. He certainly needed no lessons in the art of snubbing a remark in questionable taste or an impertinent question. A classical scholar from Berlin, who was a guest at Christ Church, ventured to say, 'Oh, Mr Dodgson, I am so glad to meet you, for I have enjoyed your *Alice* books so much.' Dodgson rebuffed the kindness. 'That is a subject which I never discuss with anybody.' He turned his back on the admirer for the rest of the meal and spoke not a word more to him. Given the amount of time he spent discussing the subject with almost any 'little miss' who cared to listen, such a reaction was apt to seem boorish.[8]

That Dodgson could be unpredictably plaintive or abrupt, as well as genial and humorous, was a symptom of the pressure of communal life upon him. He was one of a dying breed of Christ Church celibates, with no true home beyond his college rooms. He was not master as he might have been in his own house, the premises and the servants were not his to command as he wished. He was, to that extent, like a man who lived in an hotel or at his club and it was part of the price to be paid for his life fellowship. The greater part of the cost was obedience to the vestiges of a monastic rule. The frustrations of this existence were apt to appear in complaints and demands, in withdrawal and in offended silences.

By contrast, the conviviality of college life was to be found at dinner, taken in Hall during the term and in the Common Room during vacation, where he might be sure of friendship from men like Powell, Vere Bayne and Liddon. Even here, he must sometimes have felt his isolation. During the Easter vacation of 1887 there was only one other member of the Common Room at dinner. College life, as he had first known it at mid-century, was dead. 'The Fellows marry,' wrote Ethel Arnold in 1890, 'and for themselves and for their families rows of red brick villas have sprung up to the north of the town with the rapidity of mushrooms on an August night . . . it would almost seem to be the ambition of some of its younger members to transform Oxford into a sort of Brixton or Croydon . . .' Among this new class of Oxonian was young Michael Sadler, as Dodgson well knew.[9]

As a relic of the 1850s, thirty or forty years later, Dodgson lived apart from the younger men with an aloofness that was unusual even in the hierarchical distinctions of Christ Church. Claude Blagden, who regarded his elders in the 1890s with the unforgiving eye of an undergraduate, summed Dodgson up as a recluse and his friend Vere Bayne as a reactionary. He might easily have reversed the descriptions.[10]

As for undergraduates, after resigning his Lectureship in 1881, Dodgson had little to do with them. Only the fame of Alice and legends of his oddity as a tutor ensured that his presence was not forgotten. He became a totem of Oxford culture. Even an undergraduate production of *Alice in Wonderland* in Worcester College gardens during June 1895 did not quite tempt him out. He would occasionally spy upon the rehearsals but, as one of the actors remarked, 'being a shy man he never allowed himself to come forward; all we ever saw of him was a sly face peeping out from behind a tree and smiling.'

It cannot have given him much satisfaction when he was paired with Oscar Wilde in 1894 as a subject for satire by a Balliol undergraduate, Leopold Amery, a future Conservative politician who was Winston Churchill's Secretary of State for India in 1940–5. Wilde's popularity at Oxford had not been enhanced when, as G. M. Young remarked, a good many of his famous ripostes were recognized as being culled from Oxford wits of the 1880s. Amery and two friends devised *Aristophanes at Oxford*, a pastiche of Athenian comedy, on the banks of the Cherwell after the summer examination season was over. The Chorus of undergraduates, standing on the river bank with Socrates and Thucydides, see a strange vessel coming towards them:

> Why that is Lewis Carroll paddling up!
> – He takes us in Pass Logic at the House –
> But what in the Wonderland is he after now?

It was many years since Dodgson had taught Pass Logic but that was scarcely relevant. He and his 'phantom-ship' of hobgoblins and ghouls slip by while he recalls the triumph of his Snark.

> Just the place for a Snark! Good bellman toll
>   – Till the clouds come down with a shower –
> That thing-um-a-bell, the one that I stole
>   From the top of the great Tom Tower.
>
> Just the place! Yet indeed as I think of the air
>   As we passed into Magdalen preserves,
> It was only the thought of a Jabberwock's lair
>   Could console my olfactory nerves . . .

To young men like Amery, Dodgson was now less a figure of contemporary life than one of the most intriguing but elusive wraiths of Oxford legend. *Aristophanes at Oxford* breathed a patrician frivolity of high summer but also a youthful lament for the passage of time. Dodgson was to live another four years but, like his *alter ego*, he seemed already lost in an Oxford dream of the past. 'His Oxford was sleepy and early Victorian,' wrote the *Academy* in 1898, 'a haunt of people who played croquet and little girls with short frocks and smoothly brushed hair and formal politeness. It seems to me that the exact subtlety of the humour of the "Alice" books could never be caught again, for the sleepy afternoon air, the quaint grace and the mock dignity are all the property of an elder and vanishing world.'[11]

*

In his Christ Church rooms or at his Eastbourne lodgings, Dodgson was much preoccupied, as he wrote to Francis Atkinson in 1890, by the thought of death and its approach in the text, 'The night cometh when no man can work.' During the years that were left, he gave himself to activity, as if for its own sake. Frederick York Powell noted his daily routine.

> His life at Oxford was simple in the extreme. He rose early, worked nearly all day standing at his desk, with the barest apology for lunch; a brief smart walk now and then in the afternoon, or call at some friend's house, were his only diversion. Hall-dinner and a chat with a friend in his own room afterward, with more work after, till he went to bed. He rarely dined out, and only occasionally invited particular friends to dine with him.[12]

His nephew and first biographer, Stuart Dodgson Collingwood, added that early rising was followed by college chapel, as it had been since Dodgson's first arrival as an undergraduate of nineteen in 1851. On the afternoon walk, 'he would talk the whole time, telling delightful stories, or explaining some new logical problem; if he was alone, he used to think out his books ... The only irregularity noticeable in his mode of life was the hour of retiring, which varied from 11 p.m. to four o'clock in the morning, according to the amount of work which he felt himself in the mood for.'[13]

Until his death, he retained the set of rooms on two floors in the north-west corner of the Great Quadrangle, where he had moved in 1868. The large sitting-room overlooking St Aldate's, the study and the two bedrooms on the floor above, were augmented briefly in 1890 by a lease which he took on a house owned by Christ Church in Brewer Street. The oil paintings in his rooms included Arthur Hughes' *The Lady with the Lilacs*, and paintings by Dodgson's friend Thomas Heaphy. He was, as Powell said, a lover of pictures rather than a connoisseur of art.

Among additions to the rooms were tiles for the sitting-room fireplace designed for him by William De Morgan, depicting fabulous animals with some suggestion of *The Hunting of the Snark*. Collingwood, as a Christ Church undergraduate in 1888, recalled that his uncle's 'nests of pigeon-holes, each neatly labelled, showed his love of order; shelves filled with the best books on every subject that interested him, were evidence of his wide reading.' He had a bound set of *Notes and Queries*, a medical library and most of George Meredith's novels in their first editions, though he got rid of Meredith in one of his periodic clearances of items from the bookshelves.

These were the quarters of the recluse. He was not a man like Browning who 'dinnered himself away.' He announced to Mrs Feilden in 1887 that he had given up dinner parties because he returned from them tired and depressed at the waste of several hours, having heard nothing and having said nothing of any worth. On 5 May 1884, he had already noted in his diary, 'I much grudge giving an evening (even if it were not tiring) to bandying small talk with dull people.' This refusal of an invitation in 1884 was a significant loss to English gossip, though the two men had met twice before, in 1878 and in 1881. The 'dull' host was William Spooner, who spent sixty years at New College, most of them as Dean and then Warden, and who became more famous in Oxford legend than Dodgson but less so than Lewis Carroll. Perhaps Dodgson had heard without amusement of the perils which pronunciation and absent-mindedness posed for Spooner as a preacher. 'In the sermon I have just preached, whenever I said Aristotle, I meant St Paul,' or 'Which of us has not felt in his heart a half-warmed fish?' An evening of Dodgson and Spooner ought surely to have been marked by a white stone.

They shared an inability to remember faces. Dodgson, greeted by a stranger in the street, said coldly that he could not recollect knowing him. 'That is very strange,' the man said, 'for I was your host last night.' Spooner issued an invitation of Carrolingian logic: 'Do come to dinner tonight to meet our new Fellow, Casson.' 'But, Warden,' said the invitee, 'I *am* Casson.' 'Never mind,' said Spooner reassuringly, 'come all the same.'[14]

Dodgson remained a considerate host. He recorded each dinner party held in his rooms with a plan of the seating arrangements and he kept a menu book, 'that the same people might not have the same dishes too frequently.' Hospitality faltered if a man wanted to smoke. 'Tommy' Bowles of *Vanity Fair* and the *Lady* was quickly trounced when he pleaded for a pipe. 'You know that I don't allow smoking here. If I had known that you wanted to smoke, I would have ordered the Common Room Smoking Room to be got ready for you.' The future Bishop Strong later found Bowles lurking with his pipe on a cold dark stairway and gave him sanctuary. Yet Bowles learnt something from Dodgson's logic that might have brought England to bankruptcy. In 1913 he successfully argued in *Bowles v. Bank of England* that it was illegal for the government to collect tax in any year until the Finance Bill had become law. Since this would have brought government to a halt, the Asquith administration was obliged to rush through the Provisional Collection of Taxes Act before it could get its hands on the nation's money.[15]

'He sometimes gave large parties,' Collingwood recalled of Dodgson, 'but his favourite form of social relaxation was a *diner à deux*.' To these intimate dinners he invited Oxford girls now in their teens. St Hugh's College, he was pleased to say, allowed them to come individually and unchaperoned. 'If you don't come alone, you shan't come at all,' he told Edith Olivier, an undergraduate at St Hugh's in the 1890s. Reluctantly, the Principal gave her consent.[16]

As so often, he posed as the scourge of Mrs Grundy. However, when his two nieces were coming to Oxford High School he sought suitable lodgings for them. He arranged for them to stay with the Rowell family, whose daughters were among his visitors. One afternoon, Hettie Rowell saw her brother come back from school while Dodgson was having tea with the family. Dodgson's face fell and he finished his tea in silence. Next year it was intended that the Rowells' son should be an undergraduate. Dodgson had forgotten the son. He wrote to Mrs Rowell saying that he could not permit his nieces to live in a house where her son was also living. At that point, surely, Mrs Grundy gave an approving nod. Such fastidiousness did not prevent him, of course, from being the jolly dog who asked that Hettie Rowell should be his sole guest at a *tête-à-tête* dinner in his rooms.[17]

Despite what he said about the varied menu, Miss Olivier recalled having the same dishes on every occasion: lamb chops followed by meringue and then port. After this, at 8.45 p.m., Dodgson made tea. He no longer made it by walking up and down, talking and waving the kettle about. A blacksmith had fitted a long handle to the kettle, like a saucepan, so that he would neither burn his hands nor need to use a kettle-holder.

Edith Olivier also recalled his dinner-table preoccupation with logic, which he taught to the girls of St Hugh's in the last years of his life. To his young visitors, as well as towards those who were his close friends, like Bayne and Liddon, and those at little more distance like Powell and Strong, Dodgson showed a mischievous and childish cleverness. He loved to tease by propositions and puzzles. The young Claude Blagden saw him reduce some colleagues to silent fury by this while others learnt for themselves that Dodgson's relaxation was to drive others wild by logical conundrums.

T. B. Strong assumed at first that when Dodgson's scout arrived with some problem in logic that required solution, it was an appeal for help. Strong did his best and sent back what he thought was the correct answer. Without delay there came another message, either showing him that his answer was wrong or enclosing another question. Dodgson was quite content to play games of this sort for as long as his colleagues tolerated them.[18]

Publicly, this enthusiasm also appeared in such pieces as 'What Achilles Said to the Tortoise', a whimsy on the first proposition of Euclid, which Dodgson contributed to *Mind* in 1894. On other occasions his amusements were less esoteric, as when he secretly changed the labels on the bottles of wine to be tasted by the Common Room Wine Committee, in order to prove that their opinions were guided by the labels and the wine merchant's advice rather than by their own palates. His own taste in wine was not sophisticated. A glass of sherry or port was his most frequent drink. When he was Curator of the Common Room in the early 1890s and the port in the cellars ran short, he ignored the specialist merchants and simply sent out to the grocer for more supplies. Running the Common Room 'on the lines of a lower middle-class family,' as his colleagues thought.[19]

In society, he was thought unpredictable by victims whom he snubbed for some lapse of taste. He found profanity or indecency where the perpetrators had not realized that it existed and he was apt to be regarded as a prig. There was in him what his friend Henry Lewis Thompson, Vicar of the University Church of St Mary the Virgin, called 'the intense and solemn earnestness' which gave the lie to intellectual flippancy. Even those who most appreciated his gifts of wit and paradox saw the same sober qualities. 'Dodgson never forgot the realities,' wrote Frederick York Powell, 'he never played at being other than he was – a cleric, a don, a Christian clergyman with sworn duties, a Student of the House.'[20]

Among those self-imposed duties, he preached at the services held for college servants on Sunday evenings and, indeed, operated the magic lantern at the Christmas parties put on for their children, so that he might combine the Advent story with the entertainment of *Sylvie and Bruno*. He had already assisted as Curate at St Mary Magdalen and in the last fourteen months of his life was persuaded to preach three times at evensong at the University Church. He preached what seemed to Blagden an old-fashioned sermon the style of which was plain and evangelical. Whatever the religious controversies of the Victorian period, they seemed on the evidence of his sermons to have passed Dodgson by.[21]

It was not surprising that those who cared little for him found his preaching mawkish, as Michael Sadler thought it. Undergraduates came to hear him as a curiosity and Sadler confirmed the comment of Stuart Dodgson Collingwood that at times, in his sermons, his uncle was 'unable to control his emotion.' Colleagues found his preaching 'strongly emotional.' This may only be to say that the preaching style of the late Victorian period was more demonstrative than it had been half a century before, when the undergraduate Matthew Arnold in the early 1840s had watched the 'spiritual apparition' of John Henry Newman in the same church, 'gliding in the dim afternoon light through the aisles of St Mary's, rising into the pulpit, and then, in the most entrancing of voices, breaking the silence with words and thoughts that were a religious music – subtle, sweet, mournful . . .'[22]

Dodgson, in Thompson's description, was dignified but unpretentious, 'the erect grey-haired figure, with the rapt look of earnest thought,' lacking the mellifluous charm and striking theatricality of Newman. As a preacher he had a very simple view of his task: 'It is *not* good to be told (and I never wish to be told), "Your sermon was so *beautiful*." We shall not be concerned to know, in the Great Day, whether we have preached beautiful sermons, but whether they were preached with the one object of serving God.'[23]

He had won his position at Christ Church by mathematics and theology. In neither subject, as his colleagues saw it, did he come anywhere near the first rank. His theology was little more than common-sense Christian morality. In mathematics, he had been happiest with the old-fashioned certainties of Euclidean geometry. There was no evidence that he ever attempted the unconquered peaks of classical mathematics, the proof of Fermat's Last Theorem from the seventeenth century, the Goldbach Conjecture from the eighteenth, or Riemann's Hypothesis from his own time. Yet he did not, as was sometimes suggested, abandon mathematics by turning to symbolic logic. A major contemporary development in the subject was the attempt to determine whether all mathematics might be derived from logic. In Berlin, Gottlob Frege had published a system of symbolic logic in 1879. Bertrand Russell, who was a Cambridge Wrangler five years before Dodgson's final work on symbolic logic was published, examined the same hypothesis.

Proof remained elusive. In symbolic logic, Frege's *Begriffsschrift* of 1879 was described as 'a formula language, modelled upon that of arithmetic, for pure thought.' Russell was to show the innate flaw in Frege's system twenty-four years later. Unlike Dodgson, Frege believed that traditional mathematics, even Euclid's axioms, had been insufficiently rigorous. Yet, like Dodgson, he sought to put concepts into notation. Such men as these worked in isolation with little or no knowledge of one another's existence. Even Russell was not to correspond with Frege until 1903, having done most of the same work independently. As early as 1884, the twelve-year-old Russell had rejected Euclidean geometry because, with the perversity of the precocious child, he wanted its axioms justified. When Dodgson turned to the work which appeared in his two volumes of *Symbolic Logic*, he was moving from a pure Euclidean tradition towards the main direction of modern logic and mathematics. He lamented that such modern technology as the phonograph and the cinema had come too late for him. He might have been consoled to know that his last work at Christ Church on mathematical logic was a path that would later emerge on the highway of computer science.

Victorian science derived a reputation for smugness from such books as Peter Guthrie Tait's *Lectures on Recent Advances in Physical Science* in 1876, which suggested that apart from a few inconsistencies, such as the discrepancy between calculated and observed orbits of Mercury, the study of science had almost completed the circle of knowledge. It is hard to say whether what lay in store for the scientists thereafter was more Dodgsonian or Carrolingian. The *Principia Mathematica* of Russell and Whitehead seems distinctly Dodgsonian. Yet there is something Carrolingian about atoms which, like naughty children, behave differently according to whether they are being observed or not.

Dodgson's own interest in mathematics often showed a childish exuberance rather than an enquiring mind. He wore out others, if not himself, by his facility in contriving paradox for the sake of paradox. Many of his Christ Church colleagues, like T. B. Strong, were tolerant of this because they shared something of Dodgson's leisured 'onomatomania'. Others, like John Swinnerton Phillimore, were not. Phillimore evidently believed that dinner at High Table would offer sanctuary from mental persecution. He sat down, only for Dodgson to slip in beside him and say eagerly, 'Take a dodecahedron,' reducing Phillimore to speechless rage.[24]

*

So far as Dodgson cut a figure in the university at large in the latter half of his life, it was by his occasional publication of pamphlets or articles on subjects of debate. None of them struck with more force than his attack on the new science of vivisection. It was a practice instinctively repugnant to him, as it was to Robert Browning who became its more active opponent in the 1870s. On 10 March 1885, Dodgson noted in his diary that the controversy had reached Oxford that afternoon at a meeting of Convocation in the Sheldonian. 'A great Convocation assembled in the theatre, about a proposed grant for Physiology, opposed by many (I was one) who wish restrictions to be enacted as to the practice of vivisection for research. Liddon made an excellent speech against the grant, but it was carried by 412 to 244.'[25]

His own conduct towards animals, despite the whimsical cruelties of the imagination in letters and fiction, justified his vote. Two years later, for example, he consulted the eminent surgeon Sir James Paget on the most humane method of having the elderly Common Room cat put down. Sir James evidently suggested caging the animal, perhaps giving a lethal injection, or poisoning its meat. Dodgson refused any method that would cause terror to the cat, as he felt sure a cage or a hypodermic syringe would do. He countered by asking Sir James whether a painless but lethal sleep could not be induced by mixing a sufficient quantity of laudanum with the cat's meat or fish. The degree of scrupulousness, if not squeamishness, which he showed made it unthinkable that he could sympathize with the infliction of pain on any animal.

In 1875, he had already opposed vivisection first in a letter to the *Pall Mall Gazette* and then in an article, 'Some Popular Fallacies about Vivisection', which the *Pall Mall Gazette* rejected but which was accepted by John Morley and published in the *Fortnightly Review* on 1 June. Dodgson considered the two absolute views, that vivisection was right in itself and that it could never be justified. Though he regarded the rights of animals as an untenable concept he rejected the assertion that man is infinitely more important than the lower animals as a 'hideous selfishness.'

The fallacy which preoccupied him most was the assertion by the *Pall Mall Gazette* on 13 February 1875 that more pain was inflicted by sport than by vivisection. Even if true, Dodgson maintained, this would not justify vivisection. In any case, apart from shooting and fishing, 'for other forms of sport, especially hunting, I have no defence to offer, believing that they involve very great cruelty.'

The evil of vivisection 'consists chiefly in the effect produced on the operator.' He quoted, from the *Spectator* of 20 March 1875, an account of vivisection carried out in the course of teaching. 'When the unfortunate creatures cried and moaned under the operation, many of the students *actually mimicked their cries in derision.*' 'Man has something of the wild beast in him.' Worse still, there was in man a degree of what was soon to be termed sadism, of which the lower animals were innocent. 'I believe that any branch of science, when taken up by one who has a natural turn for it, will soon become as sport to the most ardent sportsman, or any form of pleasure to the most refined sensualist.'

The article ends with the chill prediction of a future when men, rather than animals, are the subject of vivisection, a horror that what Winston Churchill called Nazism's 'lights of perverted science' brought to reality within seventy years of Dodgson's prophecy.

> Will you represent to that grim spectre, as he gloats over you, scalpel in hand, the inalienable rights of man? He will tell you that this is merely a question of relative expediency – that, with so feeble a physique as yours, you have only to be thankful that natural selection has spared you so long. Will you reproach him with the needless torture he proposes to inflict upon you? He will smilingly assure you that the *hyperaesthesia*, which he hopes to induce, is in itself a most interesting phenomenon, deserving much patient study. Will you then, gathering up all your strength for one last desperate appeal, plead with him as with a fellow-man, and with an agonized cry for 'Mercy!' seek to rouse some dormant spark of pity in that icy breast? Ask it rather of the nether mill-stone.

The views of Dodgson on vivisection are characteristic of the man, but the final passage of his article goes further. It offers a rare glimpse of the moral nightmare in his heart, at a depth which nothing in *Alice* or the *Snark* had revealed. If his analysis of the physician as torturer foreshadows the butchery of totalitarianism, it also echoes that earlier vivisectionist whom Sade created as Rodin the surgeon in *Justine*. Like Dodgson's phantom with the scalpel, Rodin and the heroes of Sade pursue their inquiry into pain for its own sake as a form of pleasure to the most refined sensualist, finding the torments of hyperaesthesia 'a most interesting phenomenon.'[26]

Compared with this essay, most of Dodgson's other contributions to Oxford controversy were at the level of play and whimsy. Even his letters to the press on the examination for Responsions, or the importance of Clerical Fellowships, or resisting the proposal that Natural Scientists should be allowed to proceed to the MA degree without being examined in Latin and Greek, seemed trivial in relation to such issues of human conduct as vivisection raised in his mind.

Of his privately printed and issued Oxford satires his friend T. B. Strong remarked in 1898, 'The style of humour which prevails in these is of a distinctly academic type, and the events satirized in them do not survive in all their details, in the memory of the present generation ... for the most part Mr Dodgson's comments have shared the oblivion into which the controversies which evoked them have fallen.' An exception to this might be his comments on Jowett and his later objections to Liddell's architectural 'improvements.'[27]

It seemed that Dodgson had further distanced himself from Liddell in the 1870s by mocking publicly the improvements at Christ Church for which the Dean was given credit. In 1873, he attacked Liddell's commission given to Sir Giles Gilbert Scott and then passed on to G. F. Bodley. The bells were to be removed from the cathedral, where the structure had become too weak to support them, and were to be housed in a campanile of wood and copper over the staircase on the Hall. The campanile was not built but the bells were removed and housed in a plain wooden exterior case above the stairs.

Dodgson published an attack in 1873 on such architectural barbarism and extravagance in *Objections Submitted to the Governing Body of Christ Church, Oxford, Against Certain Proposed Alterations in the Great Quadrangle*. In the previous year he published his satire, *The New Belfry of Christ Church, Oxford*, ridiculing the work that Liddell and his colleagues had put in hand. He wrote the piece in May 1872, took it to the University Press to be printed, and issued it at his own expense. The satire caught the fancy of those who recoiled at the wooden box on Christ Church Hall and also of those who took a certain pleasure in seeing the humourless Liddell cut down to size.

With a po-faced self-importance that might have come from the Dean himself, Dodgson proceeds to describe the new marvel of the Oxford skyline.

The word 'Belfry' is derived from the French *bel*, 'beautiful, becoming, meet,' and from the German *frei*, 'free, unfettered, secure, safe.' Thus the word is strictly equivalent to 'meatsafe,' to which the new Belfry bears a resemblance so perfect as almost to amount to coincidence ... The style is that which is usually known as 'Early Debased:' very early, and remarkably debased.

In case Liddell himself thought he had been forgotten, Dodgson gave him Giles Gilbert Scott as partner, as though the latter were the Scott of the famous lexicon, and partnered them both with a wandering lunatic, Jeeby, (the G. B. of 'G. Bodley') who had been let loose on the design but was now safely 'incarcerated at Hanwell' in the lunatic asylum once more. These wise men had given a new impetus to 'Art in England' by their creation.

> Already an enterprising maker of bonnet-boxes is advertising 'the Belfry pattern:' two builders of bathing machines at Ramsgate have followed his example; one of the great London houses is supplying 'bar-soap' cut in the same striking and symmetrical form: and we are credibly informed that Borwick's Baking Powder and Thorley's Food for Cattle are now sold in no other shape ... At the approaching 'Gaudy,' when a number of old Ch. Ch. men will be gathered together, it is proposed, at the conclusion of the banquet, to present to each guest a portable model of the new Belfry, tastefully executed in cheese.[28]

The pamphlet then breaks off into a spirited parody of *King Lear* with Dean Liddell as the mad monarch. 'The little dons and all, Tutor, Reader, Lecturer – see, they bark at me!'[29]

The pamphlet was published by 'D. C. L.', initials not likely to leave Liddell in serious doubt of its authorship. Dodgson followed it in 1873 with a drama or masque, *The Vision of the Three T's*, which was more elaborate but less barbed. In the course of it, poor mad Jeeby confesses that his architectural inspiration for the new structure came from the cheese-scoop and the Stilton. In reality, however, both the wooden case and the satires were overtaken when Bodley covered the offending belfry with a foursquare stone tower.

In his *Vision of the Three T's*, Dodgson also resumed an attack upon the proposal for cloisters. The terrace in the Great Quadrangle had been lowered and the base of the shafts of Tudor cloisters had been uncovered. Dodgson was dismayed at the suggestion that a set of cloisters should now be built on these foundations, a scheme which he attacked in his pamplet and in a letter of 3 November 1874 in the *Pall Mall Gazette*. In the press he also went back to the earlier 'improvement' and described Liddell's belfry bluntly as 'the ugliest and most conspicuous monstrosity.' Because it would now have to be encased in a further tower of stone, Christ Church would be faced with costs of £5,000 or £6,000. He noted in his diary ten days earlier that the question of the cloisters had been discussed at a meeting of the Governing Body. Dodgson had proposed the removal of the Tudor foundations but his motion was not even seconded. He was not surprised. Eight years later, after what he described as a stormy four-hour meeting of the Governing Body in 1882, he expressed astonishment that a motion of his had been carried by thirteen votes to twelve, accustomed as he was to being on the losing side.

In 1874 he was back in the architectural and fiscal arena, in his pamphlet *The Blank Cheque*, which attacked the University's decision to build the new Examination Schools in the High Street without the scheme having been costed or even planned, without even a committee being formed to consider such matters or to choose an architect. Perhaps, from the creator of *Alice*, the most memorable comment in the pamphlet is on the establishment of a far greater Victorian landmark. '"Five o'clock tea" is a phrase that our "rude forefathers," even of the last generation, would scarcely have understood, so completely is it a thing of to-day ... It has already risen into a national institution.'[30]

*

Though he had become a self-confessed recluse by 1882, no senior member of Christ Church could easily escape the lumpen-patrician vulgarity of its noisier set of well-heeled undergraduates. In March 1875, for example, it had been necessary to bring forward the end of Lent term because the Christ Church men had arranged a steeplechase in defiance of authority. Later still, the walls were defaced by graffiti, the spite of young noblemen who had been refused permission to attend the Duke and Duchess of Marlborough's ball at Blenheim Palace. Far the worst of these recurrent scandals was the so-called 'Library Riot' of 1870.

Loder's, which had begun as the college debating society in 1814 with the motion 'Whether the Allies in taking Paris would be justified in destroying the Louvre', did a modest amount of destroying on its own account. The cause in 1870 was the dismissal of a porter, Timms, popular with the rowdy element in the College. Loder's sought vengeance. On the night of 10 May, after Hall, bets were made as to the possibility of breaking into the eighteenth-century library by climbing over a high railing. The break-in was accomplished by those who had apparently never seen the inside of the library before. Someone shouted, 'It's full of blooming images!' and someone else shouted, 'Have them out!'

A number of marble busts and a small statuary were handed out. At 1.30 a.m. these were ranged round the Great Quadrangle with mats and faggots piled between them and bonfires were started, 'Just to leave our mark and blacken the old Brutes a bit,' as one of the perpetrators explained. Among these 'old brutes' was the fourth-century BC copy of a Greek statue of Aphrodite and Eros. The fires spread and the statue and the busts were left to be blackened. An anonymous bust of the late Dean Gaisford stared balefully through the flames. He and the other busts were permanently blackened and disfigured, the Aphrodite and Eros was reduced to fragments. All this time, Dodgson was at home in the north-west corner of the quadrangle, his windows looking out on to the quieter prospect of the city thoroughfare of St Aldate's.

Most incidents were not on this scale. However, in May 1881, the national press reported a more violent encounter, in which the Junior Censor was set upon in Christ Church and struck by a stone thrown by one of the undergraduate rioters. News of the incident reached the middle-class press of Liberal England. Christ Church's reputation as the home of snobbery, indolence and philistine resentment was described by the *Observer* in an editorial on 29 May. 'Christ Church is always provoking the adverse criticism of the outer world . . . At Christ Church all attempts to preserve order by the usual means have hitherto proved uniformly unsuccessful, and apparently remain equally fruitless.' Dean Liddell, who 'spends the bulk of his time in Madeira,' had failed to deal with the present outrage as he had failed to deal with the library riot in 1870. He had promised that those who burnt the library busts and statues would be punished but took fright when he found that the perpetrators were 'highly connected' and he did nothing.

Dodgson's letter of 5 June was published in answer to this attack. 'The truth is,' he wrote loyally, 'that Christ Church stands convicted of two unpardonable crimes – being great, and having a name.' He pointed out that Liddell's two visits to Madeira had taken place 'more than twenty years ago,' and that the library rioters had been dealt with by the Governing Body, of which Dodgson himself was a member at the time. He insisted that 'order has been the rule, disorder the rare exception.' He invited the paper's informant to find an institution where the undergraduates were 'more gentlemanly, more orderly, and more pleasant in every way to deal with.'

Dodgson may have felt obliged to defend the College as the home of good breeding and polite conduct but he knew perfectly well that what he wrote was nonsense. Dean Liddell had said something quite contrary to the Governing Body when it decided the fate of the library rioters in 1870. 'Let me observe, that the class of young men who have long been in the habit of resorting to this place are particularly difficult to deal with ... Young men of large fortune have little to fear from such penalties as we can impose.' Indeed, even in this matter of internal college discipline the miscreants had briefed Queen's Counsel to represent them. Their first line of defence was to refuse to admit any part in the destruction. Their own lawyers then warned them that the busts and statues were the property of the Crown, not of the College. Unless the matter were dealt with internally, it would go to court, where they might be treated like other young men of their age and face sentences of six months imprisonment with hard labour.

The rioters were astonished to find that they were not exempt from the law but hastily admitted their guilt. The Governing Body expelled three of the offenders, two were rusticated for a year and two were gated after Hall. Of these seven offenders, five were either noblemen themselves or sons of nobility.[31]

Despite such unpromising incidents, Bayne, as librarian, opened an Undergraduates Reading Room in 1884, decorating it with a bust of Hermes and providing a suggestions book. The more subversive suggestions soon included a plea for the works of Karl Marx and for the *Winning Post Annual*, edited by Robert Standish Siever with limericks and innocent pictures which became uproariously indecent when partially covered. Siever and his magazine were soon to be investigated by the Joint Select Committee on Lotteries and Indecent Advertisements. The bust of Hermes also provoked entries about the 'mutilation of the Hermae' and the 'unwashen state of our Hermes,' at a time when Dodgson and Bayne may or may not have known that Hermae were the phallic signposts of Greece.[32]

*

By his own account, Dodgson allowed himself to be proposed as Curator of the Common Room in 1882 because 'it will take me out of myself a little, and so may be a real good – my life was tending to become too much that of a selfish recluse.' Next to daily chapel, Common Room was the heart of his social life in the College, as it was of many of his colleagues, notably those whose appointments dated from the era of enforced celibacy. Senior members were now more likely to be married and to live out of College in the leafy avenues of north Oxford, yet even they made a point of dining in quite frequently. In 1889, the Common Room had forty resident members, paying half a guinea a quarter, and four hundred non-resident members who paid a shilling. It was not unfairly described as a club in the Victorian tradition of gentlemen's clubs, open from eight in the morning until ten at night, where members might see the newspapers, talk, write letters or enjoy a cup of tea. Afternoon tea was introduced in 1884, during Dodgson's curatorship.[33]

It was following dinner that Common Room society came into its own. Those who had dined at High Table, accompanied by their guests, filed out of the Hall, past the undergraduates' tables, down the great staircase with its fan vaulting, and out into the lamplit vastness of the Great Quadrangle, which gave separate access to the Common Room.

On its ground level below the Hall, the Common Room had a separate drawing-room, a smoking-room and extensive cellars whose stock varied between 20,000 and 25,000 bottles. In the evening it appeared in what Blagden called its 'dim, religious light,' the panelled walls hung with paintings by Cuyp and Frans Hals and Gainsborough, and engravings of Chancellors of the University and Governor-Generals and Viceroys of India. Its members sat round a large table to take their dessert and wine. A guest would usually take the place of honour next to the Curator who presided over the company. The Curator was head of Common Room, elected by his colleagues, though the Dean and the Canons were admitted by a decision of the members. The Students followed a frequent practice in the Victorian period by taking dessert separately from dinner. The cost of dessert and wine for the evening was shared equally among those present. They were waited upon by the butler or 'Upper Servant', James Telling, with his white whiskers and choker, a Dickensian creation.

Coffee was served soon after 8.30. At 9.05 p.m. Great Tom began to ring out its one hundred and one strokes, the tolling of the one hundred and one Students who had been on the College's original foundation. This was the signal for the college gates to close and for most of the members to disperse to their own rooms, or else to share hospitality in the rooms of others. In vacation, when there were no undergraduates in residence, dinner itself was taken in the Common Room and gowns were not worn. The Curator's most onerous duty, in Dodgson's view, consisted of obtaining whatever wine, cigarettes and sundries were needed for the comfort of the members and adjusting the cost to the weekly accounts of individuals. The Common Room rules after Dodgson's election laid down that, 'There shall be a Wine-Committee consisting of five persons, including the Curator, whose duty it shall be to assist the Curator in the management of the cellar.' Dodgson remarked that the Curator was thus logically obliged to help himself and he wondered if this was to be taken literally. The day-to-day running of the Common Room was the responsibility of Michael Sadler as Steward and of James Telling and a second servant.

Despite what sounded like a convivial and civilized society of senior members, the Common Room suffered from such feuds and bickering as are apt to flourish in closed communities. Dodgson's friend Vere Bayne had been Curator for twenty-one years until he resigned at a Common Room meeting on 30 November 1882. The main problem was that Bayne had had no Wine Committee and had made purchases solely on his own judgement. He bought sherry as if by compulsion and was informed by Dodgson that at the present rate of consumption there was enough in the cellars to last three hundred years. Dodgson had worked it out by calculus. Barclay Thompson, Lee's Reader in Anatomy at Christ Church, charged Bayne at the meeting with obstinacy and extravagance and moved that there should be a Wine Committee. Dodgson came to his friend's defence, but the motion was carried and Bayne resigned. According to Sadler, Dodgson and Thompson then conferred in a corner of the Common Room and Dodgson promised that, if elected to succeed Bayne, he would not be guilty of such stiff and autocratic rule as his friend and he would form a Wine Committee.

Despite his own assurance that he was reluctant to become Curator, it seemed that he was soliciting support. On 8 December, at a further meeting, he was proposed and seconded. He agreed to this with self-confessed reluctance, and because he still sought to make some amends for the selfishness of his solitary life. He had resigned his Mathematical Lectureship the year before and now, at the age of fifty, had unlimited leisure. He therefore sacrificed something of this for the public good. That, unfortunately, was not how Dodgson's opponents saw it. Sadler claimed that Dodgson became autocratic in a couple of weeks, drawing up rules for Common Room and then breaking them himself. When Thompson, whose support he had solicited in the election, protested at this, Dodgson became angry with him. There was an exchange of letters and an account of the dispute written by Dodgson was deposited in Christ Church library, as the means of vindicating himself and discrediting Common Room opposition.[34]

His attention to detail could not be faulted. He was meticulous in keeping accounts and holding audits, drawing a map of the cellars and recording the contents. The ledgers themselves were kept for him by James Telling. As Curator he was also responsible for the Common Room furnishings, the wages of the servants, even the newspapers and the coal for the fires. He arranged for William De Morgan to design and install new tiles in the Common Room fireplace. The Common Room drawing-room was in need of modern comforts. Dodgson commissioned the purchase of basket chairs and easy chairs. Most of these matters proved to be potential subjects of dispute between himself and the other members, though like Bayne before him it was the cellar that caused him most work.

There was no doubt that Dodgson increased the power of the Curator during his tenure of office by exploiting the reluctance of his colleagues for endless meetings and exhaustive argument. In 1888, he was given authority to buy and sell at his own 'discretion' those Exchequer Bonds in which Common Room funds were invested. In 1890 he was authorized to hold a 'poll' of members on issues arising, to avoid unnecessary meetings. Attendance at the meetings was modest, usually amounting to eight or ten members. Those who attended voted on such momentous issues as whether during vacations High Table dinner should be in the New Common Room or the Old Common Room and what provision should be made for non-diners' access to newspapers during the meal. On several occasions between 1885 and 1888 Dodgson suggested that a member bringing a guest to dessert should not contribute to the general cost of wine but should pay for himself and his guest only, by using a bottle marked with his name. It was repeatedly voted down but, as his willingness to resign became more evident, in 1888 an amendment was carried 'that the proposed privilege be granted to the present Curator (Mr Dodgson)'.

On 28 February 1884, it was revealed that Dodgson, on his own initiative, had introduced 'Afternoon Tea', consisting of 'tea, cocoa, and bread and butter supplied in the C. R. between 4.30 and 5.30 on all week-days.' The meeting approved this innovation. Tea was something to be left to the Curator but wine was a more complex matter. The most important Common Room committee was the Wine Committee, which subsequently authorized the Curator to construct a new cellar and to have ventilation and gas-jets installed in the old ones. A good deal of the Common Room wine was currently in cellars under the lately constructed Meadow Buildings.

Smoking had always been a contentious issue. In 1886, Christ Church Common Room adopted the characteristic Victorian club-man's remedy of the smoking-room. A proposal that smoking should be allowed in the Old Common Room after 9 p.m. on weekdays was heavily defeated on 7 March 1889. Instead a Smoking-Room Committee was set up, including the non-smoking Dodgson. The Curator was authorized to install an asbestos gas fire in the smoking-room. Yet the smoking-room was the cause of Dodgson's only serious threat of resignation. On 9 May 1889, he asked permission to give the Common Room servants 'reasonable remuneration for the additional trouble entailed on them by the new Smoking-Room.' The meeting refused. Having enough reading in law to know that the meeting could not reverse its decision there and then, Dodgson summoned another. He announced that unless he got his way, he would resign. No one else was prepared to take his place. 'It was therefore resolved, *nem. con.*, to leave the whole matter in his hands. The Curator did not tender his resignation.'[35]

In general, he was unhappy with the tone of Common Room life, complaining to Canon William Warner in February 1886 of a party spirit which had split the members into two camps, sometimes Dodgson versus the rest, despite his attempts to sustain social harmony. He was critical of what he considered to be a flippancy among the members towards subjects that should be held sacred. Even in lesser matters of taste, the standard of Common Room had fallen. In February 1896, for example, he deplored the decision at the Annual Common Room Audit to stop taking the *Observer* and to replace it by the *Sunday Times*, which he considered 'disreputable.'[36]

Dodgson had always been apt to put his views on such issues into print. It was a good tactic because, whatever their feelings, few people wanted to be dragged into the trouble of a pamphlet war over such matters as the type of liqueur or brandy to be stocked. They were more likely to let him have his way. There was also the danger by 1883 that the pamphlet which had been addressed to them might be printed in sufficient numbers to be spread all over Oxford, as his views on Christ Church architecture had been ten years before. Dodgson's first pamphlet on the trials of a Curator appeared when he had been in office just over a year, in January 1884: *Twelve Months in a Curatorship By One Who Has Tried It.* It dealt chiefly with his problems over the Wine Committee, 'a very simple organism at first – a sort of Amaeba, with so brief a code of Rules, that it was all but structureless; but as time went on it developed; and its Rules grew ever more complex and stringent...' Four members of the committee were supposed to assist him but there had been a 'gentle fading away' and in the end he was lucky if he could get more than one. Then, when the consequences of this were not to the liking of others, they blamed him. Not least among these critics were non-resident members who lived far away from Christ Church and seldom came near it. One of the residents in Dodgson's sights was Barclay Thompson. Another was a non-resident trouble-maker in Tunbridge Wells.

I have received, during this past year, a long series of letters from one writer, of a highly critical – not to say hostile – tendency. They had been fired off at me with a monotonous regularity, having all the persistency – without the pathos – of minute-guns ... I had been weak enough to picture myself to myself as a well-worked and slightly worried individual, trying, to the best of his poor judgment, to do his duty by his friends who had entrusted their Common Room to his care ... and behold, I find I am a dark conspirator, going about in cloak and domino, with daggers and detonators, and withal liable to be put in the dark and lectured by any soi-disant judge that chooses to don the wig and gown! All this is, as Tennyson says, 'sweet and strange to me.'[37]

Matters came to a head in November 1883 in the battle of the Green Chartreuse, between Dodgson and Barclay Thompson. On 12 November, Dodgson issued a notice informing his colleagues that the Wine Committee had decided to stock only three liqueurs: Green Chartreuse, Dry Curaçoa and Maraschino. There was little demand even for these and Dodgson, on his own authority, decided not to buy the dozen bottles of Green Chartreuse. However, if members of Common Room wanted liqueurs not stocked, 'I will procure any others for which an order is given.' Barclay Thompson issued a challenge to the members. If Dodgson was simply buying liqueurs for his friends, 'the word *Curator*, after his signature, should be expunged.' If he was acting as Curator, then he was defying the Wine Committee.

Dodgson sent round a note claiming that Barclay Thompson had 'erroneously stated' the position. Thompson, well into his stride, followed with another note insisting that 'the Curator is breaking the Rules of the Club *if he uses our subscriptions* in making purchases of wines, etc., on behalf of individual members of Common Room . . . Such purchases are not only illegal, but may cause serious inconvenience and even loss to the Club.' Dodgson replied that, whatever the Wine Committee might decide, he was not going to waste money on a dozen bottles of Green Chartreuse that no one wanted. He represented the members of Common Room, 'where *what seems their interest* clashes with the *letter* of any Rule, *I take the responsibility of breaking the Rule*.' That was the source of the dispute.

As Barclay Thompson bought the wrong decanters and Dodgson got the prices of liqueurs mixed up, the battle of the Green Chartreuse threatened general war. The butler was given instructions on how to serve the liqueurs. The decanters were destined to stand on a board, against a scale marked off in various fractions of an inch. Unfortunately, the decanters were not symmetrical. Dodgson drew up a series of instructions for the butler which involved three scales and calculations in sixteenths of an inch. The entire incident might seem to have an anticipatory ring of Captain Queeg and *The Caine Mutiny*.[38]

The Wine Committee and the non-resident critics were both targets of Dodgson's ridicule. 'And if the Curator shall complain of cold,' he wrote sardonically, 'it shall be the duty of the Committee to make things warm for him.'

An old member of Common Room had just come to Oxford, who always took pale Brandy and Soda at dinner, and there was nothing but brown in the cellar. 'What *am* I to do?' groaned the agonised Curator. 'It will take 8 days to get a Committee-meeting to settle from what merchant to get samples – 4 days to get the samples – 8 days more to get a meeting to select the brandy and fix the price to put on it – and 4 days to get it. That is over 3 weeks, and the poor old man only stays a fortnight!' Beads of perspiration trickled down his manly forehead. After some hours of anxious thought, he nerved himself for a truly desperate step: *he ordered a bottle of pale brandy on his own responsibility!* And forthwith came a letter from Tunbridge Wells. 'What! you're at it again, are you? For ever trampling on the liberties of Common Room, and conspiring against the Constitution. What's the use of my anathematizing you twice a week by post, and doing my best to make your life a burden? What's the good of a Wine-Committee? What's the good of anything? And *you* pretend to be a constitutional Curator? Yah, you Cockatrice!' I don't quite know what became of that guilty Curator. I believe he fled to other climes: and they elected a new one; and Common Room was once more supposed to be governed on constitutional principles: and no hitch occurred – till the next time.

After a year in office, Dodgson proposed that his colleagues should elect another Curator, or re-elect him with 'discretionary power,' or elect 'an automaton.' He was weary of the criticism and bickering. His trump card was that no one else wanted to do the job. As if inviting dismissal, he listed the rules he had broken. He had chosen dinner-sherry himself – because only one person attended the tasting. He chose whisky on his own authority when he had 'tried in vain to get someone to come!' Still the criticisms plagued him.

An urchin on the village green, when somebody's window has been broken, and the wrathful owner has sallied forth, stick in hand, to enquire *'Who did that?'* has a certain sudden desire of self-effacement, and a certain modest shrinking from the publicity which seems to await him: but I can assure you his feelings are nothing to mine.[39]

Common Room let him have his way. His second pamphlet, *Three Years in a Curatorship By One Whom It Has Tried*, appeared in 1886 and reflected a state of truce. Dodgson had fifty copies printed for circulation to his colleagues. It was less a satire than a straightforward presentation of expenditure and receipts and an account of the existing stock of wine. Yet there was a sardonic commentary, as much on the contents of the pamphlet itself as on its readers.

Long and painful experience has taught me one great principle in managing business for other people, *viz.*, if you want to inspire confidence, *give plenty of statistics*. It does not matter that they should be accurate, or even intelligible, so long as there is enough of them.[40]

There was some justice in the complaint that by his compulsive attention to detail he turned a relatively simple task into something comparable to running a business. He spent a good deal of his time in complaints to wine-merchants about deficient corks, bottles that appeared to have been opened in transit (returned sealed by stamp-edging with 'C. L. Dodgson' endorsed across it.) He supervised the annual wine count, disputed whether an imperial pint of champagne was 9/10 or 24/25 of a bottle, whether non-members were allowed to buy from the Common Room cellar and whether the correct price was charged by the butler for liqueurs. In 1892 he accused members of taking more bottles of the rarer vintages than the rules allowed but was obliged to apologize when he realized he had misread the accounts. In addition to the Wine Committee, the Smoking-Room Committee was to assist in the purchase of cigarettes and cigars. In 1890, he passed on some samples from the Alexandra Cigarette Company of Oxford to Arthur Hassall for an expert opinion. Dodgson, the lifelong non-smoker, could only say that he had never smoked a cigarette that was superior to these.[41]

However tiresome his punctiliousness as Curator might seem to younger colleagues like Sadler, he was regarded by many as a most amiable companion at High Table and in Common Room. As one of the elders of Christ Church he gained assurance with the passing years and, far from being the silent recluse, he shone as one of the stars in that private world. It was his humour at the dinner table or in the Common Room that was remembered. Powell remembered how Dodgson's story of a child caught in an apple-pie bed, 'made me laugh once till I nearly cried.' Others recollected a famous Dodgson dinner story of a man who was so fat that he had to put his trousers on over his head. Walter Ryde, a Junior Student, watched him keeping High Table 'in fits of laughter.' Stuart Dodgson Collingwood added that 'A guest brought into Christ Church Common room was usually handed over to him to be amused. He was not a good man to tell a story to – he had always heard it before; but as a *raconteur* I never met his equal.' Confidence, born of self-knowledge, made him at last the Dodgson of Oxford legend.[42]

His curatorship lasted a little less than ten years. On 3 March 1892 in a printed *Circular about Curatorship*, Dodgson informed his colleagues, 'It is my earnest wish to be permitted to resign, at the next Audit-Meeting, the Office of Curator, with which Common Room did me the honour of entrusting me nine years ago.' The work had been 'tiring to the brain,' if unproductive. Yet he had enjoyed 'the opportunities afforded me, by the frequent practice of placing a guest next to the Curator, of coming into contact with many interesting strangers, and of doing what I could to make their visits enjoyable to them.'

His place was taken by Arthur Hassall and Dodgson celebrated his release by publishing the pamphlet *Curiosissima Curatoria*, an account of the office since the beginning of the century with a list of resolutions passed since 1859.

*

Dodgson had long since talked himself into old age and began to notice everywhere about him the omens of mortality. In November 1882, he went to dinner with Thomas Fowler, the President of Corpus Christi, and there met William Ranken again, with whom he had read mathematics as an undergraduate. The other two men were mostly bald and quite grey. It seemed to Dodgson such a little while since they had all three been members of Bartholomew Price's undergraduate coaching party at Whitby thirty years before.

The greatest break in the continuity of life at Christ Church came at the end of 1891 with the resignation of Liddell as Dean and his replacement by Francis Paget. Paget, a Canon of Christ Church, had been friendly with Dodgson for many years and seemed an agreeable successor. Dodgson had not been intimate with the Liddells for a long time. Though he did not know it, Mrs Liddell had made a point of destroying all the letters he had written to Alice. In 1891, his valedictory notes to the Dean and his wife were appreciative without being more than formal. During the autumn of that year, before Liddell's resignation took effect, the Queen's daughter-in-law, the Duchess of Albany, and her children were guests at the Deanery. Dodgson was not a fellow guest and was incapacitated by synovitis but, as though treated to crumbs from the rich man's table, he was allowed visits from the royal children on 16 November. He showed them how to fold paper pistols and blot their names in creased paper, just as though he was in his thirties again in the summers of the 1860s.

Throughout the 1880s and into the 1890s, his sun rose above Peckwater and set over St Aldate's. Even while he triumphed at High Table or in Common Room, he was a stranger to that world in which Oxford's horizons had expanded beyond all expectations of the 1850s, where new voices and new orthodoxies prevailed and the annual number of matriculations doubled between Dodgson's arrival at Christ Church and the year of his death. Occasionally his voice was heard, though not to much effect, as when the next stage of reform raised the question of admitting women to the BA degree, a proposal to which he remained opposed. He was in favour of the higher education of women, but not of their co-education with men. Dodgson believed that the mental health of women was more likely than that of men to fall prey to stress and emotional disturbance in the face of such demands as the Final Honour School in Literae Humaniores or Mathematics. He did not live long enough to judge whether the implementation of such a reform would prove him right.

In his pamphlet *Resident Women Students* in 1896 he deplored what he called 'that social monster, the He-Woman,' who denied her sex and competed with her male rivals as though one of them. His greater fear was that it was women as a whole who would be at a disadvantage by being lumped with the men at Oxford rather than being allowed an institution of their own. He did not, of course, claim to represent the wishes of women by his argument. What women – or, indeed, men – wished for was not necessarily what would do them any good.[43]

The decline of Oxford life as he had once known it was a reality of the last fifteen years of his own. On 1 March 1883 he had called on Jowett, then Vice-Chancellor. The official reason was that Dodgson wanted backs to the seats in the gallery of the University Church. More ominously, the poisoned tide of a debased culture was lapping round the precincts of the University itself. He wanted Jowett to use his authority to prevent music hall in Oxford, the town being threatened by a visit from the singer and comedian Alfred Vance, once an insurance clerk but now topping the bill everywhere as 'The Great Vance' with the song which had made him famous, 'Slap! Bang! Here we are again!' Dodgson protested at such plebeian vulgarity, while Jowett listened but took no action. An unspoken moral objection was that music hall brought with it the promenade bar at the rear of the auditorium where prostitutes paraded for hire, protected from darkness and inclement weather.[44]

In the *St James's Gazette* of 6 December 1890, Dodgson summed up the change in Oxford common rooms as illustrated by their gossip.

I have resided in this University for nearly forty years, and during that time have spent some seven or eight thousand evenings in college 'common rooms,' and have heard, at a moderate computation, some twenty thousand anecdotes ... My impression is that there has been a gradual, but very real and steady, change in the tone of the anecdotes that have thus obtained currency and won applause among the senior men. This change has been in one respect for the better, in that it is very seldom indeed now that any such anecdote depends for its point on some objectionable *double entendre*; but it has been in another respect distinctly for the worse, in that anecdotes whose point consists in a comic allusion to some Bible text, or the existence of evil spirits, or the reality of future punishment, or even the name of God, are more freely bandied about and more openly enjoyed, not only by laymen, to whom such things may possibly be mere myths not worthy of any respect, but even by ordained clergymen, to whom, if to any living man, these things are solemn realities.

He sensed change and decay in the world of the century's end. Those who spoke of him did so with increasing agreement that he was a charming anachronism. Lewis Carroll was now the most famous author of children's books who had ever lived, perhaps one of the most famous names in all England. The Reverend C. L. Dodgson belonged elsewhere. His presence faded into the recesses of an Oxford eternity, the world of summer legend created for him by Leopold Amery and the young Athenians of the 1890s, as his friend Ethel Arnold described it, where 'the rooks will still build their nests in the New College elms, the Cherwell will still glide past Addison's Walk, the ghost of Duns Scotus will still linger in Merton Library, and from her guardian towers the "enchantments of the Middle Age" will whisper still to every understanding heart.'[45]

13

The Aged Aged Man

My dear father was what is called a 'High Churchman,' and I naturally adopted those views, but have always felt repelled by the yet higher development called 'Ritualism.' But I doubt if I am fully a 'High Church-man' now. I find that as life slips away (I am over fifty now), and the life on the other side of the great river becomes more and more the reality, of which *this* is only a shadow, that the petty distinctions of the many creeds of Christendom tend to slip away as well – leaving only the great truths which all Christians believe alike.[1]

S UCH PRIVATE CONFIDENCES as this one from the mid-1880s expressed Dodgson's creed in the last ten years of his life. Indeed, in 1894, he told his sister Elizabeth that he was 'Broad Church', compared to his younger brother Edwin who was 'High Church', a shift in description which thirty years earlier would have put him shoulder to shoulder with Jowett and the heretics. His, however, was a true breadth. Ritualism was to be tolerated for the sake of others. At the opposite extreme, writing to the mother of Edith Rix, he added that he could not believe that a man was to lose heaven merely because he had never heard of Christ. When Edith Rix became a Catholic in 1897, he thought it was probably a very wise step to take and found 'much beauty' in the ceremony of St Aloysius at Oxford.[2]

Those, like the young Claude Blagden, who heard him preach and thought he had retained his family's faith unchanged, were deceived. He was reticent in matters of doctrine and gave little away in public. As he said on more than one occasion, he disliked arguing about matters of religion. 'I have a deep dread of argument on religious topics,' he told Edith Rix in January 1886, 'it has many risks, and little chance of doing good.' Had he been a priest, he might have felt obliged to debate the tenets of his faith. He had been wise to remain a deacon and a teacher of mathematics, one who regarded it as a good thing that some teachers should be in Holy Orders, even if not fully ordained.[3]

In the last fifteen years of his life, he fashioned a humane theology in which, as he wrote to Lilian Moxon in July 1895, he believed that giving happiness to others is more important than attaining heaven oneself. Heaven had customarily been offered as a crude reward, as one offers treats to children for good conduct. When Edith Rix was anxious for an unbelieving friend who lived a noble life and had a beautiful character, Dodgson assured her, 'Even though she does not as yet see any God, for whose sake she can do things, I don't think you need be unhappy about her.' He might also have invited questions about his orthodoxy in April 1890, when he wrote that Christ was not perfect to begin with. St Luke's Gospel described Him as having 'increased in wisdom and stature.' Christ's humanity was perfected only by suffering.

In his letters, he wrote privately on such topics as the paradox of divine goodness and human suffering, the nature of evil, the question of heaven and hell. To Edith Rix in 1885 he sent one of his most engaging letters on theology. He believed only in the resurrection of what St Paul called the 'spiritual body.' He could not believe in bodily resurrection, if that meant resurrecting the 'particular set of atoms' which comprised him at the time of his death. Cannibalism alone made it a *reductio ad absurdum*. If one man eats another, which will be resurrected from the single body? The cannibal or the missionary?[4]

In 1890, in his letter to an invalid, he took the familiar position that life on earth was a time of trial, a building of character and spirit, for the eternity that was to follow. Pain was not sent to punish but to raise the glorious soul to higher glory. Quoting from the first Epistle of St Peter, Dodgson describes Christ as an elder brother who has suffered Himself and is present at the side of those who share those sufferings by their pain. A year earlier he had written that the answer to the problem of pain would only be known in the 'Other World', just as there were problems in mathematics, insoluble to human reason, whose answers would then be plain.

The problem of evil was a more sensitive matter. Dodgson believed that all new-born children were innocent, baptized or not. He also confessed in July 1886 that he prayed for those who rebelled against

God. The infant Augustus Hare had never understood why he might not pray that Satan should repent and be forgiven.

At his death, Dodgson left an unpublished essay on 'Eternal Punishment', a subject he had also discussed in his letters. He reduced the argument to simple conclusions. To punish human beings infinitely for finite sins would clearly be wrong and would make God a sinner. To accept that such infinite punishment was right, though believing it wrong, would mean the abandonment of both individual conscience and of faith in the goodness of God. To believe that God would not, in truth, commit such wrong, while believing that the Bible teaches the contrary, would mean 'the abandonment of the Bible as a trustworthy book.' The truth was, surely, that the Bible had been mistranslated, since the Greek word αἰών, in describing punishment, did not mean 'eternal'. Dodgson also had an instinctive repugnance for the assertion that a man must suffer eternally in hell, however much he might repent while there. He repeated to Mary Brown in 1889 his view on having to give up the Bible if, which he did not believe, it sanctioned eternal punishment. Punishment and reward might be replaced, he suggested in 1886, by the giving of different degrees of happiness.[5]

In such matters as heaven and hell or infant baptism, Dodgson in the 1880s and 1890s had reached much the same conclusions as Jowett and the contributors to *Essays and Reviews* more than quarter of a century before. So had many others of all denominations. In the world of the Belle Epoque, Edith Wharton's friend the *bon vivant* Abbé Mugnier performed theological acrobatics worthy of Dodgson on cannibalism. He was asked by his hostess at a dinner party how so civilized and amiable a man as he was could believe in hell. 'I must, madame, because it is a dogma,' he said solemnly, then smiled and added, 'I do not, of course, believe that there is anyone there.'[6]

*

In politics and society rather than in religion Dodgson remained always conservative, often reactionary, and habitually naïve. It was characteristic of his social attitudes that, though he preached at the servants' Sunday evening services, he was uneasy when the wife of a college employee wrote him a letter of appreciation. He was happy to lecture on logic to a girls' school at Worcester, but less happy when he realized that some of the girls listening were servants. He was eager to appear at girls' schools in Oxford and Eastbourne, as well as at St Hugh's College, but disapproved of colleges like Girton as fast and mannish.

In party allegiance, he could never have been anything but Conservative, his view of Gladstone sometimes mocking and sometimes scornful. He had little sympathy for the 1868 Reform Bill or for the 'roughs' who supported it. He was opposed to Home Rule for Ireland, having approved of the execution in 1867 of three Fenians for the murder of a policeman. He welcomed Parnell's arrest over the Irish Land League in 1881. He was relieved by Parnell's downfall in 1890, when the Irish Nationalist leader was cited in the O'Shea divorce suit, and he remained contemptuous of Gladstone's Home Rule Bill. One of the first books on the shelves of his rooms was A. V. Dicey's *England's Case Against Irish Home Rule*. A minor curiosity of the Parnell scandal is that the Nationalist leader and Kitty O'Shea were living clandestinely at Heatherbell Cottage on the road from Eastbourne to Beachy Head in the same weeks as Dodgson used to pass it with his little girls in the summer of 1886. Did he know from gossip and resent it then, or only when the story was told in court?

His own political theories and requests for patronage were brought frequently to the notice of Lord Salisbury, who had become Prime Minister in 1885 and held office for most of the period until his resignation in 1902. Salisbury was also a mathematician, a Fellow of All Souls, and had been at Christ Church a little before Dodgson, going down in 1849. The two men met when Salisbury was elected Chancellor of the University in 1869. Salisbury had served under Disraeli as Secretary of State for India and then as Foreign Secretary, becoming leader of the Conservative party in opposition in 1881 on Disraeli's death.

When Salisbury was installed as Chancellor in 1870, Dodgson used the good offices of his friend Liddon, who received an honorary Doctorate of Civil Law at the Chancellor's hands that summer, and his own fame as the author of *Alice in Wonderland*, to obtain Lady Salisbury's permission to photograph her four children. He also photographed Salisbury in his robes. Two weeks later he was the Salisburys' dinner guest in London. In the years that followed, he became a favourite with the Salisbury children, particularly with the two girls, Maud and Gwendolen, for whom he devised riddles and puzzles. In 1871 and 1872, he was a house guest at Hatfield for the birthday of Gwendolen Cecil. Three times in the 1870s he was a New Year's guest and in June 1889 wrote to fifteen-year-old Isa Bowman from Hatfield, as 'Your ever loving Uncle C.L.D.,' a letter bespangled with titles and etiquette.

> This is Lord Salisbury's house ... I came yesterday, and I'm going to stay until Monday ... There are some sweet little children staying in the house. Dear little 'Wang' is here with her mother. By the way, *I* made a mistake in telling you what to call her. She is 'the Honourable Mabel *Palmer*' – 'Palmer' is the *family* name: 'Wolmer' is the *title*, just as the family name of Lord Salisbury is 'Cecil:' so that his daughter was Lady Maud Cecil, till she married.
>
> Then there is the Duchess of Albany here, with two such sweet little children. She is the widow of Prince Leopold (the Queen's youngest son), so her children are a Prince and Princess: the girl is 'Alice,' but I don't know the boy's Christian name: they call him 'Albany' because he is the Duke of Albany. Now that I have made friends with a real live little Princess, I don't intend ever to *speak* to any more children that haven't any titles. In fact, I'm so proud, and I hold my chin so high, that I shouldn't even *see* you if we met! No, darlings, you mustn't believe *that*. If I made friends with a *dozen* Princesses, I would love you better than all of them together, even if I had them all rolled up into a sort of child-roly-poly.'[7]

Despite the disclaimer, it was hard to avoid the impression that Dodgson was enormously pleased with himself. He was where he belonged, at the heart of Conservative and patrician England. He retained the friendship of Maud Cecil, as Lady Wolmer, daughter-in-law of the Christ Church lawyer Roundell Palmer, Earl of Selborne. Elsewhere he might be Mr Dodgson who never accepted invitations and never took lunch. But lunch at Lady Wolmer's with his current little friend was quite a different matter.

Most of his correspondence or conversation was with Lady Salisbury and the children but Lord Salisbury was the member of the family whose attention and interest he courted in matters of preferment. Like his father's generation, Dodgson believed that patronage was his class entitlement, obtained either for himself or for others. Though his appeals to Salisbury were sometimes for his family, they were never for himself. In 1875 he intervened with Salisbury as Foreign Secretary, asking him to use his influence with the Charity Commissioners to secure the post of Assistant Charity Commissioner for Tom Arnold, son of Arnold of Rugby, brother of Matthew Arnold, and father of the novelist Mrs Humphry Ward. Arnold had been reduced to working as a private tutor, taking in boarders, and deserved something better. He was appointed.

Encouraged by this, Dodgson tried next year to get a Board of Trade Inspectorship for his cousin Captain Henry Wilcox. He failed. In 1880 he asked for an Inspectorship of Constabulary for the friend of another cousin. He failed again. In 1884, he wrote on behalf of a poor but deserving cousin who had taught at Twyford School. Again, Salisbury did nothing.

Undaunted, Dodgson turned to a wider topic. His youngest brother Edwin, whom he thought a Ritualist, was priest-in-charge of the remote South Atlantic island of Tristan da Cunha. Life had become difficult for the one hundred inhabitants and the Dodgson brothers began a campaign to get them moved to the Cape or to Australia, with compensation for the loss of livestock. Charles Dodgson tried impressing the importance of this on Captain George Tryon at the Admiralty. Tryon, notorious ten years later as the intransigent admiral who sank the flagship of the Mediterranean Fleet during an argument over its distance from HMS *Camperdown*, had not the least interest in either Tristan da Cunha or Dodgson. He suggested bluntly that it would be better to write letters to such people as himself rather than seek interviews.

Dodgson had tried the Assistant Under-Secretary at the Colonial Office, as well as the Governor and the Prime Minister of the Cape. He now wrote to Salisbury, asking him to grant Edwin an interview. Salisbury, as leader of a minority government, undertook to see Edwin but it was plain that there was no point in agreeing to take action while the government's tenure of power was so uncertain. Indeed, Salisbury was out of office in the following month. Four years later Edwin returned to England for medical treatment. A few months more and he was sent to the Cape Verde islands by the Society for the Propagation of the Gospel. Back again in 1895, he failed to get a curacy in England, despite another intervention by Dodgson with Salisbury, now Prime Minister once more. The brothers parted finally when Edwin left in 1896 to become vicar of Jamestown on St Helena.

Dodgson's interventions with Salisbury were not always in favour of a deserving client. In 1888, he asked Salisbury to use his influence to prevent the election of Henry MacLoed as Professor of Political Economy at Oxford, on the grounds that MacLoed had served a prison term, following the collapse of a bank of which he was a director, and was mentally unbalanced. MacLoed was not elected.

As a political reformer or innovator, Dodgson was always ready with schemes to be offered to Conservative and Liberal governments alike. He disliked Gladstone, comparing him unfavourably as a leader with Disraeli. Disraeli when defeated had continued to lead his party in opposition but Gladstone resigned upon the defeat of his party and came back to its leadership only after it won an election. His dislike did not extend to the Liberal leader Lord Rosebery, Dodgson's pupil at Christ Church in the 1860s. Rosebery took his name off the books after the College refused to let him continue as an undergraduate while owning a stable of racehorses. Dodgson resumed their friendship in 1893, a year before Rosebery became Prime Minister, and wrote to congratulate his former pupil on successful mediation between colliers and coal-owners which ended the miners' strike of 1893.

Few of the schemes he sent to Downing Street won approval. At the time of the 1884 Franchise Bill, he offered a form of voting based on proportional representation and transferable votes, in a form mathematically incomprehensible to most people. It was first directed to Gladstone, still in office in the autumn of 1884. Dodgson had his pamphlet printed and sent copies to every MP. Henry Scott-Holland, a Student of Christ Church, intended to take a copy to Gladstone's daughter Mary Drew at Downing Street. His nerve failed him. He wrote to Mrs Drew instead.

> Oh, Dodgson! Have you seen his incredible paper on Redistribution! It is the wildest form of serious joking that ever was seen! ... It really is a curiosity – to come out of the same mind as *Alice* – and yet to think that that same mind does not the least see the splendour of the joke! He is frightfully in earnest ... It really is worth looking at, for this purpose of psychical study.[8]

The proposal was followed by others, suggesting such reforms as the strengthening of the House of Lords at the expense of the Commons by having first-class government bills introduced in the Lords, debated, amended and merely sent to the Commons for approval. Members of the government should have the right to appear in both houses. It seemed extraordinary that Dodgson could believe that such proposals would have the least chance of success at a time when, for example, constitutional convention already forbad any money bill from being introduced in the Lords, let alone amended and presented as a *fait accompli* to the Commons. Salisbury, well aware of the potential for crisis, politely explained to Dodgson the danger of offending what he called the *amour propre* of the House of Commons.

In similar vein, Dodgson wrote in 1897, on Victoria's Diamond Jubilee, with a plan to settle the problem of Ireland. Let the Queen make a tour of Ireland and delight the hearts of her subjects. Let her do it regularly. Let her have a home there. Had she only gone there every few years of her reign, the Home Rule Bills, which Dodgson regarded with contempt, would never have been heard of. To illustrate what Victoria might accomplish, Dodgson pinned to the letter a press cutting on 'Holiday Tours in Ireland'. As it happened, Victoria made a visit in April 1900, though without the universal success which he had predicted. Indeed, when her son made a royal tour six years later, it was chiefly remembered by someone stealing the Irish Crown Jewels, which were never recovered.

Dodgson's other suggestions included new schemes for postal money-orders and charging double for Sunday post. The one that found most favour with Salisbury came from Eastbourne, during his seaside leisure of August 1895. He advocated a system of what was to be known in the Second World War as fire-watchers. Men were to be posted on the highest accessible points in London, twenty-four hours a day, to watch for fire. They would be in instantaneous communication with the fire-stations and able to direct their resources. Forty-four years later the scheme became a reality.

*

While his views on religion grew more humane, and his political fancies more outlandish, his nose for indelicacy was as keen as ever. 'I have known him leave a theatre in the midst of a performance for a very small deviation from the line he had marked out,' wrote the dramatist A. W. Dubourg. Yet he remained a devotee of the more anodyne productions of the London stage, in which a number of his past or present little girls often performed. Though by now he could afford a box on every occasion, he still preferred to sit in the stalls.[9]

In April 1894 the London production of *The Little Squire* by Dora Greet and Horace Sedger offended him by a dialogue on baptism, followed by laughter from the audience. Worse still, Isa Bowman and her sister Empsie were members of the cast. He wrote to Mrs Greet, as Lewis Carroll, reprimanding her for treating sacred topics as themes for laughter. Mrs Greet replied, resting on the defence of realism. The example was not one of profanity but a lesson to mothers in the audience who cared too little for their children's spiritual guidance.

Dodgson, as usual on these occasions, argued in a polite but implacable tone that the lines could be cut without damage to the play. He had put by two pounds to pay for tickets to take his nieces to the production. Unless the text were cut, he could not possibly do so. As for Mrs Greet's appeal to the example of the success of that London season, Arthur Wing Pinero's *The Second Mrs Tanqueray*, he told her he had read the reviews and had no intention of going to the play. Mrs Greet was not to be moved and the matter ended.

A point not raised by Mrs Greet was that all plays on the English stage had first to be read and licensed by the Lord Chamberlain, under the Licensing Act of 1737. This was not to be repealed until 1968 and led to the banning of Oscar Wilde's *Salomé* in the year of Dodgson's complaint, on grounds of profanity. The censors of St James's Palace would have cut anything from Mrs Greet's play that they considered offensive.

But Dodgson took no risks with decency. He decided not to go to *The Dancing Girl* by Henry Arthur Jones in 1891. His friends had praised it but, just in time, he learnt that the plot involved a dissolute young nobleman and a dancing girl who was his mistress. He had seen *The Middleman* by the same author in 1889 and found it good as a production but not healthy. However moral a play, he told Winifred Stevens, its plot might pass the limit of what was desirable. *The Dancing Girl* would probably come to Oxford. If she chose to see it there, he would think none the worse of her.

Some objections brought conflict with girl-friends themselves, many of them now adult. Ellen Terry heard of his displeasure twice. In 1880, he unsuccessfully tried to persuade her and Henry Irving to cut from the Lyceum Theatre production of *The Merchant of Venice* the lines on Shylock,

... That for this favour,
He presently became a Christian.

This was 'a sentiment that is entirely horrible and revolting to the feelings of all who believe in the Gospel of Love ... a needless outrage on religious feeling.' Once again, he helpfully demonstrated how the lines might be cut and the continuity of the play preserved.

He was not sufficiently revolted to stay away from future productions of *The Merchant of Venice*. On 17 August 1892, he went to a performance by Frank Benson's company at the Devonshire Park Theatre in Eastbourne, taking Maggie Bowman, the little girl then in residence at Lushington Road. He thought the production excellent and Jessica Bateman a very pretty page.[10]

There had been a more acrimonious exchange with Ellen Terry over her performance in *Faust* at the Lyceum in 1886. The incident showed, however, the persistent effect that Dodgson could have upon his female subjects, wholesome or insidious, according to taste.

> Mr Dodgson (Lewis Carroll of the immortal 'Alice in Wonderland') once brought a little girl to see me in 'Faust.' He wrote and told me that she had said (where Margaret begins to undress): 'Where is it going to stop?' and that perhaps, in consideration of the fact that it could affect a mere child disagreeably, I ought to alter my business!
>
> I had known dear Mr Dodgson for years and years. He was as fond of me as he could be of any one over the age of ten, but I was *furious*. 'I thought you only knew *nice* children,' was all the answer I gave him. 'It would have seemed awful for a *child* to see harm where harm is; how much more so when she sees it where harm is not.'
>
> But I felt ashamed and shy whenever I played that scene.[11]

Dodgson evidently heard of Ellen's displeasure and of the difficulty he had created for her in playing that scene. The following year he wrote and apologized for giving her pain. Elsewhere he was less understanding. In 1895 he thought *The Chili Widow* was not a nice play, since it involved one man making love to the wife of another, which Dodgson regarded as a French aberration. In 1896, he was offended by a musical extravaganza at Oxford, *The Water Babes* by E. W. Bowles, in which he found profanity as well as coarseness. Two of the Bowman sisters were appearing in it. Isa Bowman recalled that Dodgson walked out of the theatre when Malcolm Scott, the comedian, came on to the stage dressed as a woman. 'He could not tolerate the idea of a man in petticoats,' charmed though he was by girls playing little boys. Men in petticoats presumably recalled to him such scandals as the Boulton and Park case of 1870–1, of which anyone who read the newspapers could scarcely be unaware. It involved two young men, accustomed to dress as women on the stage, who had posed as women in private life, being tried though acquitted for inciting an unnatural act by parading with female prostitutes in the West End. In the case of *The Water Babes*, Dodgson protested to the manager and called on the Vice-Chancellor to ensure that the company would not be licensed to perform in Oxford again.

One of his worst horrors was when, after Florence Jackson had given her childish rendition of 'The Holy City', Isa Bowman, not to be outdone, gave him a private performance of 'Ta-ra-ra-boom-de-ay!' 'He stopped me before I could get to the second verse, and was so scandalised that I almost felt as though I had done something dreadful.' Dodgson's views on female dancers were mathematically precise. 'No really good dancer, who is an artist, should ever raise her foot more than a few inches from the ground.'[12]

Others might think his taste in drama commonplace and unadventurous. Dodgson thought it morally prudent. With his enthusiasm for the London theatre, he might have seen the comedies of Oscar Wilde, the first productions of Bernard Shaw, for that matter Ibsen or Chekov. It seems he did not. His friend Marion Terry played Lady Erlynne in *Lady Windermere's Fan* at the St James's Theatre in 1892, while his acquaintance the actor-manager George Alexander played Lord Windermere and also John Worthing in *The Importance of Being Earnest* at the same theatre in 1895, though not in front of Dodgson. He tolerated Pinero and Henry Arthur Jones, with exceptions and reservations. He enjoyed Gilbert and Sullivan, though he was shocked at a children's performance of *HMS Pinafore*, when the line, 'He said "Damn me!"' was permitted to remain in the text, sullying young lips by profanity. 'In some ways, "Uncle" was curiously narrow,' Isa Bowman thought. 'He hated me playing the wicked girl in *The Wicked Squire*, and for the time it ran was never quite so nice to me.'[13]

As a reader, he was less inhibited. His shelves contained Kipling, whom he admired and, perhaps surprisingly, Hardy's *Tess of the D'Urbervilles*. In 1882, he saw a stage adaptation of *Far From the Madding Crowd*, which pained him because it involved the seduction and suicide of a girl, but was not vicious. He read Henry James' *The Portrait of a Lady*, but passed no comment. He read a great deal of Meredith but with no apparent reaction. The books in his possession by William Acton, Henry Mayhew and James Greenwood suggest that he was not unaware of the major social issues of the day. He was indeed, as

Frederick York Powell said, a great worker rather than a great reader. This seems true both in quantity and depth, so far as contemporary literature was concerned.

*

As a great worker his reputation was safe. *Alice* was in the hands of the Albany children and the daughters of Lord Salisbury, as well as somewhere on the shelves at Windsor or Osborne. By 1891, he was able to tell Alice Liddell, as Mrs Hargreaves, that her adventures had sold more than 100,000 copies. There were Alice tins and Alice biscuit-boxes, the Wonderland stamp-case, even an Alice Birthday Book, in the last decade of the century. Henry Savile Clarke had staged what Dodgson called 'the *Alice* play' in 1886, a musical version which complied with the author's first condition that it must contain no coarseness, 'no *suggestion* even of coarseness.'[14]

Four years later, the hard-edged prose of *Alice in Wonderland* was transmuted by Dodgson into the baby prattle of *The Nursery Alice* of 1889. His Preface begins with thankfulness that English 'children' of all ages have read the original of his story, even those elderly children 'in whom no waning of health and strength, no weariness of the solemn mockery, and the gaudy glitter, and the hopeless misery, of Life has availed to parch the fountain of joy that wells up in all child-like hearts.'

> And my ambition *now* is (is it a vain one?) to be read by Children aged from Nought to Five. To be read? Nay, not so! Say rather to be thumbed, to be cooed over, to be dogs'-eared, to be rumpled, to be kissed, by the illiterate, ungrammatical, dimpled Darlings that fill your Nursery with merry uproar, and your inmost hearts with a restful gladness![15]

As in *Sylvie and Bruno*, published the same year, Dodgson lapsed into a style which seemed quite the contrary of his earlier manner. Sharpness and self-discipline had gone. He began to gush. The new opening of *Alice* was an alarming contrast to the assurance and energy of the original. It promised worse to come.

> Once upon a time, there was a little girl called Alice; and she had a very curious dream. Would you like to hear what it was that she dreamed about?

Well, this was the first thing that happened. A White Rabbit came running by, in a great hurry; and, just as it passed Alice, it stopped and took its watch out of its pocket. Wasn't *that* a funny thing? Did *you* ever see a Rabbit that had a watch, and a pocket to put it in?

Nothing but the shell of the original remained. Such highlights as 'The Mouse's Tail' or

> Speak roughly to your little boy,
> And beat him when he sneezes,

were removed. The Mad Tea-Party is scarcely recognizable, stripped of its splendid dialogue. No one speaks until the end, when the Hatter stands up. 'He has just got up to say to Alice, "Your hair wants cutting!" That was a rude thing to say, *wasn't* it? And do you think her hair *does* want cutting? *I* think it's rather a pretty length – just the right length.' If proof were needed that the original of *Alice in Wonderland* was not for the nursery, this version provides it. Yet, in another respect, the new tone illustrates the difference between a harsher world of childhood in the 1860s and the more indulgent child-centred world of the English middle class at the century's end.

For Dodgson, however, the exploitation of *Alice* was a subsidiary occupation. *Sylvie and Bruno* dominated his writing in the 1880s and 1890s, by far the longest and least satisfactory of his story-books. It appeared as *Sylvie and Bruno* (1889) and *Sylvie and Bruno Concluded* (1893). In his Preface to the second part, he described it as an attempt to show 'what might *possibly* happen supposing that Fairies really existed.' In the Preface to the first part he announced it as a book drawn from fragments jotted down since 1873, building on his story 'Bruno's Revenge', written in 1867. He hoped it would introduce to readers, 'along with what will, I hope, prove to be acceptable nonsense for children, some of the graver thoughts of human life.'

His gravest thought was that death might come at any moment, even during gaiety. He revealed that the unexpected death of a friend had been announced to him while he was writing these very lines. This gave him a chance to say something about unhealthy plays on the stage. Death was everywhere and unpredictable. The reader might not return alive from an evening at the theatre. 'And *dare* you, knowing this, say to yourself "Well, perhaps it *is* an immoral play: perhaps the situations *are* a little too 'risky,' the dialogue a little too strong, the 'business' a little too suggestive. I don't say that conscience is quite easy: but the piece is so clever, I must see it this once! I'll begin a stricter life tomorrow . . ." Be sure the safest rule is that we should not dare to *live* in any scene in which we dare not *die*.' There was no hope for *The Second Mrs Tanqueray* or *The Dancing Girl*, perhaps not even for *HMS Pinafore*, whose audiences might die with 'Damn me!' ringing in their ears.

As Dodgson had pointed out, the *Alice* stories had no moral purpose whatever. *Sylvie and Bruno* was frequently mawkish, determinedly moralistic, and extremely complex in structure. It contained a political fable in which the Warden of Outland went on a journey disguised as a beggar to become King of Elfland. He was betrayed by his brother, who acted as Regent, and was then insulted and beaten by his brother's wife and her child Uggug. As there is the good Warden and the unscrupulous Vice-Warden, so there is the Professor and the Other Professor.

The principal story is the narrator's experience of discovering the invisible world of Fairyland through Sylvie and Bruno, who are sometimes natural children and sometimes fairies. The narrator is also a character in the story of Arthur Forester, a doctor who marries Lady Muriel, who at another level is Sylvie. Lady Muriel has broken off her engagement to Major Eric Lindon, a morally noble atheist, because of his unbelief. Arthur hurries off to assist the victims of a fever epidemic, only to be reported as one of those who have died of the infection. Lady Muriel stands at his memorial cross, 'for one whose dust reposed elsewhere.' The absence of his dust enables Dodgson to spring Arthur on the reader again, since the report of his death was false. He has been saved by Lindon, the noble atheist, and restored to Lady Muriel.

The novel ends as happily as anyone could wish. The Warden, like Odysseus, returns disguised as a beggar but prefers, after all, to be King of Elfland. Arthur and Muriel are reunited. The noble atheist, though still not a Christian, now believes that God answers prayers. Finally, Sylvie prepares to reply to Bruno's question, 'What makes the sky such a *darling* blue?' For the narrator, as the answer comes, the vision of Fairyland fades, 'fast slipping from my eager gaze: but, it seemed to me, in the last bewildering moment, that not Sylvie but an angel was looking out through those trustful brown eyes, and that not Sylvie's but an angel's voice was whispering, "IT IS LOVE."'

Along the complex path of this story are scattered relics that might have belonged to the earlier and happier world of *Alice*. There are railways that work by the force of gravity, since all the lines go down hill. There are sham arguments, such as an inquiry into when a dinner guest legally acquires property in a plate of soup, or curious observations such as that 'Evil' is 'Live' spelt backwards, or the Professor's advice to the Mad Gardener that it is easier to keep a potato and see if hedgehogs eat it than to keep a hedgehog in order to see if it eats potatoes. Of all the fragments in the book, none are more poignant reminders of Dodgson's earlier genius than the occasional verses of the Mad Gardener's Song.

> He thought he saw an Elephant,
>   That practised on a fife:
> He looked again, and found it was
>   A letter from his wife.
> 'At length I realize,' he said,
>   'The bitterness of Life! . . .'
>
> He thought he saw an Argument
>   That proved he was the Pope:
> He looked again, and found it was
>   A Bar of Mottled Soap.
> 'A fact so dread,' he faintly said,
>   'Extinguishes all hope!'

The preaching of much of the novel is more evident than the last flickers of true 'Lewis Carroll' in the verse, whether in 'Little birds are hiding/Crimes in carpet-bags,' or the Alicean celebration of a great Victorian institution.

> Five o'clock tea!
> Ever to thee
> Faithful I'll be,
> Five o'clock tea!

More perishable are such incidents as the new Dodgson, alias 'Mr Sir,' meeting the fairy Bruno again at the beginning of *Sylvie and Bruno Concluded*, finding 'the little creature' in the grass of Kensington Gardens and catching him in his cupped hands. Bruno is at his most winsome.

'Does oo know what the *Rule* is,' he enquired, 'when oo catches a Fairy, withouten its having tolded oo where it was?' (Bruno's notions of English Grammar had certainly *not* improved since our last meeting.)

'No,' I said, 'I didn't know there was any Rule about it.'

'I *think* oo've got a right to *eat* me,' said the little fellow, looking up into my face with a winning smile.

Bruno has 'a rogueish twinkle' in his armoury as well as a winning smile. Sylvie, by contrast, is wise, beautiful and good. These two fairy creatures, accompanied by baby talk, the dog speech of Dogland, the unremitting purveying of sentiment and morality, pose a formidable barrier to the reader tuned to the cadences of *Alice*.

As a writer of fiction, Dodgson remained fiercely protective of his true identity. On the last occasion, two months before his death, he received a letter addressed to him at Christ Church as 'Lewis Carroll'. He handed it to the Common Room butler, James Telling, and ordered him to return it to the dead-letter office. There had been a time when he took a malicious delight in dealing with letters from autograph hunters by getting his colleagues to sign themselves 'Lewis Carroll' and returning these signatures to his admirers. That was a joke of which he had grown weary.

In 1883 he refused to be included in a dictionary of English authors, either as Lewis Carroll or as C. L. Dodgson, and the following year he asked a contributor to the *World* to abandon a proposed article on him. In 1890, he protested to George's bookshop in Bristol when their catalogue linked him with a book by Lewis Carroll. Among his friends, he was 'aghast' in 1885 when Edith Rix's mother sent a letter to him as 'Lewis Carroll, Christ Church.' His demand for privacy was inflexible. In another letter to Edith Rix in 1886 he wrote,

> One of the most dreadful things you have ever told me is your students' theory of going and speaking to any one they are interested in, without any introductions. This, joined with what you say of some of them being interested in 'Alice,' suggests the horrid idea of their some day walking into this room and beginning a conversation. It is enough to make one shiver, even to think of it![16]

Too many people knew his identity by now for him to have any hope of anonymity. In 1888, William Ralph Hall Caine wrote to him as Dodgson asking permission to include in an anthology some of the verses written by him as Lewis Carroll. Dodgson replied that 'Mr C. L. Dodgson begs to say, in reply to Mr Caine's letter received this morning, that he had never put his name to any such pieces as are named by Mr Caine. His published writings are exclusively mathematical and would not be suitable for such a volume as Mr Caine proposes to edit.' It was a Carrolingian, rather than a Dodgsonian, version of the truth – and it failed. Caine not only published two of his poems but reprinted Dodgson's letter in the introduction to *Humorous Poems of the Century* in 1890.

Sometimes it was necessary for Dodgson to come before the public as Lewis Carroll. 'Of no man could it more truly be said that until he was satisfied he was dissatisfied,' wrote the *Academy* on 22 January 1898, discussing his perfectionism in the production of his books. One cause of dissatisfaction had led him to issue a public advertisement, as Lewis Carroll, in *The Times* on 2 December 1893, over the latest printing of *Through the Looking-Glass*.

> For over twenty-five years I have made it my chief object with regard to my books, that they should be of the best workmanship attainable for that price. And I am deeply annoyed to find that the last issue of *Through the Looking-Glass*, consisting of the Sixtieth Thousand, has been put on sale without it having been noticed that most of the pictures have failed so much in the printing as to make the book not worth buying.

He invited all those who had bought copies of the impression to return them to Macmillan, giving their names and addresses so that copies of the new printing could be sent to them. He also invited applications from 'mechanics' institutes, village reading-rooms and similar institutions where the means of purchasing such books are scanty' and to whom the faulty copies would be given away. He wrote to Frederick Macmillan complaining that this had cost him hundreds of pounds. He also threatened to sever his connection with the firm after almost thirty years.

Dodgson was never less than acutely aware of the business potential of his writings. The setback over the printing of *Through the Looking-Glass* led him to require undertakings from Richard Clay, the printer, in respect of *Sylvie and Bruno Concluded*, before the printing of that book began. It was now the end of November and he feared the delay in getting written undertakings would mean his new book missing the Christmas market.

*

In the life of the Dodgson family, his surviving uncle, Hassard, had died on 3 September 1884 while his nephew was in Eastbourne. Dodgson declined to take the funeral service himself because he could not trust his feelings at the passing of 'one of the kindest friends I ever had.' With the death of Uncle Hassard, the closest of the elder generation of the family had gone. He himself, of course, acted as the head of his father's family, superintending the finances and legal affairs of The Chestnuts at Guildford, where his unmarried sisters were to live until his death. They had some money and property of their own, and he still assisted over such matters as leases and unsatisfactory tenants. Yet they remained dependent upon him.

In October 1894 he wrote to his sisters explaining that he could not make his usual gifts to them in 1895 because of the financial loss of £500 which he had suffered over the printing of *Through the Looking-Glass* the previous winter. It seems they thought he regarded their response to this as unsympathetic. He assured his sister Elizabeth that he had thought no such thing. He hoped that by 1896 his earnings from the books would again enable him to support them financially. If he died before then, they would inherit the copyrights and income.

Dodgson remained a regular visitor to Guildford, though sometimes there were a good many guests at The Chestnuts and he found lodgings elsewhere in the town. On other occasions he promised to make visits when there was room in the house. He regularly spent Christmas there, except when synovitis prevented him from travelling. In the last ten years of his life, he preached from time to time at St Mary's, Guildford.

Yet family life remained an adjunct to his existence rather than the heart of it. His sisters were said to adore him but his replies to them were sometimes abrupt. As he warned Elizabeth in 1894, he had not the time to be a chatty correspondent, even on the matters of religious belief which she raised with him. In September 1893, in the gentlest manner, he told his sister Mary to mind her own business when she wrote about the gossip that his girls at Eastbourne were causing. The year before, she had sent him a tract of her own. He told her that he did not read tracts, they were not worth it. He would make an exception for hers, which was evidently written for uneducated readers, and he would correct her English which seemed to him rather slipshod.

He was far happier among his child-friends, even if they were no longer children. Nigel Playfair recalled amusement in the 1890s at 'middle-aged females who continued to come and stay in Oxford and skittishly accept the toys and packets of pear drops that Mr Dodgson still produced for them from his pockets.' He was apt to mistake grown women for children. In November 1896 at the Princess's Theatre, he admired Kate Tyndall and Sydney Fairbrother, whom he thought were fifteen and twelve respectively. He gave books to them and prepared to lay siege, only to discover that they were both married women. He had, of course, made a similar mistake in launching himself upon 'Atty Owens twenty-five years earlier and kissing her without permission because he underestimated her age.[17]

A few months before the incident with the named actresses he met the daughters of Mrs Catharine Moore at Oxford, their ages sixteen and thirteen. He wrote to Mrs Moore asking if they were 'invitable' and 'kissable.' He asked permission to kiss, unless the girl were under fourteen, when he thought it unnecessary. Mrs Moore found him 'a bit odd.' The romance foundered. Yet it was one more indication that his enthusiasms were no longer confined to the very young.[18]

Among those who had grown older in his affections, he remained the lifelong friend of Gertrude Chataway. When she was nineteen, in 1885, he accepted an invitation from her family on the assurance that she was not too old to be kissed. In 1890, he still urged her to defy Mrs Grundy and come to Eastbourne, because 'you will always be a child to me, even when your hair is grey.'[19]

Even Dodgson's little girls could not always be relied upon to avoid the moral underworld. In his fifties, he was much taken by the young actress Isa Bowman, with whom he spent what he called a 'honeymoon' at Eastbourne. Did he know the world with which he shared her in the 1890s? It gathered at the Bedford Square house of Leonard Smithers, lawyer, publisher and pornographer. The member of this group to whom Isa Bowman was surrendered in marriage was Reginald Bacchus, an Oxford-educated journalist, 'tall, thin and languid,' as Jack Smithers, the son of the house, recalled.

He was a writer, and would write the most goody-goody stories for a prominent religious weekly, still running, and at the same time write obscene stories for a French publisher. He was a good soul nevertheless, kindly, gentlemanly and quiet.

Bacchus evidently wrote his bawdy novels for Charles Carrington, a Paris publisher whose English-language fiction was a target for Her Majesty's Customs and for a Parliamentary Select Committee on the subject. How much did Dodgson know? Before she was engaged to Bacchus, Isa briefly had another fiancé. When she went to tell Dodgson of an engagement, he was extremely upset, snatched the roses from her belt and threw them from the window saying, 'You know I can't stand flowers!' Did he think, on this occasion, that she was about to announce Reginald Bacchus as her future husband? Her first platonic honeymoon had been with Dodgson but her second was to be with the creator of such gems as *Two Flappers in Paris* or *Flossie: A Venus of Fifteen*.

By 1896, he wondered what had become of her. Isa was lost in what Jack Smithers called 'The Wilde homosexual atmosphere, the Bacchus foreign translations and bawdy books . . . Dowson's obscene translations for French publishers, Wilde's syphilis, and Dowson's sexual invalidism.' Ironically, Leonard Smithers was one of those whose bookshop sold '"artistically posed" photographs of prepubescent girls,' a tribute to a darker cult than Dodgson's.[20]

In July 1888, when she was fourteen, Isa had been his guest at Oxford. Though she could not be permitted to sleep in his rooms at Christ Church, she was with him every day from breakfast until dinner, sleeping nearby in the house of an old lady, to prevent 'ill-natured gossip.' Unfortunately, as Ruth Gamlen's mother observed, the old lady was 'gossip's very fountain-head.' Dodgson subsequently wrote for Isa her own supposed memoir of the visit: the Oxford colleges, the rooms at Christ Church, turning the handle of the orguinette (an early form of pianola), seeing coloured 'ghosts' on the ceiling, dining on meringues, learning to 'print' on Dodgson's typewriter, the little adventures, her thoughts and dreams, her enjoyment of the visit. It was charming, intimate, and just a little sinister, as 'Uncle' took absolute possession of his 'sweet pet,' with all her thoughts, dreams, and secrets, Andromeda-like in his world of restraints.

After dinner, Isa got somebody or other (she is not sure who it was) to finish this story for her. Then she went to bed, and dreamed she was fixed in the middle of Oxford, with her feet fast to the ground, and her head between the bars of a cellar-window, in a sort of final tableau. Then she dreamed the curtain came down, and the people all called out 'encore!' But she cried out, 'Oh, not again! It would be *too* dreadful to have my visit all over again!' But, on second thoughts, she smiled in her sleep, and said, 'Well, do you know, after all I think I wouldn't mind so very *much* if I *did* have it all over again!'[21]

Isa was soon to be replaced by Enid Stevens, whom Dodgson first met in 1891, when she was nine and he was fifty-nine, her 'old gentleman', as he was known in her family. A previous favourite, Evelyn Hatch, recalled that 'Enid Stevens, with her dark curls and large dreamy eyes, was like one of Sir Joshua Reynolds' child-angels.' In his usual phrase, Dodgson asked permission to 'borrow' Enid from her mother. 'Borrowing a girl' to 'take about' had been his customary phrase since the 1870s. From then until the end of his life, when she was fifteen, the walks, games, theatre, *tête-à-tête* dinners with 'my darling Enid' followed their accustomed course. More than half a century later, Enid Stevens thought their friendship was more like the mutual affection of a girl and her grandfather. She judged it the most valuable experience of her life. For all that, Dodgson's repeated requests that he should be allowed to take her away with him to Eastbourne or London were met by her mother's refusals. To the end of her life, Enid regretted it. At the first refusal, in 1892, Dodgson was content instead with one of the last of his little actresses, twelve-year-old Polly Mallalieu, as his Eastbourne companion.[22]

Occasionally, Enid Stevens was accompanied to Dodgson's rooms by Margaret Mayhew, a year her junior. Margaret Mayhew was the youngest child in her family, her three elder sisters having been the occasion of Dodgson's falling out with their mother in 1879 over nude photography. Margaret was the means of a *rapprochement* with the Mayhews and was Dodgson's guest with Enid on the occasion of Victoria's Diamond Jubilee on 22 July 1897, when they went up to the flat roof above his rooms after dinner to see the fireworks and illuminations. In 1891, Dodgson told Mrs Liddell that romantic sentiment was dead in him. Enid Stevens, to whom he dedicated *Sylvie and Bruno Concluded* in 1893 and much of his affection for the remainder of his life, proved him wrong.

Alice Liddell, 'Mrs Hargreaves' as he now addressed her, was almost a stranger to him by this time. Writing to her in March 1885 to ask her permission before publishing the manuscript volume of *Alice's Adventures Underground* in facsimile, he began by saying, 'I fancy this will come to you almost like a voice from the dead after so many years of silence.' When the volume was produced, Dodgson asked if he might present a copy to the eldest Hargreaves daughter. There were no daughters. When Alice invited him to be godfather to her son, Dodgson did not reply. Yet his relations with the Liddells improved at the time of the Dean's resignation. On 25 November 1891 Rhoda and Violet Liddell were allowed to come to tea. Dodgson was suffering from synovitis and they insisted upon acting as his waitresses. Eight days later Mrs Liddell herself came to tea with her daughter Lorina, now Mrs Skene. To complete the pilgrimages to Staircase 7 in the Liddells' last weeks at Christ Church, Alice herself came over with Rhoda for a short visit on 9 December.[23]

Alice Liddell had, of course, done well by her marriage into the Hargreaves family. Yet, no less than Isa Bowman, her new life glanced against an old scandal. The Hargreaves family formed an alliance with the Hanbury-Tracys, who had enjoyed a most unwelcome moment of late-Victorian fame, when Henry Labouchere's newspaper *Truth*, on 21 November 1889, listed them among the patrons of an absurdly named 'chastising-service,' run by a lady in Bristol who beat girls and young women for money, as a service to their families. There were moments when the path of self-conscious respectability seemed to dwindle from a tightrope to a mere spider-thread, thoroughly justifying Dodgson's careful choice of those with whom he associated. It might seem, in retrospect, that he had been only a step away from the infamies of Charles Augustus Howell, the commercial pornography of Isa Bowman's husband, and the moral underworld where the troublesome female young were professionally beaten.

With his tendency to quantify, he told Isa Bowman that children were 'three-fourths of my life.' Since, as he said repeatedly, he did not care much for boys, it was little girls who had made his life worth living. It was said that he ceased to have an interest in them when they reached the 'awkward age' of puberty, and before that if they proved stupid or self-centred. In the last years of his life, however, he still loved some 'girl-children' who had reached the age of twenty-five or thirty. There were some, like Isa Bowman or Enid Stevens, who were in their teens while the relationship still flourished. It seemed that, at last, he was growing up. Or perhaps he loved each special girl for herself and, as he matured, such special love survived the passage of time. Alice was the single great disappointment.[24]

*

Among his associations with the world of the Pre-Raphaelites in the 1860s, Christina Rossetti remained his friend into the 1890s. In the 1880s and 1890s, many of his adult friendships and associations lay in the world of art. He was still an enthusiastic amateur, sketching child models in the studios of female friends, urging Gertrude Thomson to make use of her camera on his behalf. In 1885 he approached Harry Furniss, a *Punch* caricaturist whom he admired, to commission illustrations for *Sylvie and Bruno*. Sir John Tenniel had had enough of 'that conceited old don.' When Furniss told Tenniel that he had agreed to do Dodgson's illustrations, Sir John said, 'I'll give you a week, old chap, *you* will never put up with that fellow a day longer.'

They put up with one another for seven years. Furniss described Dodgson as 'a wit, a gentleman, a bore and an egotist – and, like Hans Andersen, a spoilt child.' He also thought him a liberal-minded and liberal-handed philanthropist but insisted that 'his egotism was all but second childhood.'

> Delightful and interesting as Carroll the author was, he, unfortunately, proved less acceptable in the form of Dodgson the critic. He subjected every illustration, when finished, to a minute examination under a magnifying glass. He would take a square inch of the drawing, count the lines I had made in that space, and compare their number with those on a square inch of illustration made for *Alice* by Tenniel! And in due course I would receive a long essay on the subject from Dodgson the mathematician.

The two men quarrelled without ever quite reaching a break. Dodgson suggested they might fight out their differences in something like a pamphlet war. He wanted an 'elaborate' legal agreement, which Furniss refused to sign. He developed, according to Furniss, an obsession over secrecy regarding the book. The two men sat up 'in the dead of night' cutting the manuscript into horizontal strips of four or five lines each. Dodgson put these in a sack, shook them up, then took them out and pasted them down on paper in random order, so that no one should steal and copy his work. Then he marked each strip with what Furniss called, 'numbers and letters and various hieroglyphics, to decipher which would really have turned my assumed eccentricity into positive madness.' Furniss sent the manuscript back and threatened to go on strike.

When the work was almost done, Dodgson arrived one evening,

ate little, drank a few glasses of sherry, and made for the studio door to inspect the drawings. Furniss stood with his back to the door, barring the way.

'Mr Dodgson, I am *very* eccentric – I cannot help it. Let me explain to you clearly, before you enter my studio, that my eccentricity sometimes takes a violent form. If I, in showing my work, discover in your face the slightest sign that you are not *absolutely* satisfied with any particle of this work in progress, the *whole* of it goes into the fire! It is a risk: will you accept it, or will you wait till I have the drawings *quite* finished and send them to Oxford?'

'I-I-I ap-appreciate your feelings – I-I-should feel the same myself. I am off to Oxford!' and he went.

Despite sparring of this kind, despite what Furniss regarded as Dodgson pestering him with suggestions about little girls of his acquaintance who would make perfect models for little naked Sylvie, or the further problem that Sylvie was also, at another level of reality, supposed to look like Lady Muriel; despite Dodgson's expressed aversion for such lapses in taste as the 'hind quarters' of fairy-girls being revealed, the work was completed. 'I treated him as a problem, and I solved him,' wrote Furniss philosophically.[25]

Dodgson had long since accepted that he had no talent for art beyond sketches that lacked a sense of draughtsmanship. It was at the beginning of 1888, eight years after abandoning photography, that he began to sketch nude figures of young girls in the studios of female friends like Edith Shute and Gertrude Thomson. His only previous attempts at sketching from the nude had been with Beatrice Hatch and Lily Henderson when they were about five years old. Some of the later studio models were hired and some were 'borrowed' from sympathetic mothers of his acquaintance, their ages between six and fourteen. On the first of these occasions, 28 January 1888, Dodgson spent the morning at Mrs Shute's studio in Chelsea, sketching a professional model, Ada Frost, who was fourteen years old. She would pose nude for fifteen or twenty minutes at a time, then sit by the fire in a dressing-gown during her rest periods. Dodgson was impressed by her naturalness and dignity, remarking that only someone 'in search of evil thoughts' would find her attractive in any other way than a statue is attractive.

Though he frequently asked Mrs Ward or Mrs Shute or Gertrude Thomson to provide child-models in their studios for sketching 'from the model', he remained prudent. To Henrietta Ward, he insisted that he must have models whose parents were respectable and whose ages were between eight and sixteen. Gertrude Thomson was also a photographer and Dodgson asked her either for nude photographs of girls she had taken or to take nude photographs of girls on his behalf. His last visit to a studio was apparently to Gertrude Thomson's in November 1897, less than two months before his death, when he and Miss Thomson spent a morning sketching Isy Watson, a thirteen-year-old professional model. Mrs Shute, who had no idea that she was only one of those providing this service for him, recalled Dodgson setting out his requirements.

> He confessed to having no interest in boy or grown-up female models, having the 'bad taste' to find more beauty in the undeveloped than the mature form. 'I think,' he adds, '12 would be my ideal age: children are so thin from 7 to 10.' I cannot say his drawings were very good, in spite of his concentration and enthusiasm, but I was always delighted when I got hold of a child to suit him, and he turned up. Letters as late as 1896 allude to sittings in my studio. In the rests, he would lay himself out to amuse our model, and it was interesting to see how puzzled a new child might be at first; how, gradually, she would catch on, and finally give herself wholly up to the enchantment of his stories. I made the tea; he supplied the cakes, and the lunch rest would get unduly prolonged, to everyone's satisfaction.

For some time he made use of Maud Howard, who was fourteen in 1890. He considered her to have a good figure but not a particularly attractive face. Though Maud Howard's elder sisters were also models, which might have made him hesitate, her mother kept a shop and that sounded respectable enough. He was not interested in her elder sisters, who were well past the age of perfection.[26]

When pictures were drawn for him, he did not want to waste his money on boys. In 1893 he asked Gertrude Thomson to make the fairy figures for his poems in *The Three Sunsets* more obviously girls. Boys were out of place. As he had told Mrs Shute, he had the 'bad taste' to prefer young girls, when drawing from the model, and would have required boys to be fully dressed.

He allowed that a rear view of a child standing might be beautiful, indeed he had suggested it to Mrs Mayhew when hoping to have eleven-year-old Ethel naked before his camera in 1879. There was beauty in such 'a lovely study of downward-rippling curves.' But when the girl's back was bent in, the lower part of the body became too prominent, in other words her buttocks were, as he described it archly, 'terribly *en évidence*.' The figure must be straightened at the hips. In 1894 he objected to another of Gertrude Thomson's illustrations on the grounds that the figure of the girl was not completely naked. To Dodgson, all partly clothed figures were 'unpleasantly suggestive of impropriety.' The figure was also smiling and beckoning in a manner that was too bold, 'unpleasantly so.'[27]

Dodgson showed himself at his most prudent in the case of Mrs Moberly Bell, the sister of Gertrude Chataway, and her daughters. Iris was ten and Cynthia six. Gertrude Chataway had just been his guest at Eastbourne in the summer of 1893. Dodgson, never having met the family, wrote to ask Mrs Moberly Bell if he might arrange to have Cynthia drawn in the nude by Gertrude Thomson. He told Miss Thomson that he also wanted photographs of both girls. Iris had a scar but that was immaterial to him and, as he said, she would soon be too old to be photographed in the nude.

A great attraction of the two girls was that, as he assured Gertrude Thomson on 27 September, they were upper-class children. Hired models bore the marks of their class origins, they were 'plebeian and heavy,' and their ankles were too thick. He made do with them but could not admire them. For three weeks he wrote to Mrs Moberly Bell and her children as though they were the centre of his universe. There were ebullient letters, affectionate and humorous, offers of theatre tickets, copies of his books, and an introduction to Christina Rossetti. Abruptly, soon after the photography had begun, he announced to Gertrude Thomson that it was all over. There must be no more nude pictures of Cynthia or Iris. Mrs Moberly Bell was bringing up her daughters in a manner that threatened their 'purity of mind.' He did not enlarge on this, though he wrote that the greatest risk was to the little boy of the family, who had perhaps glimpsed his sisters naked while Gertrude Thomson was drawing them at Mrs Moberly Bell's house in Portland Place. On 31 May 1880, he had written to Mrs Henderson after her daughters had spent three hours naked in his photographic studio. Delightful though the experience was, he advised her to break them of such habits at the summer's end, for the sake of their little brother.[28]

Of all the adult women in his life, Gertrude Thomson was perhaps the one whom Dodgson might conceivably have taken as a wife in his later years. When they first corresponded in 1878, he was forty-six and she was twenty-eight, the daughter of the Professor of Greek and Hebrew at Lancashire Independent College and herself a student of the Manchester College of Art. Her obituary of 'my beloved friend,' which appeared in the *Gentlewoman* in January and February 1898, was as public a display of love and devotion as Dodgson was ever to receive. The enthusiasm of his little girls, writing over half a century later as elderly ladies, is entirely eclipsed by it.

In appearance, Gertrude Thomson was a mild and androgynous-looking woman of the type who is apt to appear ageless. She adored Dodgson, admired his learning and loved his books. They had artistic interests in common, whether in drawing or photography. His enthusiasm for naked girl-children failed to shock her and was something she could share. She painted Enid Stevens' portrait for him, as well as that of May Miller, and undertook the illustrations for his last book, *The Three Sunsets*, a collection of his more solemn verse. In this relationship, however, it seemed that romance was indeed dead in him and he had no taste for a marriage based on the friendship of a mature man and woman. Yet he showed gratitude and affection to her. In 1893, when he was delayed in getting to Eastbourne, he arranged for Gertrude Thomson to spend a week in his Lushington Road rooms, even buying her return railway ticket as part of the hospitality. He did not, however, install her there while he was present. Throughout their friendship there was always something of the artist and paymaster.

Gertrude Thomson's final memory of him in November 1897, when they sketched the model Isy Watson, was one of the last glimpses left for posterity.

He had written asking me if I would go with him to the matinée of 'The Little Minister', and I had suggested that he should come to my studio in the morning for an hour's sketching. I secured a lovely little girl as model, and he promptly appeared at 11 o'clock. He was charmed with the child and they made friends at once. In the 'resting' intervals he sat with her on his knee drawing comic pictures to amuse her, and warming her little hands, for the morning was chilly. We were to lunch with some friends of his in Lowndes-square, and being rather behindhand, we hailed a hansom. Something frightened the horse and it bolted with us.

'Well,' observed Lewis Carroll serenely, 'if we are alive when we reach Lowndes-square, we certainly shall not be late.'

He was exceptionally brilliant that day at lunch, full of repartee and anecdote. He looked extremely well, and as if many years of work still lay before him. As we were driving to the theatre he confessed to me that he had been working very hard lately, sitting up till 5 o'clock in the morning. When I ventured to gently remonstrate, he smiled.

'It suits me,' he said; 'I feel very well.' Then suddenly turning to me, he said, while a wistful look grew in his eyes, 'My time is so short. I have so much to do before I go, and the call might come any day.'

Before they parted, he sent a note backstage asking if he might bring Gertrude Thomson to meet a young actress he knew. The reply came and the envelope was handed to her. By an irony not lost on her companion, it was addressed to 'Mrs Dodgson'. Even if not married they were now, as he put it, 'labelled.'[29]

*

In Dodgson's accounts of his health, he now spoke alternately of habitual fitness and of the probability that he had not much longer to live. After a medical examination in 1885, he described himself as thoroughly healthy and never having been seriously ill. He could stand at his desk and work for ten hours at a time, sometimes until five o'clock in the morning, or walk twenty-five miles without feeling exhausted. He thought that he might be able to work for another twenty or thirty years, if that was God's will for him. Little more than a year before his death, he still spoke of his splendid health. When he told his friends that he feared he might die before completing his work, it was largely because he had planned so much of it. Those who observed him, even if they could not vouch for his health, never doubted his energy.

In 1893, at sixty-one, he recorded an eighteen-mile walk from Oxford to Abingdon and back in five hours and twenty-four minutes, at eighteen minutes to the mile. The previous year he had denounced his Christ Church colleagues as too lazy, too fat or too old to accompany him, but his medical man, Dr Brooks, was game. In 1894, at Eastbourne, Dodgson walked from his rooms to St Leonard's, a distance of seventeen miles. Four months before his death, during his last summer at Eastbourne, he noted that an eighteen-mile walk to Hastings was becoming quite a regular thing, he had done it twice within three days. That summer he had also purchased a Whitely Exerciser which fitted to the wall and on which he could exercise the muscles of his arms and shoulders.

From 1888, however, he suffered a series of maladies. He had long been deaf in the right ear. In 1888 he consulted Sir James Paget for synovitis in his right knee. The next year it was in his left knee. Also in June and December 1888 he experienced migraine attacks, his vision impeded by 'moving fortifications,' but without a headache. There was another episode of this in the following year. More seriously, in 1891, he fainted at the end of morning chapel on 6 February and lay, unnoticed, on the floor of the choir stalls until he came round an hour later. His nose had bled because, he thought, he had struck it on the hassock as he fell. He felt a headache afterwards but nothing more and recorded having had a similar 'epileptic attack,' as he called it, in London at the end of 1885. Dr Walter Brooks examined him and prescribed exercise. For four months Dodgson avoided train journeys alone, in case he should be taken ill while travelling. So far as his health was concerned, it was his first true *memento mori*. In January 1892 he wrote to Gertrude Chataway about his weak circulation, the diagnosis which Brooks had made and for which twice-daily walks had been prescribed.

The attacks of synovitis or 'housemaid's knee', sometimes immobilized him for weeks and affected him permanently, giving him the abrupt and jerky movement in his walk which Isa Bowman remembered. On 19 April 1888 he complained to Michael Sadler that he had spent three weeks lying on the sofa, though still able to get to Hall. The first attack lasted over two months. It struck again while he was at Eastbourne in 1889 and again in the final weeks of Liddell's tenure of office, in the late autumn of 1891.[30]

On this last occasion, Dodgson took the advice of Dr Brooks and abandoned his plan to spend Christmas at Guildford, partly for fear that the extreme cold might cause another fainting fit. He tried iodine and bandaging for his knee, as usual, then left the bandages off, which seemed to do quite as much good. For the first time ever he spent Christmas and the New Year alone in his Christ Church rooms. It was more than three months before he recovered and, towards the end of this time, he announced his wish to resign as Curator of the Common Room.

Towards the end of 1890, he was confined to his rooms by what he called an ague-like attack. This was followed by a bronchial cold in January 1893 at Guildford, then a severe cold in March 1894 and a bad attack of influenza in February 1895, which made him unable to attend chapel or Hall for four weeks. He told his brother Skeffington that he had been left feeling very weak. In 1892 influenza had laid low the entire household at Guildford, bringing pleurisy in its wake, which suggested the possibility of an hereditary disposition to such weakness among Archdeacon Dodgson's children. As he faced the second half of his sixties, the lottery of illness might equally prove that energy would beget health for him, or that some recurrent malady would bring upon him the night 'in which no man can work.'

He possessed a considerable collection of books on human physiology and medicine. In the last twenty years of his life he showed a particular attachment to homoeopathy. Among his carefully prepared equipment for travelling was a homoeopathic medicine chest. At Eastbourne, in September 1879, he treated Agnes Hull with calendula when she cut her foot on a broken bottle. He supplied calendula lotion for Amyatt Hull's blistered feet and eight drops of nux vomica, the deadly nightshade, on a lump of sugar for Agnes's sick headache. Self-medication was to begin in earnest by 1882, when hard, pink skin formed on his side. Dodgson diagnosed it as erythema and treated it with graphites and calendula.

Six years later, when he was fifty-six, he had begun to suffer from eczema and varicosis, which did not yield to self-treatment. He went to London and consulted his homoeopathic physician, Dr Burnett, who prescribed rubia tinctoria for what he diagnosed as Dodgson's disordered spleen.

*

His instincts and habits, as opposed to some of his beliefs, seemed little modified in his later years. He practised frugality, eating sparingly and still confining his lunch to a biscuit with sherry. He was careful with money, on his guard against beggars and the undeserving poor, though generous to those he knew. To Gertrude Thomson and to his own family, he commended ways of avoiding the cost of a cab when travelling to Oxford or Eastbourne. At Oxford, for example, it was possible to make a porter wheel the luggage on a barrow to a destination in the city while the travellers followed on foot. A shilling would be ample payment. A cab driver, on the other hand, would expect two shillings and more. Dodgson was ever mindful of the proverb that a penny saved is a penny gained.

In 1890, in a letter in the *Standard* on 19 August, he offered a means of putting an end to industrial disputes and keeping the working-class in its place. He was replying to the Eight Hours Movement, whose call for the reduction of the working day to eight hours had resulted in strike action.

> Supposing that employers of labour, when threatened with a 'strike' in case they should decline to reduce the number of hours in a working day, were to reply, 'In future we will pay you so much per hour, and you can make up days as you please,' it does appear to me – being, as I confess, an ignorant outsider – that the dispute would die out for want of a *raison d'être*, and that these disastrous strikes, inflicting such heavy loss on employers and employed alike, would become things of the past.

The truth was that Dodgson was schooled in the economy of the day labourer. Charity, whether a gift of money or of books to sick children, came easily to him. When his friends were in trouble, wrote his nephew Stuart Dodgson Collingwood, he replied, 'I will not *lend* but I will *give* you the £100 you ask for.' The general notions of social welfare provision, which the Liberal party was to pioneer in the ten years after his death, seemed to him a reward that had not been earned and was not deserved.[31]

In his way, he had remained a man of business. Having invested money as well as genius in the books which Macmillan published by his leave, he expected a return. He paid the printers and the publishers and took the receipts. If he treated Macmillan as though the firm was his employee, ordering its partners to buy his theatre tickets or get his watch repaired, there seemed to be some justice in this. Printers and publishers alike had been hired by him. They owned no part of the books and no rights in them. When the Sixtieth Thousand impression of *Through the Looking-Glass* had to be withdrawn, it was Dodgson who bore the loss. He was not an unworldly aesthete but a man who knew the value of money. So his luggage travelled on a barrow with a porter pushing it from Oxford station and the owner walking behind.

He was also the best placed of the Archdeacon's children to supervise matters of family business. He dealt with legal and financial matters, appealing when necessary to his cousin, James Hume Dodgson, for advice. James Hume Dodgson, whom he addressed as 'Hume,' was the recipient of Dodgson's correspondence, as yet unpublished, in which he argued as a lawyer.

In his last ten years, the same oddities and compulsions ran through his private humour that had characterized his dealings with children since he was a boy at Croft. Children were violent to one another, children were naughty, children were punished. They threw one another in the river as fish bait. They hurt each other with knives. They found whips waiting for them on the dinner table. He imagined little girls – and indeed little boys – being violent or cruel to one another, scratching, pinching and hair-pulling, if only as a joke. He pictured Janet Terry Lewis dragging her sister Kate through Kensington Gardens with a dog collar round the victim's neck and a rope tied to it. Invoking the nursery penalty for constipation, he told the Hunter girls that when he disliked a child, it would be far worse than a dose of rhubarb and magnesia.

Naughtiness and punishment seemed to make the world go round but only when sweetened by murmurs of 'darling' and 'pet'. He was going to punish Isa Bowman 'severely' for being a 'naughty, naughty, bad wicked little girl.' Olive Chataway was another naughty little girl. Maggie Bowman was a 'naughty naughty little culprit' whose knuckles he longed to beat with a large stick. Marion Miller and Beatrice Hatch were naughty little girls at different times. To Margaret Mayhew he wrote with knowing facetiousness about the hair-pulling and scratching he imagined between her and Enid Stevens, rivals for his attention. 'To pull each other's hair perhaps doesn't matter much. It is always pleasant to be reminded, even if it hurts a little, that one's hair is real, and not a wig. But *scratching* should be, if possible, avoided – it is too much like a cat.' When he called at Oxford High School, a girl was being punished but afterwards refused to tell him all about it. He confided in Margaret Mayhew.

> Also I need not say how sorry I am that your friend Ethel Harland *won't* confess that she was the child who was being punished when I called last Tuesday at the High School. This is very sad, children should *always* confess everything they are accused of.[32]

Knowingness of this kind, soon to be unwelcome in earnest or in jest, seemed like the relic of an earlier life. Yet Dodgson also looked to the future. 'Think of me in the year 1924,' he once wrote, looking thirty years ahead. He dreamt too, as he told Mrs Kitchin, of what little girls from the world of 1874 would seem like to those who peopled the world in 1974. In gadgets and invention, he was a man of the future to the end of his life. As early as 1882, he was riding the Velociman several miles at a time, a form of tricycle invented by a fellow Oxford mathematician. Indeed, Dodgson volunteered ideas for the improvement of the steering.[33]

In the 1890s he devised a means of writing in the dark and also learnt to use a typewriter. He heard the first recordings of the phonograph and wished that he could have known its perfection fifty years later. Robert Browning had been recorded as early as 1889 and both Tennyson and Gladstone, by courtesy of Edison, in the following year. Whether Dodgson's hesitation in speech inhibited him from speaking into the cavernous horn we do not know. Aeronautically, he invented Bob the Bat, made of wire and gauze with an elastic band. Isa Bowman saw it fly round his room for half a minute. Once it flew out of the open window of his room and landed in a bowl of salad which a scout was carrying across the Great Quadrangle.

Yet whatever lay in the future, far greater change had come in his lifetime: the wonders of railway travel and steamships; the camera and electric light; the leisured world of the croquet lawn and the tennis court; the theatre and the panorama; the summer paradise of Eastbourne, the new and more indulgent world of Victorian childhood. The exact images of the dead might now be recovered by opening the pages of a photograph album and their voices might speak again from a cylinder of wax. Perhaps that would have seemed more wonderful to a previous age than railway trains or the 'writing machine.' Beyond the images of the camera were 'moving pictures', with the inception of cinema in 1895. There is no evidence that Dodgson saw anything of this but for many years he had attended displays of 'dissolving views' at the Polytechnic and elsewhere.

*

In 1894 he was told that the High School girls were too busy for his logic lessons and the story was much the same at St Hugh's. He gave private tuition to girls who were seldom very keen on the subject, and he was still welcomed at Mrs Barber's school in Eastbourne. He also preached, or rather gave addresses with improving stories, at the children's services which were held at Christ Church, Eastbourne, and at St Mary Magdalen at St Leonard's, where an Oxford friend was now rector.

The passage of time was marked increasingly by the deaths of those whom he had known. The mothers of Gertrude Chataway and Ellen Terry died in 1892–3 and he hastened to comfort their daughters. To Kate Terry, who had been the captive Andromeda of his photographs, he signed himself 'with an old man's love.' In 1890, his companion on the Russian journey, Henry Parry Liddon, died while convalescing at Weston-super-Mare. In July 1897 he heard of the death of one of his oldest Christ Church friends, George Woodhouse, the first fellow undergraduate to speak to him at their table in Hall in 1851 and whose daughter he had befriended while she was at Lady Margaret Hall.[34]

He had lost one or two of his child-friends. Edith Liddell had died far back in 1876 of appendicitis. His reconciliation with Mrs Liddell was fostered when they exchanged photographs of her dead daughter.

In 1896 he wrote to his sister Louisa, on the death of their cousin Clara Hitchcock, of the sense of unreality which the news of bereavements brought.

> It is getting increasingly difficult now to remember *which* of one's friends remain alive, and *which* have gone 'into the land of the great departed, into the silent land.' Also, such news comes less and less as a shock, and more and more one realises that it is an experience each of *us* has to face before long. The fact is getting *less* dreamlike to me now, and I sometimes think what a grand thing it will be to be able to say to oneself, 'Death is *over* now; there is not *that* experience to be faced again.'[35]

Dodgson had been a member of the Society for Psychical Research since its foundation in 1882 and his bookshelves contained a set of its proceedings. He was a believer in telepathy and thought that one day it would be shown to be determined by the laws of a science not yet understood. He had once known in advance what the number of the next hymn would be in chapel and had turned to the page before it was announced, but this was far from proving telepathy. On other matters he kept an open mind. His shelves contained works by authors like the American medium D. D. Home but they also contained Browning's exposure of Home as a charlatan and cheat in '"Mr Sludge:" The Medium', from *Dramatis Personae*. In his own Preface to *Sylvie and Bruno Concluded*, Dodgson 'supposed a Human being to be capable of various psychical states, with varying degrees of consciousness.' There was the ordinary state; the 'eerie' state of awareness of fairies and of actual surroundings; and consciousness of fairies while unconscious of the real world. He wrote of fairies but it was his nearest approach to an account of belief in psychical phenomena.

When his own death came, he would be packed and ready for the journey but there was also the matter of what would be left behind. There were, for example, the nude photographs from the 1870s. He had kept them all, though their subjects were now grown women. He wrote to Beatrice Hatch during his illness of 1895 asking her what she would like done with five studies of her. It was plain that on his death there must be a bonfire of many papers, sketches, photographs and other items. When the time came, part of his diary was found to be torn out, covering the troubled Oxford summer weeks of 1879 and the gossip circulated by Mrs Owens. Perhaps it was done by his executors but more likely Dodgson himself had removed it.

In the autumn of 1897, he was preoccupied by working out rules for a new system of long division. After his meeting with Gertrude Thomson on 20 November he returned to Oxford. Ten days before Christmas, the weather was so warm that he was working in his sitting room without a fire and with the window open. The temperature was still fifty-four degrees. On 19 December he sat up until 4 a.m., trying to solve a problem that had been sent him from New York and which involved finding three equal rational-sided right-angle triangles. He found two and then went to bed.

Two days before Christmas, he caught the afternoon train for Guildford and spent much of the time over Christmas working on the second part of *Symbolic Logic* and correcting the proofs of *The Three Sunsets*. On 5 January 1898, a telegram arrived announcing the death of the Reverend Charles Collingwood of Southwick near Sunderland, the husband of Dodgson's sister Mary. Dodgson wrote back, enclosing £50 to cover immediate expenses. To his nephew Stuart Dodgson Collingwood he wrote a business letter, warning him to get a signed agreement from the undertakers on the cost of the funeral and reminding the young man that he and his mother 'have no money to throw away.'[36]

In his letter of 5 January to his sister Mary, he added that he would not be able to travel north for the funeral, though she had asked him to come at once. He had a bronchial cold and Dr Gabb had forbidden him to undertake the journey. In a few days, the bronchial symptoms were worse and Dr Gabb ordered him to bed. A nurse was brought in. Dodgson lay propped on the pillows and his breathing 'rapidly became hard and laborious.' He asked one of his sisters to read him a hymn whose verses ended with the refrain, 'Thy Will be done.' He described the illness as 'a great trial of his patience.' On 13 January, he said to the sister who was with him. 'Take away those pillows, I shall need them no more.' On the following day, at about half past two in the afternoon, as Stuart Dodgson Collingwood described it, 'One of his sisters was in the room at the time, and she only noticed that the hard breathing suddenly ceased.' She called the nurse who came at once and 'hoped that this was a sign that he had taken a turn for the better.' When she saw him, it was evident that he was dead. They summoned Dr Gabb. The doctor looked at the smooth and unlined face, then went down to the sitting-room where Dodgson's sisters were waiting and said, 'How wonderfully young your brother looks!'[37]

He was buried in the graveyard on the hill at Guildford, after a service at St Mary's, taken by the rector and Francis Paget, now Dean of Christ Church. The ceremony was simple and inexpensive, as he had stipulated, remembering the difficulties caused at probate by extravagance in his father's funeral. There were relatively few mourners. Dean Liddell and family were absent for, by an irony of fate, Liddell himself died four days after the Christ Church colleague who had been his friend, ridiculer, defender in the press, and who had in the end made the Liddell name more famous than royal visits, social pretension, or even the celebrated *Greek–English Lexicon*.

Gertrude Thomson accompanied her 'Beloved Friend' and at his death showed publicly a degree of attachment which had been concealed during twenty years of his life.

A grey January day, calm, and without a sound, full of the peace of God which passeth all understanding. A steep, stony, country road, with hedges close on either side, fast quickening with the breath of the premature spring. Between the withered leaves of the dead summer a pure white daisy here and there shone out like a little star. A few mourners slowly climbed the hill in silence, while borne before them on a simple hand-bier was the coffin, half hid in flowers. Under an old yew, round whose gnarled trunk the green ivy twined, in the pure white chalk earth his body was laid to rest, while the slow bell tolled the passing –

Of the sweetest soul
That ever looked with human eye.[37]

To this his nephew added,

> A marble cross, under the shadow of a pine, marks the spot, and beneath his own name they have engraved the name of 'Lewis Carroll,' that the children who pass by may remember their friend, who is now – himself a child in all that makes childhood most attractive – in that 'Wonderland' which outstrips all our dreams and hopes.[38]

*

The suddenness of his death seemed to confirm that a fetish for physical fitness may be more lethal than a life of indolence. Though it was no comfort to those who mourned him, medical science might soon afterwards have ensured that he need not have died at sixty-six from bronchial pneumonia. Even the taking away of the pillows was more likely to precipitate the end than prevent or postpone it. For some years he might have been spared to continue with his symbolic logic and long division, interspersed with summer days at Eastbourne, intimate dinners in his Christ Church rooms with girls now in their teens, and happy mornings in the studios of Mrs Shute or Gertrude Thomson.

Those who wrote of his death made much of the patron saint of children rather than of a troubled soul now at rest. In letters to the Dodgson brothers, George Jelf recalled their friendship at Christ Church since 1852 and Dodgson's genius for 'the brightening of our lives with pure innocent fun'; Frederic Harrison called him 'mainly as a sort of missionary to all in need.' From Oxford came tributes to 'the kindest and gentlest of friends' and 'countless acts of kindness.'[39]

From a number of his child-friends who were now adults, the response to his death was the same. 'I shall never forget all his kindness to us, from the time he first met us as little mites in the railway train, and one feels glad to have had the privilege of knowing him.' To this another added, 'He was to me a dear and true friend, and it has been my great privilege to see a good deal of him ever since I was a tiny child, and especially during the last two years.' One who had first met him as a little girl on the beach at Eastbourne sixteen years earlier met him again as a young woman. 'I think, that the childish delight in his kindness, and pride in his friendship, changed into higher love and reverence, when in our long walks over the downs, I saw more and more into the great tenderness and gentleness of his nature.' Two Sundays after his death, Dean Paget paid tribute at Christ Church in a sermon on the 'Virtue of Simplicity.'[40]

The Three Sunsets, illustrated by Gertrude Thomson, appeared a month after his death. Collingwood wrote, 'One cannot read this little volume without feeling that the shadow of some disappointment lay over Lewis Carroll's life . . . But those who loved him would not wish to lift the veil from these dead sanctities.' Nothing was better calculated to prompt speculation as to what the veil hid. In 1932, Collingwood made a belated retraction. His words had been based only on what Frances Dodgson, the dead man's sister, thought.[41]

The sanctities were safe again. Dodgson's executors, his brothers Wilfred and Skeffington, struggled with a mass of papers in his Christ Church rooms. Their bonfires were his true funeral pyre. An auction at Holywell Music Room in Oxford dispersed his books and possessions. Over thirty years later his diaries were found on a cellar floor, four of the thirteen volumes missing and another mutilated. He left his family the modest sum of £4,596. In an age bereft of much free medical provision, a subscription was raised to endow in perpetuity a Lewis Carroll Cot at Great Ormond Street Hospital for Children.

Punch sped him to a paradise which was of his own making.

> Farewell! But near our hearts we have you yet,
>   Holding our heritage with loving hand,
> Who may not follow where your feet are set
>   Upon the ways of Wonderland.

The family and the press were agreed that Dodgson's eternity was to be a heavenly Wonderland, presumably without the grotesques that his own had contained. Yet Wonderland also flourished on earth, giving to his most famous creation a future fame that might have puzzled him and sometimes would have outraged him. Heaven was the love and simplicity of perfect childhood. On earth his creation was the companion of Baudelaire and Sade, of Adolf Hitler and Winston Churchill, of Frank Harris and those little heroines of literature or art whose bestial ignorance was matched only by their utter lack of innocence. Having striven to provide wholesome fare for the little ones, it might have seemed to him that he had begotten a monster.

14

Wonderland

THE SMOKE FROM sackfuls of burning papers marked the funeral pyre of the Reverend Charles Lutwidge Dodgson rather than of Lewis Carroll. There was no suggestion that this was a destruction of documents unfit for other eyes, rather that the Christ Church rooms had to be emptied. Of the thirteen volumes of diaries used by Stuart Dodgson Collingwood in writing his uncle's biography in 1898, most were extant in 1932, the others known only by the extracts Collingwood had quoted. Thousands of letters from almost 100,000 he had written had also survived.

At his death, the *Pall Mall Gazette* calculated that Lewis Carroll's two most famous books were more often quoted or alluded to in English public life than those of any author but Shakespeare. E. V. Lucas saluted his immortality by celebrating the Walrus and the Carpenter as the Grownup and the Prillilgirl – or Pretty Little Girl.

> The Grownup and the Prillilgirl
>   Were walking hand in hand;
> They were as pleased as Punch to be
>   Alone in Wonderland:
> 'If there were other books like his,'
>   They said, 'It would be grand . . .'
>
> 'But will,' the Prillilgirl inquired,
>   'His writings ever die?
> Will people always love his books
>   The same as you and I?'
> 'There is no doubt at all of that,'
>   The Grownup made reply.[1]

The centenary catalogue of 1932 suggested that there had been considerable doubt. Maud Ffooks 'almost alone has watched for and collected Carrolliana ever since Dodgson's death ... after his death in 1898, say from 1900 to 1917, he came to be regarded as, after all, only a Victorian, whose significance began and ended with that age.'[2]

This was true at the time of Victorians in general and Dodgson shared their collective fate. His heroine did not. Alice was out of the nursery or schoolroom and into politics within a few years of her creator's passing to a Wonderland of his own. No English author, in the century following Dodgson's death, nor even Karl Marx or Winston Churchill, left such a legacy in the language of public life as he had done. It is true that a relatively few phrases were the most used or adapted: 'Curiouser and curiouser ...', 'Off with his head! ...', 'Sentence first – verdict afterwards ...', 'Now *here*, you see, it takes all the running *you* can do, to keep in the same place ...', 'The rule is, jam tomorrow and jam yesterday – but never jam today ...', '"When *I* use a word," Humpty Dumpty said in a rather scornful tone, "it means just what I choose it to mean – neither more nor less ..."', 'It's as large as life and twice as natural.' No less frequent are references to an 'Alice in Wonderland' situation or policy. The Tenniel illustrations, as well as Dodgson's text, have formed a frame of reference for the political cartoonist.

Two years after Dodgson's death, H. H. Munro, 'Saki', the creator of *The Unbearable Bassington*, began a serial in *The Westminster Gazette*, lampooning Lord Salisbury's government in 'The Westminster Alice'. J. A. Spender, the magazine's editor, later wrote, 'Parodies of the famous original had several times been submitted to me (as I suppose to most editors) and nearly all had been dismal failures.' Saki's was in a class of its own. Alice appears in Downing Street, at St Stephen's, with the Liberal Party and, at last, has tea at the Hotel Cecil, where Lord Salisbury is the Dormouse, A. J. Balfour the March Hare, and Joseph Chamberlain the Mad Hatter.

'The Dormouse must tell us a story,' said the Hatter, giving it a sharp pinch.

The Dormouse awoke with a start, and began as though it had been awake all the time: 'There was an old woman who lived in a shoe –'

'I know,' said Alice, 'she had so many children that she didn't know what to do.'

'Nothing of the sort,' said the Dormouse, 'you lack the gift of imagination. She put most of them into Treasuries and Foreign Offices and Boards of Trade, and all sorts of unlikely places where they could learn things.'

'What did they learn?' asked Alice.

'Painting in glowing colours, and attrition, and terminology (that's the science of knowing when things are over), and iteration (that's the same thing over again), and drawing –'

'What did they draw?'

'Salaries. And then there were classes for foreign languages. And such language!' (Here the March Hare and the Hatter shut their eyes and took a big gulp from their tea-cups.) 'However, I don't think anybody attended to them.'

The Dormouse broke off into a chuckle which ended in a snore, and as no one seemed inclined to wake it up again Alice thought she might as well be going.[3]

The propulsion of Alice into public life owes more to Saki than to any other author. By 1904, in the politics of motoring, Horace Wyatt's *Alice in Motorland* replaced the White Knight's horse with an early car and the seven-year-old Alice with a pubescent in black stockings.

'But you've got a big number on the front of the car,' said Alice.

'Yes,' said the Knight, brightening up, 'it's an invention of my own. It has hinges at the top, so that when I go fast it swings back and disappears under the radiators.'

'But then,' Alice said, 'the police would stop you for having no number.'

'They do,' said the Knight, 'Often. But I tell them to look again. Of course, when the car stops the number swings down, so they have to let me go on.'[4]

As the gloom of constitutional crisis and European war deepened, the character of Alice was never more in demand. In 1909, defying the constitutional convention by which it did not reject money bills passed by the Commons, the House of Lords voted down the so-called 'People's Budget', introduced by Lloyd George as Chancellor of the Exchequer in Asquith's Liberal government. The Parliament Act of 1911 ensured the passage of such legislation in future. Among the lampoons on the government in 1910 was one by the anagrammatical 'Loris Carllew', *Alice in Plunderland*, which featured Lloyd George as the Welsh Rabbit. Winston Churchill, Home Secretary in Asquith's cabinet, is the Mad Hatter and the Queller of Tonypandy, having sent troops to the Rhondda in November 1910 to confront the 30,000 striking miners in the Tonypandy riots. Churchill, however, is ushered off the stage after a handshake and a hurried inquiry 'whether Alice had any germs of Suffragettism about her.' Lloyd George, as the Welsh Rabbit with the Finance Bill rolled under his arm, the plunderer of the middle classes, is allowed to explain himself.

> 'You see I'm not the *White* Rabbit, he's only a sort of cousin-german. I'm *the* Welsh Rabbit, "quite the cheese" in fact, and where I live isn't Wonderland but Plunderland, except when I take my summer holidays in Blunderland, and amuse myself by preparing forms and setting holiday tasks for my enemies.'[5]

The outbreak of war in 1914 was the ideal opportunity for Alice's literary guardians to donate her services to propaganda. Horace Wyatt's *Malice in Kulturland* combined denunciation of Germany, suspicion of Ulster's advocates of partition in the face of the Government of Ireland Act, and fear that the peacetime Prime Minister, Asquith, would be no use in war. Asquith's characterization is unsurprising: 'As a matter of fact, I am a Dodo. I used to call myself a Liberal, some other people used to call me a Radical, and plenty of others used to call me anything they could lay their tongues to.'

Wyatt lets Asquith down gently, and reserves his hostility for Germany and the leaders of 'Ulster will fight and Ulster will be right', specifically the two illustrious lawyers Sir Edward Carson and F. E. 'Galloper' Smith.

> 'Twas dertag, and the slithy Huns
> Did sturm and sturgel through the sludge;
> All bulgous were the blunderguns,
> And the bosch bombs outbludge.
>
> 'Beware the Ulsterman, my son –
> The jaws that bite at kith and kin;
> Beware the Carsonclan, and shun
> The frumious Ridersmith.'

In Europe there is 'The Duel [*sic*] Monarchy' in which the Austrian Emperor becomes both Francis and Joseph as Tweedledum and Tweedledee. German foreign policy is derived from the successors to the Walrus and the Carpenter.

> The Kaiser and the Chancellor
> Were walking hand in hand;
> They wept like anything to see
> Such lots of foreign land;
> 'If this were only Germanised,'
> They said, 'it *would* be grand.'

Of Bethmann-Hollweg, '"I like the Chancellor best," said Alice, "because he was a *little* sorry for the poor Austrians."'[6]

*

Dodgson himself, 'The Patron Saint of Children', was not at first a target of ridicule. Edmund Wilson, surveying the anniversary in 1932, the respectful and worthy commemorations by academics and devotees, concluded, 'If the Lewis Carroll centenary has produced anything of special interest, I have failed to see it.' Dodgson – as opposed to Lewis Carroll – had not been done justice, in Wilson's view. There remained the paradox of a man who protested about the stage 'in a tone of indignation worthy of Mr Podsnap,' yet whose studies in the dream psychology of *Alice* was the equal of 'Strindberg or Joyce or Flaubert's *Tentation de Saint Antoine.*'[7]

Yet among the waste land of lectures and catalogues and bibliographies, one contribution to the centenary shone out from the rest. It was mischievous, impious and cruelly accurate in tone. Hugh Kingsmill, a scourge of pedantry and pomposity, published in the *New York Bookman* an account of a meeting with Lewis Carroll by the memoirist, philanderer and braggart Frank Harris. Kingsmill's parody appears as a lost fragment of Harris's *My Life and Loves*, still banned on grounds of obscenity in 1932 in England and the United States. Harris describes meeting Dodgson at a reception and launching into a conversation on the subject of Oscar Wilde at Oxford.

> 'You know Oscar, of course?' I questioned, 'and I suppose like the rest of us have yielded to his irresistible seduction?'
> He knit fretful brows. 'Oscar? I don't know whom you mean.'
> 'I mean Oscar Wilde. We who are his friends speak of him as Oscar, simply.'
> 'I know nothing about him,' he squeaked, 'I never knew him. I resent, I very much resent ...'

A quarter of a century before *Lolita*, Kingsmill then lets Frank Harris loose on the delights of the female sex at puberty, an age at which Harris in reality had found girls sexually appealing. What did the great philanderer think of *Alice in Wonderland*? He dismisses the book as drivel but sees certain possibilities in it which he thinks Dodgson may – or may not – have considered.

> Did Carroll see her as a child, or, as I should have preferred, a girl of thirteen or so, at that age when awkwardness itself is adorable, and budding breasts and limbs shaping to roundness take on, as it were, the entrancing curves of womanhood?'

Kingsmill's Frank Harris wastes no time on the book apart from this, finding it dull and wooden, most of all in the character of its heroine. He concludes of Dodgson that he was just the sexless bachelor type whom the English with their fear of Eros would take to their hearts.[8]

Whatever the purists of the 1932 centenary celebrations might feel, there was little evidence that Dodgson's most famous creation had lost anything of her influence, even in the twenty years following his death. In political rhetoric and cartoon iconography her reputation seemed secure. As much of Europe fell to Fascism in the 1930s, Stanley Baldwin announced in the autumn of 1934, 'For a statesman today to try and lead or bring into agreement whole groups of foreign and independent countries is about as difficult a task as it was for Alice in Wonderland when she tried to play croquet with a flamingo as a mallet.' The *Daily Express* responded on 31 October with the cartoon 'Europe's Croquet Ground', in which the dictators strut, a suitably Hitlerian Alice clutches a flamingo and the Cheshire Cat as the League of Nations grins from its tree before it vanishes.

Thereafter, the dark mid-century was punctuated by such offerings as *Alice in Rationland* in 1939; or the Walrus and the Carpenter, represented by Goering and Hitler in 1942, or the Carrolingian political cartoons of Vicky in the post-war *News Chronicle*. The *Punch* cartoon series of 'The Voter in Wonderland' at the time of the 1950 General Election, offered Alice as puzzled voter the identical figures of Tweedledum and Tweedledee chanting contradictory political messages: 'Britain faces extinction' versus 'Britain was never so prosperous.' Nor was the influence of Alice confined to the cartoonist's view of political leadership. Hugh Trevor-Roper describes the meeting of the Nazi leaders with Mussolini, after the failed plot of 20 July 1944, Hitler foaming and Bormann screaming, waited on by white-uniformed footmen with tea-pots, as 'this Mad Hatter's Tea-Party.'[9]

Further enhancement was given to Alice as a political icon by the revelation that Harold Macmillan, whose family firm had published Dodgson's books, made a point of continuing his political education as Prime Minister by reading Alice's adventures once a year. Nor has her influence waned. In 1995 she vied for tabloid attention with topless models in the *Sun* newspaper.

THE SUN SAYS
Blunderland
They can call the single currency what they like ... We still
don't want it. John Major's warning that the Euro could turn
into an 'Alice in Wonderland plan' was spot on.[10]

In quantifying such allusions in public life, it might now prove that references to Alice are more frequent than those to any other literary creation.

From shorthand to Swahili, it is difficult to find a language into which the two famous tales have not been translated. Shakespeare is internationally the most read English author. Despite its intimate little world of an Oxford summer afternoon, *Alice in Wonderland* seems not far behind. A curiosity is that censorship of Alice is unusual even under despotic regimes. A rare exception was the banning of *Alice in Wonderland* by the Governor of Hunan Province in China in 1931, on the ground that 'Animals should not use human language, and that it was disastrous to put animals and human beings on the same level.' 'The Lobster Quadrille' from *Alice in Wonderland* was banned incidentally in France in 1940, when the Pétain government suppressed André Breton's *Anthologie de l'humour noir*, in which it was included.[11]

Because he wrote for children, Dodgson invested his story with a plain style. Shakespeare's style, however widely read, is dated. By comparison with *Alice in Wonderland* and however estimable in themselves, Dickens, Conan Doyle, D. H. Lawrence or Virginia Woolf are dated. Dodgson, rather like P. G. Wodehouse, created a style, and more important a world, as immune to the passage of time as the motionless watch at the Mad Tea Party. For more than a century, and across more territory than was known of when he told his story to the Liddell sisters, that summer day of 4 July 1862 has yet to end.

*

As Humpty Dumpty might think, Alice and the Snark mean what the world wants them to mean. While impervious to literary criticism, they were a gift to the hungry psychoanalysts. Indeed, so far as literary criticism is concerned, Dodgson received one of the most sincere tributes that any author might expect when two of his minor works were issued in forged first editions.[12]

The psychoanalysts, however, provided an entertainment that might be a missing chapter from Dodgson's work, had the terminology been less offensive to him. In 1936, Paul Schilder, of the Medical College of New York University's Department of Psychiatry addressed the American Psychoanalytical Society, warning its members against 'exposing children to the dangerous corruption of Lewis Carroll's books.' In his contribution to *The Journal of Nervous and Mental Disease* in 1938, Professor Schilder described Dodgson's writing as the expression of 'enormous anxiety.' He noted that 'Oral aggressiveness is found everywhere,' and that the behaviour of the Walrus and the Carpenter displays 'astonishing cruelty . . . We find, also, preponderant oral sadistic traits of cannibalistic character.' Dodgson had been a profoundly disturbed personality: 'What was his relation to his sex organ anyhow?' Citing Otto Fenichel's theory of little girls as symbolic phalluses, Dr Schilder was quick to see how Alice, significantly, grows and shrinks. Dodgson was 'a particularly destructive writer,' subject to an unconscious wish to play the part of his own mother or sister.

In 1947, John Skinner cited Professor Schilder's view of the 'anal-sadistic' content of *Alice in Wonderland*, matching Dodgson's compulsions of neatness and precision, 'the retentive, hoarding, inflexible character of the anal personality.' Kenneth Burke in 1966 noted the 'anal-oral reversibility' of the Mad Tea Party, and Alice as the 'prim, well-trained potty-girl.'[13]

The pioneer of such wisdom was A. M. E. Goldschmidt, who wrote and published '*Alice in Wonderland* Psychoanalysed' at Oxford in 1933, as a Balliol undergraduate. His critique is rich in Freudian sexual appreciation of such phenomena as the entry into the rabbit hole, the door whose curtain has to be lifted, and the insertion of the key into the lock. He left to others such unconsidered trifles as the bowsprit getting mixed up with the rudder in *The Hunting of the Snark*. Despite his youth, he was the father of this line of criticism, followed solemnly, not to say seriously, by his senior academic disciples on both sides of the Atlantic.

Mr Goldschmidt was not the first of his kind, however. Dr Emil Busch of the University of Frankfurt had packed Oxford Town Hall with senior members of the University, including Heads of Houses, for a lecture on the latest news from Vienna. This envisaged the mind as a cinema projector, throwing the images of each individual's multiple and profoundly conflicting personalities on to a 'screen' which was constituted of 'a fluid' of some sort. The lecture was received with respect in the press and with enthusiasm by its audience. Unfortunately, Dr Emil Busch had never been anywhere near Vienna. Indeed, he did not exist, except as George Edinger, another Balliol undergraduate with a false moustache and a persuasive manner. Had the more earnest of the theorists investigated the work of young Mr Goldschmidt in this context, they might have thought themselves victims of an Oxford hoax which did great honour to the shade of Lewis Carroll.[14]

Elsewhere, Dodgson the mathematician and Carroll the creator of Alice surfaced in histories of philosophy and Oxford examination questions, in Bertrand Russell's *Principles of Mathematics* (1903) and in the *Principia Mathematica* (1910–13) of Russell and Whitehead. Both the Red Queen and the White Knight are cited by Arthur Stanley Eddington in *The Nature of the Physical World* (1928), as is the White Knight by Bertrand Russell in *The ABC of Relativity* (1925), on the question of whether the earth's motion may affect the speed of light. Of the Cambridge mathematicians, Russell, at least, was credited with a certain physical resemblance to the Mad Hatter.[15]

*

Among those who might have regarded themselves as heirs to his genius, it seemed that a new art of the new century was particularly suited to adapting or purloining his most famous works. He had been dead only five years when Cecil Hepworth's *Alice in Wonderland* appeared on the cinema screens of England in 1903 in a ten-minute version. It was remade twice as a silent film in the United States, in

1910 and 1915. With the advent of sound, a number of versions appeared, including the Paramount production of 1933 with W. C. Fields as Humpty Dumpty, Cary Grant as the Mock Turtle and Gary Cooper as the White Knight. Dodgson's original became the vehicle for others to display their talents. The Walt Disney feature-length cartoon version of 1951 owed more to the culture of popcorn and bubble-gum than to the genius of either Dodgson or Tenniel. For the first time, the self-confidence of Alice was touched by the vulgar assertiveness of Lolita.

At every attempt to imprison it in this manner, Dodgson's master-piece eluded the hunters, leaving only a wraith behind. The BBC television version of 1966 proved more of a tombstone than a mile-stone, despite the promise that famous people would entertain the watching millions of ordinary folk by impersonating the characters of the original. The heroine, portrayed as a rather sullen adolescent whose affinity was closer to Brigitte Bardot than to Alice Liddell, spoke in the pampered accents of Sloane Square with a background of ethnic zither and the chiming melody of the Welsh hymn-tune 'St Serio'.

The hard-worked description 'inimitable' has protected the stories against such adaptations, no less than against the hopeful quest of drug-culture for a heaven in Wonderland. Poems like 'The White Rabbit', by Jefferson Airplane's Grace Slick,

> Remember what the Dormouse said:
> Feed your head,
> feed your head,

or Thomas Fensch's *Lewis Carroll – The First Acidhead*, bloomed into self-parody before the ink was dry on the paper. Taking acid and tripping out are said to be the message, though Dodgson – 'even for his time he was freaky' and his book 'echoes' the LSD trip – probably knew nothing of 'the nineteenth-century equivalent of LSD.' As it happens, one of the books on his shelves at Christ Church was Frederick Anstie's *Stimulants and Narcotics*.[16]

The stern voice of critical philistinism was raised more loudly than usual in 1967, when Brigid Brophy, Michael Levey and Charles Osborne dismissed Dodgson and Carroll in *Fifty Works of English Literature We Could Do Without*, which itself became almost instantly one of the many works of literary criticism that the world found it could do without.

Dodgson's legacy has been to admirers rather than to critics or imitators. Nowhere was he more readily welcomed than in the international surrealist movement. His two most prominent champions among its members, André Breton and Max Ernst, both described formative experiences which suggested the dream of Wonderland. For Breton in 1919 it was 'the more or less fragmentary phrases which, when one is alone and about to fall asleep, begin to run through the mind, though it is impossible to say what shaped or framed them.' For Ernst in the same year it was the memory of reading an illustrated catalogue on a rainy afternoon and the vision of the implements overlaying one another, 'with the persistence and rapidity peculiar to love memories and the visions of half-sleep.'[17]

As in vision, so in life. Alice herself might have thought she was on familiar territory at the Salon des Indépendants in February 1920, when the audience was expecting the advertised appearance of Charlie Chaplin but got instead forty manifestos of Dadaists read aloud simultaneously by their authors. 'What is beautiful?' declaimed Ribemont-Dessaignes into the din with the self-assurance of a supernumerary inhabitant of Dodgson's Wonderland. 'What is ugly? What is great, strong, weak? What is Carpentier, Renan, Foch? Never heard of them. What am I? Never heard of him. Never heard of him. Never heard of him.' As surely as in Worcester College gardens, the shade of Dodgson might have peeped and smiled.[18]

By the 1930s his title as an honorary surrealist seemed secure. In André Breton's *Anthologie de l'humour noir* the names of Lewis Carroll and 'The Lobster Quadrille' stand next to Swift and Sade, Baudelaire and Lautréamont, with moral rebellions far more profound than anything which the Reverend C. L. Dodgson found unwholesome in *The Little Squire* or *The Second Mrs Tanqueray*. What united him with his strange bedfellows in Breton's anthology was a sense of anarchy and a streak of cruelty. Louis Aragon, who had been a manifesto-reader at the Salon des Indépendants in 1920 and was now Dodgson's translator, saw the significance of *The Hunting of the Snark* as a child of the same locust years as Lautréamont, *Les Chants de Maldoror* and Arthur Rimbaud, *Un Saison en enfer*.

In Breton's view, the nonsense of Alice and the Snark was Dodgson's escape from 'the profound contradiction between the acceptance of faith and the exercise of reason on the one hand, and on the other, between the pangs of poetic conscience and rigorous professional duties. The spirit, confronted by every kind of difficulty, may find an escape in the absurd.' Yet in this analysis, the nonsense of Alice is total anarchy, not the mere revolution which substitutes one regime for another. 'It comes from that fundamental resistance which the child always opposes to those who try to shape it, and so to reduce it, by limiting more or less arbitrarily its splendid field of experience. All those who harbour a spirit of rebellion would recognize in Lewis Carroll their first master in truancy.'[19]

Aragon saw in the creator of Alice a figure who had defended liberty in a manner that contradicted Dodgson's own politics. That Carroll accomplished what Dodgson could scarcely have intended was not the point.

> In the shameful fetters of those days of massacre in Ireland, nameless oppression in the manufacturing industries, where lay the ironic balance of pleasure and suffering foretold by Bentham, when Manchester raised in challenge the theory of free trade? What became of human liberty? It remained intact in the frail hands of Alice, where this strange man had placed it.[20]

The art of surrealism, like its literature, reflected Alice's dream and the sinister voyage of the Bellman's crew, in the illustrations of Max Ernst for *The Hunting of the Snark*, Clovis Trouille's 'Wonderland' paintings or the kingdom of death as a looking-glass in Cocteau's film *Orphée*, 'With these gloves you can pass through mirrors.' The theme of passing through the mirror was also used to tragic purpose by Jacques Rigaud in *Lord Patchogue*.

Clovis Trouille's painting of 1958, *Alice au pays des merveilles*, is the work of a surrealist primitive and fellow pupil of Mucha, set against Breughel-like sea and mountains. In the foreground, a modern Alice-Lolita drifts in a swan's neck boat among water lilies, Dodgson a robed and hooded figure of religion behind her, above them a girl in a tutu on a tightrope, on the shore a boy flying a kite.

In Trouille's painting of 1945, *Le Rêve d'Alice*, there is the outline of a castle on a hill above the figures. It appears again fourteen years later in Trouille's *Luxure*, where it has the unmistakable outline of the Château de Sade at La Coste, as indeed the figures of the latter painting are those of Sade and three of his female subjects. The only two literary heroines in Trouille's paintings are Alice and Justine.

Jean-Marc Campagne describes the world to which Dodgson's heroine is translated by the artist.

> The lavish flora, playthings in the air, deep waters and visions of Scottish castles, the Rhine, the Palais Borromée – these were the foundation, the adornments were dreamed by the child-Clovis. 'Dreaming while the summers die . . . Life what is it but a dream?' Trouille, the admirer of Rimbaud and Sade, answers Lewis Carroll's question by a view beyond the looking-glass, the mirror whose poetry eludes the casual glance.[21]

A later generation of literary surrealists was represented by Boris Vian and Fernando Arrabal. Arrabal's *Picque-nique en campagne* was cited as a homage to Tweedledum and Tweedledee, while the heroine of *Barrabas* became a talking animal as equine victim, harnessed and mounted by her own father. If Dodgson had been dismayed at the thought of being seen in the same landscape as Sade or Arrabal, he might have shuddered at the connection with Boris Vian in Jennifer Walters' essay 'The Disquieting Worlds of Lewis Carroll and Boris Vian'. Vian was not only the author of *L'Ecume des jours* (1947) with its room which changes shape according to mood, and *L'Arrache-Coeur* (1953) with its Carrolingian timescale of 39 Junuary or 59 Janpril. As 'Vernon Sullivan' he was the author of the bestseller of 1947 *J'Irai cracher sur vos tombes*, translated as *I'll Spit on Your Graves*. Prosecuted in France and banned almost universally, its innocent abroad is a young black in the southern United States who avenges his humiliation by the savage and meticulously described sexual murder of a spoilt daughter of the white middle class. The weapon of cruelty passes from the hands of the monsters, whose scorn Alice had known, into the possession of the voyager.[22]

More generally, the proceedings of the courts of Wonderland were to be echoed, not imitated, by Kafka and Orwell. In America and Europe there were also child heroes and heroines who might reflect something of their famous forbear, the wisdom of the innocents. Vladimir Nabokov's *Lolita* owes nothing to Dodgson and remains of its own time. Even if, as Elizabeth Prioleau suggests in 'Humbert Humbert *Through the Looking-Glass*', Lolita might be seen as an Alice-figure and her mother Mrs Haze as the Red Queen, their immaculate vulgarity would surely evoke the angel with the flaming sword at the gates of Dodgson's paradise. Holden Caulfield in J. D. Salinger's *The Catcher in the Rye* (1951) might more plausibly fill the role but does not play it.[23]

Of all such candidates, perhaps the most likely is Zazie, the creation of Raymond Queneau, himself a critic of Dodgson's use of dog-language in *Sylvie and Bruno* and a surrealist during the 1920s. The title of *Zazie dans le métro* suggests something of *Alice's Adventures Underground*, though Zazie when abandoned by her mother to her uncle's care in Paris finds her ambition thwarted by a strike of workers on the Métro.

'And me,' says Zazie, 'would I suit you?'
'Why, you're only a little girl.'
'Some girls get married at fifteen, sometimes even fourteen. There are guys who like that.'
'So? How about me, then, would I attract you?'
'Hell no,' answers Zazie with simplicity.
Charles swallows the bitter truth, then proceeds:
'You know,' he says, 'you got some mighty funny ideas for a brat your age.'

There is a poise and self-awareness in Zazie that, allowing for changes in language and fashion, are not far removed from those of Alice. The comments of the Caterpillar and the Red Queen, if not their terminology, suggest that the brat has some mighty funny ideas for her age.[24]

A gentler homage to Dodgson's heroine than any from the surrealists came with the English school of Ruralists in the 1960s, whose paintings and photographs sought the tranquillity and innocence of Wonderland and Looking-Glass House. The Brotherhood looked back to figures of English art and literature as sources of a new culture, Dodgson, Samuel Palmer, Edward Elgar, John Clare, Francis Kilvert, Thomas Hardy and Edward Thomas among them. Children in clouded and enclosed garden landscapes offered a suitably Alicean theme. Both Graham Ovenden's paintings of 1969–70 on the theme of *Through the Looking-Glass* and Peter Blake's gouaches, 'full of topiary gardens and mysterious landscapes,' as well as the work of Jann Haworth were the basis of a memorable exhibition in tribute to Alice at the Waddington Galleries in 1970.[25]

*

Many of the uses made of his creation seem grotesquely at odds with the genius of the troubled dreamer in the grim little Victorian grave at Guildford. The white marble cross on its tiered base was not so much inscribed as placarded with epitaphs. None of them truly matched the man or his genius. 'Thy will be done . . .', 'Where I am, there shall my servant be . . .', 'Father in thy gracious keeping, here we leave thy servant sleeping . . .' The elevation of common terms into memorial phrases, in this case, missed the mark. Dodgson had been born into a rank which made him temperamentally the master of servants rather than the servant of a master, and in which he was able to please himself for most of his life.

If the survivors found it hard to say the right thing at the right time, that was understandable. Despite his frequent meditations on mortality, the Bellman had called for him at a most unexpected moment. A few days earlier he was still preparing two books for publication, the second volume of *Symbolic Logic* and *The Three Sunsets*. 'The summons,' as he was apt to call it, had given those who mourned him little time to consider the monumental inscriptions. At Eastbourne a few months earlier and at his meeting with Gertrude Thomson only a few weeks earlier, he had been in full vigour. Some who heard of his passing might have wondered if he had not commemorated the occasion himself in his epitaph for the Baker who, at his life's end, at last met the Snark. Dodgson never knew where the lines came from, only that everything must lead up to them. They now seemed a promise of the easy manner of his own death.

> In the midst of the word he was trying to say,
> In the midst of his laughter and glee,
> He had softly and silently vanished away,
> For the Snark *was* a Boojum, you see . . .'

It would hardly have done for Guildford and yet he had slipped quietly away, like a guest leaving a party before the appointed hour. It might have pleased him to know that despite his forty-seven years at Christ Church, there was surprise and sadness among Common Room elders for one cut off practically in boyhood. 'I was very fond of Dodgson,' said one ancient resident of the Common Room on hearing of his death, 'although he was a junior man.'[26]

For all the praise of his benevolence and his literary genius, no one seemed much interested in the collections and inventions of this uniquely curious man. While sackfuls of documents shrivelled in the flames kindled by his legal representatives, what could be sold was bundled off to the auction room. His younger Christ Church friend Frederick York Powell attended the sale of Dodgson's possessions in the Holywell Music Room at Oxford in May 1898, four months after his death. The verses which Powell wrote on the occasion described a scene that was melancholy and macabre, and from which Dodgson was fortunate to be travelling further with every moment.

> Fast ride the Dead! Perhaps 'tis well!
> He shall not know, what none would tell,
> That gambling salesmen bargain'd o'er
> The books he read, the clothes he wore.

The bonfire of the early year had sent a mass of his private papers, secret images and thoughts to the Oxford sky. Powell wished only that they had taken the rest, sparing 'the poor playthings' and 'the toys he loved in quiet' this public and mercenary spoiling.

> Better by far the Norseman's pyre,
> That burnt in one sky-soaring fire
> The man with all he held most dear.
> He that hath ears, now let him hear.[27]

Dodgson was no Norseman. His true reward for a life of piety would better have been an eternal summer in an ideal Eastbourne of the late 1870s. No Mrs Grundy, no serpent-masked psychopathologist in a seaside Eden, no news of moral horrors in the urban slums, no posterity recasting him in its own tawdry image. Perhaps, when he stepped forward into this new world with the thought that 'Death is over now,' the décor might have owed a little to his friend Sir Joseph Noël Paton, painter of the fay, in a single canvas of whose work Dodgson once counted 165 fairies. Paton was also a poet and several lines 'To D. O. H.' matched Dodgson's dream so accurately that he rewrote the verse for himself. Beyond the reach of contemporary gossip or future scorn, the dawning of a new world was to be both sublime and happily familiar.

> For there, upon the glimmering marge,
> Between the sea and sea-worn rocks.

> Stood, mother-naked in the sun,
> A little girl with golden locks.

But that would hardly do for Guildford either – or for his future reputation.

In a world now bereft of him, however, not all feelings of grief were spoken or displayed. One of them, at least, might settle for ever the feelings of Dodgson and his child-friends for one another. Ethel Rowell was by this time in her third year as a student at Royal Holloway College. She saw in *The Times* a notice announcing his death, and at first refused to believe it: 'He had always been so vividly alive to me and I had never imagined life without him.' To wear mourning seemed impossible, without inviting inquiries and speculation. Yet Edith Rowell at twenty-one showed the same intensity of affection and loyalty to her friend as she had done when a child. To satisfy this, she adopted a strangely intimate symbol of mourning for him.

> I made a large badge out of some black ribbon I had by me, and I fastened this black badge to my petticoat in front just under my shirt blouse. I felt I could not wear the badge outside; people would ask what it was and after all he was no relation; yet I knew I must in some manner 'wear black' for Mr Dodgson.[28]

Of all the tributes paid him, none was more poignant nor more apt than this.

Notes

Abbreviations

Aspects of Alice – *Aspects of Alice: Lewis Carroll's Dreamchild as seen through the Critics' Looking-Glasses 1865–1971*, ed. Robert Phillips, Harmondsworth: Penguin Books, 1974

Bill – E. G. W. Bill, *University Reform in Nineteenth-Century Oxford: A Study of Henry Halford Vaughan 1811–1885*, Oxford: Clarendon Press, 1973

Bill & Mason – E. G. W. Bill and J. F. A. Mason, *Christ Church and Reform 1850–1867*, Oxford: Clarendon Press, 1970

Bowman – Isa Bowman, *The Story of Lewis Carroll Told for Young People by the Real Alice in Wonderland Miss Isa Bowman*, New York, E. P. Dutton & Company, 1900

Child-Friends – *A Selection from the Letters of Lewis Carroll (The Rev. Charles Lutwidge Dodgson) to his Child-Friends*, ed. Evelyn Hatch, London: Macmillan, 1933

Clark – Anne Clark, *Lewis Carroll: A Biography*, London: J. M. Dent, 1979

Collingwood – Stuart Dodgson Collingwood, *The Life and Letters of Lewis Carroll*, London: T. Fisher Unwin, 1898

Diaries – Lewis Carroll, *The Diaries of Lewis Carroll*, ed. Roger Lancelyn Green, London: Cassell & Company, 1953

Greville – Charles Greville, *The Greville Memoirs 1814–1860*, ed. Lytton Strachey and Roger Fulford, London: Macmillan & Co., 1938

Hudson – Derek Hudson, *Lewis Carroll*, London, Constable, 1954

Kitchins – *Lewis Carroll and the Kitchins*, ed. Morton N. Cohen, New York: Lewis Carroll Society of North America, 1980

Letters – *The Letters of Lewis Carroll*, ed. Morton N. Cohen and Roger Lancelyn Green, London: Macmillan, 1979

A Long Time Burning – Donald Thomas, *A Long Time Burning: The History of Literary Censorship in England*, London: Routledge and Kegan Paul, 1969

373

Picture Book – The Lewis Carroll Picture Book, ed. Stuart Dodgson Collingwood, London: T. Fisher Unwin, 1899

Reed – Langford Reed, *The Life of Lewis Carroll*, London: W & G Foyle, 1932

Russian Journal – The Russian Journal and other Selections from the Works of Lewis Carroll, ed. John Francis McDermott, New York: E. P. Dutton & Co., 1935

Works – The Complete Works of Lewis Carroll, ed. Alexander Woollcott, London: The Nonesuch Press, 1939

1   The Prisoner of Conscience

1. Jean Gattégno, *Lewis Carroll: Fragments of a Looking-Glass*, tr. Rosemary Sheed, New York: Thomas Y. Crowell, 1976, p. 80
2. *Diaries*, p. 246; *Picture Book*, p. 195; Leonard E. Naylor, *The Irrepressible Victorian: The Story of Thomas Gibson Bowles*, London: Macdonald, 1965, p. 130
3. Richard von Krafft-Ebing, *Psychopathia Sexualis, with Especial Reference to Contrary Sexual Instinct: A Medico-Legal Study, Authorized Translation of the Seventh Enlarged and Revised German Edition* tr., Charles Gilbert Chaddock, M. D., Philadelphia: The F. A. Davis Company: London: F. J. Rebman, 1894, pp. 17n., 35n., 44–5; C. L. Dodgson, *Pillow Problems Thought Out During Wakeful Hours*, Fourth Edition, London: Macmillan, 1895, xv; Collingwood, p. 242; A. S. Russell, 'Lewis Carroll: Tutor and Mathematician,' *Listener*, 13 January 1932, p. 55
4. Karl Robert Eduard von Hartmann, *Philosophie des Unbewussten*, Berlin, 1869, p. 583
5. A. S. Russell, 'Lewis Carroll: Tutor and Mathematician,' *Listener*, 13 January 1932, p. 56; Hudson, pp. 323, 324
6. *Child-Friends*, p. 25
7. Gordon Thomas, *Enslaved: An Investigation into Modern-Day Slavery*, London: Bantam Press, 1990, p. 155
8. *The Independent Magazine*, 4 September 1993, p. 28
9. Ibid., p. 32
10. *Letters*, pp. 981, 987–8
11. Wolf von Eckardt, Sander L. Gilman, J. Edward Chamberlain, *Oscar Wilde's London*, London: Michael O'Mara Books, 1988, p. 248
12. *Criminal Law Amendment Act, 1885. Vigilance Committees and their Work*, London: Pall Mall Gazette Office, 1885, p. 22; *The Maiden Tribute of Modern Babylon*, London: Pall Mall Gazette Office, 1885, p. 9
13. *Vogue*, December 1966, p. 281
14. Helmut Gernsheim, *Lewis Carroll Photographer*, Revised Edition, New York: Dover Publications, 1969, p. v

15. *Harper's Magazine*, CLXXXVI (1943), 320, 323
16. *The Letters of Queen Victoria Second Series: A Selection from Her Majesty's Correspondence and Journals between the Years 1862 and 1878*, ed. George Earle Buckle, London: John Murray, 1926, I, 124, 250; Greville, VII, 203
17. J. W. Mackail, *James Leigh Strachan-Davidson*, Oxford: Clarendon Press, 1925, p. 52
18. *Criminal Law Amendment Act, 1885. Vigilance Committees and their Work*, p. 10
19. *Letters*, p. 338
20. *A Long Time Burning*, p. 470
21. *Picture Book*, p. 195
22. *Catalogue of the Personal Effects of the Rev. C. L. Dodgson, 'Lewis Carroll'*, Oxford, 1898, Nos. 309, 538, 570, 573, 850
23. Lewis Carroll, *Lettres à ses amies enfants*, tr. Henri Parisot, Paris: Aubier Flammarion, 1977, p. 43
24. Collingwood, p. 429

2   Ancient and Modern

1. *Cornhill Magazine*, LXXIII NS, (1932), 560
2. Thomas Hughes, *The Vale Royal of England: or, The County Palatine of Chester*, London: John Gray Bell, 1852, p. 98
3. Leslie Stephen, *Hours in a Library*, 1893, III, 214
4. Collingwood, pp. 3–5
5. Ibid., p. 8
6. QU. Clark, p. 23
7. Collingwood, p. 15; *Diaries*, p. 6
8. Collingwood, p. 8
9. *A Long Time Burning*, pp 380–1; James Woodforde, *The Diary of a Country Parson, 1758–1802*, ed. John Beresford, London: Oxford University Press, 1956, p. 57
10. *Works*, p. 451
11. Greville, II, 161, 212–14
12. Augustus J. C. Hare, *The Story of My Life*, London: George Allen, 1896, I, 59
13. Raymond Richards, *Old Cheshire Churches*, London: B. T. Batsford. 1947, p. 142
14. Collingwood, pp. 11–12; *Works*, 355, 383, 639
15. *Works*, p. 701
16. Collingwood, pp. 13–14
17. *Letters*, p. 4

18. *Letters to Skeffington Dodgson from his Father*, ed. Anne Clark Amor, The Lewis Carroll Society, 1990, p. 24
19. Hare, *The Story of My Life*, I, 41–2
20. Ibid., II, 481
21. *Works*, 396–7
22. BL. Add MS., 40489 ff. 191–2
23. Lord David Cecil, *Melbourne*, Indianapolis and New York: The Bobbs Merrill Company Inc., 1966, pp. 348, 402
24. Henry Mayhew, *London Labour and the London Poor*, London: Charles Griffin, 1851–62, I, 268
25. BL. Add. MSS 40489 ff. 187–8, 193–4; 40522 ff. 195, 197–8, 371–2
26. *A Sermon Preached at the Minster in Ripon*, Oxford: J. H. Parker, 1837, p. 19
27. Ibid., p. 26
28. Charles Dodgson, *The Sacraments of the Gospel*, London: Rivingtons, 1864, pp. 53, 55
29. W. Goode, *The Doctrine of the Church of England*, London: Hatchard, 1864, p. 3; Charles Dodgson, *The Sacraments of the Gospel*, p. 4
30. Charles Dodgson, *The Sacraments of the Gospel*, p. 42; W. Goode, *A Reply to Archdeacon Dodgson's Statement*, London: Hatchard, 1864, pp. 5, 28
31. Charles Dodgson, *Ritual Worship*, Leeds: T. Harrison, 1852, p. 9

3   Facing the World

1. T. B. Macaulay, *Critical and Historical Essays Contributed to the Edinburgh Review*, new edn., London: Longman's Green, Reader & Dyer, 1880, p. 605
2. *Northern Echo*, 5 January 1932
3. *A Short Account of the First Establishment of the Croft National School*, Darlington, 1846, p. 9
4. Ronald Pearsall, *The Worm in the Bud: The World of Victorian Sexuality*, London: Penguin Books, 1971, p. 333
5. Collingwood, p. 22
6. Ibid., pp. 23–4
7. Ibid., p. 25
8. *The Works of William Cowper*, ed. H. S. Milford, London: Oxford University Press, 1934, p. 246
9. Collingwood, p. 30
10. Sir William Hardman, *A Mid-Victorian Pepys*, ed. S. M. Ellis, London: Cecil Palmer, 1923, p. 71
11. *Nineteenth Century*, XV (1884), 457, 464
12. *Works*, p. 718; *Cornhill Magazine*, LXXIII (1932), 9; Collingwood, p. 28

13. Collingwood, pp. 30–1
14. C. A. Wilkinson, *Reminiscences of Eton*, London: Hurst & Blackett 1888, pp. 321, 324, 326; A. P. Stanley, *Life and Correspondence of Thomas Arnold*, Third Edition, London: Fellowes, 1844, II, 234
15. Hare, *The Story of My Life*, I, 168–9
16. Geoffrey Faber, *Jowett: A Portrait with Background*, London: Faber and Faber, 1957, p. 65
17. Collingwood, p. 29
18. Bill, p. 8
19. Collingwood, p. 28
20. Ibid., pp. 28–9
21. Ibid., p. 29
22. Ibid., p. 20
23. *The Harcourt Amory Collection of Lewis Carroll in the Harvard College Library*, ed. Flora V. Livingstone, Cambridge, Mass: Privately Printed, 1932, pp. 128–9; Hudson, p. 35
24. *The Queen*, CLXX (1931), 37–40, 66
25. *Works*, p. 737
26. *Picture Book*, p. 16
27. C. A. Sainte-Beuve, 'Quelques verités sur la situation en littérature,' *Revue des deux mondes*, III (1843), 14; PRO, KB28/515/13
28. *Works*, pp. 290–2
29. Ibid., 613–14
30. Collingwood, pp. 48–9

4   Shooting the Dean

1. Collingwood, p. 57
2. *Cornhill Magazine*, IV N. S. (1898), 303; S. H. Williams and F. Madan *A Handbook of the Literature of the Rev. C. L. Dodgson*, London: Oxford University Press, 1931, p. 212
3. *Nineteenth Century* XLV (1898), 210
4. Collingwood, p. 56
5. *Cornhill Magazine*, October (1879)
6. John Ruskin, *Praeterita. Outlines of Scenes and Thoughts Perhaps Worthy of Memory in My Past Life*, Orpington: George Allen, 1886, I, 349–50
7. Macaulay, *Critical and Historical Essays*, p. 465
8. Jan Morris (ed.), *The Oxford Book of Oxford*, Oxford: Oxford University Press, 1979, pp. 237–8
9. Bill, pp. 21n., 64; Ruskin, *Praeterita*, I, 374
10. *Praeterita*, I, 355–6
11. W. Tuckwell, *Reminiscences of Oxford*, London: Cassell, 1900, p. 134

12. W. Tuckwell, *Reminiscences of Oxford*, p. 39; Ruskin, *Praeterita*, I, 376–7
13. Tuckwell, *Reminiscences of Oxford*, pp. 39–40
14. George C. Bompas, *Life of Frank Buckland*, sixth edition, London: Smith, Elder, 1885, p. 48
15. Collingwood, p. 341
16. Ibid., pp. 53–5
17. Ibid., p. 55
18. Ibid., p. 59
19. Ibid., p. 61
20. W. Tuckwell, *Reminiscences of Oxford*, p. 20
21. Bill & Mason, p. 13
22. *Works*, p. 821
23. Oxford University Commission (1852), Evidence 45

5 An Oxford Chiel

1. BL. Add. MSS 44387 f. 44; 44381 f. 31
2. Hare, *The Story of My Life*, II, 10
3. W. G. Hiscock, *A Christ Church Miscellany*, Oxford: Oxford University Press, 1946, p. 100
4. *The Times*, 30 January 1932
5. *Picture Book*, p. 199
6. Collingwood, pp. 64–5
7. *Cornhill Magazine*, N. S. IV (1898), 303–4; *Pillow Problems*, pp. xv, 1; *Aspects of Alice*, p. 221
8. *Listener*, 13 January 1932; *The Times*, 19 December 1931
9. *The Times*, 12 January 1932
10. Bill & Mason, p. 63
11. Faber, *Jowett*, p. 145
12. Sir William Hardman, *The Letters and Memoirs of Sir William Hardman, Second Series: 1863–1865*, ed. S. M. Ellis, London: Cecil Palmer, 1925, p. 147
13. Faber, *Jowett*, pp. 266–72
14. *Works*, pp. 812–14
15. Collingwood, p. 91
16. *Works*, pp. 1011–16
17. Collingwood, p. 74
18. Ibid., p. 86

6   The Lion Hunter

1. Collingwood, pp. 65–6
2. Ibid., p. 293; *Diaries*, p. 246; *Letters*, p. 667; *Standard*, 18 August 1890
3. Collingwood, p. 66
4. *Diaries*, p. 72
5. Ibid., p. 117
6. C. L. Cline (ed.), *The Owl and the Rossettis*, London: Pennsylvania State University Press, 1978, p. 2
7. Ibid., p. 26; T. J. Wise, *A Bibliography of the Writings in Prose and Verse of Algernon Charles Swinburne*, Privately Printed, 1919–20, I, 220
8. Collingwood, pp. 60, 68
9. James Pope-Hennessey, *Monckton Milnes: The Flight of Youth 1851–1885*, London: Constable, 1951, p. 122
10. Helmut Gernsheim, *Lewis Carroll Photographer*, p. 36
11. R. D. Wood, *The Calotype Patent Lawsuit of Talbot v. Laroche, 1854*, Lacock: The Fox Talbot Museum, *passim*
12. Collingwood, p. 102
13. Ibid., p. 69
14. *Strand Magazine*, XXI (1901), 543–4
15. *Letters*, 49–50; 53
16. *Diaries*, p. 76; Francis Kilvert, *Kilvert's Diary*, ed. William Plomer, London: Jonathan Cape, 1977, II, 276–8
17. William Ll. Parry-Jones, *The Trade in Lunacy*, London: Routledge and Kegan Paul, 1972, p. 236
18. Krafft-Ebing, *Psychopathia Sexualis*, 1894, p. 17n. James C. Prichard, *A Treatise on Insanity*, London: Sherwood, Gilbert and Piper, 1835, pp. 4–5; Henry Maudsley, *Body and Mind*, second edn., London: Macmillan, 1873, pp. 128, 136, 137
19. Collingwood, p. 82
20. PRO., KB28/690/2

7   Alice in the Golden Afternoon

1. *Works*, p. 826
2. Ibid., p. 1018
3. Ibid., p. 1022
4. Ibid., pp. 823, 825
5. Ibid., p. 824
6. Ibid., p. 1010

7. H. L. Thompson, *Henry George Liddell*, London: John Murray, 1899, p. 170

8. F. Max Müller, *My Autobiography: A Fragment*, London: Longmans, Green, 1901, p. 258

9. QU. *Diaries*, p. 51

10. *Balliol Rhymes*, ed. W. G. Hiscock, Oxford: For the Editor, 1955, p. 29

11. *Cornhill Magazine*, LXXIII N. S. (1932), 9; *The Poems of Catullus*, ed. Guy Lee, Oxford: Oxford University Press, 1991, p. 120

12. *Cornhill Magazine*, LXXIII N. S., p. 6

13. Ibid., p. 6

14. Ibid., p. 2

15. Ibid., p. 9

16. *Picture Book*, p. 165

17. *Cornhill Magazine*, LXXIII N. S., 7

18. Collingwood, pp. 93–4

19. *Cornhill Magazine*, LXXIII N. S., 8; *Picture Book*, pp. 165, 358–60; Collingwood, p. 96

20. *Picture Book*, pp. 168, 360

21. Ibid., p. 360

22. *Letters* p. 77n.

23. Clark, p. 131

24. *Picture Book*, p. 171

25. Paul Harvey, *Oxford Companion to Classical Literature*, Oxford: Clarendon Press, 1951, p. 279; [Bibliotheca Classica, ed. George Long] *P. Vergili Maronis Opera: The Works of Virgil*, ed. John Conington, London: Whittaker, 1863, II, 488

26. *The Aeneid of Virgil: Books I–VI*, ed. T. E. Page, London: Macmillan, 1894, p. 480

27. *Diaries*, pp. 199, 227; *Letters*, pp. 269, 1132

28. Greville, II, 10, 89–90; Lord David Cecil, *Melbourne*, p. 265

29. Collingwood, p. 150

30. Henry Maudsley, *Responsibility in Mental Disease*, London: Henry S. King, 1874, p. 86

31. Ibid., Chapters III & V, pp. 81, 153

32. William Raeper, *George MacDonald*, Tring: Lion Publishing, 1987, pp. 176–7

33. *Annotated Alice*, ed. Martin Gardner, p. 238; William Berkeley, *Three Dialogues between Hylas and Philonous* in Isaiah Berlin (ed.), *The Age of Enlightenment*, New York: New American Library, 1956, p. 154

34. *Aspects of Alice*, London: Penguin Books, 1970, pp. 208–9

35. Greville, II, 2, 18, 120

36. Collingwood, pp. 142, 146; Lewis Carroll, *The Wasp in a Wig: A Suppressed Episode of Through the Looking-Glass and What Alice Found There*, ed. Martin

Gardner, London: Macmillan, 1977, *passim*; Walter De La Mare, *Lewis Carroll*, London: Faber and Faber, 1932, p. 45

37. *Harper's Monthly Magazine*, XX (1890), 254
38. John Howe Jenkins, *Cakeless*, Oxford: Shrimpton, 1874, Act II, Scene 1, 20–33; Act III, Scene 1, 21–29
39. *The Times*, 23 December 1931
40. W. G. Hiscock, *A Christ Church Miscellany*, p. 46
41. Bill & Mason, p. 137
42. A. Hassall, *Christ Church*, London: Hodder and Stoughton, 1911, p. 42
43. Sir William Hardman, *The Hardman Papers*, ed. S. M. Ellis, London: Constable, 1930, p. 77
44. *Works*, pp. 818, 822

8   Man about Town

1. Hardman, *A Mid-Victorian Pepys*, p. 283; Collingwood, p. 81; G. M. Young, *Victorian England: Portrait of an Age*, London: Oxford University Press, 1960, p. 126n.
2. Henry Mayhew, *London Labour and the London Poor*, IV, 213, 359
3. *Diaries*, p. 281; *Letters*, p. 335
4. Hardman, *A Mid-Victorian Pepys*, p. 297; *The Hardman Papers*, p. 251; Edmund Gosse, *Portraits and Sketches*, London: William Heinemann 1912, p. 4
5. Albert Schweitzer, *J. S. Bach*, London: A & C Black, 1955, I, 89–90
6. Hardman, *A Mid-Victorian Pepys*, p. 236
7. Francis Kilvert, *Kilvert's Diary*, I, 21, 39, 127
8. Henry Mayhew, *London Labour and the London Poor*, I, 43; *A Long Time Burning*, pp. 456–60
9. *Picture Book*, pp. 188–9
10. Ibid., p. 191
11. Henry Knepler (ed.), *Man About Paris: The Confessions of Arsène Houssaye*, London: Victor Gollancz, 1972, p. 85
12. Henry Treffery Dunn, *Recollections of Dante Gabriel Rossetti and his Circle*, London: Elkin Matthews, 1904, pp. 52–3, 66; Helen Rossetti Angeli, *Pre-Raphaelite Twilight: The Story of Charles Augustus Howell*, London: The Richards Press, 1954, pp. 48, 164
13. William Michael Rossetti, *Some Reminiscences of William Michael Rossetti*, London: Brown Langham and Co., 1906, p. 329; Marya Zaturenska, *Christina Rossetti: A Portrait with Background*, New York: Macmillan, 1949, p. 187; E. F. Benson, *As We Were: A Victorian Peep-Show*, London: Longmans, Green, 1930, p. 272
14. Gernsheim, *Lewis Carroll Photographer*, p. 56

15. QU. Hudson, p. 140
16. Collingwood, pp. 224–5
17. Raeper, *George MacDonald*, p. 169
18. Ibid., p. 171
19. Mark Twain, *Autobiography*, New York and London, Harper & Bros., 1924, II, 232
20. *Gentlewoman*, 29 January 1898, p. 147
21. Ellen Terry, *Ellen Terry's Memoirs*, ed. Edith Craig and Christopher St John, London: Victor Gollancz, 1933, p. 75
22. Basil Willey, *More Nineteenth Century Studies*, London: Chatto and Windus, 1963, p. 162
23. *Letters*, pp. 246–7
24. Collingwood, p. 138
25. *Letters*, p. 208
26. Bowman, pp. 35–6
27. *Works*, p. 828
28. *Letters*, p. 75
29. *Child-Friends*, pp. 40, 79, 98; Collingwood, p. 380
30. John Octavius Johnston, *Life and Letters of Henry Parry Liddon*, London: Longmans, Green, 1904, p. 100; *Russian Journal*, p. 76
31. *Russian Journal*, pp. 77–81
32. Ibid., p. 89
33. Ibid., pp. 92–3
34. Henry Parry Liddon, MS. Diary for 1867 (Pusey House, Oxford), 18, 28 July; 11, 13, 14, 15 August
35. *Russian Journal*, p. 115
36. Collingwood, p. 131
37. Ibid., p. 132; *Letters*, p. 1155
38. W. S. Jevons, *The Principles of Science*, London: Macmillan, 1892, p. 43
39. *The Times*, 15 January 1932
40. *Diaries*, p. 277
41. *Picture Book*, pp. 357–8
42. Collingwood, p. 152
43. Ibid., pp. 152–3

9   The Man of Letters

1. Charles Morgan, *The House of Macmillan (1843–1943)*, London: Macmillan, 1944, p. 81; Collingwood, pp. 227–8
2. *Picture Book*, p. 167
3. William Shakespeare, *Macbeth*, II, ii, 3–4; John Webster, *The Duchess of Malfi*, IV, ii, 173–5

4. Reed, p. 86
5. *The Logic of Personal Knowledge: Essays Presented to Michael Polanyi on his Seventi-eth Birthday*, London: Routledge and Kegan Paul, 1961, p. 186; J. A. Wechsler, *The Age of Suspicion*, New York: Random House, 1953, p. 287
6. *Picture Book*, pp. 215–16
7. *Child-Friends*, p. 245
8. *Aspects of Alice*, p. 371
9. H. L. Thompson, *Henry George Liddell*, p. 258
10. Collingwood, p. 209
11. Ibid., p. 174
12. Bowman, p. 81
13. *New York Times*, 28 January 1932

10   Dreaming as the Summers Die

1. Francis Kilvert, *Kilvert's Diary*, III, 35; Collingwood, pp. 279–80; *Hampshire Chronicle*, 13 March 1948
2. *Letters*, pp. 238, 253
3. Francis Kilvert, *Kilvert's Diary*, I, 387, III, 37–8
4. *Letters and Memoirs of Sir William Hardman*, pp. 80–81; Cyril Pearl, *The Girl with the Swansdown Seat*, Indianapolis and New York: The Bobbs-Merrill Company Inc. 1955, p. 223
5. Pearl, *The Girl with the Swansdown Seat*, p. 223; *Eastbourne Gazette*, 14 July 1880
6. *Child-Friends*, p. 9
7. *Diaries*, pp. 365–6; *Letters*, p. 545n.
8. *Child-Friends*, pp. 124–5
9. Ibid., p. 110
10. *The Lewis Carroll Centenary in London*, London: J. & E. Bumpus, 1932, p. 135; *Child-Friends*, p. 167
11. *Eastbourne Gazette*, 14 September 1881
12. *Eastbourne Chronicle*, 11 August 1877
13. *Works*, pp. 1083–5
14. *Eastbourne Chronicle*, 22 January 1898
15. Ibid., 31 July 1897
16. *Works*, p. 679
17. *Picture Book*, p. 231
18. *Child-Friends*, p. 169; *Letters*, p. 686
19. *Child-Friends*, pp. 177–8
20. Ibid., p. 169
21. Bowman, p. 8
22. *Eastbourne Gazette*, 2 July 1879, 20 July 1881, 13 August 1884

23. Ibid., 5 October 1878, 14 July 1886, 21 July 1886
24. Ibid., 15 July 1885
25. Bowman, pp. 12–14; *Criminal Law Amendment Act, 1885. Vigilance Committees and their Work*, p. 10
26. *Eastbourne Gazette*, 7 September 1887, 23 September 1896
27. Bowman, p. 177
28. Leonard E. Naylor, *The Irrepressible Victorian: The Story of Thomas Gibson Bowles*, p. 130
29. *Eastbourne Chronicle*, 11 July 1891, 18 July 1891
30. *Diaries*, p. 528; *Child-Friends*, pp. 235–7
31. Bowman, p. 31; *Child-Friends*, p. 216
32. Bowman, p. 11

11   Mrs Grundy and the Baron

1. *Diaries*, p. xxv
2. *The Hardman Papers*, p. 99
3. E. F. Benson, *As We Were*, p. 64
4. Greville, VII, 387–90
5. *The Hardman Papers*, pp. 44–5n.; 'Walter,' *My Secret Life I* (Vols. 1–4), ed. Donald Thomas, London: Arrow Books, 1994, p. 419
6. Hudson, p. 323
7. *Kitchins*, p. 43
8. *A Long Time Burning*, pp. 263, 282–3; Franz Hubmann, *The Habsburg Empire*, London: Routledge and Kegan Paul, 1972, pp. 42–3; Serge Nazarieff, *Jeux de dames cruelles: Photographies 1850–1960*, Köln: Benedikt Taschen Verlag, 1992, pp. 23, 25; Graham Ovenden and Peter Mendes, *Victorian Erotic Photography*, London: Academy Editions, 1973, pp. 76–7
9. *Aspects of Alice*, p. 220; *Gentlewoman*, 5 February 1898, p. 166; Krafft-Ebing, *Psychopathia Sexualis*, 1894, pp. 35n., 44–5
10. *St James's Gazette*, 22 July 1885. Edward Monro (1815–66) published tales, allegories and sermons. *Purity of Life* appeared in 1850.
11. Bowman, p. 56
12. Helmut Gernsheim, *Lewis Carroll Photographer*, p. 62
13. Hudson, p. 318; *Fortnightly Review*, CL (1941), 282
14. *Child-Friends*, p. 101
15. *The Quiver*, 1899, p. 411
16. Collingwood, p. 402; *Catalogue of the Personal Effects of the Rev. C. L. Dodgson, 'Lewis Carroll,'* Nos. 309, 537, 538, 570, 573, 587
17. Collingwood, p. 355; *Letters*, pp. 309n., 416; Duncan Black, 'Lewis Carroll and the Cambridge School of P. R; Arthur Cohen and Edith Denman,' *Public Choice*, VIII (1970), 1–28; Qu. *Letters*, p. 309

18. University College, London, Papers of Edwin Chadwick, Depositions, Box 129
19. Fyodor Dostoevsky, *A Gentle Creature and Other Stories*, Tr. David Magarshack, London: John Lehmann, 1950, p. xiii
20. *Harper's Monthly Magazine*, XX (1890), 254
21. *Report from the Select Committee of the House of Lords on the Law Relating to the Protection of Young Girls*, 25 August 1881, p. 64
22. Faber, *Jowett*, p. 93
23. *Gentlewoman*, 5 February 1898, p. 166
24. *Fortnightly Review*, CL (1941), 282
25. *St James's Gazette*, 15 July 1885
26. Émile Zola, *Germinal: or, Master and Man. A Realistic Novel*, London: Vizetelly, n.d. p. 115
27. *National Vigilance Association. Third Annual Report*, London 1888, p. 4
28. Charles Terrot, *The Maiden Tribute*, London: Federick Muller, 1959, p. 215
29. *The Criminal Law Amendment Act, 1885. Vigilance Committees and Their Work*, p. 10
30. Henry James, *The Middle Years*, London: William Collins, 1917, pp. 99–100; *The Complete Ronald Firbank*, ed. Anthony Powell, London: Gerald Duckworth, 1961, p. 73
31. Francis Kilvert, *Kilvert's Diary*, I, 123
32. Krafft-Ebing, *Psychopathia Sexualis*, 1894, p. 17n.
33. Michael Kettle, *Salomé's Last Veil: The Libel Case of the Century*, London: Hart-Davis, MacGibbon, 1977, p. 173; *Bernard Shaw and Alfred Douglas: A Correspondence*, ed. Mary Hyde, London: John Murray, 1982, p. 126
34. Krafft-Ebing, *Psychopathia Sexualis*, 1894, p. 379; Richard von Krafft-Ebing, *Psychopathia Sexualis with Especial Reference to the Antipathic Sexual Instinct: A Medico-Forensic Study. Only Authorised English Adaptation of the Twelfth German Edition*, Tr. F. J. Rebman, London: William Heinemann, 1914, p. 498–9, 526
35. Krafft-Ebing, *Psychopathia Sexualis*, 1914, p. 553
36. Ibid., pp. 552, 554; Collingwood, p. 369
37. Krafft-Ebing, *Psychopathia Sexualis*, 1914, pp. 555–6
38. Ibid., p. 560
39. Krafft-Ebing, *Psychopathia Sexualis*, 1894, p. 432
40. Ibid., pp. 1–2, 12
41. Ibid., p. 55
42. Henry James, *What Maisie Knew*, (The Novels and Tales of Henry James, New York Edition, Vol. XI) New York: Charles Scribner's Sons, 1908, p. ix; Henry James, *The Awkward Age*, (The Novels and Tales of Henry James, New York Edition, Vol. IX), pp. viii-ix, 84 (Bk. II, Ch. 4)
43. Hudson, p. 320

12   Christ Church Hall

1. Tuckwell, *Reminiscences of Oxford*, pp. 161–2
2. Collingwood, p. 218
3. Oliver Elton, *Frederick York Powell: A Life and a Selection from his Letters and Occasional Writings*, Oxford: Clarendon Press, 1906, II, 361–2; *Cornhill Magazine*, IV N. S. (1898), 309
4. Collingwood, p. 351; Tuckwell, *Reminiscences of Oxford*, pp. 162–3
5. Michael Sadleir, *Michael Ernest Sadler: A Memoir by his Son*, London: Constable, 1949, p. 90
6. Ibid., p. 91
7. Oliver Elton, *Frederick York Powell*, I, 427; II, 363, 365–6
8. Hudson, p. 312; Claude M. Blagden, *Well Remembered*, London: Hodder and Stoughton, 1953, p. 114
9. *Harper's Monthly Magazine*, XX (1890), 247, 249
10. Claude M. Blagden, *Well Remembered*, pp. 112–15
11. Alan Mackinnon, *The Oxford Amateurs*, London: Chapman & Hall, 1910, pp. 200–1; G. M. Young, *Victorian England*, p. 163n.; L. S. Amery, F. W. Hirst, H. A. A. Cruso, *Aristophanes at Oxford, O. W. by Y. T. O.* Oxford: J. Vincent (1894), pp. 56–7
12. Oliver Elton, *Frederick York Powell*, II, 365
13. Collingwood, pp. 266–7; William Hayter, *Spooner: A Biography*, London: W. H. Allen, 1977, pp. 71–2, 136, 140–1
14. Collingwood, pp. 232, 267
15. Claude M. Blagden, *Well Remembered*, pp. 114–15
16. Edith Olivier, *Without Knowing Mr Walkley*, London: Faber and Faber, 1938, p. 176
17. Hudson, pp. 320–1
18. Claude M. Blagden, *Well Remembered*, p. 115
19. Ibid., p. 114
20. *Oxford Magazine*, 26 January 1898, p. 159; Oliver Elton, *Frederick York Powell*, II, 364
21. Claude M. Blagden, *Well Remembered*, p. 116
22. Michael Sadleir, *Michael Ernest Sadler*, p. 95; Collingwood, p. 78; Matthew Arnold, 'Emerson' in *Discourses in America* (1885)
23. Collingwood, p. 77
24. Pierre Fermat's Last Theorem, of which he noted he had 'a wonderful proof,' never disclosed, states that $x^n + y^n = z^n$ has no whole number solution when n is greater than 2. In 1742 Christian Goldbach conjectured that all even numbers may be expressed as the sum of two primes. Georg Riemann's Hypothesis of 1859 stated that all non-trivial roots

of ζ have the real part ½. The complex function ζ is defined by an infinite series with the *n*th term e $^{-z\log n}$ J. S. Phillimore's ordeal is described in Claude M. Blagden, *Well Remembered*, p. 115

25. Collingwood, p. 238
26. *'Assurément, je le suis, réprit Rodin: il est odieux que de futiles considérations arrêtent ainsi le progrès des sciences: les grands hommes se sont-ils laissé captiver d'aussi méprisables chaînes?'* *Oeuvres Complètes du Marquis de Sade*, Paris: Cercle du Livre Précieux, 1966–7, III, 151; *Works*, pp. 1075, 1076, 1078, 1081–2
27. *Cornhill Magazine*, N. S. IV (1898), 308–9
28. *Works*, pp. 1026, 1030
29. Ibid., p. 1033
30. Ibid., p. 1054
31. W. G. Hiscock, *A Christ Church Miscellany*, pp. 97–101
32. Ibid., pp. 108, 110
33. Collingwood, p. 221
34. Claude M. Blagden, *Well Remembered*, p. 117; 'Rude Donatus', *Curiosissima Curatoria*, Oxford: G. Sheppard, 1892, pp. 29–32; Michael Sadleir, *Michael Ernest Sadler*, p. 95
35. *Curiosissima Curatoria*, pp. 9, 12, 23, 24, 26, 32–5
36. *Diaries*, pp. 440, 523
37. *Twelve Months in a Curatorship. By One Who Has Tried It*, 1894, pp. 28, 31, 38, 40; *Works*, pp. 1061, 1062
38. *Twelve Months in a Curatorship*, pp. 23–7
39. *Twelve Months in a Curatorship*, pp. 42, 43–4; 62; *Works*, pp. 1063–4
40. *Three Years in a Curatorship. By One Whom it Has Tried*, Oxford: E. Baxter, 1886, p. 3; *Works*, p. 1064
41. *Letters*, pp. 514–15, 811
42. *Picture Book*, p. 356; *Listener*, 6 February 1958, p. 239; Collingwood, p. 270
43. *Works*, p. 1070
44. *Diaries*, p. 415; Hardman, *A Mid-Victorian Pepys*, pp. 257–8
45. *Harper's Monthly Magazine*, XX (1890), 248

13   The Aged Aged Man

1. Collingwood, p. 340
2. Ibid., p. 339
3. Ibid., p. 251
4. Ibid., pp. 241–2, 251; *Letters*, p. 783
5. *Picture Book*, p. 355

6. Cornelia Otis Skinner, *Elegant Wits and Grand Horizontals*, London: Michael Joseph, 1963, p. 100
7. Bowman, pp. 119–20
8. S. L. Ollard (ed.), *A Forty Years' Friendship: Letters from the Late Henry Scott Holland to Mrs Drew*, London: Nisbet & Co., 1919, pp. 79–80
9. *Picture Book*, p. 162
10. Collingwood, p. 183
11. Ellen Terry, *Ellen Terry's Memoirs*, ed. Edith Craig and Christopher St John, London: Victor Gollancz, 1933, pp. 141–2
12. Reed, pp. 77–8
13. Ibid., p. 84
14. Collingwood, p. 253
15. *The Nursery Alice*, London: Macmillan, 1889, pp. 9–10
16. Collingwood, pp. 252, 411
17. Verily Anderson, *The Last of the Eccentrics: A Life of Rosslyn Bruce*, London: Hodder and Stoughton, 1972, p. 88
18. *Letters*, p. 1095
19. Collingwood, p. 380
20. Jack Smithers, *The Early Life and Vicissitudes of Jack Smithers*, London: Martin Secker, 1939, pp. 17, 40–1
21. *Picture Book*, p. 331; Hudson, p. 317
22. *Child-Friends*, p. 219
23. Collingwood, p. 237
24. Bowman, p. 57
25. Harry Furniss, *Confessions of a Caricaturist*, London: T. Fisher Unwin, 1901, I, 104, 105, 111–12; *Strand Magazine*, January 1908
26. *Cornhill Magazine*, LXXIII N. S. (1932), 560
27. *Letters*, 981, 987–8, 1027–8
28. Ibid., p. 992
29. *Gentlewoman*, 5 February 1898, pp. 166–7
30. Bowman, p. 10
31. Collingwood, pp. 293, 325
32. *Child-Friends*, p. 238
33. *Listener*, 30 January 1958, p. 202; *Kitchins*, p. 15
34. Collingwood, p. 341
35. Ibid., p. 330
36. *Letters*, p. 1156
37. Collingwood, pp. 347–8, 363–4
38. *Gentlewoman*, 5 February 1898, p. 167; Collingwood, p. 349
39. Collingwood, pp. 353–4
40. Ibid., pp. 351, 354
41. Ibid., p. 355

14   Wonderland

1. *The Lewis Carroll Centenary in London*, pp. 128–9
2. Ibid., pp. vii, ix
3. Saki (H. H. Munro), *The Westminster Alice*, Illustrated by F. Carruthers Gould with a Foreword by J. A. Spender, London: John Lane, The Bodley Head, 1927, p. 119
4. Horace M. Wyatt, *Alice in Motorland*. Drawings by Charles R. Sykes, London: The Car Illustrated (The 'Car Magazine' Series No. 1), 1904, p. 9
5. Loris Carllew, *Alice in Plunderland*. Illustrated by Linton Jehne, London: Eveleigh Nash, 1910, pp. 6, 83
6. Horace Wyatt, *Malice in Kulturland*. With Illustrations by W. Tell, London: The Car Illustrated, 1914, pp. 4, 12, 16, 19
7. *Aspects of Alice*, pp. 243–4, 246
8. Hugh Kingsmill, *The Table of Truth*, London: Jarrolds, 1933, pp. 68, 70, 72
9. H. R. Trevor-Roper, *The Last Days of Hitler*, London: Pan Books, 1952 p. 40
10. *Sun*, 16 December 1995
11. Anne Lyon Haight, *Banned Books*, London: George Allen and Unwin, 1955, p. 66; Gaëton Picon, *Surrealism 1919–1939*, London: Macmillan, 1977, p. 183
12. Nicolas Barker and John Collins, *A Sequel to an Enquiry into the Nature of Certain Nineteenth-Century Pamphlets by John Carter and Graham Pollard*, London & Berkeley: Scolar Press, 1983, pp. 107–8, 186, 187, 195–6, 267–8
13. *Aspects of Alice*, pp. 335, 336, 341, 342, 352, 398, 508
14. *The Oxford Book of Oxford*, ed. Jan Morris, Oxford: Oxford University Press, 1978, pp. 350–1
15. *The Annotated Alice*, ed. Martin Gardner, London: Penguin Books, 1970, pp. 207, 311–12
16. *Aspects of Alice*, pp. 483, 486; *Catalogue of the Personal Effects of the Rev. C. L. Dodgson, 'Lewis Carroll'*, Oxford, 1898, No. 923
17. Gaëton Picon, *Surrealism 1919–1939*, p. 11
18. Ibid., p. 37
19. André Breton, *Anthologie de l'humour noir*, Paris: Jean-Jacques Pauvert, 1966, pp. 140–2
20. Ibid., pp. 141–2
21. Jean-Marc Campagne, *Clovis Trouille*, Paris: Jean-Jacques Pauvert, 1965 p. 58

Notes

22. Jennifer R. Walters, 'The Disquieting Worlds of Lewis Carroll and Boris Vian', *Revue de littérature comparée*, XLVI (1972), pp. 284–94
23. Elizabeth Prioleau, 'Humbert Humbert *Through the Looking Glass*', *Twentieth Century Literature* XXI (1975), 435
24. Raymond Queneau, *Zazie dans le Métro*, Paris: Olympia Press, 1959, p. 95
25. Nicholas Usherwood, *The Brotherhood of Ruralists*, London: Lund Humphries, 1981, p. 28
26. *The Times*, 27 January 1932
27. Oliver Elton, *Frederick York Powell*, II, 393
28. *Harper's Magazine*, CLXXXVI (1943), 323

Index

Index

Meredith, George, 151, 180, 185, 187, 236, 294–5, 328

Merryman's Magazine, 153

Middleton, Conyers, *Life of Cicero*, 56

Millais, Euphemia, née Grey, 189, 195, 268

Millais, John Everett, 8, 133, 189, 191, 193, 195

Millard, Magdalen, 200

Miller, Edith Mary, 255, 266

Miller, Louisa Maria, 255

Miller, Marion Louisa, 'May', 255, 344, 349

Milnes, Richard Monckton, *Life, Letters and Literary Remains of John Keats*, 108, 115

Milton, John, 91

Mind, 297

Mode Enfantine, 6

Modern Society, 254

Monier-Williams, Ella, 9, 267

Monro, Edward, 267, 277

Moore, Catharine Maria, 255, 336

Moore, George, 12

Moore, Thomas, 129

More, Hannah, 30

Morgan, Charles, 214

Morning Post, 134

Morris, William, 17, 130, 180, 185, 187

Morton, John Maddison, *Box and Cox*, 194–5

Morton, Thomas, *Speed the Plough*, 11

Moulin, Jacques, 265

Moxon, Edward, 151, 180

Moxon, Lilian, 319

Mozart, Wolfgang Amadeus, *Don Giovanni*, 115; *The Magic Flute*, 181

Mucha, Alphonse, 367

Mugnier, Abbé, 320

Müller, Friedrich Max, 2, 127, 137–8, 283

Mulock, Dinah Maria (Mrs Craik), 126, 153; *The Ogilvies*, 109

Munro, Alexander, 185

Munro, H. H. *see* 'Saki'

Murdoch, Alice, 119

Mussolini, Benito, 362

Nabokov, Vladimir, 1, 8, 14; *Lolita*, 361, 365, 367, 368

Nash, Edith, 242

National Society for the Prevention of Cruelty to Children, 10, 252, 287

National Vigilance Association, 10–11, 12, 280

New Monthly Review, 157

Newby, Mary, 255

Newman, John Henry, 50, 70, 222, 298; *Tract XC*, 50, 100, 248

Newry and Morne, Charles Francis Needham, Viscount, 148

News Chronicle, 361

Nightingale, Florence, 131, 275

Northern Echo, 47, 204, 275

Northumberland, Hugh Percy, 2nd Duke of, 20, 24

Notes and Queries, 19, 155, 158, 294

Nottidge v. Ripley (1849), 126

'Novalis', Friedrich Leopold von Hardenberg, 163

Oakley, Frederick, 72

Obscene Publications Act, 1857, 265

Obscene Publications Squad, 5–6

Observer, 2, 305, 310

Offences Against the Person Act 1861, 161, 260

Oliver, Ron, 5–6

Olivier, Edith, 296

O'Malley, John, 4

Orton, Arthur, 197

Orwell, George, 368

Osborne, Charles, 365

O'Shea, Katharine, 321

Ovenden, Graham, 369

'Ouida', (Marie Louise De La Ramée), 180

Owens, Henrietta, 'Atty', 264, 336

Owens, Mary Ellen, 264, 336

Owens, Sidney James, 264, 352

Oxford Act 1854, 87, 88, 98

Page, T. E. 159

Paget, Lady Frances, 66

Paget, Dean Francis, 197–8, 289, 315, 353, 355

Paget, Sir James, 206, 228, 300, 346

Palgrave, Francis Turner, 122

Pall Mall Gazette, 11, 47, 96, 154, 253, 275–80, 300, 303, 356

Palmer, Sir Roundell, 1st Earl of Selborne, 175, 207, 220, 322

Palmer, Samuel, 369

Palmerston, Henry John Temple, 3rd Viscount, 75, 85, 90, 144

Parisot, Henri, 221

Park, Frederick, 327–8

Parke, Sir James, Baron Wensleydale, 162

Parliament Act 1911, 358–9

Parliamentary Select Committee on the Treatment and Care of Lunatics 1859, 126

Parnell, Charles Stewart, 321

Paterson, Miss, 138

Paton, Sir Joseph Noel, 191, 371–2

Patten, Wilson, 24

Pattison, Mark, 87

Paul Pry, 236–7, 239

Peel, Sir Robert, 35–8, 41, 73

Penn, William, 72

Pétain, Henri Philippe Omer, 362

Phillimore, Sir Robert Joseph, 101

Phillimore, John Swinnerton, 299

Phillips, Halliwell, *see* Halliwell-Phillipps, James Orchard

Philpotts, Dr Henry, Bishop of Exeter, 38, 179

Physical Life of Women, 13

Pinero, Sir Arthur Wing, 247, 328; *The Second Mrs Tanqueray*, 326, 331

Playfair, Nigel, 336